AF607948

THE DRAMA OF THE ASSIMILATED JEW

Giorgio Bassani's *Romanzo di Ferrara*

LUCIENNE KROHA

The Drama of the Assimilated Jew

Giorgio Bassani's *Romanzo di Ferrara*

UNIVERSITY OF TORONTO PRESS
Toronto Buffalo London

Toronto Buffalo London
www.utppublishing.com

ISBN 978-1-4426-4616-2

Library and Archives Canada Cataloguing in Publication

Kroha, Lucienne, 1947–, author
The drama of the assimilated jew : Giorgio Bassani's
Romanzo di Ferrara / Lucienne Kroha.

Includes bibliographical references and index.
ISBN 978-1-4426-4616-2 (bound)

1. Bassani, Giorgio – Criticism and interpretation. 2. Jews in literature. I. Title.

PQ4807.A79Z64 2014 853′.914 C2013-906184-3

This book has been published with the help of a grant from the Canadian Federation for the Humanities and Social Sciences, through the Awards to Scholarly Publications Program, using funds provided by the Social Sciences and Humanities Research Council of Canada.

University of Toronto Press acknowledges the financial assistance to its publishing program of the Canada Council for the Arts and the Ontario Arts Council.

Canada Council for the Arts Conseil des Arts du Canada

University of Toronto Press acknowledges the financial support of the Government of Canada through the Canada Book Fund for its publishing activities.

To the memory of my paternal grandparents, Oswald Katz and Elsa Cohen, who, like the Finzi-Continis, have no tombs.

Contents

Preface and Note on Translations ix

Introduction 3

1 Jews and Gender 23

2 *Dentro le mura*: Men of Resentment 40

3 *Gli occhiali d'oro*: Jews and Homosexuals Revisited 72

4 *Il giardino dei Finzi-Contini*: A Jewish Family Romance 110

5 *Dietro la porta*: The Body in History 152

6 *L'airone*: A Case of Mistaken Identity 194

7 *L'odore del fieno*: On Becoming What One Is 217

Conclusion 240

Notes 261

Bibliography 291

Index 301

Preface and Note on Translations

This study of the works of Giorgio Bassani has been a long time in the making, most certainly longer than its results would lead one to believe. This is due to the fact that I did not set out to write a book on Bassani, but only gradually came to realize that I had enough material for a book. The ideas for it came together over a long period of gestation and after much reading into areas well beyond my comfort zone as an Italianist, as readers of this study will undoubtedly be able to discern. This was, for me, the most time-consuming and most fascinating part of my intellectual journey, and despite their inevitable shortcomings, I do believe that my findings break some new ground in Bassani studies, which more qualified minds may be able to mine for further results. This is essentially a study of intentionality, which, though not currently fashionable, is nonetheless an important part of understanding an author on his own terms and still a worthwhile enterprise in my opinion.

A few previously published articles form the nucleus from which this book has emerged, but only two can be said to have been partially reproduced here: "The Structures of Silence: Re-reading Giorgio Bassani's *Gli occhiali d'oro*," which appeared in *The Italianist* 10 (1990): 71–102, forms a part of chapter 3. A small part of another essay, "In the Aftermath: Modalities of Memory in *Il Romanzo di Ferrara*," in *Poscritto a Giorgio Bassani: Saggi in memoria del decimo anniversario della morte*, edited by Roberta Antognini and Rodica Blumenfeld, forms part of chapter 7. I thank the editors for permission to use them here.

A further note is required concerning the English translations of Bassani's texts that appear here. Bassani not only reworked his writings several times but also rearranged his stories, added to them, and collected them in different ways over the years. The only translations available until recently were of versions of his work that he subsequently modified. The project of translating the *Romanzo di Ferrara* in its final and definitive version is now under way, however, and two volumes have been published by Penguin. I have drawn on Jamie McKendrick's translations of *Gli occhiali d'oro* (Penguin, 2012) and of *Il giardino dei Finzi-Contini* (Penguin, 2007) for the quotations from those novels. For *L'airone* I have used the existing translation by William Weaver (Harcourt, 1970) because this is the novel that has experienced the fewest changes, and I have found the translations satisfactory for the most part. In a very few cases where I have found the existing translations inadequate, I have inserted my own words in square brackets. The translations from *Dentro le mura*, *Dietro la porta*, and *L'odore del fieno* are my own and are not followed by page numbers. However, I have consulted the existing translations of earlier versions of those works. All other translations of interviews, essays, and articles are my own. All references to Bassani's works in the original Italian, unless otherwise indicated, are to Giorgio Bassani, *Opere* (1998), edited by Roberto Cotroneo (Mondadori, 2009), with page numbers provided within parentheses directly in the text.

I would like to thank my former student Jean-Pierre Primiani for his help with the translations, as well as for his comments. I would also like to remember the teachers and mentors who encouraged and supported my work and were instrumental in my own early formation and career: the late Antonio D'Andrea (McGill), the late Fernando Ferrara (Istituto Universitario Orientale, Naples), and Dante Della Terza (Harvard). Most recently, I would like to remember the late Ron Schoeffel of University of Toronto Press, who dealt with me always graciously and patiently throughout the sometimes frustrating and lengthy waiting times associated with publication; Carla DeSantis, who has proven to be a very thorough and exacting copy editor; Akiva Kenny Segan, who so generously allowed his wonderful drawing to grace the cover of this book.

I have dedicated this book to the memory of my paternal grandparents, whom I never knew. I would also like to recognize my own dear Egyptian family and lovely Sarah, who continues to be a source of wonder as I watch her grow up. To family and friends who doubted that this book would ever see the light of day and, in some cases, even doubted its very existence, voilà!

THE DRAMA OF THE ASSIMILATED JEW

Giorgio Bassani's *Romanzo di Ferrara*

Introduction

In an interview granted in 1958, Giorgio Bassani said, "Ogni opera d'arte deve voler dire almeno due cose: una apparente e una riposta" (Every work of art should say at least two things, one apparent, the other concealed).[1] When I first encountered the writings of Bassani, although as yet unaware of this statement, I was indeed left with the feeling that I had missed something: there was more going on in these stories than could be gleaned from even a not-so-cursory reading. The thrust of this book derives from that initial impression.

The central thesis of this study is that in the process of unfolding, the works that make up the *Romanzo di Ferrara* produce an additional level of meaning – a palimpsest of sorts – which none of the stories or novels alone allows us to grasp and which constitutes its "concealed" subject. The *Romanzo* takes as its apparent subject the relations between Jews and Gentiles, as well as between Jews themselves, in Bassani's native Ferrara, from the end of the nineteenth century to just after World War II but primarily during the years of Fascism, with a particular focus on the years of persecution following the passage of the Race Laws in 1938. Its "concealed" subject, its unifying palimpsest, I claim, is the psychological hurdle Bassani felt that a Jewish male coming from his particular background had to overcome in order to make what was indeed an unlikely decision at the time and one not supported by any models in his own immediate entourage: the decision to fight for freedom, in an atmosphere of widespread passivity and denial, by joining the Resistance. Moreover, this hurdle is never definitively cleared; made up of his own internal demons, it demands an ongoing struggle that is never quite over, a struggle that is evoked in terms of Nietzsche's concept of "self-overcoming"[2] and extends to the difficult road to recovery and to reintegration in the postwar years, with a new understanding of his place as a Jew in Italian society and in history.

Access to this palimpsest is not direct. The analysis through which I tease out its presence involves a close reading that focuses primarily, though not exclusively, on the specifically gender-based intertexts and discourses that echo in the pages of the *Romanzo*. My reading identifies and grounds itself in three such overarching narratives: the Nietzschean narrative of *ressentiment*, the Freudian family romance, and Thomas Mann's diagnosis of the distortions wrought by emancipation on the Jewish psyche in his relatively little-known story "The Blood of the Walsungs" (1905). Their point of intersection is the gendered discourse of Jewish identity in vogue in the late nineteenth and early twentieth centuries.[3]

Few critics have commented on the role of gender and sexuality in Bassani's works and even then have paid it only cursory attention. The sexual deviations and difficulties that plague many of his characters are normally glossed over and downplayed as mere metaphors for social disorders. Anna Dolfi, one of the most important Italian critics of Bassani, sees all manifestations of sexual deviance or dysfunction as symptomatic of an existential malaise and dismisses any other more literal interpretations as "facile Freudianism."[4] According to Marilyn Schneider, whose *Vengeance of the Victim: History and Symbol in Giorgio Bassani's Fiction* (1986) remains a cornerstone of Bassani criticism,

> In the Bassani narratives homosexuality signals moral weakness, both personal and social. It represents an impotence or infertility that blocks all potential for social health. In its initial expression in *Una notte del '43*, the "sick" association between the pharmacist Pino Barilari and the Fascist Sciagura determines the negative coordinates of the social forces that will operate in one way or another throughout Bassani's fiction. ... Once written into his fiction, the idea of homosexuality takes possession of the author. Whether elegant and sensitive or pathetic and dull-witted, the homosexual becomes a metaphor of the diseased social body.[5]

What Schneider does not explain is why "the idea of homosexuality takes possession of the author."

Other than Bassani himself, only two American critics completely extraneous to the Italian critical context have explicitly addressed sexuality as such in the context of his work. Writing in 1973, Stanley Eskin, a professor of French reviewing *The Garden of the Finzi-Continis* and

Behind the Door, says quite bluntly, "Sex (in its normal English usage) is one of the two principal subjects of both novels."[6] More recently John Champagne (2010), another American scholar who is, again, not an Italianist, has addressed the question of the protagonist's sexuality in *The Garden of the Finzi-Continis* from the perspective of queer studies. Basing himself on a very partial knowledge of the Bassani corpus, Champagne arrives at conclusions with which I do not entirely agree but which do have the merit of drawing attention to the primacy of this question in Bassani's work.[7] As for Bassani himself, in a 1984 interview he says:

> J'ai écrit *Dietro la porta* pour donner une réalité au personnage qui dit "je" depuis *Gli occhiali d'oro.* Le narrateur avait besoin de tout dire sur lui-même, de dire toute la vérité sur son passage de l'enfance à l'âge adulte. Rien de plus. Je n'avais jamais parlé de ma virilité, de mon propre sexe auparavant. ... Après l'atroce histoire des *Lunettes d'or*, après la description des jeux érotiques du *Jardin des Finzi-Contini*, j'avais besoin de donner une image véridique de moi-même.[8]

> I wrote *Dietro la porta* to give a real dimension to the character saying "I" from *Gli occhiali d'oro* onward. The narrator needed to express everything about himself, to tell the whole truth about his passage from childhood to adulthood. Nothing more. I had never before spoken about my virility, about my own sexuality. ... After the atrocious story of *Gli occhiali d'oro*, after the description of the erotic games in *Il giardino dei Finzi-Contini*, I needed to provide a true image of myself.

In the words of Eskin, that image involves "a fearful, glum sense of sexuality involving shadowy hints of homosexuality, incest and impotence."[9]

Eskin omits masochism. What still haunted Bassani in the aftermath of the war was the extent to which the Jews of Ferrara had supported Fascism even in the face of persecution and the degree to which both Jews and Gentiles had seemingly acquiesced passively to their marginalization and eventual deportation. The nature of Jewish reaction to persecution was a subject of heated debate among Jewish historians after the war. According to Raul Hilberg, whose massive and masterful history of the Holocaust came out in the early 1960s, more Jews did not react forcefully to the round-ups of their people because they lacked a military tradition: he believed that "Jews had traditionally, because of their history, abandoned the art of communal self-defence and therefore no significant armed Jewish resistance took place during the Holocaust."[10] Other historians have since refuted this claim, but the fact that so many Jews in Bassani's own milieu had failed to oppose their persecution, going quietly to their deaths after having been obstinately faithful to the Fascist regime, loomed large in his mind. As Bassani himself points out, the Jews of Italy had gone from emancipation and integration (and in some cases assimilation) to exile in their own land and then to extermination in a little under eighty years:

> Quegli stessi ebrei che poi sarebbero finiti in così gran numero nelle camere a gas naziste, erano stati in gran parte fascisti. ... Eh sì, purtroppo, la tragedia vera degli ebrei ferraresi, e di grandissima parte degli ebrei italiani, può dirsi quella di essere stati dei borghesi, coinvolti dapprima nel fascismo, e poi, in fondo senza sapere perché, finiti nel nulla dei campi di sterminio.[11]

> Those same Jews who would end up in such great numbers in the Nazi gas chambers were for the most part Fascists. ... Indeed, the real tragedy of the Ferrara Jews, and of the great majority of Italian Jews, can be said to be, regrettably, the fact that they had been part of the bourgeoisie, involved at first in Fascism and then, without actually knowing why, had ended up annihilated in the extermination camps.

It is in connection to this problem that Bassani engages with the discourses of Jewishness and gender common to Nietzsche, Freud, and Mann. By casting the Jewish people as the originators of *ressentiment*, Nietzsche focuses on them as a weak, feminized people forced to idealize passivity by their own helplessness in the face of the powerful. In an interview with Ferdinando Camon, Bassani in fact uses a distinctly Nietzschean vocabulary: in speaking of his relationship to Thomas Mann, in particular of the difference between Micòl and Alberto Finzi-Contini and the protagonists of the "Blood of the Walsungs," he refers to himself as a "recovering decadent," so to speak, who has tried to "overcome" his decadence through understanding. He says: "Non che io rifiuti il decadentismo: ci siamo ancora tutti dentro. Però ho cercato di guarirne possedendolo criticamente fino in fondo." (Not that I reject decadentism: we are all still immersed in it. However, I have tried to recover from it, by getting to the bottom of it.)[12] In the same interview he speaks of the protagonists of *Il giardino dei Finzi-Contini* as all "fiacchi" (weak, exhausted). He attributes this weakness or exhaustion to Fascism, which he sees as a disease that has contaminated everyone, including those who claim to oppose the regime, but the repeated emphasis on the term *fiacco* cannot help but suggest a Nietzschean intertext:

> La tabe corrode tutti, e questo spiega che la reazione di tante vittime sia debole, fiacca: il protagonista è fiacco, Malnate è fiacco, i Finzi-Contini sono fiacchi: si sta attraversando questa galassia, e tutti quanti non possono non essere toccati da essa, anche per delle ragioni sociali, perché tutti sono borghesi, perché tutti sono proprietari, sono radicati lì.

> The disease corrodes everyone, and this explains why the reaction of so many victims is weak, faint: the protagonist is weak, Malnate is weak, the Finzi-Continis are weak: they are all passing through this galaxy, and cannot help but be touched by it, also for social reasons, because they are all bourgeois, because they are all property owners, because they are rooted there.[13]

The Freudian Oedipal narrative is, of course, all about shedding the feminine identification for a more properly heterosexual, masculine gender position, while Thomas Mann's story about the German-Jewish Ahrenhold family provides a brilliant, satirical condensation of how this process has been undermined by the contradictory position in which Jews find themselves after emancipation. Though far from an exhaustive inventory of the wealth of materials and discourses Bassani has drawn upon in the *Romanzo di Ferrara,* these authors are the ones, however, that I believe Bassani uses to evoke his own internal struggle to mobilize himself in an atmosphere of passivity and denial. Nathaniel Hawthorne, Stendhal, Dante, Pirandello, Lampedusa, Joyce, Otto Weininger, and the stereotypes of anti-Jewish propaganda, to name only some of his interlocutors, provide other elements that interact with the three principal intertexts. Bassani appropriates, absorbs, and recasts them all in such a way as to tell another story: his own.

Bassani is notorious for having obsessed over his novels and stories well after their initial publication, continuing to revise them over a period of approximately forty years, until he was satisfied that he had created a compact, unified body of work. Written, rewritten, titled, retitled, collected, rearranged, re-collected, published, and republished, they finally appeared in 1974 as one volume under the umbrella title

Il romanzo di Ferrara, only to be reworked again between 1978 and 1980.[14] And yet, notwithstanding all that has been written about the *Romanzo* since then, no serious attempt to provide a unified interpretation of this final product appears to have been made; nor should it be, if one is to heed the warning of Roberto Cotroneo, editor of the superb Mondadori Meridiani volume of Bassani's complete works (1998). Cotroneo sees the *Romanzo* as a work that Bassani "ha tessuto con pazienza, e ha riempito di trappole" (has woven patiently and has filled with traps):

> *Il romanzo di Ferrara* è il lungo racconto di una città e di un mondo, di una borghesia, di una comunità ebraica ricca e contraddittoria: è un'analisi sul fascismo, e in particolare su *quel* fascismo ferrarese. Ma su tutto questo c'è una nebbia che avvolge i motivi più profondi per i quali Bassani ha concepito la sua produzione narrativa come un'unica opera, fatta di fili che si annodano, di storie che s'intrecciano, anche per poco, quanto basta per far tornare alla mente un personaggio, un angolo di Ferrara, un pensiero di un racconto precedente. …
>
> Rimane il lavoro di uno scrittore che ha fatto della sua opera, soprattutto di quella narrativa, un capolavoro di maestria, di intuizione, di ambiguità, lasciando ai suoi lettori più accorti una vertigine interpretativa che nessuna ermeneutica futura potrà chiarire fino in fondo e che pone Giorgio Bassani tra i grandi scrittori italiani di questo secondo Novecento.[15]

> The *Romanzo di Ferrara* is the saga of a city and of a world, of a bourgeoisie, of a rich Jewish community, full of contradictions: it is an analysis of Fascism and more particularly of its specific Ferrarese expression. But over all this there is a fog that obscures the deeper motivations behind Bassani's conception of his narrative output as a unified whole, made up of knotted threads, interwoven stories – albeit subtly, just enough to evoke a character, a corner of Ferrara, a thought of a previous story. …
>
> It remains the work of a writer who has made of his oeuvre, but especially his narrative work, a masterpiece of execution, of intuition, of ambiguity, leaving to his more attentive readers a work of vertiginous interpretative possibilities, which no future hermeneutics will manage to decipher fully and which places Giorgio Bassani among the great Italian writers of this second half of the twentieth century.

The interviews that Bassani gave over the years certainly seem to support Cotroneo's position. Though useful, they are not without their glaring inconsistencies,[16] as well as a certain amount of coyness and posturing. Bassani attributes the apparent opacity of his stories,[17] – the fact that he does not delve beneath the surface of things to "explain" his characters' behaviour – to his desire to avoid invading their privacy: "J'éprouve une répugnance à entrer au-delà du 'coeur' du personnage" (I feel a great reluctance to penetrate the "heart" of a character).[18] At the same time he tells us that these very characters, with their secrets and inviolable boundaries, represent "parts" of him[19] and as such are vehicles for his own veiled confessions:[20] "Non è immaginabile un libro come il *Romanzo di Ferrara* se non lo si vede come storia dell'*io*: il personaggio più importante di tutta la mia opera è l'*io*, uomo e artista. Un *io* che parla, che si confessa, si svela, anche in segreto."[21] (One cannot imagine a book like the *Romanzo di Ferrara* if not as the story of the narrating "I": the most important character of my whole oeuvre is the "I," man and artist. An "I" who speaks, confesses, reveals himself, even secretly.) To complicate matters further, sometimes he claims that the real confession is in his poetry but not in his novels,[22] at other times he says that it is in his last two novels as well.[23]

And yet if it is true, as Cotroneo points out, that the *Romanzo* is made up of a self-referential body of texts that gesture back and forth to each other quite forcefully, then it follows that the whole must be greater than the sum of its parts. In a late interview (1991), Bassani explained his obsessive revision of his works in the following terms:

> Io credo nella realtà spirituale come unica realtà. ... Ci credo sul serio. Ed è anche per questo che mi sono accanito sulle mie scritture per farne un'opera sola. È soltanto per questa ragione che ho scritto e riscritto ogni pagina dei miei libri. Ho scritto e riscritto allo scopo di dire, attraverso la mia opera, la verità, tutta la verità.[24]

> I believe in spiritual reality as the only reality. ... Seriously. And this is also why I laboured so persistently to turn my writings into a unified whole. It is only for this reason that I wrote and rewrote every page of my books. I wrote and rewrote with the aim of telling, through my works, the truth, the whole truth.

A copy of philosopher Guido Calogero's *La scuola dell'uomo* (1939), annotated by Bassani presumably between 1940 and 1943, makes clear what Bassani meant by "spiritual reality."[25] Calogero was more or less an orthodox follower of Benedetto Croce, to whose secular *religione della libertà* (religion of freedom) Bassani attributed the fact that he was able to defy his own milieu and join the Resistance in 1937, even before the Race Laws were passed. For Calogero and Croce, and consequently Bassani, the spirit has nothing to do with transcendence. A marginal notation on Calogero's text in Bassani's hand explicitly reads, "Lo spirito si attua non per una sorta di trascendenza ma per consapevole atto morale" (The spirit comes to life not as a form of transcendence but rather as a deliberate moral act). Bassani underlined twice a passage about history containing Calogero's affirmation that "per vasta e profonda e grande che possa essere questa storia, essa storia sarà in me e non io in essa"[26] (However vast and profound and powerful this history may be, it is a history that will be in me and not I in it). In an interview Bassani also speaks of "spirito inteso come realtà unica da cui qualsiasi dittatura non può non sentirsi minacciata"[27] (spirit understood as the only reality by which any dictatorship cannot help but feel threatened). Thus "spirit," in this particular context, is the conscious decision to oppose the Fascist dictatorship, and the *realtà spirituale* (spiritual reality) that the *Romanzo* evokes is the process of overcoming passivity in order to resist. A submerged story that originates in his own psyche and gradually takes shape over the course of the *Romanzo*, it points to everything that he himself, as an overprotected and pampered Jewish male growing up in an affluent and essentially conformist bourgeois family in a community such as that of Ferrara, had had to struggle with in order to mobilize himself in the dark days of the Fascist dictatorship.[28]

Not the least of his problems was the fact that among the Jews of Ferrara who had been strangely silent in the face of persecution was his own father. Like so many other Jews of his class, the elder Bassani had been reluctant to confront head-on the threat to the Jews posed by the new legislation, preferring to deny or to minimize its devastating effects. If we are to believe what Bassani tells us in *Il giardino dei Finzi-Contini*, he even turned to his son for guidance, losing all credibility in the young man's eyes.[29] In a 1961 speech Bassani described his father's beliefs and the milieu in which he grew up in the following terms:

> Io ... uscivo da una famiglia perfettamente allineata ai tempi. Mio padre, lui, aveva preso la tessera del fascio addirittura nel '20: e ciò nondimeno era tra gli uomini più onesti che abbia mai conosciuto, puro e candido nel suo ingenuo patriottismo. Nel 1940, nel '41, durante gli anni furenti del mio primo antifascismo io definivo "stolido patriottismo" il suo. Tuttavia si trattava di patriottismo: vero, ingenuo, appassionato, puro.
>
> Uscivo da una famiglia di questo tipo: ebraica e fascista. Ma sia ben chiaro: infinite altre famiglie ebraiche erano a quell'epoca come la nostra,

normali (e banali) come la nostra. Eravamo dei piccoli borghesi, caratterizzati, anche noi, dagli stessi difetti, dalle stesse colpe, dalle stesse insufficienze della contemporanea piccola borghesia moderata cattolica. Sembrerà strano: eppure erano pochissimi, prima del 1938, gli ebrei italiani che non fossero devoti di Casa Savoia, mentre il duce, che aveva conquistato l'impero, rappresentava per molte delle nostre madri, zie e sorelle una specie di idolo. Dopo il 1938, dopo le famigerate leggi razziali, *quasi* tutti capirono, naturalmente. Ma prima di questa data fatidica, ripeto, fra gli ebrei italiani dominava il conformismo più totale.[30]

I ... came from a family perfectly in line with the spirit of the times. My father had joined the Fascist Party as early as 1920: and nonetheless, he was one of the most honest men I have ever known, pure and candid in his naive patriotism. In 1940, 1941, during my first furious anti-Fascist years, I defined his patriotism as "foolish." Even so, it was in fact patriotism: true, ingenuous, passionate, pure.

This is the type of family I came from: Jewish and Fascist. But I must stress this: that an infinite number of other Jewish families were at that time similar to ours, normal (and banal) like ours. We belonged to the petty bourgeoisie, characterized by the very same flaws, faults, and failings as the contemporary moderate Catholic petty bourgeoisie. It will seem strange: nevertheless, before 1938, very few Italian Jews were not devotees of the House of Savoy, while the Duce, who had conquered the empire, represented for many a mother, aunt, sister, a sort of idol. After 1938, after the infamous racial laws, *almost* everyone understood, naturally. However, before that fateful date, I must stress how prevalent among Italian Jews was this attitude of total conformity.

From his interviews and essays it is clear that Bassani was particularly proud of the fact that he had distinguished himself from his community by joining the Resistance even before the passing of the Race Laws in 1938:

A quell'epoca [1940] ero già implicato da parecchi anni nella lotta contro il fascismo. ... Ero quindi ben conscio di quel che stava accadendo. Anzi, ti dirò di più: fiero di essere come ero, cioè diverso non soltanto dalla grande maggioranza degli italiani, che erano quasi tutti fascisti, ma diverso anche dai miei correzziali (come li chiamavo io), cioè appartenenti alla stessa razza ma non alla stessa religione. La mia religione era quella della libertà. Credevo nella libertà come religione: seguace anche in questo di Benedetto Croce, e perciò ben difeso, diciamo così.[31]

> At that time [1940] I had already been involved for a number of years in the fight against Fascism. … I was therefore very well aware of what was going on. In fact, I would add this much: I was proud of being the way I was, different from the majority of Italians, who were almost all Fascists, but also from my "coracials," as I liked to call them, that is to say, those belonging to the same race as I but not to the same religion. My religion was that of liberty. I believed in liberty as a religion: I was a follower of Benedetto Croce also in that sense and, as such, well defended.

Elsewhere he says:

> Bien avant les lois raciales je suis devenu un antifasciste actif. C'était très rare, car à cette époque, israélites compris, ils étaient tous fascistes. Je suis resté un militant, un conspirateur … jusqu'en 1943. Ces années, si tristes pour tout le monde, ne l'étaient pas pour moi. Je possédais ma vérité, ma double vérité, de militant et (sans l'avoir bien réalisé encore) de barde de la réalité.[32]

> I became an active anti-Fascist well before the Race Laws. This was very rare, because at that time, everyone was a Fascist, Jews included. I remained an activist, a conspirator … until 1943. Those years, which were very miserable for everyone, were not so for me. I had my own truth, my double truth, as an activist and – without yet being aware of it – as a bard of reality.

And yet, with all the pride that he took in his anti-Fascist activism, the one topic Bassani never addresses directly in his fictional autobiography is his own role in the Resistance and how he came to make the decision to break with his milieu.[33] The narrator of *Il giardino dei Finzi-Contini* makes only one oblique reference to the time he spent in prison during the war years, in spite of the fact that Bassani claimed that his political experience was the sine qua non of his literary career – without it he would not have been able to write what he did:

> Per ciò che riguarda esclusivamente me, gli anni dal '37 al '43, che dedicai quasi del tutto all'attività antifascista clandestina … furono tra i più belli e più intensi dell'intera mia esistenza. Mi salvarono dalla disperazione a cui andarono incontro tanti ebrei italiani, mio padre compreso, col conforto che mi dettero d'essere totalmente dalla parte della giustizia e della verità, e persuadendomi soprattutto a non emigrare. Senza quegli anni per me fondamentali, credo che non sarei mai diventato uno scrittore.[34]

> As for me exclusively, the years from 1937 to 1943, which I devoted almost entirely to clandestine anti-Fascist activity … were among the best and most intense of my entire existence. They spared me the desperation that so many Italian Jews faced, my father included, giving me the solace of being totally on the side of justice and of truth and persuading me especially not to emigrate. Had it not been for those years, fundamental for me, I believe that I would have never become a writer.

Perhaps seizing on these last words, Marilyn Schneider has said: "The project of the entire *Romanzo*, in the process of breathing life into a universe of individuals and communities afflicted by historic upheaval, is to record the birth of its poet."[35] I would qualify this by adding that, to the extent that the birth of the poet depended on the birth of the militant anti-Fascist, the labour pains accompanying the birth of the anti-Fascist are also recorded here, symbolically, in all the stories that make up the *Romanzo*. By anti-Fascist I refer not only to the formation of an ideological stance – though that too, of course, is discussed, particularly in *Il giardino dei Finzi-Contini* – but to the birth of the adult male, the individual capable of severing his attachment to parent figures and all that they stand for in order to become an individual in his own right.[36] It carries also traces of the Nietzschean process of self-overcoming, of leaving the "crowd," of finding one's own voice and the courage to make it heard.

It is important to emphasize that Bassani sees himself as a historian of his community and of himself as a member of that community, the specific Jewish agrarian bourgeoisie of Ferrara, and it is within this context that he seeks answers to the questions that haunted him. Why did the Holocaust happen? How was it possible? How does one become a victim? How does one become a victimizer? And why did so many Gentiles sit by passively, why did so many Jews react passively as well, and why was it so difficult for them to admit what was happening in time to save themselves? And last but certainly not least, how does one go on in the aftermath?

Bassani, the Jews of Italy, and the Literary Establishment

Italian Jews, who constituted the longest continuous Jewish presence in Europe, had struggled with the vagaries of persecution and acceptance over the centuries, and although the first ghetto is said to have been the one established in Venice in 1516, by the time Bassani was born, exactly four hundred years later, they were comfortably ensconced in Italian society – or so it seemed.[37] Italian Unification had taken place in the years between 1860 and 1871. These were the years during which the Jews, fervent supporters of the Risorgimento, left behind the ghettos to experience the heady euphoria of admittance into mainstream Italian society. Many Italians experienced a conflict between their local regional identities or their Catholic identity and the new Italian one, the pope having excommunicated all supporters of the new secular state after the defeat of his army and the capture of Rome. However, for Jews previously confined to their ghettos no such conflict is deemed to have existed, or certainly not to the same extent.[38] Although the individual communities throughout Italy differed in terms of their local characteristics, as a group the Jews embraced Italian citizenship with a vengeance and, according to the distinguished historian and author Dan Vittorio Segre, could be considered the quintessential Italians, perhaps even to their own detriment as Jews:

> During the Risorgimento the Italian Jews had the feeling that they had not been admitted to a preexisting economic, social, and political system but had created it, they were co-founders together with the other Italian patriots of something totally new. To be a Jew in Italy meant, like for many Jews in America, to feel or believe oneself to be fully integrated in the non-Jewish society, whereas for the other Jews in Europe and the Islamic world, being a Jew meant never being 100% German, French or Arab, because they could not claim to be part of the host nation from its origin. The identity of interest and ideas between Jews and Italian nationalists up to the conquest of Rome in 1870 was so complete that it is not surprising to find that they idealized their new and transitory situation even when they realized that the Risorgimento, as a secular, emancipatory, and assimilatory movement, was bound to destroy their own particularism.[39]

Indeed, Jewishness was increasingly experienced as a private identity, lived largely in the home, while the public face was entirely Italian: "Ebrei in casa e cittadini fuori" (Jews in the home and citizens outside).[40] This was particularly the case among the Jews of the upper reaches of society. If it is true, as Segre suggests, that their Jewishness was quickly eroded, sacrificed to acculturation and to the mirage of integration, it is certainly also true, especially in northern and central Italy, that they prospered financially, professionally, and otherwise, quickly becoming prominent in politics, in journalism, and in the arts. By the time the Fascists came to power in 1922, the Jews were so integrated that one or two were among Mussolini's ministers. (His mistress Margherita Sarfati was also a Jew. She functioned as an adviser in cultural and artistic matters until she too fell from grace with the rise of official anti-Semitism.) Of course not all Jews supported Fascism; but certainly their patriotism was very strong, and for many this meant allegiance to the regime in power, especially in the class to which Bassani belonged. When Mussolini and Hitler officially became allies in 1936, the campaign against the Jews began in the Italian press. Nonetheless, the passage of the Race Laws in November 1938 – which meant, among other things, the removal of Jewish names from telephone directories, the expulsion of Jewish students and teachers from public schools and universities, restrictions on professional and business rights, prohibitions against marrying Aryans, having Aryans as servants in their homes, holding public office, and publishing – left the large majority of Italian Jews completely stunned, and they remained incredulous despite the reality.[41] For while the German Jews had been aware that there existed in Germany and Austria a strong current of racial anti-Semitism from the second half of the nineteenth century onward, the Italian Jews were entirely unprepared for their persecution: though anti-Semitic sentiment certainly existed in Italy, it had been largely religious in nature and not as threatening as the racial variety that was now rearing its head.

Bassani experienced this sudden change in status at a particularly important point in his life: the end of his university years. The doors to society were closing to him just as he was about to enter adulthood. Forced to abandon whatever plans he may have had, Bassani began teaching in the Jewish community school of Ferrara, to which Jewish children were relegated after having been banned from the public system. However, at the time he was already active in the Resistance and was later to become one of the founders of the Partito d'Azione, one of the most effective political parties in the fight against Fascism. In May 1943 he was imprisoned for subversive activity but was freed in July after the Allied invasion of Sicily and the arrest of Mussolini. He then moved to Rome with his parents and his new wife, Valeria Sinigallia, only to be forced into hiding in September, when German troops occupied northern and central Italy and returned Mussolini to power, at least nominally, in the Republic of Salò. Partisan warfare began, as did the rounding up and deportation of Jews by the Nazis and their local collaborators.

Although he had already published under a pseudonym in the early forties, Bassani began writing in earnest in the postwar years and continued to do so until the appearance of the final version of the *Romanzo di Ferrara* in 1980. In addition to his literary pursuits, he enjoyed an illustrious career in public service, briefly as director and vice-president of RAI, the national broadcasting network, and as founder of Italia Nostra, an organization dedicated to the protection of natural and cultural monuments. Bassani also taught, wrote film scripts, worked as an editor for the publishing house Feltrinelli (where he was responsible for the publication of Tomasi di Lampedusa's *Gattopardo*), won literary prizes, and generally participated fully in the cultural and political debates of his time. Everything would seem to suggest that he was thoroughly integrated into the life of his country. His work, however, suggests otherwise.

Though apparently recovered from the shock of his experiences, his preoccupations in the postwar years were clearly not those of the majority. Out of step under Fascism, he was out of step again after its demise. Few of Bassani's contemporaries, Jews and non-Jews alike, were willing to address the horrors of the recent past in any real way. "Memory" and "trauma" not being the common currency they are today,[42] once perfunctory homage had been paid to the dead, most Italian Jews, as historian Guri Schwartz explains, were anxious simply to move on:

> With a few exceptions, there was no convincing effort to reconsider the Jewish minority's relationship with the national culture, history and society. Rather, what emerges from the Jewish press, from memoirs and diaries as well as from declarations of community leaders, is the marked inclination to deny Italian responsibility in the origin and implementation of persecution, both for the period 1938-1943 as well as for the period of mass murders and deportation that followed the armistice with the Allies. This behaviour, in many ways similar to that adopted by Jews in other Western countries – such as, for example, France, Holland and Belgium – can be understood if we consider the intense desire to reintegrate into society and the conviction that such a process would have been easier by avoiding attracting too much attention to their specific tragedy. Reminding the nation of the Jewish plight would have contributed to the confirmation of a separateness, a distinction which most Italian Jews simply wished to erase as rapidly as possible. These were the dominant

> feelings of Jewish communal institutions of the generation that led in the post-fascist era and that supported, with great emphasis, a consolatory interpretation of fascist antisemitism destined to influence the political, cultural, as well as historiographical, debate for decades to come.[43]

Deemed defeatist and melancholy, Bassani's insistence on dwelling on the past flew in the face of attitudes of intellectual circles as well. The Marxist orthodoxy admitted only of heroic depictions of opposition to Fascism.[44] The neo-avant-garde represented by the members of Gruppo '63 was equally rigid and demanded formal experiments as a means of resistance to "bourgeois" literary conventions. Reading his work within the parameters of its own programme and prejudices, the Italian literary establishment condemned Bassani's writing as antiquated and self-indulgent,[45] preoccupied with memorializing as opposed to understanding,[46] while the Jews in his milieu objected to his depiction of their reactions to Fascism and the Race Laws.

Undaunted by his detractors, Bassani persisted, determined to pursue his own artistic and intellectual agenda. He made very clear what this agenda was in a 1991 interview with Anna Dolfi:

> Dentro di me c'era il desiderio che i miei racconti avessero un significato nuovo, più ricco e profondo di ciò che produceva la letteratura italiana d'allora, anche la più importante. A differenza degli altri, di tutti gli altri, io pretendevo di essere, oltre che un cosidetto narratore anche uno storico di me stesso e della società che rappresentavo. ... Intendevo essere uno storico, uno storicista, non un raccontatore di balle.[47]

> My desire was that my stories have a new meaning, richer and more profound than what Italian literature, even the most important, was producing at that time. Unlike the others, all the others, I wanted to be not only a so-called narrator but also a historian of myself and of the society I represented. ... I aimed to be a historian, a historically minded narrator, not just a teller of fibs.

Bassani's rejection of the essentialist view of Jews and their place in society was responsible, he claimed, for the fact that the Jews of Ferrara were hostile to his work. Of Jewish reception of his stories he says:

> *Le roman de Ferrare*, au fur et à mesure que je l'écrivais (et je n'avais aucune idée, au début, qu'il formerait un ensemble) a toujours trouvé

> parmi les israélites de Ferrare en particulier et chez les israélites italiens, des ennemis. Dans leur majorité, ils n'ont pas accepté la version que je donnais des événements qui se passaient à Ferrare. Ils étaient tous de l'Holocauste et non de celui de l'histoire et de la perspective historique.[48]

> As I was writing the *Romanzo di Ferrara* (and at first, I had no idea it would form a whole), I found that it encountered much hostility from Italian Jews, and particularly from the Jews of Ferrara. Most of them did not accept my version of the events taking place in Ferrara. They saw things only in terms of the Holocaust itself, not in terms of history and historical perspective.

When he chose *Il romanzo di Ferrara* as the the umbrella title for his works, he may have had in mind the "historical" definition of romance proposed by Nathaniel Hawthorne. Bassani is known to have been a great admirer of Hawthorne, in particular for *The Scarlet Letter* (1850), but his personal library also held two copies of the subsequent novel, *The House of the Seven Gables* (1851),[49] which Hawthorne termed a "romance." While it is true that Bassani would not have had to justify himself in the same way as Hawthorne, since the Italian term for novel, *romanzo*, connects the modern novel very explicitly to its roots in the medieval and Renaissance romance tradition, the following portions of Hawthorne's preface to *The House of the Seven Gables* might nonetheless have caught Bassani's attention:

> When a writer calls his work a Romance, it need hardly be observed that he wishes to claim a certain latitude, both as to its fashion and material, which he would not have felt himself entitled to assume, had he professed to be writing a novel. The latter form of composition is presumed to aim at a very minute fidelity, not merely to the possible, but to the probable and ordinary course of man's experience. The former … has fairly a right to present that truth under circumstances, to a great extent, of the writer's own choosing or creation. …
>
> … The point of view in which this Tale comes under the Romantic definition, *lies in the attempt to connect a by-gone time with the very Present that is flitting away from us.* It is a Legend, prolonging itself, from an epoch now gray in the distance, down into our own broad daylight, and bringing along with it some of its legendary mist, which the Reader, according to his pleasure, may either disregard, or allow to float almost imperceptibly about the characters and events.[50]

That Bassani had indeed been struck by Hawthorne's preface is also suggested by the following statement that Hawthorne makes about the Pynchon home, the House of the Seven Gables, a statement that cannot help but bring to mind the imaginary house of the Finzi-Continis: "[The author] trusts not to be considered as unpardonably offending, by laying out a street that infringes on nobody's private rights, and appropriating a lot of land which had no visible owner, and building a house, of materials long in use for constructing castles in the air." In the Hawthorne novel the root of the family's misfortune is seen as past ill-gotten gain, which in successive generations "divesting itself of every temporary advantage, becomes a pure and uncontrollable mischief."[51]

While there is no question that Bassani sees the prosperity of the Jews in the post-emancipation period, whether ill-gotten or not, as partly responsible for their hubris and thus their failure to react to their persecution, his underlying historical perspective goes back much farther than the nineteenth century. The famous prologue to *Il giardino dei Finzi-Contini* takes place in the Etruscan cemetery at Cerveteri. When Giannina innocently says that in her history book the Etruscans are placed at the beginning, together with the Jews and the Egyptians, Bassani is reminding us that the Jews are an ancient people and that their present cannot be abstracted from their past. By juxtaposing Etruscans and Jews he is also reminding us that while the Etruscans are extinct, having been brutally put down by the Romans, the Jews, notwithstanding a similar attempt to annihilate them, continue to defy the odds. However, repeated persecutions and centuries of ghetto living must have left their mark on the modern Jewish psyche: that the Etruscan cemetery is also an archaeological site suggests that the story about to be told involves a "digging" into this past.

In *Moses and Monotheism* (1939) Freud proposed a "theory of Jewishness – what it is, how it is transmitted, and how it continues to survive," which Eliza Slavet, author of *Racial Fever: Freud and the Jewish Question*, has called "a racial theory of memory":

> Certain events in the distant past were so traumatic that their memories were inherited by successive generations. Freud theorized that Jewishness is constituted by the inheritance of a specific archaic memory which Jewish people are inexorably compelled to transmit to future generations, whether consciously or unconsciously.[52]

Giusi Oddo De Stefanis, among the first to focus on Bassani's work as symbolic and to understand *Il giardino dei Finzi-Contini* as a spiritual autobiography, voices the questions Bassani appears to have had in mind in terms that suggest a Freudian derivation:

> Che cosa c'era nel passato degli ebrei ferraresi che ha permesso che avvenisse quello che è avvenuto? Avevano forse quegli eventi un'inconsapevole radice in fattori costituzionali della razza ebraica o in elementi fatalistici: auto-isolamento, vittimismo, predestinazione?[53]

> What was it, in the past of the Ferrara Jews, which allowed what happened to happen? Did those events have some unconscious origin in the constitutional makeup of the Jewish race or in fatalistic elements: self-seclusion, victimization, predestination?

Bassani looks for the answers as they are inscribed in him, a Jewish male living in Italy at a particular time, in a particular place, and from a particular background. Logically, he concentrates not so much on events themselves but on events as conduits into the emotions and fantasies of individuals and communities, whose inner, often unconscious and unarticulated experience is woven skilfully into indirect free discourse, first-person narration, and dialogue. Since we can only know the past from the way it is inscribed in the present, and since the way it manifests itself is often cryptic, we are left to fill in the blanks ourselves. His particular skill lies in the subtlety with which he captures the dynamic of self-delusion[54] as it manifests itself in a specific historical context, in conjunction with complex issues of class, race, and sexual orientation. He challenges the reader to find within the conflicts, contradictions, ambivalences, and biases of the narrative, as well in its leitmotifs, recurring patterns, and particular combination of "blindness and insight," clues as to what the actual reality might have been.[55]

It is important for an understanding of the present reading of Bassani's work to focus briefly on the status of the narrator. There are essentially three kinds of narrators in Bassani's oeuvre. In the earlier short stories the third-person narrator is both an insider and an outsider. He does not come forward except to occasionally remark on something, often from the perspective of the sort of narrator who inhabits the short stories of Pirandello. He uses for the most part indirect free discourse. The second type of narrator is the narrator of three first-person novels, who remains nameless throughout but is clearly meant to be the same person.[56] Telling his story retrospectively, he is not, however, the contemporary Bassani but a creation of

Bassani, a part of himself that he has objectified to the point of being able to analyse it; but what the narration gives us, on the surface, is the narrator's limited, subjective, and sometimes unreliable version of things. Bassani the writer has had to overcome or at least bring to consciousness not only the conflicts of his young protagonist but also the ongoing struggles of his older narrator, writing in the postwar period after the trauma of the Race Laws and the Holocaust. George Güntert speaks of this as an aesthetic solution influenced by Croce's concept of the *sentimento contemplato* (contemplated sentiment), in which "lo scrittore, nella misura in cui rinuncia al proprio compiacimento autobiografico per conferire autonomia al testo, applica a se stesso un procedimento ironico"[57] (The writer, insofar as he renounces his own autobiographical complacency to lend autonomy to the text, is submitting himself to a process of irony). While I concur with Güntert's view of Bassani's attention both to Crocean aesthetics and to the lessons of Thomas Mann, for my own purposes I would simply call this the use of a limited almost "unreliable narrator," as so termed by Wayne Booth in his classic *The Rhetoric of Fiction* (1961), to the extent that the narrator is still caught up in his personal viewpoint and cannot contemplate events, and himself, objectively, even though he is speaking retrospectively: it is his subjectivity that is at issue here for Bassani more than the chronicle of events. The third type of narrator appears in the last novel, *L'airone*, as simply a third-person narrator exclusively inside the main character's head.[58]

The three types of narrators correspond to different degrees of openness: in the early stories that make up *Dentro le mura* the third-person narrator is still reluctant to speak directly, while in the first-person trilogy he speaks directly, but still only obliquely, of himself. In *Gli occhiali d'oro* the narrator uses the homosexual Dr Fadigati as the mirror of his condition, in *Il giardino dei Finzi-Contini* the Finzi-Continis are his "doubles," so to speak, and in *Dietro la porta* his adolescent classmates and tormentors, Pulga and Cattolica, are the terms of his conflict. In *L'airone*, there is no mediating presence other than the heron: Limentani is a still lingering but completely objectified "part of him"[59] that has yet to be eliminated – and is – by suicide. For Limentani it is suicide; for Bassani it is surmounting the residual resentment that he may have carried with him and that could still poison his being as a Jew. In *L'odore del fieno*, the collection of assorted fiction and nonfiction short pieces that closes the *Romanzo*, he finally emerges as himself, the contemporary author and man, but again only partly unveiled. Sometimes he is himself, sometimes he is hiding behind fictional characters who are projections of him.

The idea of stratification is also fundamental for an understanding of Bassani's writing, as suggested by the archaeology metaphor evoked by the Etruscan cemetery (this will be discussed in greater detail in the analysis of *Il giardino dei Finzi-Contini*). In the case of the first-person trilogy, the stratification is first of all spatial. Each novel represents a different level of awareness, alluding to the Nietzschean process of "going inside"[60] and "unmasking,"[61] peeling away layer after layer of whatever it is that needs to be laid bare. Each of the last two novels illuminates the previous one, uncovering new dimensions of the protagonist/narrator's psyche; but within each novel there exists also a temporal stratification in which memory traces, representing different epochs in the psychic life of the narrator, are superimposed or intertwined. Moreover, everything that Bassani's narrator recalls is filtered by hindsight, through the experience of the Race Laws and his awareness of the Holocaust, including his account of anything that might have taken place before.[62] Thus, concentration camp imagery is sometimes unconsciously evoked by apparently unrelated descriptions in which, however, associations are formed that hark back to this trauma, resulting in the two time frames being embedded on top of each other in the same soil, so to speak.[63] In other cases, the use of archetypal imagery such as the door and the threshold will point back to individual "ancient or pre-historic memories of childhood"[64] that have been repressed but are still operative, as well as to archaic structures of the collective Jewish psyche created by centuries of persecution and ghetto living.

When he assembled *Il romanzo di Ferrara* in its final form, Bassani eliminated all but one of the epigraphs originally contained in the individual works: Manzoni's famous "Ma che sa il cuore? Appena un poco di quello che è già accaduto."[65] (But what does the heart know? A mere fraction of what has already occurred.) In other words, there are no exhaustive or entirely objective answers to the question of what makes certain events possible at any given time. Ultimately, why something happens remains a mystery lodged in the human heart.[66] While what goes on there cannot be represented directly, it can be evoked: it is this unspoken and elusive dimension of his own history as a Jew, as the son of his "fathers," that Bassani's fiction tries, symbolically, to capture.[67] What contribution the work of Nietzsche, Freud, and Mann may have made to his understanding of this history and how their insights are worked into his own story form the subject of the first chapter.

1 Jews and Gender

It is no secret that doubts about the masculinity of Jews were rampant in post-Darwinian pseudoscientific literature in the late nineteenth and early twentieth centuries and that they were a distinct part of the discourse that led up to the Nazi genocide of the Jews as an inferior race. Ann Pellegrini, in an article on race, gender, and Jewish bodies, summarizes the issue very well:

> The intersection of race and gender at and as the site of Jewishness can be seen in much of the popular and "scientific" literature of nineteenth and early twentieth-century Germany and Austria, where the Jewish male was ubiquitously assimilated to the category "woman." Indeed, the feminization of the Jewish male body was so frequent a theme in this period that Jewishness – more precisely the Jewishness of Jewish *men* – became as much a category of gender as of race. ... Accordingly, the Jewish male's supposed effeminacy became one of the essential signposts of the Jewish people's racial difference. ... The feminization of the Jewish male body took on especial significance for the health of the body politic, which was identified with masculine vigor. Otto Rank, a prominent and Jewish member of Freud's Viennese circle, called Jews "women among the people," who must "above all join themselves to the masculine life-force if they are to become productive."[1]

Historian Ritchie Robertson offers specific examples:

> The equation of Jewishness and femininity appears in Nietzsche's work as early as section 9 of the *Birth of Tragedy* (1872), where the active, Aryan, masculine myth of Prometheus and his crime of stealing fire from heaven

> is contrasted with the passive, Semitic, feminine myth of Eve and the sin of the Fall. In 1869 the distinguished Viennese rabbi Adolf Jellinek published a book, *Der Judische Stamm* (*The Jewish Tribe*), with a chapter headed "*The Femininity of the Jewish Tribe*" [in which] the relationship of Jews to non-Jews is made analogous to the passive, submissive relationship of women to men. …
>
> A feminized Jewish man features in the play *Karla Bühring* (1895) by "Laura Marholm" (the pseudonym of Laura Hansson, 1854–1905), where the violinist Karla Bühring is attracted to the Jewish intellectual Dr. Siegfried Collander. … His enemy Eschenmeyer describes him [as] "a kind of half-way house and intermediate formation, to put it in scientific terms, between us and the female, and that is why women like him as a daily stimulant." This Darwinian language proposes the feminized Jew as a kind of missing link between the Aryan man and the woman.[2]

Of course the most notorious of Germanic writers to enshrine the Jewish male as "feminine" was the Austrian Jew and homosexual Otto Weininger, whose *Sex and Character* (*Geschlecht und Charakter*, 1903)[3] enjoyed great popularity among European intellectuals and in Italy particularly among those associated with the prestigious journal *La voce*. Weininger's work was published in Italy in 1912 and reprinted five times under Fascism. Alberto Cavaglion's *Otto Weininger in Italia* documents the immense influence of this treatise on Italian intellectuals in the period coinciding with Bassani's formation, that is, well into the thirties.[4] It is certainly no coincidence that this infamous text is mentioned in *Dietro la porta* as one of the books in Pulga's father's library.

That Bassani was sensitive to the purported Jewish lack of manliness in the face of persecution is made explicit in "Una lapide in via Mazzini," in his portrayal of the way in which the citizens of Ferrara viewed the postwar prefect of Ferrara, Dr Herzen. Fearful of being called to account for their collaboration with the Fascists, instead of defending themselves directly, they implicitly accuse the Jewish Herzen of a similar complicity for having failed to protest when his factory was seized by the Fascists: "Eh sì, lo conoscevano bene, loro, quel tipo che nel '39 si era lasciato buttar fuori come niente fosse, senza dire bai, dalla fabbrica di scarpe che allora possedeva a un paio di chilometri lungo la strada di Bologna" (91; Ah yes, they knew him well, they did, that character who in '39, without saying a word, had allowed himself to be thrown out of the big shoe factory he owned a couple of kilometres down the road on the way to Bologna).

In this connection, Bassani was certainly also familiar with a famous Freudian passage from the *Interpretation of Dreams* (1899) in which the particular dilemma of the Jewish male in a hostile Christian society is evoked by Freud himself. The passage concerns Freud's deep love for Rome and a series of dreams he had about his longing to visit that city. His analysis of these dreams leads him to associate to Hannibal, whom he calls "the favorite hero of my high school days," and eventually to an actual childhood memory of a conversation with his father:

> I may have been ten or twelve years old, when my father began to take me with him on his walks and reveal to me in his talk his views upon things in the world we live in. Thus it was, on one such occasion, that he told me a story to show me how much better things were now than they had been in his days. "When I was a young man," he said, "I went for a walk one Saturday in the streets of your birthplace; I was well-dressed and had a new fur cap on my head. A Christian came up to me and with a single blow knocked off my cap into the mud and shouted: 'Jew! Get off the pavement!'" "And what did you do?" I asked. "I went into the roadway and picked up my cap," was his quiet reply. This struck me as unheroic conduct on the part of the big, strong man who was holding the little boy by the hand. I contrasted this situation with another which fitted my feelings better: the scene in which Hannibal's father, Hamilcar Barca, made his boy swear before the household altar to take vengeance on the Romans. Ever since that time Hannibal had a place in my phantasies.[5]

The Freud anecdote illustrates clearly the difference in attitude between a secularized Jew, such as the younger Freud, and an older Jew closer to his ghetto roots and therefore less prone to acknowledge the desire for revenge. The reluctance of the Jewish male to give vent to his anger is addressed by Warren Rosenberg and seen not only as the result of centuries of oppression but also as the consequence of a culture of passivity developed in response to it:

> The vast divergence between biblical narratives that depict Jewish men as militarily heroic, with God the Father demanding violence from his Jewish sons, and the historic reality of Jewish victimization continues to shape Jewish male conflicts over violence. … The compensatory image of the Jew as non-violent, intellectual, fatalistic and accepting others' violence results in part from a two-thousand year exclusion from positions of power, but it

> also results from inconsistent messages transmitted by the Hebrew scriptures themselves, complicated by the diversity of rabbinic interpretation.[6]

In short, standards of manliness in the ghetto were very different from those in Christian society.[7] Recent work on gender and Jewishness points out that such standards comprised "a set of performances that are culturally read as non-male within a given historical context. This culture can be very broadly described as Roman in its origins and as European in its scope and later history."[8] It is even suggested that ghetto Jews, immersed in rabbinic culture, valorized the feminine in their make-up, that "the feminization of the male, in part symbolized (or effected?) through truncation of the penis, was experienced as a positive phenomenon, as a positive sense of self-identification and differentiation from the Romans (and their descendants)."[9] However, in the move from the ghetto to the broader world, this positive valorization, if ever it existed, was lost. Moreover, before emancipation, the connection of Jewish men to the outside world had naturally been rather fragile and tenuous. As a result, in the early post-emancipation period, moving from a Jewish "private" sphere to a Christian "public" one – or even a secularized one – meant not only taking one's place in society without a strong, socially embedded male figure to emulate but also renouncing, to some degree, one's Jewish roots and hence adopting a very different standard of manliness.[10] When seventy or so years later the Race Laws (1938) closed the official public sphere to Jews altogether, the problem for "marginal Jews" such as Bassani[11] became that of choosing to fall back on an often reviled Jewish identity associated with the ghetto, as is clearly the case for the protagonist of *Gli occhiali d'oro* – "*Goi, goìm*: che vergogna, che umiliazione, che ribrezzo a esprimermi così! Eppure ci riuscivo già – mi dicevo – : diventato simile a un qualsiasi ebreo dell'Europa orientale che non fosse mai vissuto fuori dal proprio ghetto" (291). (Goy, goyim; what a sense of shame, what a humiliation, what a loathsome falling-off to think in those terms. And yet I had already managed this – I told myself – become like any Jew whatsoever from Eastern Europe who had never lived outside his own ghetto [96].) – or of fighting back by joining an alternate public sphere, that of resistance. Neither choice, as Bassani depicts it, came naturally.

The Family Romance

In a 1979 interview Bassani is quoted as having said that the best titles are those that have at least two meanings: "I titoli che funzionano sono quelli che vogliono dire almeno due cose."[12] The *Romanzo di Ferrara* serves the purpose admirably, alluding as it does to several possible works and genres. We have already mentioned Nathaniel Hawthorne's definition of romance and how it may pertain to Bassani's work. In an Italian context, the first definition that comes to mind is the romance tradition that flourished in the court of Renaissance Ferrara. Such works as *Orlando Furioso* staged episodes of fancy and invention in historical contexts. The nineteenth-century tradition of cyclical realist novels, such as Balzac's *Comédie humaine* or Verga's *Vinti*, is also suggested by the term *romanzo*, although Bassani did not share these authors' ambition to create a wide fresco of society.[13] For our purposes, the most relevant kind of romance, especially if one considers the wording of the original Italian title, is the family romance as described by Freud in his famous essay by that name (1908). The Italian title *Il romanzo di Ferrara* readily evokes *il romanzo di famiglia*, the Italian translation of family romance. Bassani has frequently denied having been influenced by Freud, in conjunction with his own belief that human beings are ultimately unknowable.[14] However, in a 1966 interview published only very recently, he admitted very openly having used Freud, but only in reference to *Dietro la porta*, and one senses that the reluctance to acknowledge the use of Freud is tied to the ambition to be seen primarily as a social novelist:

> Io sono stato accusato di non indagare nelle viscere, ma ad un certo punto il tentativo di istituire un rapporto anche su una base freudiana, viscerale, con il cosidetto io narrante l'ho fatto: chi è costui? Perché racconta ciò che gli è accaduto nella lontana adolescenza, perché questa storia del tutto privata, personale, eccetera? Però anche in questo libro, il più viscerale che ho scritto, c'è l'impegno morale e politico di definire un ambiente, di restituire una situazione valida per tutti: il libro non è soltanto una esibizione di viscere, è anche la rappresentazione di un certo mondo, di un preciso ambiente sociale.[15]

> I have been accused of failing to inquire into the depths of the psyches of my characters, but at a certain point I did make the attempt to create a Freudian, visceral relationship with the so-called narrating self [of *Behind the Door*]: who is he? Why is he telling this story of something that happened to him so long ago, in his adolescence, why this very private, personal story, etc.? However, in this book, the most visceral I have written, there is also the moral and political commitment to define a milieu, to bring to life a situation valid for everyone: the book is not only an exposure

> of the visceral, it is also the representation of a certain world, of a precise social milieu.

In a later interview one can even detect a certain Bloomian "anxiety of influence" in the admission that he made use of Freud's ideas: "Même quand je me suis servi de la psychanalyse je suis resté fidèle à moi-même"[16] (Even when I used psychoanalysis, I stayed faithful to myself).

In the brief but very influential text entitled "Family Romances," Freud develops his well-known theory regarding the rather convoluted and fanciful processes by which psychic separation from parental figures is attained or not. The first paragraph reads thus:

> The freeing of an individual, as he grows up, from the authority of his parents is one of the most necessary though one of the most painful results brought about by the course of his development. It is quite essential that this liberation should occur and it may be presumed that it has been to some extent achieved by everyone who has reached a normal state. Indeed, the whole progress of society rests upon the opposition between successive generations. On the other hand there is a class of neurotics whose condition is recognizably determined by their having failed in this task.[17]

Failure to negotiate this difficult passage meant, in the Freudian paradigm, remaining forever in the thrall of the mother, forever on the cusp of manhood, without ever crossing completely into that territory. It is no coincidence that the *Romanzo di Ferrara* begins and ends with maternal imagery. In the opening sequence of the first short story, "Lida Mantovani," the female protagonist is about to give birth, while the last novel, *L'airone,* ends with the main character saying goodnight to his elderly mother in her bedroom just before he retires to his own room to commit suicide with his hunting rifle. Ferrara is a state of mind, the prison of the maternal embrace, and leaving "Ferrara" means overcoming passivity and even paralysis, to which denial often seems preferable. In fact, figures of passivity and paralysis, both figurative and literal, are rampant and explicit in the *Romanzo,* as are images of arrested development. The profusion of primal imagery, in which characters are seen on different thresholds and indeed kept there, will allude to many things – not the least of which is the increased difficulty of moving into manhood, of living out the Bildungsroman, in a society whose doors are closed to some, as they are to the young Jew at the heart of these stories, who, according to this account, will have to reinvent himself almost overnight in order to leave the psychological ghetto he inhabits. The title of the third first-person novel, *Dietro la porta*, is an explicit reference to the primal scene. The threshold also alludes to the position of Jews in society, poised precariously between Jewish and Gentile worlds and unable to extricate themselves from their families of origin.

In keeping with the theme of separation, the ultimate desired outcome of the family romance phase, Bassani repeatedly emphasizes in his interviews the separation from both family and friends that the decision to join the anti-Fascist movement entailed:

> Guardi tuttavia che nel corso di quegli anni per me fatali, quelli, ripeto, che vanno dal '37 al '43, io mi staccai completamente sia dalla mia famiglia, sia dalla mia città, diventato per certi versi straniero a tutto quanto mi aveva circondato prima d'allora, compresi gli amici bolognesi e sardi di cui si è parlato sopra. La mia famiglia d'origine e i miei amici di giovinezza li avrei ritrovati sì, ma più tardi, molto più tardi, quando avrei cominciato in qualche modo a scriverne.[18]

> Still, note that in those years, that span of time from 1937 to 1943 so fateful for me, I detached myself completely both from my family and from my city, becoming in some ways a stranger to everything that had surrounded me until then, including the Bolognese and Sardinian friends I mentioned earlier. Yes, I would return to my family of origin and to the friends of my youth, but later, much later, when I would somehow start writing about them.

Elsewhere he again returns to the themes of transformation and separation:

> L'incontro a Bologna con Carlo Ludovico Ragghianti avvenne nel '37 ... , e per me significò moltissimo. Dal giovane letterato che ero, mi trasformò in breve tempo in attivista politico clandestino, sottraendomi sia alle amicizie letterarie ferraresi sia a quelle bolognesi. L'unico sodale a seguirmi in questa nuova vicenda della mia vita fu Antonio Rinaldi.[19]

> I met Carlo Ludovico Ragghianti in Bologna in 1937 ... , and that encounter meant a lot to me. In a short time it transformed me from a

> young man of letters into a clandestine political activist, removing me from my literary friendships in both Ferrara and Bologna. The only comrade to follow me in this new direction of my life was Antonio Rinaldi.

Marthe Robert, of course, has taught us that the family romance lies at the origin of all storytelling and thus of the novel, which might serve to neutralize my claim for it as a particularly fruitful and germane conduit to an understanding of the *Romanzo*.[20] However, the case I will be trying to make is that Bassani deliberately adapts Freud's symbolic narrative of the tortuous process of individuation and transformation, leading to emotional maturity, to his own work. *Il giardino dei Finzi-Contini*, located at the centre of the *Romanzo*, is an explicit articulation of this genre,[21] in which Bassani applies Freud's theory to the problem of how a privileged and overprotected member of the Jewish bourgeoisie[22] attains manhood in an environment that exposes him only to examples of passive submission to the Race Laws.

The Man of Resentment

It is commonly believed that popular understanding of Nietzsche's contempt for the culture of his times fed the climate of hostility towards the Jews, which eventually would lead to the Holocaust. Whether or not this is the case, it is certainly true that "Jews and Judaism are completely central to Nietzsche's work; in both his hostile and friendly deliberations, he insisted upon their absolutely fateful historical role within European civilization."[23] In fact, Nietzsche's critique of culture may be viewed as having arisen out of the climate of tension between Jews and Germans.[24] I am not suggesting that Bassani endorsed all of Nietzsche's controversial thought. He does, however, appear to have drawn on some of Nietzsche's ideas and diagnosis as to what ailed the culture of his times, appropriating and adapting these insights to inform the long-range historical perspective that he wished to create; specifically, echoes can be found of Nietzsche's concepts of the "man of resentment" and "slave revolt in morality" as elaborated in the *Genealogy of Morality* (1887), which he attributes to the Jews of the rabbinical era. Although it originated with Kierkegaard, the concept of *ressentiment* gained widespread currency because of Nietzsche's invocation of it.[25] Moreover, "the *Genealogy* is largely a political text opposed to a general decline of vitality throughout Europe,"[26] and thus Nietzsche's views would have been of interest to Bassani, given his own concern with the passivity of the Jews in the face of persecution. Bassani's avowed *maître-à-penser*, Benedetto Croce, had engaged with Nietzsche himself, and in not entirely unfavourable terms.[27]

According to Nietzsche's version of the evolution of morality as described in the *Genealogy of Morality*, the distinction between good and bad began in Homeric times: the powerful, not content with the fact of their power, decided that they must have earned it, while the weak must have deserved their fate as well. The problem with this logic, according to Nietzsche, lies in the fact that strength and weakness represent impersonal forces to which language erroneously attributes subjectivity: the strong are strong because they cannot be otherwise, and so too the weak – with no merit involved.[28] Nonetheless, the powerful considered themselves the good, while the powerless were the bad, despite the fact that these terms imply nothing other than the "well born" and the "less well born." Essentially "good" and "bad" were social distinctions, devoid of moral connotation.

Later on, after the destruction of the Second Temple by the Romans and with the beginning of the Talmudic era, the Jews, by then a weak, priestly caste, became jealous of the powerful. Their weakness prevented them from retaliating with physical force, and thus they retaliated instead with their wits by operating "the slave revolt in morality," a clever sleight of hand that turned the former social distinction between good and bad into a value-laden distinction between good and evil; thus the roles were inverted: the weak became "good" while the strong became "evil." The invention of moral superiority was the priestly caste's ingenious response to its physical impotence: "The beginning of the slaves' revolt in morality occurs when *ressentiment* itself turns creative and gives birth to values: the *ressentiment* of those beings who, being denied the proper response of action, compensate for it only with imaginary revenge."[29] After Christianity adopted this distinction, it became the basis of Judeo-Christian morality: the weak shall inherit the earth. However, Nietzsche warns, one must not be deceived:

> When the oppressed, the downtrodden, the violated say to each other with the vindictive cunning of powerlessness: "Let us be different from evil people, let us be good! And a good person is anyone who does not rape, does not harm anyone, who does not attack, does not retaliate, who leaves the taking of revenge to God, who keeps hidden as we do, avoids all evil and asks little from life in general, like us who are patient, humble and upright" – this means, if heard coolly and impartially, nothing more than

> "We weak people are just weak; it is good to do nothing *for which we are not strong enough*" – but this grim state of affairs, this cleverness of the lowest rank which even insects possess (which play dead, in order not to "do too much" when in great danger) has, thanks to the counterfeiting and self-deception of powerlessness, clothed itself in the finery of self-denying, quiet, patient virtue, as though the weakness of the weak were itself – I mean its *essence*, its effect, its whole unique, unavoidable, irredeemable reality – a voluntary achievement, something wanted, chosen, a *deed*, an *accomplishment*.[30]

Jacob Neusser, a contemporary rabbinic scholar and student of the Talmud, without making any reference to Nietzsche, has called this very same attitude the "affective program of the Rabbis," which pious Jews were encouraged to cultivate by their superiors:

> A simple catalogue of permissible feelings comprises humility, generosity, self-abnegation, love, a spirit of conciliation to the other, and eagerness to please. A list of impermissible emotions is made up of envy, ambition, jealousy, arrogance, sticking to one's opinion, self-centeredness, a grudging spirit, vengefulness ... aiming at the cultivation of the humble and malleable person, one who accepts everything and resents nothing. ... Temper marks the ignorant person, restraint and serenity, the learned one. ... A mark of humility is the humble acceptance of suffering. ... Submit, accept, conciliate, stay cool in emotion as much as in attitude, inside and outside. ... To turn survival into endurance, pariah-status into an exercise in Godly-living, the sages' affective program served full well. Israel's hero saw power in submission ... ultimate degradation was made to stand for absolute power.[31]

Nietzsche's *ressentiment* is a by-product of this process of inversion: since the desire for revenge is as natural and instinctive as the desire for power, mere rationalization does not destroy it; having been deprived of a healthy outlet, the desire for revenge turns in upon itself and festers, becoming bitterness and impeding the capacity for action:

> The "well-born" *felt* that they were the "happy"; they did not need first of all to construct their happiness artificially by looking at their enemies, or in some cases by talking themselves into it, lying themselves into it (as all men of *ressentiment* are wont to do); and also as complete men bursting with strength and therefore *necessarily* active, they knew they must not

> separate happiness from action – being active is by necessity counted as part of happiness. ... All very much the opposite of happiness at the level of the powerless, the oppressed, and those rankled with poisonous and hostile feelings, for whom it manifests itself as essentially a narcotic, an anesthetic, rest, peace, "sabbath," relaxation of the mind and stretching of the limbs, in short as something *passive*. While the noble man is confident and frank with himself ... , the man of *ressentiment* is neither upright nor naive, not honest and straight with himself. His soul *squints*; his mind loves dark corners, secret paths, and back doors; everything secretive appeals to him as being *his* world, *his* security, *his* comfort; he knows all about keeping quiet, not forgetting, waiting, temporarily humbling and abasing himself. A race of such men of *ressentiment* will inevitably end up cleverer than any noble race, and will respect cleverness to a quite different degree as well.[32]

Further on, in an imaginary dialogue, he tells an interlocutor that the weak operate "in a dark workshop" where they transmute "weakness into an *accomplishment*," and "impotence, which doesn't retaliate, into *goodness*":

> The inoffensiveness of the weakling, the very cowardice with which he is richly endowed, his standing-by-the-door, his inevitable position of having to wait, are all given good names such as "patience." ... They tell me that their misery means they are God's chosen and select, after all people beat the dogs they love best; perhaps this misery is just a preparation, a test, a training.[33]

Nietzsche's main target was contemporary Christianity, and he counted the anti-Semites of his time among the "men of resentment," whose scapegoating of the Jews was a result of their own failings: "The anti-Semites do not forgive the Jews for possessing 'spirit' – and money. Anti-Semites – another name for the 'underprivileged.'"[34] He admired what he saw as the heroic, vital, and life-affirming spirit of ancient pre-Christian cultures, among which he counted biblical Judaism. He also admired the German Jews of his own time, whom he saw as harbingers of the new, aristocratic culture he wanted to bring about. Nonetheless, Nietzsche could not forget that Christianity was the product of rabbinic, second-temple Judaism, which by rationalizing its weakness, had created the premise for an overspiritualization and denaturalization of Jewish life and, by extension, of Christianity. The rabbinic Jews "were the priestly nation of *ressentiment par excellence*"[35] and the forefathers of the "failed, sickly, tired and exhausted people of whom today's Europe is beginning to reek."[36]

Theodor Lessing (1872–1933), the originator of the term "Jewish self-hatred," wrote his famous treaty on the subject *Der Jüdische Selbsthass* (1930) inspired by Nietzsche's version of the origins of Judeo-Christian morality. Jacob Golomb summarizes it thus:

> In this book Lessing describes the Jews as people who have been forced to live unnatural lives. After separation from their land, they turned to an excessively spiritual life which they live "together with their dead ones." Lessing claims, in language that is definitely Nietzschean, that in their internalized lives, as the result of external pressure and out of fear of their hostile surroundings, the Jews began to direct their spiritual resources against themselves, manifesting self-doubt, insecurity and self-torture. This agonizing state of affairs was so unbearable that they attempted to liberate themselves from it by despising anything that had to do with Judaism and Jewishness, especially themselves.[37]

Perhaps Bassani begins his story in the Etruscan cemetery not only because both Jews and Etruscans were subjected to brutal genocides but because the Etruscans were known to have been in the habit of visiting their ancestors in their elaborate tombs, to spend time "together with their dead ones."[38] In *Gli occhiali d'oro*, the protagonist seeks comfort in the sight of the tombs in the Jewish cemetery, while Ermanno Finzi-Contini tells the narrator that he proposed to his wife in one of his favourite haunts, the Jewish cemetery in Venice, which he urges the protagonist to visit. In the figure of Professor Ermanno, who spends his time compiling lists of the names in the Venetian Jewish cemetery, we can also detect Nietzsche's disparagement of the "antiquarian historical consciousness."[39]

Bassani uses images of degeneracy and weakness freely in his characterization of both Jews and Nazi-Fascists, echoing Nietzsche's view that anti-Semites were also men of "resentment."[40] The passivity that characterizes his alter ego Bruno Lattes can also be found in the Gentile Pino Barilari, the literally paralysed and syphilitic protagonist of "Una notte del '43," who, though he witnessed the execution of eight anti-Fascists, refuses to incriminate the killer Sciagura in his postwar trial. Meanwhile, the Jew Bruno Lattes, as we see in the final scene of "Gli ultimi anni di Clelia Trotti," is as full of resentment upon his return to

Ferrara after the war as he was ten years earlier when his Aryan girlfriend, Adriana Trentini, ended their relationship (this is described in "Altre notizie su Bruno Lattes"). Significantly, Bruno flirts with activism but, unlike Bassani himself, ultimately emigrates. Ireneo, the son of David and Lida Mantovani in the first of the *Storie ferraresi*, is also characterized as inept and lacking initiative and energy, as is David himself, who sleeps away the afternoons in the apartment he shares with Lida for a brief time. Elia Corcos, the doctor in "La passeggiata prima di cena," is equally inert and stays in provincial Ferrara in spite of the possibilities that the world offers, trapped in a prison of his own making; moreover, he resents his wife and his Gentile in-laws, from whom he isolates himself. Even more significant is the fact that he has chosen to marry beneath himself as a means to avoid having to confront his weakness: the early marriage becomes an excuse to remain in Ferrara and spare himself the arduous task of achieving scientific success in the broader world. The narrator of the first-person trilogy is full of resentment as well, towards the Gentiles who refuse him admittance to their society after the Race Laws are passed, towards his father who fails to take a stand that his son can emulate, and even in the postwar period towards the lower classes whose rise and whose demands are threatening his position and his values. This resentment leads him not to action but to brooding, isolation, paralysis, and masochistic submission to the prevailing climate. In *Gli occhiali d'oro* both he and his father submit silently to the insults of Signora Lavezzoli as she quotes an article from *Civiltà cattolica*, which explains anti-Semitism as the just fate of killers of Christ. The Finzi-Continis also display all the signs of resentment in their grandiose isolation, which nonetheless mimics the lifestyle of the Christian aristocracy, their internalized ideal. By the same token, the Finzi-Continis are characterized as "priestly" by their association with their pious Venetian cousins and Professor Ermanno's revival of the Spanish synagogue (an allusion to "second synagogue" priestly Judaism?). Alberto Finzi-Contini is a closeted homosexual, pale, weakly, devoid of energy, who bears all the characteristics of "degeneracy" as it was used in late nineteenth-century discourse.[41]

As he moves progressively through the three first-person novels, the narrator is himself confronted each time by his own passivity in the face of different situations. At the beginning of the third novel, *Dietro la porta*, he finally states that he will never be able to "overcome" his experiences.[42] At the end of the story, it becomes clear that what he will never be able to face is the encounter with the toxic part of himself, as represented by the antagonist Pulga: he is unable, in the words of Nietzsche, to "go inside," but Bassani does.

The protagonist of *L'airone,* in which Bassani returns to the third person, is so consumed by *ressentiment* that he commits suicide after coming face to face with the famous stuffed birds whom he aspires to join in the taxidermist's window. Frozen in their fate as hunted animals, they are the figures of his own internal life. It is here that Nietzsche's symbolic vengeance is enacted literally, when Limentani presents a former Fascist with the corpses of the birds his guide has killed. With this last novel Bassani himself emerges on the other side of the abyss, having "overcome" the rancour that might have poisoned him. One can see in the progression of Bassani's work the enactment of Nietzsche's philosophy of "unmasking," as he peels off the layers until he reaches the core, represented by the delusional and schizoid Limentani.

The Blood of the Walsungs

If Freud and Nietzsche provide Bassani with the theoretical underpinnings for his meditation on the Jewish condition, it is Thomas Mann who is his most important literary source for this aspect of his work. One of the most significant intertexts in the *Romanzo di Ferrara,* and one not identified thus far, is that provided by Thomas Mann's relatively little-known story entitled "The Blood of the Walsungs."[43] A satirical depiction of a parvenu Jewish family, its protagonists are the highly refined and inseparable Ahrenhold twins, Sieglund and Siegfried. When the story opens, Sieglund is about to marry the Gentile Beckerath. On the eve of the wedding, the twins conspire to have an evening to themselves, an outing to the opera, to see Wagner's *Die Walküre.* When they return home, in another instance of life imitating art and as a farewell gesture marking the end of their exclusive relationship, they commit incest, just like the characters in the opera after whom they are named.

The story was written in 1905, just before Mann's own marriage to Katia Pringsheim, also a twin and the daughter of wealthy and cultured assimilated German Jews. Regardless of whatever it may say about Mann's own sentiments towards this family and his impending nuptials, "The Blood of the Walsungs" also portrays what he perceived as the extreme ambivalence felt by parvenu Jews themselves towards the Germans they so desperately wanted to resemble. The twins are ashamed of their parents' eastern European origins and characteristics, but on the other hand they resent the non-Jews in their midst and want to outwit them. They feel both superior and inferior, illustrating the contradictions of emancipation Jewry, who, according to this account, want to have it both ways: full acceptance on the part of the Gentile world but the right to maintain their own sense of difference, superiority, and intimacy. In fact, the last line of the original version of the story contained a rather vicious slur on the part of the twins against the unsuspecting Gentile bridegroom, depicted as a lamb about to go to the slaughter. Mann's future father-in-law objected strenuously to the tale, particularly the last line, and Mann halted its publication in deference to his wishes. The story was eventually to see the light several years later, with a new ending.

Interestingly, Bassani's last novel, *L'airone*, though not actually containing a slur on the part of Jewish characters against Christians, seems to have been inspired in part by an imagined one, also at the end. In the interview about the writing of this novel, Bassani himself describes mother and son in the final scene of the novel as united by their common resentment of the Gentiles in their home. It is this image, Bassani says, that gave him the momentum to complete the novel:

> Ogni sera si recava dalla madre, e insieme, questi due esseri, già esclusi, già cadaveri, arrocati in una camera della vecchia casa invasa dai "gentili" (la moglie di Edgardo, l'amministratore) si sfogavano a dir male degli occupanti. Quando ho capito questo, tutto è stato facile.[44]

> Every night he went to see his mother, and together, these two beings, already excluded, already corpses, barricaded in a room of the old house invaded by the "Gentiles" (Edgardo's wife and the administrator), they would vent against the occupiers. When I understood this, the rest was easy.

The centrepiece of the *Romanzo di Ferrara, Il giardino dei Finzi-Contini*, contains several rather blatant allusions to "Blood of the Walsungs." One cannot help but see in Micòl and Alberto, who share with their models a private language and a luxurious and idle lifestyle, a reference to the Ahrenhold twins. Says Mann: "They were like self-centered invalids who absorb themselves in trifles, as narcotics to console them for the loss of hope. With an inward gesture of renunciation, they doffed aside the evil smelling world and loved each other alone, for the priceless sake of their own rare uselessness."[45] In the Mann story there is a hint of homosexuality when Siegmund says to his twin sister, "Everything about you is just like me – and so – what you have – with Beckerath – the experience is for me too."[46] Alberto's ambiguous attachment to the Gentile Malnate mirrors Siegfried's suggested homosexuality, while Bassani himself refers to Malnate as the "tramite forse inconsapevole del sotterraneo rapporto incestuoso che lega l'uno all'altro i due fratelli"[47] (perhaps unconscious go-between in the covert incestuous relationship that ties brother and sister to each other). In an interview with Ferdinando Camon, Bassani as much as acknowledges the connection to this story without mentioning it explicitly: "Fortini mi rimproverava di non aver esaurito tutto il potenziale erotico che poteva scaturire dai rapporti tra Alberto, l'io scrivente, Micòl e Malnate ... È assurdo fare dei doppioni manniani trenta-quarant'anni dopo."[48] (Fortini thought I hadn't quite exhausted the erotic potential latent in the relationships between Alberto, the narrating "I," Micòl, and Malnate ... It is absurd to make Mannian doubles thirty, forty years later.)

The "Blood of the Walsungs" is radically different in tone and intent from anything that Bassani wrote, but the story clearly struck him in a profound way because of its brilliant condensation of the dilemma of the emancipated Jew, trapped between the need for the narcissistic mirroring of the ghetto experience[49] – hence the twins – and the desire for validation by the Gentile world. Following Mann's lead, Bassani eroticizes the institutional structures of power through the suggestion that both Micòl and Alberto desire Malnate because he is a Gentile, while the Jewish narrator desires Micòl because of her class superiority. Although this is the only direct allusion to the Mann text, the same permutation between relations of power and erotic dynamics is at play in almost all of Bassani's stories. As a caricatured representation of the "troubled psychology of the assimilated German Jew" and a "complex vision of the paralyzing tragedy of deracination,"[50] "The Blood of the Walsungs" provides the thematic centre of irradiation of the entire *Romanzo di Ferrara*, which, through various combinations and metaphorical permutations, tells a story of emotional and sexual maladjustment deriving from an inability to move into manhood, as understood in the Freudian paradigm. However, the Mann story conflates Jewishness, homosexuality, and incest in a clear reflection of the anti-Semitic discourses circulating in the culture of the time. In an apparent paradox, Bassani's narrative follows the same path but in a different spirit. For Bassani, Thomas Mann is the diagnostician of a malaise, but he offers no real understanding of it. Moreover, Mann's story itself is a symptom of a greater malaise in German society itself, which was to play itself out in tragic terms. In Bassani's post-Holocaust perspective this malaise is not essentialized but historicized; through his own story, he shows through what circumstances discourses of anti-Semitism have been internalized, the damage they have wrought, and through what processes they can be overcome.

2 *Dentro le mura*: Men of Resentment

My intention was to write a chapter of the moral history of my country and I chose Dublin for the scene because the city seemed to me the centre of paralysis.

James Joyce, Letter to Grant Richards, 5 May 1906[1]

The family romance begins in "Lida Mantovani," the first of the original *Storie ferraresi*. It opens, fittingly, as Lida, the protagonist, is about to give birth. Perhaps Bassani's most belaboured story (no pun intended), it underwent four rewrites and has been carefully scrutinized by at least one critic trying to understand what Bassani was aiming for in these successive versions.[2] Despite the differences, however, this first story constitutes an *entrée en matière* to the *Romanzo*, in all its versions, encapsulating the essence of a failed attempt to break out of the psychic parental stranglehold.

On the surface, the story focuses on a poor, young working-class girl who lives with her single mother and fantasizes about escaping her dull existence as a seamstress, as the two struggle to eke out a living together. Their shabby, enclosed basement home clearly signifies their social and economic marginality, but it is also a fitting metaphor for the suffocating stranglehold of the mother-daughter relationship. When Lida first meets and becomes involved with David Camaioli, a young Jew from a middle-class family, her dream suddenly seems within reach; but an ironic twist of events leads her to reproduce rather than to escape her mother's life: she becomes pregnant, and David abandons her to her fate as an unwed mother. However, her subsequent marriage of convenience to Oreste Benetti, an older, prosperous artisan and father figure, partially grants her wish. As devout a Catholic as he is a Fascist, Oreste persists in his pursuit of Lida until, despite her initial reservations, she finally yields to his forceful personality. After her mother's death, they leave Ferrara, and she has a more dignified and comfortable life, but not a happier one, as the memory of her Jewish lover lingers on forever. Her son by David, Ireneo, a rather inept and unambitious young man who seems to have inherited his father's slothful temperament, also turns out to be a disappointment. Oreste, who ardently desired a child of his own, dies without seeing his wish fulfilled.

Lida's story is essentially that of her struggle to free herself, to extract herself from the clutches of her mother and the destiny she represents in order to shape her own future. The ambivalence she feels towards her mother is only part of her problem, amplified by the very circumscribed range of action she is allowed as a woman. In a sense, in terms of the family romance, she escapes the clutches of her mother only to fall into those of the father she never knew. Perhaps that is why her marriage to Oreste is barren, as a means of signalling the nature of this relationship.

Like all of Bassani's tales, the story is told through the perceptions, misperceptions, and fantasies of its characters, whether individual or collective (as in the narrator's reports of gossip or commonly-held opinion in Ferrara), in the attempt to capture actual experience. In the opening scene, Lida is about to give birth. The narration moves from the present to the past and back again, with much space devoted to Lida's recollection of David's emotionally sadistic treatment of her and her submission to it, as well as to her later acquiescence to Oreste's will. Of David we know only what she tells us, but he too appears to be trying to separate from his family, uncertain of how to do so other than by using a lower-class Gentile girl as a means of rebellion. He uses and abuses Lida, even living with her briefly and pretending to seek work in a factory; at the same time David tells her very callously about his relationship with a girl from the Gentile upper class, presumably invented, which also serves the purpose of alerting the reader to his aspirations and reasons for his exploitation of poor Lida.

In this closed little world, we find all the dynamics of the power relationships that shall play themselves out in Bassani's subsequent works. Lida submits to David's treatment for obvious reasons: class and culture. He is desirable for all that he represents, not for who he is. Her own power vis-à-vis Oreste is her youth, since she can bear him a child, while his appeal lies in his fatherly, take-charge manliness, which prevents Lida from having to deal alone with her mother's death and also saves her from the shame and marginality of unwed motherhood. The most powerless person, incapable of eliciting desire from anyone, is Lida's mother. Oreste, who is her contemporary, does not hesitate to humiliate her by repeatedly mentioning the subject of her abandonment by Lida's father, while she insists on maintaining the image of herself as a victim of circumstance rather than of her lover's cruelty and indifference.

The story takes place over a period of approximately ten years, ending with Oreste's death in 1938, the year of the Race Laws. Popular opinion among the Catholic majority is rendered through Oreste's feelings, his optimism and buoyancy after the signing of the Lateran Pacts (1929), which saw the reconciliation of church and state after years of mutual hostility. Oreste is the only working-class character to receive such an elaborate treatment in the *Romanzo*. Working-class figures populate the margins of all of Bassani's fiction, but mostly as threatening or mysterious presences that figure sporadically in the imaginations of his more protected and fearful bourgeois characters. In this debut story, the centre is occupied by the working class, while the margins are haunted by the elusive Jewish male, about whom Lida will ask herself, "Chi era David? ... Che cosa voleva? Perché?" (42). (Who was David? ... What did he want? Why?)

David Camaioli, the Jew, is a shadowy and enigmatic figure who never appears directly in the story, set after the end of their relationship. When the story opens, Lida remembers how she lay alone at the end of a long corridor, staring at a magnolia tree outside her window, waiting for her child to be born: "Per oltre un mese era vissuta stesa su un letto, in fondo a un corridoio, e per tutto quel tempo non aveva fatto altro che fissare attraverso la finestra di contro, in genere spalancata, le foglie della grande magnolia secolare che sorgeva giusto nel mezzo del giardino sottostante" (9; For over a month she had lived lying on a bed, at the end of a corridor, and for all that time she had done nothing but stare out the usually open window at the leaves of the huge, centuries-old magnolia tree that stood right in the middle of the garden below).

A magnolia tree had been planted in front of Bassani's own home in Ferrara. Lida's view of the magnolia represents the first of the tree's several appearances in the *Romanzo* and, along with the corridor, signals Lida as the first of Bassani's many doubles. In fact, in the earlier versions of this story Lida was named "Debora," very much a Jewish name.[3] Although the enigma of David is not resolved for Lida, it is clear that her struggle to escape the prison of her situation, emblematized by the small, subterranean flat she inhabits, mirrors David's submerged story since both are trying to break away from their families of origin. And just as he represents the status to which she aspires, so too for David does the imaginary woman of the upper class whom he mentions to poor Lida constitute the prestigious tie he longs for. As for David's mistreatment of Lida, his passive aggression, his sloth, and the afternoons spent sleeping – "Annoiato, scontento, non le parlava quasi mai: rimaneva a letto giornate intere, la faccia nascosta dietro un libro oppure dormendo" (10; Annoyed, discontented, he almost never spoke to her: he spent entire days in bed, his face hidden behind a book or else sleeping) – are all the symbolic expression of the hostility he harbours both towards his own family and towards the Gentile elite to whose ranks he so ardently desires to belong and about which he fantasizes. He is truly a "man of resentment," who has had all the energy sapped out of him by his misplaced anger and unresolved conflicts, and who inhabits a liminal space between worlds.

The Jewish character begins to emerge from the shadows in the second story, "La passeggiata prima di cena," set in the immediate post-Unification years. Its protagonist, Elia Corcos, belongs to the first generation of post-emancipation Jewry in Ferrara[4] and is clearly represented as a victim of the loss of identity caused by the end of ghetto civilization and the abrupt thrust into secular modernity. His character is based partially on Bassani's own grandfather, Cesare Minerbi, once an important physician in Ferrara and indeed an almost legendary figure, about whom many wondered why he had never left this small provincial town to seek the opportunities that the broader world could offer. Like David and Lida, Elia is "trapped," and, like David, has his counterpart in a female figure, here the spinster sister-in-law Ausilia.

The story begins from a photograph, on the basis of which a moment in the past gradually comes alive. In this photograph one can detect a human figure, assumed to be Gemma, the girl that Elia marries. The first thing we are told is how insignificant she is: "È da supporre che anche a un occhio meno indifferente di un obbiettivo fotografico il passaggio di una ragazza come questa sarebbe forse sfuggito" (56–7; It's conceivable that even a gaze less indifferent than a photographic lens would have failed to notice a girl such as her). The implication, of course, is that she is neither beautiful nor in any way exceptional enough to explain why Elia would have courted, impregnated, and then married her, especially since, according to the custom of the time, it was not strictly necessary. Their courtship is presented through the eyes of Ausilia, Gemma's sister, who, along with her mother, spies on the couple from her window, all the while fantasizing about their relationship. After the marriage, the perspective shifts from that of Ausilia and her family, to whom the doctor represents an awesome, intimidating figure, to include the perspective of the members of the Jewish community of Ferrara, who consider Elia somewhat of a pariah. They speculate about Elia and about the reasons behind his inappropriate marriage and his decision to remain in Ferrara rather than seek out a better position elsewhere, one perhaps more suited to his considerable – and wasted – talents. This too is the story of a failure to "break out," in this case of Ferrara and of all that it represents in the conflict-ridden internal world of the protagonist: "Neppure a Gemma, benché moglie e padrona, era mai riuscito di oltrepassare il muro invisibile dietro il quale Elia si estraniava da tutto quanto lo circondasse" (77; Not even Gemma, though wife and mistress of the household, had ever succeeded in breaking through the invisible wall behind which Elia estranged himself from everything that surrounded him).

The story is told obliquely, but the veil of mystery surrounding Elia is not so opaque that one cannot glean some information as to his plight: that he is caught in a trap of his own making. His decision to marry the pregnant Gemma, we are to understand, suits him. On the surface it appears to have been a sacrifice, but in reality it has provided him with a convenient excuse not to leave Ferrara. At the moment of decision when he asks Gemma's father for her hand, Elia also asks himself why he is subjecting himself to this marriage and concludes that he has two options: the first, to leave Gemma and Ferrara and to pursue goals commensurate with his abilities in the outside world; the second, to resign himself to the life of a modest small-town physician, all the while insinuating that it was because of his marriage that he was forced to stay in Ferrara. Of the two, the first he sees as risky and difficult; after all, what if he fails to live up to his promise? The second provides an easy way out, allowing him to mask his fear of having to struggle and compete outside the protective cocoon of Ferrara. He does, however, have some doubt as to how easy remaining in Ferrara will actually be.

Once Elia has made the decision to stay, he in fact absents himself in a different way. He becomes aloof, ironic, hidden behind a distant demeanour that contributes in part to the mystique that surrounds him. Slowly we see that he is uneasy and insecure, the very opposite of his father, Salomone, introduced later in the story clearly as a foil to his son's lack of confidence. A humble grain merchant who has lived most of his life in Ferrara's Jewish ghetto, Salomone is a far more reachable, warm, and open man, the only one of the Jews with whom Ausilia will feel comfortable after her sister's marriage: "Con Gemma era sempre stato umano, gentile, pieno di attenzioni. E anche nei confronti di lei, Ausilia, quanta affabilità aveva mostrato in ogni occasione, quanta cortesia!" (80). (With Gemma he had always been warm, kind, considerate. And even with her, Ausilia, how affable he had always been, how courteous!)

The deliberate and sharp contrast between father and son corresponds to the spaces with which they are associated. While Salomone refuses to leave the ghetto and only does so when forced by old age, Elia chooses to build a house on the edge of town, with two entrances and two facades, one urban in the front for his own relatives and guests and a second rustic one in the back facing the country fields for his in-laws.[5] While Salomone is secure in his identity as a Jew firmly rooted in his traditions, his son finds himself in limbo, in a no-man's-land, poised precariously between the country and the city, between Jewish and Christian worlds, between the peasant and professional worlds, between the past and the future. Elia is a victim of emancipation, of the opening up of broader horizons that are at once tantalizing and intimidating. The social-climbing Jewish community has nothing but contempt for both Salomone and Gemma. Gemma is seen as a dead weight holding Elia back, Salomone as an inept, negligible, small-time merchant, who has never amounted to anything. Elia's uncertainty as to his identity, with his aspirations unmatched by the courage to pursue them, keeps him at a distance from both his father and his wife, onto whom he projects the resentments that would more properly be directed at himself. Perhaps his marriage was a way to create walls in the absence of a ghetto, to tie himself to Ferrara forever, and to compensate for the insecurity of being a Jew by associating with a socially-inferior Christian family perpetually in awe of him, while he barely deigns to acknowledge them, so much so that all except Ausilia do everything they can to avoid him. And when Ausilia does approach him, she regrets it: "Aveva ragione sua madre che lì in quella casa si era sempre rifiutata di venirci! E suo padre e i suoi fratelli ... non avevano ragione anche loro di evitare qualsiasi intimità e confidenza?" (77). (Her mother was right to have always refused to come to the house! And her father and brothers ... weren't they right too, to avoid all familiarity with them?)

Later in life, Elia becomes the personal physician to a local aristocratic woman and is rumoured to be her lover; this possible liaison suggests that just as he is the unattainable object of desire for Ausilia, so the countess represents his own unfulfilled social aspirations. In the passage below, the image of Elia looking out the window to the horizon beyond which lies Bologna suggests a longing that remains unfulfilled but was not sufficiently strong to help him overcome the fear of entering into broader society. Years later we see him through Ausilia's eyes and memories, sitting at the window every time he returned from his trips with the duchess more than ever in need of peace and solitude, moving his eyes "di là dall'orto, di là dal muro di cinta che separava l'orto dai bastioni, di là dai bastioni medesimi, e per fissarli infine, sorridendo vagamente sotto i baffi, sulle grandi nuvole dorate che occupavano il cielo dalla parte di Bologna" (77; beyond the garden, beyond the walls that separated the garden from the bastions, beyond the bastions themselves, resting them finally, smiling vaguely under his mustache, on the big, gilded clouds that occupied the sky towards Bologna).

He remains Ausilia's idol, though she is far more comfortable with his down-to-earth father, whose warmth and emotional immediacy she will remember long after his death and after Elia and his son Jacopo have been deported to Buchenwald. In particular her memory of Salomone is associated with the smell of his clothes:

> Misto di vaghi effluvi di agrumi, di fieno appassito e di grano, era il medesimo odore che sfogliando certi libretti di devozione ebraica, da lui portati con sé nella casa di via della Ghiara in vista d'una loro "eventuale" distribuzione fra i convitati delle due successive cene di Pasqua, lei aveva sempre sentito sprigionarsi da quelle vecchie pagine indecifrabili, illustrate da incisioni azzurrine un poco sbiadite le quali rappresentavano, secondo quanto si leggeva sotto ciascuno di essa stampato in italiano, le dieci piaghe d'Egitto, Mosè dinanzi a Faraone, il passaggio del mar Rosso, la caduta della manna, Mosè sulla vetta del Sinai a colloquio con l'Eterno, l'adorazione del vitello d'oro: e così, di seguito, fino allo svelarsi a Giosuè della Terra Promessa. La *redingote* di Elia non aveva saputo mai d'altro che di sublimato e di acido fenico. Dai panni e dall'intera persona di Salomone Corcos spirava invece un profumo che, pur diverso come era, faceva subito pensare a quello dell'incenso. (80–1)

> A mixture of the perfumes of citrus fruits, dried hay, and wheat, it was an odour that she smelled each time she leafed through certain little Jewish prayer books he had brought with him to the house in Via della Ghiara,

> in case they were ever needed for distribution to the guests at the two successive Passover meals, emanating from those indeciferable pages illustrated by somewhat faded blue engravings depicting, according to what could be read underneath in Italian, the ten plagues of Egypt, Moses before the pharoah, the crossing of the Red Sea, the manna falling from heaven, Moses on Sinai talking to the Eternal Being, the worshipping of the golden calf, and so on, up to the appearance of the Promised Land to Joshua. Elia's frock coat never smelled of anything but corrosive sublimate and carbolic acid. From the clothes and the whole person of Salomone Corcos there emanated instead an aroma that, though different, was immediately reminiscent of incense.

The connection of Salomone to the Passover prayer books confirms that Salomone's far less neurotic personality is connected to his unwavering identity as a Jew. It is also interesting and not entirely coincidental, I believe, that Bassani connects him to the grandiose moments of ancient Jewish history, before the advent of the priestly culture that gave rise to the "slave revolt in morality," according to Nietzsche, and of which Nietzsche wrote: "The *Old* Testament – all honour to [it]! I find in it great human beings, a heroic landscape, and something of the very rarest quality in the world, the incomparable naiveté of the *strong heart*; what is more I find a people."[6]

The very last segment of this story is the most important one, in that it confirms the true nature of this story as one about the loss of identity. Ausilia's memories return to Elia's penetrating yet empty stare and then to his account of the turning point in his life, the night when he asked for Gemma's hand and then had to return home to face his father. The father-son confrontation, positive and negative, returns frequently in the *Romanzo* as one of a repertoire of recurring situations. Here, it is a negative one. Elia experiences his decision to marry a Gentile as a break with his father's ways and dreads having to inform him of it. That night he comes home late and finds his father waiting up for him. He is about to gather his courage and reveal his engagement to Gemma but then changes his mind. At the same time he adopts "science" as his new religion, thus abandoning the old faith and moving into the secular world. He seals the "conversion" to science by going off to study in his room despite the late hour. This decision, obviously the pivotal one in Elia's life, will clearly fail to provide the "fullness" that Bassani attributes to Salomone: the absence, the blank stare, the loveless marriage, the false persona Elia Corcos was to adopt all signal the extent of his malaise.

As for Ausilia, to whom Elia recounts the story of that fateful night one evening at supper and through whose eyes it is told, she lives her life vicariously through her sister, stationed at the window of life, not unlike Elia himself. The first of a series of characters who will be explicitly associated with the primal image motif, we first encounter her as she watches Gemma and Elia from above and fantasizes about what is going on between them:

> L'amore era un'altra cosa – pensava Ausilia –: nessuno meglio di lei poteva saperlo.
>
> Era qualcosa di crudele, di atroce, da spiare da lontano; o da sognarne a palpebre abbassate.
>
> E infatti il sentimento segreto che fin da principio l'aveva tenuta legata ad Elia, tanto da costringerla per tutta la vita a una presenza continua, fatale, indispensabile, quel sentimento non era certo mai stato fonte della minima gioia, no davvero, se ogni volta, entrando nella grande cucina della casa di via della Ghiara dove lui, presso la finestra d'angolo, si attardava a studiare fino all'ora di cena ..., lei sentiva il bisogno di evitare il calmo sguardo che per un attimo, al suo ingresso, si era distolto da un libro, e di suscitare prontamente a difesa l'immagine buona e gentile di Salomone Corcos. (82)

> Love was something else - thought Ausilia -: no one knew that better than she did.
>
> It was something cruel, horrible, to spy on from a distance; or to dream about, closing your eyes.
>
> And in fact the secret feeling that, from the beginning, had tied her to Elia, so strongly that it forced her to become a continuous, fatal, indispensable presence, that feeling had never been the source of a moment's joy, really not, if every time she entered the large kitchen of the house in Via della Ghiara where he studied by the window in the corner until the supper hour ... she felt the need to avoid the calm gaze that he raised from his book for a moment; and she had to summon up, immediately, as a defence, the image of the kind and gentle Salomone Corcos.

Much as Lida's struggle with her mother is a projection of David's internal life, of which we are not informed in any conventional way by the narrative, so too Ausilia, as a passive character caught on the threshold of life, is a literal figuration of Elia's own internal emotional struggle; Ausilia acts as an eternal spectator, spying on her sister and imagining the details of her relationship with Elia, whose struggle again is only barely suggested by the glimpse provided of him staring out the window at the horizon beyond Ferrara. In the final scene the two are pictured sitting opposite each other at the dinner table, each unknowingly mirroring the other's state of arrested development. Interestingly, as Ausilia relives that evening, the thought of "povera Gemma" (poor Gemma) interposes itself between her and Elia, coming between them even in death:

> Le stava di fronte di là dal tavolo, la faccia presa in pieno dal lume del lampadario centrale. E intanto, parlando e sogghinando appena sotto i grandi baffi bianchissimi, sembrava guardarla.
>
> Ma la vedeva, in realtà? la vedeva *veramente*?
>
> Certo un'espressione ben strana, povera Gemma, quella dei suoi occhi in quel momento! Neanche se lui, a partire dal mattino successivo alla sera che aveva promesso a sua sorella di sposarla, cose e persone le avesse sempre guardate proprio così: dall'alto, e in qualche modo da fuori del tempo. (83)

> He sat across the table from her, his face fully lit by the central chandelier. And, as he talked and sneered slightly from below his great white mustache, he seemed to be looking at her.
>
> But did he see her, really? could he *really* see her?
>
> Certainly the look in his eyes at that moment was a strange one, poor Gemma! As if from the morning after the evening he had promised his sister to marry her, he was to see people and things always in that way: from above, that is, and as if from outside of time.

The compulsive, self-destructive behaviour that will be the lot of several subsequent protagonists is suggested in Lida's submission to David but makes its first explicit appearance in this story, in Ausilia's inability to avoid the situations that hurt her. Here we see her on the threshold of her sister's home, surrounded by Elia's relatives and intimidated by them yet drawn instinctively to the site of her pain:

> Si poneva di lato, la vecchia ragazza, abbassando gli occhi. Come avrebbe preferito in quel momento tornarsene indietro a casa propria e dei suoi!

> E invece macché. Finiva anche lei con l'entrare ...: secondo un moto istintivo che per quarant'anni almeno fu sempre più forte, sempre, di qualsiasi volontà di resistergli, di proibirselo. (75)
>
> She drew to the side, the old spinster, lowering her eyes. How she would have preferred, at that moment, to go back to her own house and family! But instead, no. She also finally entered ...: following an instinctive impulse that for at least forty years was always stronger, always, than any will to resist, to fight against it.

In these two first stories, Bassani is delving into the prehistory of the autobiographical Jewish male figure that he will focus on in much greater depth later on. At the same time, he is looking at the world of Jewish-Gentile relations in Ferrara before the era of persecution but from the perspective of the knowledge of what was to come; he arrives at the rather bitter conclusion that such relations were governed by envy, resentment, and false consciousness. From the perspective of Nietzsche's theory of *ressentiment*, one might say that both David and Elia are in the grips of an internal struggle: desperate to connect to the world of Gentiles, they can only do so through lower-class women whom they treat with contempt. These women act both as their "doubles," in that they mirror their own sense of inferiority, and as the objects of their symbolic revenge, which would more rightly be directed at the upper-class Gentile world from which they remain essentially barred, except through imaginary or rumoured illicit relationships.

While the two previous stories centre on the character distortions brought about by the loss of identity, the third story, "Una lapide in via Mazzini," treats the reclaiming of that identity – through the Holocaust. Moving abruptly forward in time to the immediate aftermath of the war, it focuses on Geo Josz, a survivor of Buchenwald presumed dead by the remaining Jews of Ferrara. He arrives back in his hometown just in time to see a workman putting the finishing touches on a plaque that has been applied to the wall of the synagogue – a plaque intended to commemorate the Jews of Ferrara who lost their lives in the Holocaust. Geo sees his name inscribed on it along with the names of his family members who were in fact murdered. The rest of the story recounts his failed attempt to readapt to normal life and his ultimate disappearance, but not before he has exacted his own personal form of revenge on one of his persecutors.

Historically, the story illustrates the climate of immediate postwar Ferrara: the justified paranoia of former collaborators and the arrogance of the new powers-that-be, the Resistance fighters of various stripes who are now holding trials in an attempt to punish those responsible for the crimes perpetrated under the Nazi occupation. Nonetheless, Geo's return is unsettling to all, even to those intent on punishing war criminals, since the purpose of doing so is to put the past to rest and to move on, something that Geo is ultimately unable to do, try as he may. After the initial shock of finding himself back in Ferrara, he goes through the motions of resuming his previous life, but the experience he has just endured makes this impossible. It is not enough to trade in the bizarre clothing he wore upon arrival for suits from the prewar days or to lose the weight gain caused by starvation edema (but seen by others as a sign of a possible trick on his part; who had ever undergone such an experience and gained weight?). One day something happens that mystifies everyone. It involves a well-known Fascist collaborator and informer, Count Scocca, who after two years spent in hiding under a false name, now deems it safe enough to return to Ferrara, given the air of reconciliation that is beginning to replace the hostile climate of the initial settling of accounts. The Count and Geo meet up by chance on a street corner. At first they seem to be chatting amicably, but then Geo suddenly and unceremoniously slaps the Count in the face. The incident is witnessed from various physical perspectives by several persons, each of whom offers a different version of the event that proves as momentous as it is scandalous. This face-to-face encounter becomes a turning point for Geo, the beginning of his resumption of his survivor persona. After this incident, he sheds his prewar suits and dons once more the clothes he wore upon his return. Everywhere he goes, he speaks of nothing but Buchenwald, much to the irritation and indeed anger of his fellow citizens, who quickly tire of his obsession and of making allowances for him.

While this is primarily a story about remembering and forgetting, it is also a story about identity. While Geo remains an "enigma" (121, 122) in the eyes of the townspeople, it becomes clear that a previously lukewarm Jew has finally found an identity and a voice as a survivor and full-time witness whom no one wants to hear (reminiscent of Primo Levi, who had such difficulty finding a publisher initially for *Se questo è un uomo*, his now-classic account of the months he spent in Auschwitz). When Geo finds himself chatting politely with the Count, as if nothing had ever happened, as if the Count's past as an informer perhaps responsible for his family's extermination had now become irrelevant, he suddenly sees himself as if from the outside: "Che cosa faccio io qui con costui? Chi è costui? E io che rispondo alle sue domande, e intanto mi presto al suo gioco, io, chi sono?" (122). (What am I doing here, I, with this man? Who is he? And I, who answer his questions, and at the same time allow myself to play his game, who am I?)[7] Geo has suddenly become profoundly aware of who he is and, more importantly, of who Count Scocca is, overcoming the confusion to which he had been prey ever since his return from the camp. The old Geo Josz, whoever he was, is gone forever, having been sacrificed somewhere in the ashes of Buchenwald along with his parents. Here we find the only instance in the entire *Romanzo* of an attempt to describe explicitly the experience of the deported, to speak the unspeakable:

> E lui, Geo, che cosa stava raccontando nel frattempo? Senza darsene per inteso, tornava magari a ripetere, tali e quali, le frasi che suo padre, prima di abbattersi sfinito sul sentiero che portava dal *Lager* alla miniera di sale dove insieme lavoravano, gli aveva mormorato in un soffio. Oppure, levando la mano, rifaceva nell'identico modo di cento altre volte precedenti il piccolo cenno d'addio che la madre … gli aveva indirizzato mentre veniva sospinta via, confusa nel gruppo delle donne. Oppure, con l'aria di esser sul punto di comunicare qualche importante novità, ricominciava con Pietruccio, il fratellino minore, seduto accanto a lui nel camion completamente buio che dalla stazione li stava trasferendo alle baracche, e a un tratto scomparso, così, senza un grido, senza un lamento, per sempre. (115)

> And he, Geo, what was he saying in the meantime? Without paying any attention to the others, he repeated again, exactly, the words that his father had murmured to him in a whisper, before collapsing exhausted onto the path that led from the *Lager* to the salt mine where they worked together. Or else, raising his hand he imitated, as he had done a hundred times before, the little gesture of farewell his mother had made to him … as she was pushed along with the other women. Or else, as if he was about to communicate something new and important, he went on again about Pietruccio, his little brother, seated beside him, in the dark, in the truck transporting them from the station to the barracks, and all of a sudden nowhere to be seen, just like that, gone, without a cry, without a moan, forever.

For all intents and purposes, Geo has returned from the dead, and is a *morto-vivo*, like the protagonist of Luigi Pirandello's famous 1906 novel *Il fu Mattia Pascal* (*The Late Mattia Pascal*) who reads his obituary and decides to disappear, only to return years later. After having lost his previous identity through the Race Laws, Geo does, in a sense, the same as Pirandello's Mattia Pascal when he finally returns home, by claiming and embracing his identity as a survivor and not that which the community would have him assume. Having been deprived of his wife and declared dead, Mattia decides to remain so, at least for the registry office, thus refusing to recognize the conventions of his society and becoming an "outsider" in the fullest sense of the term. Upon his return, Geo has also refused to take his place in society. Once he has declared openly who he is, for all to see, by slapping the Count in the town square, Geo has made a public statement and called his enemy by his name, thus rendering impossible the continued feigned acceptance of the climate of consensus that enables at least a semblance of peaceful coexistence. He has changed forever, he has become the witness, the return of the repressed, the gaping wound in the fabric of reconstructed civil society.

Bassani's "Una lapide in via Mazzini" is also reminiscent of two of Pirandello's short stories, "Il treno ha fischiato" ("The Train has Whistled") and "La maschera dimenticata" ("The Forgotten Mask"), both of which deal with issues of identity and the relationship between identity and community, between who we are and who others think we are. In "Il treno ha fischiato," Belluca "suddenly" goes mad, but the true dramatization is the heartless reaction of the community to this seemingly unexpected and mysterious event, which, as the narrator points out, is not mysterious at all, given the conditions of Belluca's life. Similarly in the Bassani story, the narrator is an unidentified member of Ferrara society but more empathetic than most. As the conduit for the various opinions and reactions of the citizenry, he points out their cruelty and indifference, as well as how little it would really take to understand Geo's behaviour, under the circumstances, if only one were to really try: "Proprio l'episodio del conte Scocca non avrebbe offerto niente di enigmatico, niente che non potrebbe essere inteso da un cuore appena solidale" (122; Precisely that episode with Count Scocca would have revealed nothing particularly enigmatic, nothing that couldn't be understood by a slightly sympathetic heart). Instead, the citizens are without pity, going so far as to accuse Geo of exaggeration or even of subterfuge and refusing to accept his need to talk: "Invece che comportarsi così, avrebbe fatto meglio a spiegare come mai fosse talmente grasso. Dato che di un edema *da fame* non si era prima d'ora mai sentito parlare" (90). (Instead of behaving like this, he would have done better to explain why he was so fat. Since no one had ever heard of *starvation* edema before.)

In Pirandello's "La maschera dimenticata," a man tries to change by moving to a new town, but eventually his old personality re-emerges, because it is impossible to change, according to Pirandello, when who and what we are is largely determined by the community's expectations. In "Una lapide in via Mazzini," what remains unchanged in spite of the upheaval caused by war is Ferrara as a whole, the community itself, the people of Ferrara:

> Ma dopo che furono rimossi i cumuli più alti di macerie e si fu sfogata una iniziale smania di cambiamenti in superficie, anche la città veniva a poco a poco ricomponendosi nel profilo assonnato, decrepito, che i secoli della decadenza clericale, succedutisi di colpo ai remoti e feroci e gloriosi tempi della Signoria ghibellina, avevano ormai fissato in maschera immutabile. Ogni cosa girava insomma. Geo, da un lato; Ferrara e la sua società (non esclusi gli ebrei scampati ai massacri), dall'altro lato: tutto e tutti risultavano a un tratto coinvolti in un moto vasto, ineluttabile, fatale. (106)

> After the biggest piles of rubble were removed, and an initial rage for superficial changes had been satisfied, the city, too, settled back into its sleepy, decrepit, old self, by now moulded into an unchangeable mask by the centuries of clerical decadence that followed abruptly on the heels of the remote and ferocious and glorious times of the Ghibelline Seigniory. Everything was in motion: Geo on one side; Ferrara and its society (including those Jews who had escaped massacre) on the other; in a vast, slow, fatal motion, impossible to escape.

Other Pirandellian traits of the story are to be found in the way in which the defining encounter between Geo and Count Scocca is presented as a theatrical moment whose objective reality is almost in doubt, reminiscent of Pirandello's play *Così è (se vi pare)*, which may also be read as a parable about the riddle of identity: "Il piccolo palcoscenico di via Mazzini presentava da una parte, provenienti contro sole, i ranghi serrati e luminosi delle ragazze in biciclette, e dalla parte opposta, grigio come l'antico stipite a cui si addossava, il conte Lionello Scocca" (107; The little stage of Via Mazzini displayed on one side, emerging against the sun from the end of the street, the closed and radiant ranks of the girls on bicycles; and on the opposite side, as gray as the wall he was leaning against, Count Lionello Scocca).

The actual confrontation portrays Geo as leaping out suddenly, like a predatory animal, to slap the Count twice sharply across his withered, old cheeks, in full view of the townspeople. Though witnessed by many, the incident seems nonetheless highly unlikely to the people of Ferrara, and different versions of the encounter begin to circulate, resulting in the elevation to almost legendary status of an actual and very recent occurrence.

Bassani's story clearly presents us with a meditation on the specific vagaries of Jewish identity. Instead of relying on their own tradition for identity, like Elia Corcos's father, post-emancipation Jews embraced an identity that in fact had been "granted" to them. When stripped of their civil rights and privileges, Italian Jews came face to face with the fact that their Italian identity was not naturally theirs by birthright, as they had assumed. Geo, marked forever by his Buchenwald experience, refuses to play the game of musical identities that characterized the postwar period and that is emblematized through the motif of the beard; the beard becomes a fixture in postwar Ferrara (also reminiscent of Mattia Pascal's attempt to change by shaving off his beard), a trend that particularly annoys Geo, along with everything else.

"Adesso non c'era quasi più nessuno che non gli si tenesse alla larga, che non lo sfuggisse come un appestato" (116; By now, there was almost no one that didn't stay out of his way, that didn't avoid him like the plague): in some ways, this story foreshadows that of Dr Fadigati in *Gli occhiali d'oro*, in its focus on the interaction between the inhabitants of Ferrara and someone who refuses to play by the rules and becomes a pariah as a result. The story also foreshadows Bassani's last novel, *L'airone*, which describes a day in the life of another survivor; though not a survivor of the camps, this character also has a sudden epiphany during a hunting expedition, in which he realizes that he is feeling more like the hunted than the hunter. However, unlike these two characters who both commit suicide, Geo speaks up for himself and his kind. In terms of *ressentiment*, Geo still takes only a symbolic revenge, the only kind that the modern world allows, according to Nietszche, since a slap in the face is hardly compensation for what he has endured; but at least he publicly displays his anger, and this causes him to leave Ferrara forever. Bassani did the same, never to return permanently, becoming a professional witness whose account of life in Ferrara under Fascist rule was as unwelcome as it was disturbing. Perhaps his oeuvre may be read as a slap in the face to the society from which he emerged and as a slow reclaiming of a normative persona and life through the process of telling and retelling, until a new equilibrium was reached.

The next story, "Gli ultimi anni di Clelia Trotti," might well have been entitled "A Flirtation with Socialism." It focuses not so much on the last years of the title character's life as on her role in a particularly difficult time in the life of Bruno Lattes, the young Jewish man who will appear in several other works. Based on the real-life figure of Alda Costa, Clelia Trotti is a famous schoolteacher in Ferrara, known for her unwavering commitment to the Socialist Party and her continuing courageous activism under Fascism, until the authorities put a stop to it by placing her under house arrest and confining her to her sister's home. The bulk of the story is a flashback set in 1939, but it opens in 1946 at Clelia's funeral. Her remains have been unearthed in order to grant her a heroine's funeral, which was denied her under Fascism. The pomp and circumstance orchestrated by the Left now in power is viewed with much cynicism by Bruno, who sees only hypocrisy in this exercise in rhetoric and propaganda: the Socialists did nothing to help Clelia when she needed them, and now they are using her as a symbol of the triumph of their ideology. It is no small irony that her eulogy is delivered by Mauro Bottecchiari, a Socialist member of parliament rumoured to have been her lover before he opportunistically made the accommodations and compromises needed to survive – and even flourish – under Fascism, one of which was dropping Clelia, who had remained naively and rigidly faithful to her ideals. Bruno, now an orphan, is visiting from America, to which he had escaped just in time to avoid deportation and extermination, the fate of his parents and other family members. He has become a lecturer in Italian at an American university and is about to be considered for tenure.

From the funeral we go back in time to 1939 when Bruno, a young victim of the Race Laws and a university student, suddenly finds himself adrift and uncertain where to turn now that he has been abruptly shut out of his former life and the larger community on which it depended. Isolated and frustrated by his own father's failure to adopt a clear stance in the face of events, Bruno is unable as yet to act on the family's insistence that he emigrate and is groping around desperately for a lifeline. In his confusion, he seeks out another community of outcasts, the local Socialists, and specifically Clelia Trotti, who has become somewhat of a legend. He eventually finds her and begins to meet with her regularly in the hope of finding a new identity and a new milieu, only to realize that he is not, and never will be, a Socialist.

The structure of the story renders it a prelude in some ways to *Il giardino dei Finzi-Contini*, with which it shares the characteristics of both the family romance and the quest novel. When Bruno first decides to look for Clelia, who has dropped completely out of circulation, he turns to Mauro Bottecchiari, the Socialist lawyer who will eventually preside at her funeral. Not coincidentally, Bottecchiari had been both Clelia's lover and a close friend of Bruno's father, and when he sees Bruno, he refers to him as one would to a child: "Ecco qua il nostro piccolo Lattes!" (136; And here is our little Lattes!). Moreover, Bruno is depicted as lingering at the doorway, afraid to enter the room: "'Ma avanti, avanti,' aggiunse allegramente, vedendolo sostare incerto sulla soglia. 'Come stà il papà?'" (136). ("Why, come in, come in!" he added happily, seeing Bruno stop uncertainly on the threshold. "And how is your papa?") It is clear that the Socialist Bottecchiari functions as a new "father," and that Clelia, having been his mistress, will function as a new "mother," in what amounts to a "mini–family romance." Before Bruno succeeds in finding Clelia, however, he will have to overcome a number of obstacles, as in any quest story.

The first obstacle is represented by the shoemaker Cesare Rovigatti, who was once part of the original group of Ferrara Socialists and to whom Bottecchiari sends Bruno, after claiming that he himself has no knowledge of Clelia's whereabouts. As Bruno makes his way to Rovigatti's shop, we learn that he is adrift not only politically but also emotionally; in the wake of the Race Laws, his upper-class Aryan girlfriend, Adriana Trentini, has dropped him, and he is full of bitterness and rage at this rejection. He finds the shoemaker and obtains Clelia's address with no difficulty, but many visits are required before he actually gains access to her. Her sister comes to the door and each time keeps him at bay with a litany of excuses, in the hope that he will eventually tire and give up: Clelia is busy tutoring, she has gone away for a while, she is unwell, and so on. Bruno spends weeks repeatedly stalled on the threshold of the apartment, unable to gain entry. And each time that he is sent away, he returns to Rovigatti's shoe-repair shop, where he undergoes a kind of apprenticeship meant to make him "worthy" of being received by Clelia Trotti herself. In the course of a series of conversations with Rovigatti, who expounds the Socialist point of view on everything from politics to literature, Bruno comes to sympathize with him but also intuits that his attraction to Socialism derives not from any shared ideological concerns with the working class but from an identification with their exclusion from society: "Come non mai, di colpo, si sentì solidale con Rovigatti" (147; More than ever before, he suddenly felt a solidarity with him, Rovigatti).

It is on this false basis that his relationship with Clelia herself develops. After weeks of frustration, he is finally granted an audience:

> Doveva succedere.
>
> In qualsiasi favola che si rispetti ... è raro che la vicenda non si concluda con la sparizione del Mostro o la sua metamorfosi. D'un tratto l'incantesimo si era spezzato, la signora Codecà era scomparsa. Ebbene, chi poteva mai essere se non Clelia Trotti la persona venuta ad aprire in sua vece? (148)

> It had to happen.
>
> In any self-respecting fairy tale ... it is rare for the story not to end with the disappearance of the Monster or of his metamorphosis. All of a sudden, the spell had been broken, Signora Codecà had vanished. And who, if not Clelia Trotti, could be the person who came to the door in her stead?

Clelia, however, is not a lovely, radiant princess, but a withered, ill-kempt old maid and her quarters a shabby little room at the end of a long, damp hall, where she tutors her private students and in which she is essentially held captive with her own sister and brother-in-law as prison guards. As he looks at her disappointedly, Bruno thinks about how sharply her miserable life contrasts with that of Mauro Bottecchiari, whose flexibility and opportunism have led him to flourish even under the Fascist regime, while Clelia's staunch loyalty to the principles of her Socialist faith have brought her to this. At this point Bruno again understands that Socialism is not his way and that he has arrived late at a party that has been over for a long time. The family-romance narrative becomes explicit as the scales fall from his eyes, and he contemplates his fantasy "parents" in their respective cynicism (Bottecchiari) and irrelevance (Clelia); at this point Bruno begins to think about paying more attention to his own father's urgings that he emigrate to either America or Palestine. As his thoughts turn to these possibilities, Bruno's eyes fall on Clelia's neck:

> La guardava, la patetica perseguitata antifascista, la pietosa prigioniera, e non gli riusciva di staccare gli occhi dalla riga scura, chiaramente visibile, che appena al di sotto dei bianchi capelli raccolti in un nodo sulla nuca le segnava torno torno l'esile collo rugoso. ... Perché una buona volta non gli avrebbe dato retta, lui, a suo padre? (151–2)

He looked at her, the pathetic, persecuted anti-Fascist, the pitiful prisoner, and he couldn't take his eyes off the dark line, clearly visible, that, just below the white hair gathered in a knot at her nape, marked her thin, wrinkled neck all around. ... Why not listen once and for all to his father's advice?

Nonetheless, Bruno is not ready to make his exit. He spends the next few months absorbed by this "flirtation" with the almost repulsive Clelia, whom he has awakened from her deep sleep and who begins to construct a delusion of her own, seeing in him a hope for the future of Socialism in Ferrara. Their meetings acquire an increasing patina of clandestinity, as she as well as her family, which disapproves of his visits, are supposedly under surveillance. Finally, Clelia's sister forbids him to return to their home, and the relationship is abruptly cut off until, one day, Clelia herself finds the courage to seek out Bruno at the Jewish school in the ghetto where he is now teaching. Soon the roles are reversed, and it is she who comes to his home to continue their conversations about Socialism:

Abbandonò la nuca contro la spalliera di velluto verde e chiuse gli occhi. Non era la prima volta che, approfittando dell'oscuramento e sfidando ogni divieto, veniva a trovare Bruno. Ma l'eccitazione che le avevano dato fin da principio queste visite clandestine non accennava a scemare di intensità. (162)

She let the back of her neck fall against the green velvet headrest and closed her eyes. This wasn't the first time that, taking advantage of the blackout and defying every prohibition, she had come to see Bruno at his home. But the excitement that these clandestine visits had produced in her from the beginning showed no signs of dying down.

The sexual undercurrent is made ever more explicit as the narration continues. But if Bruno "un po' se ne compiaceva ... [di] quell'aria di sotterfugio erotico che assumevano per forza i loro incontri sempre dopo cena" (163; was not entirely displeased ... by that air of erotic subterfuge that their after-dinner meetings necessarily took on), Clelia, though full of hope that he will carry on the Socialist struggle, is also well aware of other taboos that haunt their relationship:

[Era] lei la prima – lei che poteva essere sua madre! – a vietarsi qualsiasi confronto fra il ragazzo che le stava davanti e Mauro Bottecchiari, il

> compagno della sua gioventù, al quale l'entrata in guerra dell'Italia aveva suggerito il pretesto politico, nel lontano 1915, per piantarla e liberarsi. (163)

> She – who could have been his mother! – was the first to forbid herself any comparison between the boy that stood before her and Mauro Bottecchiari, the companion of her own youth, whom Italy's entry into the war in 1915 had provided with a political excuse to leave her and be free.

After the police come to Clelia's home, their nightly encounters are curtailed for the second time, and they begin, paradoxically, to meet in the open, signalling the fact that they are entering the downward curve of the relationship. Their rendezvous takes place in Piazza della Certosa, which is described at the beginning of the story as the ideal meeting place for persons who want to get to know each other but are not quite certain what they want: it serves as a threshhold of sorts, a place to stop before taking the plunge or reconsidering:

> Dove si va mai a Ferrara, anche oggi, quando si abbia voglia di parlare con una persona un tantino in disparte? In piazza della Certosa, prima di tutto. Ché se la cosa procederà per il suo verso, sarà faccenda da niente raggiungere più tardi i vicini bastioni, dove di luoghi riparati ... ce ne è quanti se ne vogliono, mentre, al contrario, se l'idillio non vorrà andare avanti, sarà altrettanto agevole e insieme lontano dall'apparire compromettente il ritorno in compagnia verso il centro della città. (124)

> Where does one go, in Ferrara, even today, to find a little privacy to talk to someone? To Piazza della Certosa, first of all. For if things then take their proper course, it's nothing to get to the bastions afterwards, where sheltered spots are easy to find; and if, on the contrary, the romance is not to be, it is just as easy, and at the same time far from appearing compromising, to return together towards the centre of town.

Interestingly, their relationship does not begin but rather ends there, placing Bruno where he rightly belongs, on a threshold, in limbo, on the outside looking in. While Clelia drones on obliviously about her plans for his future as a militant anti-Fascist, Bruno is completely mesmerized by the sight of a young couple nearby, both blonde and clearly from the upper reaches of the Gentile Ferrara bourgeoisie, whose playful, erotically charged interaction elicits his impotent rage and jealousy:

> Bruno non si saziava di guardarli. "Chi sono, come si chiamano?", continuava a mormorare fra i denti. Più che belli gli apparivano meravigliosi, irraggiungibili. Eccoli dunque là i campioni, i prototipi della razza! – si diceva con odio e amore disperati, socchiudendo le palpebre –. Il loro sangue era migliore del suo, la loro anima migliore della sua. …
>
> Oh, essere con loro, dei loro, nonostante tutto! (171–2)

> "Who are they? What are their names?" he went on muttering between his teeth. More than beautiful, they seemed to him awesome, out of reach. There they were, the exemplars, the prototypes of the race! – he said to himself, with desperate hatred and love, lowering his eyelids –. Their blood was better than his, their soul was better than his. …
>
> Oh, to be with them, one of them, in spite of everything!

This scene is foreshadowed by a similar one that unfolds in the same place in the opening scene at Clelia's funeral, after Bruno's return from America in 1946. Here he is distracted by the sight of a young girl who is revving the motor of her scooter, happily unaware of the significance of the ceremony taking place in the piazza. She is making eye contact with a young man across the way "come lei biondissimo e con la medesima espressione dura e indifferente nelle iridi chiare" (132; like her very blonde and with the same hard and indifferent expression in his light-coloured eyes). Bruno catches the look they exchange and immediately identifies them as a couple. Again he is mesmerized and consumed by jealousy and curiosity: "I due era chiaro filavano insieme – pensò Bruno Lattes – : per questo si erano dati appuntamento lì, in piazza della Certosa! Ma chi era, lei, di chi era figlia? – seguitò, attratto improvvisamente, spasmodicamente, dal nastro rosso che legava i capelli della fanciulla" (132). (The two, it was clear, were seeing each other – thought Bruno Lattes – : that was why they had made a date to meet in Piazza della Certosa! But who was she? Whose child? – he wondered, attracted suddenly, and spasmodically, by the red ribbon that bound the girl's hair.)

The repetition of this situation, and the fact that the story itself begins and ends in the same location, signals that emotionally Bruno has made no progress since the time of the Race Laws. He is again on the outside looking in, still full of impotent rage and jealousy. He has left Ferrara physically but not emotionally and is still trapped in Piazza della Certosa. As in the previous stories, Clelia's plight will project symbolically the male protagonist's state of mind: the real prisoner here is Bruno. Piazza della Certosa and the name Clelia clearly allude to Stendhal's *Charterhouse of Parma* (1839), a story of erotic and ambitious frustration. Its protagonist, Fabrizio Del Dongo, is a young man in search of a cause to champion, who runs off to join the Napoleonic forces against his father's wishes. Eventually Fabrizio is imprisoned, and from the window of his cell in the Farnese Tower he catches glimpses of his jailer's daughter, the pure and beautiful Clelia. He falls in love with her and thus begins to enjoy his imprisonment. The significance of this particular intertext emerges very clearly in the following comments of a contemporary reviewer of Stendhal's novel:

> Like so many of us, Fabrice is always measuring his life against the poems and novels he has read. With a self-consciousness more typical of the late 20th than the early 19th century, he keeps checking up on himself, as if trying to conform to some hidden master plan for being, or for loving – a plan that, as the novel tragically demonstrates, he is never quite able to follow. No wonder he so often expresses himself in the interrogative: "Had what he'd seen been a battle? ... Had this battle been Waterloo?" "Am I such a hypocrite?" "What about a minor affair here in Parma?" One ironic measure of Fabrice's inability to master the art of living as a free man is that he finds true happiness only in the womb-like security of his prison cell in the Farnese Tower (as many critics have noted, he's jailed for exactly nine months), from which he is loath to escape after he falls in love with Clelia.[8]

Like Fabrizio, Bruno is unable to master the art of living as a free man. At least Fabrizio finds love with a beautiful young woman, even though she is his jailer's daughter. In contrast, Bruno has been cast out into the world and has no such refuge to which he can retreat. Moreover, his Clelia is a withered old maid, and he is not physically but mentally imprisoned.

The last story of the group, "Una notte del '43," also takes actual historical facts as its point of departure, but, as in the previous story, Bassani modifies them in such a way as to indicate that his version is not intended primarily as a realistic one. It is, in a sense, a particularly Manzonian story. For Manzoni, the writer's duty was to illuminate the emotional or psychological circumstances in which historical decisions are made by illustrious characters. Bassani's characters in this story are not illustrious, of course, but the events in question are indeed historical, or at least the point of departure is – the summary execution of eleven citizens of Ferrara, anti-Fascists and Jews, on 15 November 1943, in retaliation for the assassination of Iginio Ghisellini, the Repubblica di Salò's commander in chief in Ferrara. It is unclear whether he was killed by anti-Fascists or by members of his own party following a disagreement, but Bassani's interest does not lie in the details of the case itself. In fact, in an interview Bassani claims to have changed the date of the execution from November to December in order to be able to have snow as the backdrop; but equally to the point is the significance of the changed facts as the author's indication of a different kind of truth here.[9]

The story itself is complete invention and takes place in 1946 in the aftermath of the shootings and of the war, when collaborators were being tried for their participation in war crimes. One of these collaborators is Carlo Aretusi, known to the townspeople by the nickname Sciagura (meaning "disaster") and considered to have been not only the informant who betrayed the identities and hiding places of the citizens chosen for this vendetta but also the person in charge of the execution itself, which took place on the sidewalk opposite the Caffè della Borsa "in una notte del dicembre del '43" (174; one night in December of 1943). The conviction and sentencing of Sciagura depends entirely on the willingness of the sole eyewitness to the massacre, the former town pharmacist Pino Barilari, to testify against him. Paralysed and confined to a wheelchair in his apartment above the pharmacy that is located directly opposite the site of the shootings, Barilari was privy to the massacre from a privileged vantage point. However, his former relationship to Sciagura complicates the situation. In his youth Barilari had been an active Fascist and had accompanied Sciagura on the March on Rome. Seventeen, naive, and not particularly virile, during that trip he was forced by Sciagura into a brutal initiation to sexuality in a brothel – with Sciagura holding a gun to his head – and contracted syphilis as a result. His paralysis is the outcome of the disease.

The story begins, like so many of Bassani's stories, with the recollection of an event that takes its cue from a physical space, in this case the sidewalk opposite the Caffè della Borsa. The narrator is an insider who knows that Barilari is often seen stationed at his window overlooking Corso Roma and the infamous site of the massacres; he has observed Barilari addressing the passers-by almost imperceptibly in a voice resembling that of a prepubescent boy, which seems to come from on high:

> La voce dice, "Badi a lei, giovanotto!"; oppure: "Attenzione!"; oppure: "Ehi!". E non è, ripeto, che ciò venga urlato. Suona piuttosto come un avvertimento bonario, come un consiglio espresso col tono di chi non si aspetti di essere udito, né, in fondo, abbia molta voglia di farsi udire. (174)

> The voice says: "Watch out, young man!" or else: "Mind where you put your feet, sir!" or else: "Be careful!" or simply: "Hey!" And I repeat: it isn't that these words are shouted. They sound more like a friendly warning, like a piece of advice offered in the tone of one neither expecting to be heard nor really wanting very much to be heard.

This particular story, even more than the earlier ones, abounds with primal images, images of seeing with the eye and with the mind's eye:

> Di scatto, dinanzi agli occhi di ogni mente, l'immagine del farmacista affacciato a una finestra dell'appartamento superiore. Per questa volta dunque lui c'è: seduto al davanzale, in vedetta, con le braccia magre, bianchissime e pelose levate a puntare in direzione di chi passa e non sa le lenti scintillanti di un binocolo da montagna. (175)

> Abruptly, in every mind's eye, the image of the pharmacist at a window of the apartment above. This time, then, he is there: sitting at the window, in full view, with his thin, very white and hairy arms raised and aiming towards an unknowing passer-by the glistening lens of a pair of mountain climber's binoculars.

After this introduction, the narration returns to 1939, then 1936, then 1937, as it attempts to flesh out a portrait of Pino Barilari on the basis of the few events in his life to which the citizens of Ferrara could be privy. Here Bassani uses much the same technique adopted in "La passeggiata prima di cena" when evoking the enigmatic figure of Elia Corcos. Like Corcos, Barilari is seen through the inquisitive eyes of the citizenry, who can only guess at what his life has been. His father was a Fascist sympathizer, the town pharmacist, and a widower. In 1936, when Pino first appeared behind the counter of the pharmacy after his father's death, everyone was stunned because no one was aware that he had even attended university. Even more surprising was his ensuing marriage to the loose, reckless, and incredibly sensuous Anna Repetto, hardly a suitable match for the shy and inept Barilari, at least according to the males of Ferrara, who almost felt as if she had been stolen out from under them by this unworthy opponent. The rest of the story oscillates between recollections, always from the perspective of the collectivity, of the events of 15 December and of Pino Barilari's situation. What connects the two in their minds is, of course, the knowledge that Barilari will be testifying at the trial of Sciagura: the possibility of arriving at the truth and assigning some responsibility for this massacre will depend on Barilari's eyewitness account of the shooting.

Instances of looking and seeing or not seeing, as already mentioned, haunt this text. Seeing, paradoxically, is often accompanied by its opposite, not seeing, or by imagining:

> Chi non ricorda, a Ferrara, la notte del 15 dicembre 1943? Chi potrà mai dimenticare le lentissime ore di quella notte? Fu per tutti una veglia angosciosa, interminabile: con gli occhi che bruciavano fissi a scrutare attraverso le fessure delle persiane le vie immerse nel buio dell'oscuramento. (186)

> Who in Ferrara doesn't remember the night of 15 December 1943? Who will ever be able to forget the slowly creeping hours of that night? It was an anguishing, seemingly endless vigil for everyone; with eyes that burned, peering intently through the cracks in the blinds at the streets plunged into the darkness of the blackout.

As if already aware that they will bow to the intimidation of the Fascists, the citizens begin to rationalize their own behaviour:

> I fascisti ... limitandosi dal settembre in poi a rastrellare quel centinaio di ebrei su cui erano riusciti a mettere le mani, e a rinchiudere in Piangipane una decina scarsa di antifascisti, avevano in fondo dato prova di notevole mitezza. ... Se i fascisti facevano un po'di baccano ... lo facevano più che altro per tenere a bada i tedeschi. ... Poveri diavoli, i fascisti! Bisognava cercare di capire il dramma loro e quello personale di Mussolini. ... E a essere schietti, come bisognava giudicarlo l'assassinio del console Bolognesi, un padre di famiglia, fra l'altro, uno che in vita sua non aveva mai torto un capello a chichessia? (187–8)

> The Fascists who, since September, had limited themselves to rounding up the hundred or so Jews they had managed to lay their hands on and to imprisoning barely ten anti-Fascists in Via Piangipane had displayed, all things considered, remarkable restraint. ... If the Fascists made a bit of a racket ... they did it mostly to keep the Germans at bay. ... Poor devils, the Fascists! You had to try to understand their drama and Mussolini's personal one, too, poor man. ... And to be honest, how was one to judge the assassination of Consul Bolognesi – a family man who, among other things, had never so much as hurt a fly in his whole life?

When the night is over, the hours of speculation and fear are replaced by the knowledge that the corpses of eleven innocent people are lying on the sidewalk opposite the Caffè della Borsa, face down and with their limbs entangled so that they have to be separated and turned over on their backs in order to be identified. The immediate reaction is one of outrage, but it quickly yields to indifference and even consent. After the war, the knowledge that they had acquiesced to the crimes of Sciagura and his cohorts haunts them, as do the images of the dead "come se l'immaginazione collettiva avesse bisogno di ritornare sempre là, a quella notte tremenda, e di riavere uno per uno dinanzi agli occhi i volti degli undici fucilati quali nel punto supremo il solo Pino Barilari li aveva avuti" (198; as if the collective imagination needed to return there over and over again, to that terrible night, to have before its eyes, one by one, the faces of the eleven murdered men, as, at the supreme moment, only Pino Barilari had seen them). The collectivity assigns Barilari the task of speaking out – of doing what they had been unable to do – and thus lifting the veil of hypocrisy with which they themselves had concealed the acts of the collaborators amongst them. In the weeks leading up to the trial, they give free rein to their fantasies about the witness who is to redeem their sins, wending their way in their imaginations from the outside into Pino's childhood room, to the single bed in which he now sleeps, and finally to the objects lying on the night table beside it:

> Immaginavano.
>
> Penetravano, immaginando, dentro ... la stanzetta che Pino, dopo averla occupata da ragazzo, era tornato a occupare da quando lo aveva colpito la paralisi ... dove, subito dopo cena, Pino si ritirava per dormirci, con un lettuccio di ferro in un angolo. (196–7)

> They imagined.

> They penetrated, imagining, … the little room Pino had occupied as a boy, and to which he had returned when he was paralyzed … where, immediately after supper, Pino went to sleep, with a small, iron bed in one corner.

On the night table beside the small bed they see a series of objects: a stamp collector's album, a cheap pencil sharpener, a cluster of coloured pencils in a tumbler, a half-used eraser, and finally a book: Edgar Allan Poe's *Narrative of Gordon Pym*. We are told that this particular edition displays a ghost holding a scythe on the cover, but that the book lies face down on the table, so that the ghost "pur continuando a essere presente, *a essere lì*, fosse invisible, non facesse più la minima paura" (196–7; while still present, *still there*, was invisible, and no longer frightening in any way).

Poe's *Narrative of Arthur Gordon Pym of Nantucket* (1838) is a macabre adventure story that takes place at sea. Its protagonist is a stowaway who witnesses all sorts of horrors – violence, mutiny, massacres, cannibalism. By focusing in particular on the book, which is turned over so that its frightening cover is invisible, the narrative indicates what Pino and the citizens who are imagining what is behind the door to his room do not want to see. Moreover, the objects that surround the book, all of which might be found in a schoolboy's desk, reinforce the notion that Pino is not a man but a child. In fact, when nine o'clock arrives, he is "già rannicchiato nel suo lettuccio di ragazzo, le coperte tirate fin sopra le orecchie. Chiudere gli occhi, dormire. … Sprofondarsi nel sonno" (197–8; already curled up in his child's bed, the blankets pulled up to his ears. To shut his eyes, to sleep. … To lose himself in sleep).

The book is prophetic. When the time for his testimony arrives, in fact, Barilari refuses to reveal what he knows, answering the judge's question with a simple "Dormivo" (198; I was sleeping). As he utters this blatant lie – since we know him to have been awakened by the screams of one of the victims just before the shootings took place and to have witnessed the ensuing massacre "[da] dietro le lastre della finestra che sovrastava la scena" (198; from behind the panes of the window, overlooking the scene) – he exchanges a telling look with Sciagura, "un ammicco, già, un quasi impercettibile ammico d'intesa" (204; a wink, yes, an almost imperceptible, complicitous wink).

The last chapter of the story contains a postscript about Anna Repetto and also clarifies the truth about Barilari's refusal to speak. It emerges that when he woke up to the screams of the victims, just prior to the shootings, he saw not only Sciagura but also his own wife Anna, who happened to be returning home from one of her nocturnal assignations at the same moment. Their eyes met briefly, she in the street and he at the window. Expecting to be confronted by him and wondering what excuse to invent this time, she hurried upstairs only to find him asleep, or pretending to be asleep, face to the wall with the blankets pulled up over his ears.

Paradoxically, it is after witnessing this scene that Barilari experiences the transformation that sees him become a fixture armed with binoculars at the window of his apartment, mumbling and sneering to himself, another form of Dantean *contrappasso*: he who does not want to see is now condemned to spend his life looking through binoculars. At this point Anna decides to leave him, fearing that he has gone mad and that she will as well if she stays. She leaves to live on her own and is frequently seen in the streets of Ferrara with a string of female room-mates rumoured to be from Rome, Bologna, or Florence. These ambiguous friendships of hers become the talk of the town, though they do not prevent her from also offering her favours to the males of Ferrara, generally married men who had known her since their school days.

This rather extensive coda about Anna Repetto and her post-separation sexual promiscuity makes little sense unless we see it as a reference to the phase of the family romance in which the child becomes aware of his parents' sexuality and begins to fantasize that his mother is sexually promiscuous. He thus passes from the foundling stage of the Romance, in which the child imagines himself to be an orphan, to the bastard stage, in which he imagines himself to be the result of one of his promiscuous mother's anonymous sexual couplings.[10] In fact, we are told that Anna's clients are not happy since she is very temperamental. It is even difficult to know whether or not she expects to be paid; the confusion of her sexual partners is, of course, that of the son in the clutches of the bastard phase of the Romance, disoriented by his mother's sudden transformation in his eyes from respectable married woman to harlot and uncertain as to whether she is merely promiscuous or actually a prostitute. In fact, the men with whom she consorts, and who never tire of talking about her among themselves, attribute the difficulty of dealing with Anna to the fact that "fino a poco tempo prima era stata una signora per bene" (207; until recently, she had been a respectable married woman).

It is to one of her clients that Anna finally reveals what happened that fateful night, that Pino never acknowledged having seen either the massacre or Anna herself, who was returning home after having been with another man. She, on the other hand, saw everything very clearly and remembers it in graphic detail: the corpses lying in the middle of Corso Roma, the full moon illuminating the scene, and Pino standing at the window of their apartment, looking down at her.

The story of Pino conflates two things: the horror of the massacre and of adult female sexuality – both of which Pino denies by pretending to be asleep; perhaps this conflation resulted from his brutal initiation to the realities of life during the March on Rome, when he was forced into a sexual encounter with Sciagura looking on and a pistol pointed at his head. The accumulation of images of mental and physical vision – of seeing and not seeing – corresponding to the child's fantasies of adult sexuality and of a threshold position, indicates a state of damaged or arrested manhood that Bassani attributes not only to Pino Barilari but to the collectivity as well. The basic underlying equivalence here is not so much sexual perversion and moral depravity but arrested development and moral passivity. Sciagura and Pino stand in fact at opposite ends of a continuum, with Sciagura representing perversion and depravity and Pino adolescence and passivity. In Pino's case, the lack of manliness is made more than explicit, with Anna stating that "lui in fondo era un bambino, e lei la sua mamma" (210; he was a child, basically, and she was his mamma).

Sciagura and Barilari are at issue in this story only inasmuch as they represent realistic incarnations of the brutality and complicity for which all have pretended, up to now, not to have been responsible. On trial here is the Ferrara that failed to stand up to the Nazi-Fascist thugs in its midst and that gained the unenviable reputation of having had the largest number of adherents to the Repubblica di Salò of all the towns in Nazi-occupied Italy. Pino embodies the mental and moral paralysis of the citizens of Ferrara. His literal paralysis is a Dantean *contrappasso*, the punishment that befits the sin of passivity. The idea of the *contrappasso*, in which the punishment is either the opposite of the sin committed on earth or else analogous to it, is very clearly alluded to in the passage below, in which the image of the "mezzo busto" recalls Farinata in *Inferno* X, visible to Dante only from the waist up.[11] A Ghibelline associated with the civil strife that plagued Dante's Florence, Farinata objected to having Florence razed to the ground by his allies, claiming that he was a Florentine first and a Ghibelline second. Pino, had he spoken up, would have been a citizen of Ferrara first and a former Fascist second, but he is unable to rise to the occasion:

> Soltanto l'improvvisa paralisi che di lì a nemmeno due anni aveva colpito Pino Barilari alle gambe, col conseguente effetto di cominciare a sospendere lassù in alto, come da un palco di proscenio, il mezzo busto in pigiama al di sopra dell'animato teatro di corso Roma, aveva avuto il potere di richiamare ancora una volta l'attenzione generale su di lui. ... Lui infatti era sempre là, ormai, seduto dalla mattina alla sera al davanzale di una finestra dell'appartamento sovrastante la farmacia ... con uno sguardo nel quale brillava una luce ... come se fosse stata appunto la sifilide che per tanti anni aveva sonnecchiato subdolamente nel suo sangue, e infine era insorta di colpo a stroncargli le gambe, a trasformare la sua scialba vita in qualcosa di chiaro, di comprensibile a lui stesso, insomma di *esistente.* (178–9)

> Only the sudden paralysis that less than two years later had struck Pino Barilari in the legs had the power to attract attention to him again. After this he began, a bust in pyjamas, to be seen suspended up there as if in a stage box over the bustling theatre of Corso Roma. ... In fact he was always there now, seated from morning to night at a window of the apartment over the pharmacy ... with a new glow in his eyes ... as if it had been the disease, which for so many years had lain dormant in his blood and then risen abruptly to strike his legs, to finally turn his lacklustre, insignificant life into something clear, comprehensible to himself: something *existent*, in other words.

If his punishment is the paralysis, the punishment of the citizens of Ferrara is knowing that he is there on high, judging them for their conduct, having refused to be the scapegoat, the one who would publicly point the finger to Sciagura and exonerate them all for their passive acquiescence to the horrible trials inflicted upon the Jews and anti-Fascists among them. Moreover, by presiding over the sidewalk where the shootings took place and preventing anyone from walking there, he keeps the past alive, making it impossible to forget or to deny. Unlike the plaque placed in Via Mazzini in order to put the past to rest, Pino is a fixed but living monument to the sins of his fellow citizens.

Although it has been suggested that Pino's paralysis brought on by syphilis is inspired by a character in Joyce's *Dubliners,*[12] it may also be relevant that a similar incident is at the origin of Nietzsche's paralysis and subsequent descent into madness. According to an often-repeated but disputed account, Nietzsche was also taken to a brothel, either by mistake or deliberately, by a taxi driver or some university classmates in Cologne in 1865, but in either case against his will. Sexually innocent, he was traumatized and reacted by sitting at a piano and playing. Some say he remained abstinent all his life, others that he contracted syphilis on that or another occasion and subsequently became paralysed. It has also been speculated that it was a homosexual brothel. Thomas Mann was to make use of this incident in his novel *Doctor Faustus*.[13]

3 *Gli occhiali d'oro*: Jews and Homosexuals Revisited

The themes of homosexuality, abuse, passivity, and denial that emerge in relation to each other in the last of the *Storie ferraresi* are expanded upon in *Gli occhiali d'oro,* which inaugurates the trilogy of first-person novels at the heart of Bassani's "confession." Bassani explained his decision to turn to the first-person in the following terms:

> Non appena ultimata la stesura di *Una notte del '43,* avevo cominciato a sentire di avere esaurito un ciclo. ... Al punto in cui mi trovavo, Ferrara, il piccolo segregato universo da me inventato, non avrebbe più saputo svelarmi nulla di sostanzialmente nuovo. Se volevo che tornasse a dirmi qualcosa, bisognava che mi riuscisse di includervi anche colui che dopo essersene separato aveva insistito per molti anni a drizzare dentro le rosse mura della patria il teatro della propria letteratura, cioè me stesso. Chi ero, io, in fondo? ... Riflettori dunque anche su me, d'ora in poi, scrivente e non scrivente: su tutto me. A partire da adesso valeva forse la pena che l'autore ... provasse anche lui a uscire dalla sua tana, si qualificasse, osasse dire finalmente "io."[1]

> As soon as I finished writing *Una notte del '43,* I began to feel like I had completed a cycle. ... At that point, Ferrara, the small, segregated universe I had invented, could not reveal anything substantially new to me. If I wanted it to keep telling me something, I had to be able to include that individual who, after having separated himself from that world, had insisted for many years on staging within those city walls the theatre of his own literature: myself. Who was I, truly? ... Henceforth, the spotlight would also be on my own person, writer and not: on all of me. From now on, it was perhaps worthwhile for the author as well ... to try to come out of hiding, to qualify himself, to dare finally to say "I."

Tempting as it may be to treat these works as autobiography (especially in the light of statements such as the one above), it is important to keep in mind the distinctions that the author himself has made, in speaking of the first-person trilogy, between "l'io scrivente" (narrator), "l'io personaggio" (protagonist), and "l'io vivente" (author):

> In quelli la mia fatica massima era stata quella di mettere in rapporto l'io scrivente, che scrive a Roma, in un luogo centrale della lingua e del paese, con l'io di molti anni prima, l'io personaggio. In sostanza lo sforzo dei romanzi e racconti precedenti [all'*Airone*] era stato quello di mettere in rapporto i due io, e al tempo stesso di stabilire la distanza temporale e spaziale fra l'io narrante e l'io vivente.[2]

> In those novels, my greatest difficulty was the interplay between the narrator – writing in Rome, in a central locus of the country and of the Italian language – and the protagonist, that "I" of many years ago. Essentially, the effort of the novels and stories [preceding *L'airone*] was to create the relationship between those two "I"s (the protagonist and the narrator), while establishing the temporal and spatial distance between the narrator and myself – the living author.

In other words, while Bassani's protagonist in these novels may or may not coincide with Bassani as a young man ("l'io personaggio"), his adult narrator, the person saying "I" in the novel, most definitely does not coincide with Bassani the living author ("l'io vivente"). The author knows things that the narrator does not, while the narrator is recalling himself as a young man in the protagonist through the only lens of memory available to human beings: memory conflated with the distortions of residual conflict, desire, and affect.

Nowhere is this more obvious than in *Gli occhiali d'oro*. Set in the period leading up to Mussolini's decision to adopt Hitler's racial policies, this masterful short novel at first appears to be the story of a respected physician, Athos Fadigati, who falls from grace in the eyes of the bourgeoisie as a result of his decision to "come out" as a homosexual in Fascist Ferrara. After years of the utmost discretion in the conduct of his private life, the highly admired, urbane, and cultured doctor suddenly, and against all logic, chooses to enter into an open affair with a much younger and vulgar university student who was part of the narrator's entourage in the spring of 1937. The affair, openly displayed in the seaside town of Riccione in full view of all the vacationing citizens of Ferrara, takes place in the summer of that year, just as the young

Jewish student, now telling Fadigati's story retrospectively as an adult, was coming face to face with the anti-Semitic campaign that preceded the passing of the Race Laws. The shared experience of social ostracism brings them together, but not enough to prevent Fadigati from committing suicide after he loses his patients, his position at the hospital, and his lover. The young Jew is left to contemplate his own uncertain future as the political climate continues to deteriorate.

The shared fate of the homosexual and the Jew in Western society is a topos with a long and distinguished literary history.[3] Why has Bassani chosen to retell it? And why in this particular manner? The relevant intertext here, flaunted by Bassani much as Fadigati flaunts his relationship with his lover Deliliers on the beaches of Riccione, is Thomas Mann's *Death in Venice* (1912), and yet relatively little critical attention has been paid to it.[4] Bassani's chosen title, *The Gold-Rimmed Spectacles*, is actually lifted directly from Mann's famous description of his protagonist Gustav von Aschenbach: "The bow of a pair of gold spectacles with rimless lenses cut into the base of his strong, nobly curved nose."[5]

In many ways, Athos Fadigati can be said to be a middle-brow version of Aschenbach. Though not an artist himself, he prides himself on being a connoisseur of the arts, a sort of "culture vulture" whose rarefied tastes and pursuits, together with his professional status, make him the object of veneration in the largely philistine world of Ferrara. Bassani goes to great lengths to emphasize how much of Fadigati's public persona is tied up with his capacity for aesthetic appreciation. His conversation is continuously peppered with references to painting, music, and literature and his office is described in great detail as a sort of miniature museum and cultural *locus amoenus*. In reality it is meant as a monument to the Enlightenment belief in the capacity of culture to function as a centripetal force in society: through his fanatic devotion to the arts, Bassani seems to be saying, Fadigati can convince himself, and others, that he is part of the mainstream, while his patients, as they wait to be seen in his anteroom, can bask briefly in their own illusion that they share in the aura of prestige that surrounds him. None of this suffices to redeem him in their eyes, however, once he violates what are considered to be the boundaries of good taste and decorum in his personal life, once he ceases to adhere to the code of behaviour that had up to then ruled his life. If he had sexual relationships, they were carefully hidden and conducted with the utmost discretion, and always with persons who sought to avoid scandal as much as he did. His uncharacteristic liaison with the unscrupulous and vulgar young student Eraldo Deliliers abruptly unmasks the sensual and masochistic longings beneath the "cultured" surface and leads to his ultimate demise.

The scenes that are drawn from the Mann text emphasize Fadigati's status as an outsider. Particularly poignant are those in which he contemplates his love object from afar, just like Aschenbach gazes at Tadzio on the shores of the Lido. There are also long sequences in which we see Fadigati repeatedly trying to cozy up to the group of students on the daily Ferrara-Bologna train (where he meets both the narrator and Deliliers, both of whom are part of the group), which recall those scenes on the boat to Venice in which Aschenbach notices a group of young people accompanied by an older man and is struck by the dissonance in this spectacle. The older man is trying to act as if he were one of them, but no amount of ostentatious camaraderie can mask the sharp contrast between his grotesque appearance and the youthfulness of his entourage. So, too, there is something pathetic about Fadigati's attempts to curry favour with the carefree young people on the train, with whom he will never fit in, no matter what. Another point of contact between the two texts is to be found in the scenes in which Fadigati meanders aimlessly and anonymously through the narrow, poorer streets of Ferrara, revelling in the smells of the foodstalls and in the bodily contact with the crowds, in search of something that is not quite clear even to him. Though Aschenbach is less relaxed in this environment in Venice, the atmosphere in the streets is very much the same.

Strange as it may seem, *Death in Venice* was not openly acknowledged in Mann criticism as a homosexual text until quite recently: "As Mann became an established international classic ... the stylistic mastery of *Death in Venice* went on being emphasized. Arguably this was at least in part a displacement activity of critics that allowed them to pass over in silence the story's taboo subject, or at any rate not to probe the author's own relation to it. Mann gave scarcely a public hint of how close that relation was."[6] Anthony Heilbut, Mann's most recent biographer, puts it very succinctly: "The history of its [*Death in Venice*'s] reception comprises an astonishing chapter of sexual politics. Although a certain public has never had trouble with the text, it rapidly acquired an intellectual patina that overwhelmed the affair that comprises its very heart. *Death in Venice* has been treated as purest symbol – to paraphrase Mann, a treatise whose subject is a matter of indifference."[7]

Clearly Bassani did not share this opinion. Long before the appearance of the Mann diaries, in a brief review of Mann's *Mario and the Magician*, Bassani stated quite clearly that, in his view, the protagonists of Mann's short stories and short novels, including Aschenbach, could all be said to bear a resemblance "all'uomo Mann, al suo privato destino di intellettuale deluso e insidiato"[8] (to Mann the individual, to his private fate as a frustrated and trapped intellectual). In the same review, Bassani also refers to another of Mann's stories, *A Man and his Dog*, in which the protagonist is a writer who, in the words of Bassani, "riconosce negli istinti del proprio cane tanta parte di un sé stesso ignorato forse per viltà, e scorge nella povera bestia, umiliata dalla catena e dalla noia, il simbolo vivente della propria infelicità"[9] (recognizes in the instincts of his dog a large part of himself, suppressed perhaps out of cowardice, and sees in the poor beast, humiliated by its leash and its boredom, the living symbol of his own unhappiness). This dog appears in *Gli occhiali d'oro* in a scene that takes place after Fadigati's public humiliation and once Mussolini's Race Laws are firmly in place. The young Jew and Fadigati, now both outcasts, meet by accident at night in the streets of Ferrara. Fadigati is being followed by a dog who has attached herself to him and seems to be masochistically ignoring his rejection of her:

> "Picchiami, uccidimi pure, se vuoi!", sembrava voler dire. "È giusto, e poi mi piace!" …
>
> "La guardi," diceva intanto Fadigati, indicandomela. "Forse bisognerebbe essere così, sapere accettare la propria natura. Ma d'altra parte come si fa? È possibile pagare un prezzo simile? Nell'uomo c'è molto della bestia, eppure può, l'uomo, arrendersi? Ammettere di essere una bestia, e soltanto una bestia?" (299–300)

> "Beat me, kill me if you want," she seemed to be saying. "It's only right, and besides, I like it!" ...
>
> "Will you look at her!" said Fadigati, pointing. "Perhaps one ought to be like that, able to accept one's own nature. But on the other hand, how does one accomplish that? Isn't the price too high? There's a great deal of the animal in all men and yet can we give in to it? Admit to being an animal and only an animal?" (106–7)

From the perspective of the glaring difference between the two stories, Bassani's rewrite constitutes what might be considered an "outing" of Mann's story as early as 1957, with Fadigati "acting out" Aschenbach's (and Mann's) repressed homosexuality. While Aschenbach initially attempts to elevate his desires onto an aesthetic plane and infuses the object of his longing with all the attributes of a Greek statue, Fadigati embraces his underside with a vengeance. And while Tadzio is a young aristocrat, largely innocent though perhaps not entirely unaware of the effect he has had on his admirer, Deliliers is a sadistic and ruthless working-class thug who exploits and humiliates the pathetic Fadigati at every turn; Fadigati appears to acquiesce to this treatment and at times even to revel in it. Since the Bassani story is presented from the limited perspective of the Jewish narrator, we are not told why Fadigati has suddenly departed so radically from his previous behaviour. Thus one chapter ends with Fadigati and Deliliers being spotted in a café in Bologna after the description of Fadigati's first humiliation at the hands of his lover-to-be in the train from Ferrara, and the next takes us directly to Riccione, where their liaison has become both common knowledge and public spectacle. To understand what has transpired in the interim to transform Fadigati, the most discreet of professionals, into the willing prey of a vulgar gigolo and then to turn up with him at the family resort where his peers (as well as Mussolini) gather en masse every summer, one has only to refer directly to Mann's text, to the struggle between the so-called Apollonian and Dionysian, and assume that the Dionysian has won out.

Fascinating as all of this may be, it does not explain Bassani's interest in this famous story or his particular take on it – after all, there are no Jews in *Death in Venice*. A further avenue to pursue may be found in a long essay Bassani published in 1964 on representations of Venice in literature. Entitled *Le parole preparate* (loosely translated as "ready-made words" or "discourses"), it traces and deplores the abyss between the reality of Venice's history over the centuries and its literary distortions, with Thomas Mann cited prominently among the guilty:

> Riguardo poi al colera che serpeggia nascostamente nella Venezia manniana (anche a Gustav von Aschenbach, che vi si trasferisce ogni giorno dal dorato arenile del Lido obbedendo all'oscuro richiamo della Bellezza e della Morte, essa appare come indecifrabile intrico di calli afose, di canali da cui spira lezzo di cadaveri e di disinfettante, un labirinto abitato da una sorta di abbietto pulviscolo umano con cui non si deve, per decenza, stabilire altri contatti che non siano puramente strumentali: una specie di *suk* medio-orientale, di viscido bordello, o addirittura di impietrata cifra del sesso), è chiaro, questo colera, non si sa poi se reale o ipotetico, a quale altra malattia allude, della psiche e dell'anima.[10]

> As for the cholera that surreptitiously winds its way through Mann's Venice (to Gustav von Aschenbach, too, who travels there every day from

> the golden sands of the Lido, obeying the obscure call of Beauty and Death, it appears as a confused maze of narrow, suffocating laneways giving off the smell of corpses and disinfectant, a labyrinth inhabited by a sort of abject human atomy with whom one must not, out of propriety, establish any contact that is not purely utilitarian: a kind of Middle Eastern souk, or slimy bordello, or even petrified cipher of sex), it is clear to what other disease of the psyche and the soul, this cholera, whether real or hypothetical, alludes.

In a paradoxical, unconscious reproduction of Mann's own reticence, Bassani does not name the "disease": homosexuality. However, his long parenthetic description of Mann's Venice and of its inhabitants clearly alludes to anti-Semitic images of the Jews as carriers of disease – in fact the two have been condensed into one. Not to be forgotten, Bassani seems to be telling us, is the fact that Venice was the first city to officially close off its Jewish population in a ghetto,[11] precisely because the Jews were seen as a threat:

> The Venetian authorities, like other rulers in Christian Europe, did not want to allow Jews – the "leaven of disbelief" – to live permanently in their city. Jews were seen as bearing something like an infectious disease – they were dangerous, they might contaminate Christians and their very existence seemed to represent a challenge and an insult to Christianity.
>
> But on the other hand the Venetian state did not want to forego the economic advantage that the Jews brought – particularly the low-interest loans they provided the urban poor through pawnshops. … The invention of the ghetto was the perfect solution. … In 1516 the Serenissima found a place for the segregation of the Jews that was far from the geographic, political and spiritual center of the city, Piazza San Marco. The choice of location itself appears to have been a symbolic statement, conscious or not – an objective correlative to the alien, "infectious" status of the Jews. … The authorities chose a peripheral area – a tiny island called the "the new foundry" because of the iron foundry that previously existed there. "New foundry" in Italian was "ghetto nuovo" – a fateful name not just for Jews in Venice but for other minorities ever since.[12]

Mann wrote his story in 1911, Bassani his in the 1950s. What Bassani may well have intuited in a post-Holocaust reading of *Death in Venice* was a subliminal Jewish presence in the Mann text, leading him to focus on something that has received little or no attention from the critics but was made explicit in Luchino Visconti's 1971 film version of Mann's story: that Mann had based the figure of Gustav von Aschenbach on his contemporary, the great Jewish composer and conductor Gustav Mahler, known, among other things, for his desperate but ultimately futile attempts to be a considered a true German artist in spite of his Jewishness. In a letter to Wolfgang Born, the illustrator of *Death in Venice*, Mann expresses his amazement at Born's uncanny ability to recognize Mahler in his description of Aschenbach:

> Just one more word about the last picture, entitled *Death*. That one strikes me as strange and almost mysterious because of a similarity. In the early summer of 1911 the news of Gustav Mahler's death played into the conception of my story. I was able to make his acquaintance earlier in Munich and his consumingly intense personality made the strongest impression upon me. From the island of Brioni, where I was staying at the time of his death, I followed the bulletins in the Viennese press, written as if for a prince, concerning his last hours. And while later this shock mingled with the impressions and ideas out of which the novella grew, I gave my hero, who had succumbed to orgiastic dissolution, not only the first name of the great musician, but also his physical description, Mahler's visage. *Still, I wanted to be certain that in the case of such a casual and hidden correlation one would not be able to talk at all about recognition on the part of the readership. Even in your case as the illustrator no one spoke about it. For you neither knew Mahler personally, nor had I confided anything about that secret personal correlation* to you. Nevertheless – and this is what startled me at first sight – Aschenbach's head portrayed in your picture unmistakably manifests the Mahler type. That really is strange. Is it not said (Goethe said it) that language cannot express the individual and the specific, and therefore it is not possible to be understood, if the other person does not have the same view? The other person, it is said, has to pay more attention to the intention of the speaker than to his words. But because you, the artist, as the result of my words were able to hit upon the individual, language must not only have a direct impact from one person to another, but, as a literary artistic means, be able to retain the powers of intention, the suggestive powers that make a transfer of visual perception possible. This is so interesting to me that I did not, at this opportunity, want to be completely silent about it. Best wishes for your work and thanks for your noble effort concerning mine![13] (emphasis added)

Mann's reticence with regard to the Mahler/Aschenbach identification reflected both his own highly ambivalent admiration for the Jews and the hostility towards Mahler on the part of a significant segment of the musical establishment. Richard Wagner's influential essay "Judaism in Music" (1850) had stated that "when the Jew tries to compose music, what he produces is ultimately inspired by synagogue music."[14] As a "Jewish Wagnerite in antisemitic Vienna,"[15] Mahler did everything he could to overcome this contradiction, going so far as to convert to Roman Catholicism. In his youth, towards the end of the 1870s, Mahler had joined the Vienna Nietzsche Society, full of Jews fuelled by assimilationist hopes and anxious to "participate in what they saw as a more cosmopolitan culture than that of their ancestors."[16] The extent to which he attempted to embrace Nietzsche's philosophy is testified to by the Third Symphony (1895–6), centred around the theme of "self-overcoming," with a poem from *Thus Spoke Zarathustra* providing the text for the fourth movement. Publicly, Mahler appeared indifferent to Jewish issues, to say nothing of his overt contempt for "eastern" Jews:

> At almost no stage did he show any special interest in Jewish matters, let alone back Jewish causes. Although he and Theodor Herzl, the founder of political Zionism, were contemporaries in Vienna, they never seem to have met. Mahler took on Bruno Walter after a few years in Vienna because he knew of his exceptional talent, but in general he did not treat Jewish musicians with special favour. Rather the contrary. In the pre-Walter era he turned down the idea that he should engage Leo Blech, a converted Jew, as a conductor because "for the anti-Semites, I still count as a Jew despite my baptism, and more than one Jew is more than the Vienna Court Opera can bear." As for his attitude to the "Ostjuden," Mahler was as harsh as any of his assimilated brethren in the capital. During a visit in 1903 to Lemberg (Lvov, now in the Ukraine) he wrote to Alma, "Life here has an unusual look. Oddest of all are the Jews who run around here the way dogs do elsewhere. It is extremely entertaining to watch them! My God, am I supposed to be related to them?"[17]

Nonetheless, despite all his efforts to downplay his Jewishness and to mould himself into a "traditional musical idealist,"[18] he could not persuade those critics determined to malign him.[19] One of Mahler's biographers describes the aftermath of the Vienna performance of his Fourth Symphony:

> What would later be regarded as Mahler's most modestly proportioned and approachable symphony had sparked off a furor of often explicitly antisemitic criticism. Reviewers referred to fake naivety that masked decadent modest irony. Worse still it was "entertaining," with its outwardly attractive melodies, licentious orchestration and elaborately worked-up "*Trugschlusse*" (literally "deceptive conclusions": the term also implies sophistry, "fallacies"). The young Swiss art-lover William Ritter, later one of Mahler's most devoted younger supporters, summed it all up in his description of its confusingly polyglot music whose supposedly Viennese themes were so "moist and persuasive, tantalizing and seductive" that they occasioned "lewd glances in the concert halls, the salacious dribble at the corners of the mouths of some of the old men, and above all the ugly, whoring laughs of certain respectable women!" But where the Third Symphony seemed exceptionally to approach the pornographic, the Fourth confirmed the disreputable mass appeal of such music by achieving a resounding public success.[20]

Thomas Mann was present at the climax of Mahler's public career at the performance of the Eighth Symphony in Munich on 12 September 1910, the year of Mahler's fiftieth birthday. After this he sent Mahler a copy of his latest novel, *Royal Highness*, "with a short letter in which he hailed the man who 'embodied the most serious and sacred artistic will of our age.'"[21] Mann's work notes for *Death in Venice* relating to Mahler speak of the "development of his style: towards the classical and settled, traditional, academic conservative. ... His works achieved greatness not only against the pressure of his delicate constitution, but also against his *mind*, against scepticism, mistrust, cynicism directed at art and artists themselves. The heroic Hamlet."[22] And yet, notwithstanding this admiration, Mann was reluctant to advertise the "secret personal correlation" acknowledged in the letter to his illustrator; moreover, like the anti-Semites, in his letter he associates Mahler with "orgiastic dissolution."

Mann identified with Mahler precisely because he saw his own struggle with homosexuality as parallel to Mahler's with his Jewishness, but this Jewishness both attracted and repulsed him.[23] Ritchie Robertson devotes several pages specifically to Mann's ambivalent identification with the Jews and quotes the following passage from a 1907 article by Mann entitled "On the Jewish Question": "Recognizable everywhere as a stranger, with the pathos of the exception in his heart, [the Jew] represents one of the extraordinary modes of existence that survive within civil life, distinguished from the common norm in a sublime or sordid sense, despite all human and democratic levelling-down." Robertson points out that this "romanticized portrayal of the Jew"

> is a projection of Mann's conception of the artist; one need only think of the permanent outsider Tonio Kroger. It suggests another figure: the homosexual. Mann's homosexuality is amply clear from his diaries and, when one reads it without prejudice, from his fiction. The stigma attached to Mann's artist figures covertly describes that of the homosexual. Mann's artists are stigmatized by conventional society as sick and degenerate, if not criminal; they have to be continual play-actors in order to disguise their inner nature ... The homosexual needs a mask in order to pass in a homophobic society, just as the Jew must suppress his original traits to be accepted in Western society. [24]

In discussing this same article by Mann, his biographer Anthony Heilbut points out some of the sources, and limitations, of Mann's identification with the Jews:

> By now Mann knew that he did not cut a charming figure, that something about his presence irritated almost everyone. He recognized a similarly forbidding personality in the arrogant Jew with his "frequently annoying superiority." The Jew does not hide his talents. Mann had argued on Schiller's behalf that the truly great possessed a right to their ambitions. Therefore, when he expressed "an artist's affinity for the Jews," he was praising a mirror image of his own personality, audacious and forlorn.
>
> In 1907 he saw "progress" as the only solution to the social prejudices of Western Europe and the far bloodier pogroms occurring in "barbarous" Russia (only its literature was "holy"). Once the Jew was fully assimilated, he would lose his disagreeable habits, the whiny, davening voice, the nervous eyes and hands, those unhappy products of "two thousand years of terrible exclusion." The stereotype could be retired now that the Jew was permitted to become a full-fledged German, if not a European. Of course the Jews Mann admired were members of an elite, whether financial or Nietzschean. He was a philo-Semite only by their standards ...: he allows the Jews only those offences that resemble his own.[25]

Bassani obviously knew that Mann and Mahler shared something more than just their artistic vocations – they shared the desperate desire to "pass," Mann as a heterosexual, Mahler as a Christian, and thus the same self-hatred. That Bassani had identified and was drawn to the veiled Mann-Mahler identification in *Death in Venice* is confirmed by several facts. As mentioned earlier, the title *The Gold-Rimmed Spectacles* is lifted from the very same description that caused Born to recognize Mahler in *Death in Venice* (33). Bassani also ends his story on the same note as Mann's. We know that Mann was provoked into writing *Death in Venice* by Mahler's death, which was revealed to him while reading the newspaper in Venice: this revelation, in fact, is incorporated into Mann's text - it is not just an external circumstance. The last sentence of *Death in Venice* reads: "And later that same day the world was respectfully shocked to receive the news of his death" (88). In Bassani's story, the narrator/protagonist also learns of Fadigati's death from the local newspaper and, in shock, announces quietly to his family, "È morto il dottor Fadigati" (314; Doctor Fadigati is dead [123]). Furthermore, in a comment about his musical tastes, Fadigati himself alludes to Mahler indirectly by mentioning Bruno Walter, one of Mahler's favourite musicians and also a Jew. He then goes on to refer to Walter as "il maestro germanico" (226; the Teutonic maestro [15]), a phrase that Bassani, with more than a touch of irony, puts in quotation marks.

From the perspective of its appropriation of the Mann story, *Gli occhiali d'oro* can be read at least partly as a veiled "setting straight" of the literary historical record: as a recuperation of the "lost" or submerged origins of *Death in Venice* in the illustrious literary tradition that documents the common fate of the Jew and of the homosexual in Western society. In other words, Bassani's novel constitutes a gloss to the Mann story, in Bloomian terms a creative – and corrective – misreading that exploits and suggests solutions to some of the interpretative conundrums posed by this famous text.[26]

An enduring commonplace of *Death in Venice* criticism is, not surprisingly, the problem of the narrator's position, the question of how to interpret this "enigmatic text without the assured and assuring guidance of a reliable narratorial voice."[27] David Luke points out that "in Mann's presentation of Aschenbach's experience the reader is constantly invited to take two opposite views simultaneously ... Mann projects into Aschenbach not only his homosexuality but also his puritan repudiation of it."[28] Lilian R. Furst speaks of the "narrator's blatant treachery."[29] T.J. Reed in "The Art of Ambivalence" sees the text's ambiguity as "rooted" in its genesis,[30] while Dorrit Cohen opts for a solution that restores full control of the text to Mann, claiming that "the author *behind* the work is communicating a message that escapes the narrator he placed *within* the work."[31]

Bassani adopts this last solution in his own first-person trilogy, and nowhere more clearly than in *Gli occhiali d'oro*: the ambivalent, textually submerged identification of the self-hating homosexual Mann with Mahler's tormented Jewishness evident in his third-person narrator is inverted and objectified by Bassani through the use here of a first-person narrator, a self-hating Jew reluctant to identify with the homosexual Fadigati. Most readings of this novel have suggested a sense of solidarity between the protagonist and Fadigati, as if it were a straightforward account of their coming together as a result of their "growing awareness" of their common plight.[32] Without explicitly collapsing the narrator into the author, these interpretations, as has been pointed out, fail to differentiate sufficiently between them. While Mann's third-person narration is clearly a source of difficulty, in Bassani's case the use of the first-person makes the distinction clear, at least from a narratological perspective.

From this vantage point, *Gli occhiali d'oro* can be considered a very subtle portrayal of a young Jew's unwitting contribution to the marginalization and eventual suicide of a highly respected homosexual physician, in spite of their shared experience of ostracism and persecution – and, in spite of what Bassani himself said about this novel in a 1991 interview, over thirty years after he had written it.[33] Fadigati considers the young Jew an ally, if not a friend, and turns to him for support in their darkest hour. But the young Jew is unable to respond sympathetically and ultimately shuns Fadigati, just as he himself is being shunned by his own Gentile cohorts, all the while failing to see the irony of the situation.[34]

Twenty years later, and for reasons that are never made explicit, he feels compelled to tell Fadigati's story. Slowly, however, Fadigati's story turns into the young Jew's story, as the adult narrator gradually and unwittingly betrays his own sense of responsibility for the doctor's suicide. Moreover, as he recalls his progressive recognition of his fate as a Jew and only a Jew, intertwined with the story of Fadigati's downfall, his memory of the unfortunate doctor emerges as still fraught with tensions and ambiguities, even after so many years have passed. Frequently, when he speaks of Fadigati's suffering at the hands of the citizens of Ferrara, it is difficult to tell with whom he sides. Sometimes his voice is that of the outsider, sympathetic to Fadigati's plight, sometimes it is that of the bourgeois *benpensante*, scandalized by Fadigati's unbecoming conduct and especially by his refusal to "play by the rules," that is, to hide his homosexuality so as not to offend his fellow citizens.

Gradually the source of the narrator's unease in speaking of Fadigati becomes clear. Though undoubtedly hostile to the bourgeois society of Ferrara and many of its attitudes, the narrator still cannot acknowledge his shared experience as a Jew with Fadigati's as a homosexual. It is this difficulty, this enduring ambivalence towards Fadigati twenty years after the fact and fifteen years after the Holocaust, that the reader comes to understand as the ultimate irony in this story. The narrator's conscious goal may well be to recall "the events of 1937 and to assess them critically in the light of Fadigati's suicide and of the fate of the Italian Jews,"[35] but what he actually does is *avoid* assessing them for as long as possible in order to obscure his role in these events and his share of moral responsibility for Fadigati's tragic fate. This accounts for the fact that the narrator's *prise de conscience* takes place only on the last page. Contrary to what has been often taken for granted – by virtue of the confusion between author and narrator – the rest of the novel is the story of his attempt to ignore these similarities, an effort that finally collapses not under the weight of the accumulating evidence (1937) but under the weight of his own suppressed guilt as it emerges in the telling (1957).

This reading of the novel shifts the emphasis from "the events of 1937" to the modalities of their discursive reconstruction by the narrator in 1958, modalities that are orchestrated by what has come to be known in the theory of narrative as the "implied author." To quote Seymour Chatman's *Story and Discourse*, the implied author is "a structural principle" that is "reconstructed by the reader from the narrative":[36] "He is not the narrator, but rather the principle that invented the narrator, along with everything else in the narrative, that stacked the cards in this particular way, had these things happen to these characters, in these words or images. Unlike the narrator, the implied author can tell us nothing. He, or better *it*, has no voice, no direct means of communicating. It instructs us silently, through the design of the whole, with all the voices, by all the means it has chosen to let us learn."[37]

In *Gli occhiali d'oro* the "implied author" or "structural principle" may reflect what the narrator knows at a subconscious level but does not wish to recognize, which manifests itself as "discourse." The parallel between Fadigati's situation and that of the young Jewish protagonist emerges from the orchestration of the "discourse" and from what it suggests "silently, through the design of the whole." This "discourse" often contradicts the "story," or what the narrator actually tells us. The significance of the novel lies, I believe, precisely in this contradiction between "story" and "discourse," and not in the supposed resolution of this contradiction, the *presa di coscienza,* the moment of epiphany, which is, at most, suggested and, if so, only at the end.[38]

The narration begins by reproducing the collective view of Athos Fadigati held by the citizens of Ferrara, many of whom, we are told, still remember him. However, immediately following in the second paragraph, the narrator calls attention to himself – more specifically, to his inability to provide an accurate portrait of the period in which Fadigati first arrived in Ferrara from his native Venice: "Per ragioni di età, io che scrivo non ho da offrire che una immagine piuttosto vaga e confusa dell'epoca" (215; Because of my age, I who write can give only a rather vague and confused picture of the period [1]). And yet he goes on to provide a detailed portrait of Fadigati's public image, followed by an even more precise account in the following chapter of those habits and aspects of his routine that first led the inhabitants of Ferrara to suspect that there might be more to his life than could be surmised from his reassuring appearance and manners. The third chapter is dedicated to a heavily ironic description of the tacit "social contract" adhered to by Fadigati and the citizenry, who even see themselves as tolerant. Divided by sexual orientation, they and the good doctor are nonetheless united in the common bourgeois goal of preserving appearances: "Di giorno, alla luce del sole, fargli tanto di cappello; la sera, anche a essere spinti ventre contro ventre dalla calca di via San Romano, mostrare di non conoscerlo. Come Fredric March nel *Dottor Jekyll,* il dottor Fadigati aveva due vite. Ma chi non ne ha?" (224–5). (By day, in the light of the sun, to show him every respect; at night, even if pressed chest-to-chest against him in the throng of Via San Romano, to show no sign of recognizing him. Like Fredric March in *Dr Jekyll and Mr Hyde,* Dr Fadigati had two lives. But who doesn't? [13].)

In this chapter we find the first reference to the gold-rimmed spectacles of the novel's title in connection with Fadigati's suspicious habit of frequenting the plebeian pit stalls of the cinemas of Ferrara, as opposed to the bourgeois balconies. When he was known to be in the theatre, the citizens could not rest, we are told, "finché non avessero colto il tipico luccichìo che i suoi occhiali d'oro mandavano ogni tanto attraverso il fumo e l'oscurità: un piccolo lampo inquieto, proveniente da una lontananza straordinaria, davvero infinita ..."[39] (225; until they had glimpsed the fitful, characteristic glint of his gold-rimmed spectacles in the smoke and darkness: a tiny, restless flash emitted from an astounding, really an infinite distance … [13]).

There is only one direct reference by the narrator to himself in this chapter: "Intorno al '35, rammento bene che al nome di Fadigati andava di solito associato quello di tale Manservigi" (228; In 1935, or thereabouts, I can clearly recall that Fadigati's name was often linked to a certain Manservigi [17]). A reader attempting to assess the position of the narrator at this point deduces only that he is an "insider" privy to a great deal of information and an "outsider," who distances himself, at least intellectually, from the self-serving hypocrisies of the bourgeoisie through irony. This is not to suggest that he sides with Fadigati in any way, but merely that he sees both attitudes for what they are. Other than his reference to this specific recollection, we know nothing of our raconteur: who he is, why he is telling this story, to whom he is addressing it.

The fourth chapter begins with a sentence that alerts us to the fact that there are, at this point, twenty-two years between the time of narration and the time of action: "Nel 1936, vale a dire ventidue anni fa" (19; In 1936, some twenty-two years ago), he specifies, the early morning Ferrara-Bologna train took at least an hour and twenty minutes to reach its destination. Here the narrator leaves the townspeople behind and narrows his focus to concentrate on the group of university students who took the train almost daily from Ferrara to Bologna. As he does so, he reveals more of his own identity as well, referring to himself as one of the students on that train.

The chapter is notable for its repeated references to the process of recollection, to the fuzziness of certain details, and particularly to the narrator's difficulty at remembering exactly who, among the students, first noticed that Fadigati, too, was travelling on this train:

> Chiudo gli occhi. Rivedo il gran varco asfaltato del viale Cavour …
>
> Chi sarà stato di noi, a richiamare per primo la curiosità generale sul signore del tassì: sul signore piuttosto che sul tassì? È vero che in tram, con la bionda testa ricciuta riversa sulla spalliera di legno, per solito Deliliers dormiva. Eppure mi sembra proprio che sia stato lui, una mattina intorno alla metà di febbraio del '37, … giurerei che sia stato proprio Deliliers ad annunciare che la seconda classe aveva trovato nel tipo dell'Astura un cliente fisso, fisso e pagante, e che questo tale era, nientemeno, il dottor Fadigati. (233–4)

> I close my eyes. I see once more the wide, asphalted avenue of Viale Cavour …
>
> Which of us, I wonder, was the first to direct our general curiosity towards the gentleman in the taxi: the gentleman rather than the taxi itself? It's true that in the tram, with his curly blond head flowing over the wooden back of the seat, Deliliers was usually asleep. And yet I'm inclined to think it was actually him, one morning about halfway through February 1937 … I'd swear it was actually Deliliers who announced that the second-class carriage had found in the guy in the Astura, a permanent and paid-up passenger, and that he was none other than Dr. Fadigati. (22–3)

The somewhat affected manner in which the vagaries of memory are evoked recalls some of the ways in which Mann's narrator recounts Aschenbach's sighting of the snub-nosed stranger who functions as his double at the very beginning of *Death in Venice*: "It was not entirely clear whether he had emerged through the bronze doors"; "Aschenbach's half-absent-minded, half inquisitive scrutiny of the stranger had no doubt been a little less than polite"; "But whether his imagination had been stirred by the stranger's itinerant appearance or whether some other physical or psychological influence was at work."[40] In Bassani's case, the young protagonist's doubts are followed by a detailed reconstruction of the circumstances in which Fadigati was first noticed by the narrator and his companions; accompanied by the use of "giurerei" (I could swear) to imply a shade of uncertainty, it nonetheless casts some doubt on the actual difficulties encountered by the narrator in the process of recollection. The affectation of speech attributed to the narrator might even be seen as a touch of irony suggesting the self-conscious use of a conventional literary topos – the defective memory – to allude, in fact, to its opposite. This interpretation is reinforced by "chiudo gli occhi" (I close my eyes), which evokes an analytic session and a reluctant patient torn between his defences on the one hand, and his desire to get to the bottom of things on the other.

The defective memory signals not only resistance at this point but also the narrator's need to maintain a certain moral distance from Fadigati. He wishes to create the impression that, certainly at the beginning, he was not sufficiently interested in Fadigati to pay much attention to the details of their first encounter, which now, therefore, elude him:

> Tuttavia non fu in treno che vennero stabiliti fra noi i primi contatti, direi proprio di no. Mi resta l'impressione che la cosa sia accaduta a Bologna, per istrada, anche se poi, come si vedrà qui di seguito, io non sappia

> indicare con sicurezza in quale strada precisa. (Forse in quei giorni fui assente da scuola, e la cosa mi venne variamente riferita dopo, dagli altri? Oppure sono io, a tanti anni di distanza, a non distinguere, a non ricordare con precisione?) (236)

> All the same, I'm absolutely sure it was not on the train that the first contacts between us were established. My impression remains that it happened at Bologna, on the street, even if, as will be seen before long, I could not be sure in precisely which street. (Perhaps at that time I was away from my studies, and was informed about the occasion later by others? Or else, so many years afterwards, it's my own failure to distinguish, to remember with any exactitude?) (26)

As the narrator continues his attempt to reconstruct the circumstances under which the first encounter with Fadigati took place, again the minutiae that emerge belie the claims to vagueness of memory. The reiteration of affected hypothetical constructions followed by paradoxically precise recollections of detail and dialogue call our attention to the narrator's discursive position vis-à-vis events, as opposed to the events themselves:

> Può darsi che sia stato uscendo dalla stazione, mentre aspettavamo il tram di Mascarella.
>
> ... Ebbene, non è impossibile che una mattina di queste, ... non è affatto impossibile, dicevo, che una di queste mattine di tardo inverno, ... il dottor Fadigati, che da tempo ci seguiva, venga d'un tratto ad affiancarsi a qualcuno di noi. ... Ronzandoci, per così dire, continuamente attorno, Fadigati ci ha seguiti finora passo passo. Ce ne siamo accorti benissimo. Sogghignando, dandoci di gomito, ne abbiamo anche parlato. (236–8)

> It could well be that it happened as we were leaving the station, or waiting for the Mascarella tram. ... It is not inconceivable that one of those mornings, ... it's not at all inconceivable that one of those late-winter mornings ... Dr. Fadigati, who for some time had followed us, suddenly came up alongside one of us. ... Constantly buzzing around us, Fadigati had been following us step by step till then. We were well aware of it. Grinning, nudging each other, we had even spoken of it. (26–9)

Also worthy of note in these two chapters is the narrator's insistence on dates: 1936, the winter of 1936–7, February 1937. The narrator makes no direct references to historical events at this point, but they loom progressively larger as they are repeatedly alluded to: 1936 was the year the Rome-Berlin Axis was declared; 1937 saw the beginning of anti-Jewish propaganda in the Italian press, a prelude to the 1938 Race Laws. Moreover, the words "nel 1936, vale a dire ventidue anni fa" (19; in 1936, some twenty-two years ago) point, but again in silence, to years of unspeakable horror followed by an apparent normalization. The significance of these inarticulated references to events lurking ominously in the background becomes clearer in the sixth and seventh chapters, in which the narrator describes the relationship between Fadigati and the students as it evolved during the twice-weekly encounters on the Ferrara-Bologna train.

At this point, the narrator suddenly drops any overt references to the process of recollection. Whatever doubt lingers as to the manner in which significant events may or may not have unfolded has suddenly evaporated. Whether it is because he was a direct participant in these events instead of a mere bystander, as in the phases of Fadigati's approach, or because as a narrator he has overcome some of his initial reticence, it is clear that as his memory improves, his ability to maintain critical distance deteriorates.

It is important to remember that the narrator's presentation of the tacit agreement between Fadigati and the bourgeois citizens of Ferrara to maintain appearances at all costs was fiercely ironic, thus differentiating his own attitude from the hypocrisy and value-laden "tolerance" practised by the collectivity in their "cordial relations" with the doctor. This critical distance disappears entirely in his treatment of the relations between Fadigati and the group of students to which he himself belonged. Whatever the reason, he is completely unable – or unwilling – to criticize the contemptuous cruelty of his peers as they taunted Fadigati for his "vice," and for his pathetic attempts to gain acceptance into their midst. Following the recollection of a particularly offensive remark on the part of Deliliers, the narrator says of Fadigati's ensuing humiliation only that "un attimo solo di abbandono gli era costato caro. Adesso, si capisce, temeva il ridicolo più che mai" (244). (A tiny unguarded moment had cost him very dear. From then on, you can imagine, he feared ridicule more than ever [36].) What's more, rather than a judgment on his companions' vulgarity or on his own passive complicity in this shameful abuse of the doctor, he offers only a reflection that places the blame for the various incidents squarely on Fadigati's shoulders: "Per la verità fu di nuovo lui a sbagliare. … Per una parola buona, uno sguardo di consenso, un sorriso divertito … avrebbe fatto davvero qualsiasi cosa" (246). (To be honest, it was he who once again made a mistake. … To win one kind word, a nod of agreement, an amused smile … he would have done practically anything [38–9].)

Nowhere does he comment that Jews were the target of similar attacks in Nazi Germany at the time. If one recalls that these incidents are taking place against the backdrop of Fascist persecutions of Jewish populations – the second half of 1937 was precisely the period of the rise of anti-Semitism in the Italian press – then this third-class compartment of the Bologna-Ferrara local train, with its persecutors and victims, takes on all the markings of a theatre for a microcosmic re-enactment of another tragedy of a magnitude unimaginable perhaps at the time of these events, but certainly not in 1958 to the narrator who has taken it upon himself to tell this story, for reasons as yet undisclosed. That he fails to acknowledge the parallel overtly is obvious: that he fails to see it is less so. The issue of blame is clearly omnipresent, and his need to assign this blame to Fadigati echoes the theories of Jewish "complicity" in their persecutions throughout history. While the irony of the situation may be lost on him, it certainly resonates in his description of the manner in which he and his companions, before the onset of open hostilities from Deliliers and Bottecchiari, stared silently at Fadigati "cercando su quel volto familiare le prove, i segni, starei per dire le macchie visibili del suo vizio, del suo peccato" (241; in search [of] the proof, the signs – I was about to say the visible stains – of his vice, of his sin [32]). It is again unclear whether he realizes that in thus describing this attitude towards Fadigati he is in fact evoking a well known and, at the time, revived myth about Jews: that their sometimes recognizable physiognomy was proof of their "sins." The more specific historical irony, of course, is that the year is 1937 and that his own companions may well have been looking at him in the same way; but nowhere is it suggested that he is aware of this even now.

The eighth chapter sees the setting of the novel shift to the seashore at Riccione, where the bourgeoisie of Ferrara normally settled for the summer months. It is here that the narrator finally brings into play his Jewishness and acknowledges the prevailing political climate, as well as his unease with his father's ambiguous position vis-à-vis the Fascist regime:

> Romantico, patriota, politicamente ingenuo e inesperto come tanti altri ebrei italiani della sua generazione, anche mio padre, tornando dal fronte

> nel '19, aveva preso la tessera del Fascio. Era stato dunque fascista fin dalla "prima ora," e tale in fondo era rimasto nonostante la sua mitezza e onestà. (263)

> Romantic, patriotic, politically naive and inexperienced like so many Jews of his generation, my father, returning from the front in 1919, had also enrolled in the Fascist party. He had thus been a Fascist from the "very beginning," and at heart had remained one, despite his meekness and his honesty. (60)

The narrator's Jewish identity emerges, not coincidentally, shortly after he discovers what has been revealed on the beaches of Riccione: "Lo stesso giorno del nostro arrivo seppi subito di Fadigati e Deliliers. Sulla spiaggia ... non si parla che di loro, della loro 'amicizia scandalosa'" (253). (The same day we arrived we immediately heard about Fadigati and Deliliers. On the beach ... they spoke of nothing else but them and their 'scandalous friendship'" [47].) As Fadigati comes out of the proverbial closet, so does the narrator. References to memory return, but, contrary to their association with elements of doubt in the first chapters, here they are accompanied by affirmations of certitude: "Ricordo molto bene. Io, la mamma, e Fanny, la nostra sorella minore, ci muovemmo da Ferrara il 10 di agosto, insieme con la donna di servizio" (253). (I remember it all perfectly. My mother, Fanny, our younger sister, and I left Ferrara on the 10th of August, accompanied by our maid [47].) Elsewhere, "Come se fossero state incise sopra un nastro magnetico, ritrovo nella memoria ad una ad una tutte le parole di quella lontana mattina" (264; As though they had been etched on a magnetic tape, I find in my memory, one after the other, all the words that were said on that distant [morning] [61]).

Having broken his pact with the citizens of Ferrara, Fadigati now becomes an open target for their suppressed venom. As Fadigati removes his mask of respectability, so the bourgeoisie removes its kid gloves. What had passed previously for tolerance reveals itself now for what it is: hatred, contempt, hypocrisy. The attack on Fadigati is led by Signora Lavezzoli, the wife of a prominent local lawyer and an enthusiastic supporter of the regime and of Mussolini, who pontificates daily from under her umbrella on the shores of the Adriatic. She considers Fadigati responsible for the spectacle that the citizens of Ferrara are being forced to endure: Deliliers is just a spoiled brat who needs military service to set him straight, but Fadigati is "a dirty old man" and a "degenerate" (52), who should have known better than to put his vices on display.

Naturally, Signora Lavezzoli also sings the praises of Hitler's Germany, as if completely unaware that the protagonist and his family are Jews. The narrator tells us that he listened silently. She also spearheads the attack against the Jews and cites an article from a recent issue of *Civiltà Cattolica*, according to which "le ricorrenti persecuzioni, di cui gli 'israeliti' venivano fatti oggetto in ogni parte del mondo da quasi duemila anni, non potevano esser spiegate altro che come segni dell'ira celeste" (270; the recurrent persecutions to which the "Israelites" had been subjected everywhere in the world for almost two thousand years could not be explained other than as a sign of celestial ire [69]). Again the protagonist maintains his silence, but this time he leaves abruptly: "A questo punto mi tirai su dalla poltroncina di vimini, e senza tanti complimenti mi eclissai" (270; At that point I got up from the wicker sofa and without too many courtesies made myself scarce [69]). His reaction to Signora Lavezzoli's words recalls a similar reaction a mere six pages back on the part of Fadigati, wounded to the quick by one of her insults: "Fadigati si alzò in piedi di scatto. Umiliato dalla frase velenosa della signora Lavezzoli, da quel momento in poi non aveva più aperto bocca" (265). (Fadigati suddenly stood up. Humiliated by Signora Lavezzoli's poisonous remark, from that moment on, he had not opened his mouth [62].)

It is obvious that at this point the narrator ought to be confronted with the similarity of his position to Fadigati's. It is he himself who in the telling constructs this parallel, and yet he never quite recognizes it and continues to maintain his distance with regard to the doctor as he tells his story. Not only does he never come to the doctor's defence, actively, as a protagonist of the story, but in his account of it, he never questions his own attitudes at the time. Perhaps the most glaring example of this contradiction is his reaction to Signora Lavezzoli's indignation at Fadigati's audacity in confronting the respectable citizens of Ferrara with his relationship with Deliliers. Though the narrator does not share her opinion that the responsibility for the shameless spectacle they are making of themselves is Fadigati's, blaming instead Deliliers, he does not come to Fadigati's defence as a human being deserving of some compassion but says only that Fadigati, left to his own devices, would never have been so indiscreet:

> Fadigati mi dispiaceva, senza dubbio, ma non era da lui che mi consideravo offeso. Conoscevo alla perfezione il carattere di Deliliers. In quella

scelta delle spiagge romagnole, così prossime a Ferrara, c'era tutta la sua cattiveria e strafottenza. Fadigati non c'entrava, ne ero sicuro. Per me lui si vergognava. Se non salutava, se anche lui fingeva di non riconoscermi, doveva essere soprattutto per questo. (257)

Fadigati, it's true, annoyed me, but it was not by him that I found myself offended. I knew Deliliers's character perfectly. In that choice of the Romagnolo beaches, so close to Ferrara, all his malice and arrogance could be seen. Fadigati was irrelevant, I was quite certain. [I think that he was ashamed.] If he failed to greet me, or even pretended not to see me, it was for that reason. (52)

The difficulty encountered by the narrator at this point in situating himself vis-à-vis Fadigati is evident. Fadigati is now an object of derision both for his homosexuality and for his submission to the arrogant and heartless Deliliers who, once he has Fadigati in his thrall, makes no secret of his intention to do as he pleases. He often disappears for hours at a time, leaving Fadigati to confront his double solitude, as a homosexual and as a rejected lover. On the one hand, the narrator appears very sensitive to Fadigati's anguish: "Mentre mi alzavo … notai che il dottore lanciava verso la linea dei capanni, di dove da un momento all'altro sperava, o temeva, di vedere spuntare l'amico, una rapida occhiata piena di inquietudine" (258; While I got up … I noticed the doctor threw a rapid glance full of disquiet towards the line of beach huts, from which at any moment he expected, or feared, to see his friend emerge [54]); "Camminava a fatica, … il volto disfatto dal sudore e dall'ansia (262; He walked uneasily, … his face discomposed by sweat and anxiety [63]); but on the other, the closest this sensitivity comes to being translated into solidarity is in his rejection of Deliliers's invitation to accompany him to Rimini, where he had supposedly met two sisters from Parma. However, even this gesture of apparent compassion reveals itself as self-serving and self-righteous, with the narrator earnestly patting himself on the back: "Io almeno non lo avevo fatto fesso. Anziché associarmi a chi lo tradiva e lo sfruttava, avevo saputo resistere, conservargli un minimo di rispetto" (272–3). (At least *I* hadn't treated him as a dupe. Rather than assisting someone keen to betray and exploit him, I had had the strength to resist, and had showed him at least a minimum of respect [73].)

The narrator's ambivalence is in part a reflection of the attitude of his parents towards Fadigati as well. On the one hand they make it clear that they do not like seeing their son with Fadigati, but on the other hand they treat the doctor with the utmost cordiality once Signora Lavezzoli disappears. Unlike his father, however, the protagonist is never capable of demonstrating anything even approximating genuine sympathy towards Fadigati. The text reproduces three conversations between them during the course of the stay at Riccione. All three are characterized by the tension deriving from the protagonist's defensive stance, from his fear of reaching out to Fadigati or allowing him in any way to unburden himself. They are conversations punctuated by strategic silences, which point to the protagonist's reluctance to allow any complicity to emerge between them, or by his laconic answers to Fadigati's attempts, never reciprocated, to engage him in a personal exchange.

> "Ha visto come fumo?," disse.
> "Già."
> Una domanda mi bruciava: "E Deliliers?." Ma non ne fui capace.
> Mi alzai in piedi e gli tesi la mano.
> "Prima non fumava affatto, se non sbaglio."
> "Cerco anche io di dare il mio modesto contributo alla diffusione del … mal di gola,"[41] ridacchiò miserabilmente. "Ho pensato che mi conveniva."
> Mi allontanai di qualche passo. (268)

> "Have you seen how much I'm smoking?" he asked.
> "Indeed."
> I was longing to ask him a question. "And Deliliers?" But I wasn't up to it.
> I got to my feet and made to shake hands.
> "If I'm not wrong, you didn't use to smoke at all."
> "I'm trying to make my own modest contribution to the spread of … maladies of the throat," he laughed miserably. "I thought it might help me."
> I walked a few paces away. (67)

The most revealing moment, however, takes place towards the end of the summer, after Fadigati has been abandoned by Deliliers. When Fadigati tells the young man that Deliliers has also robbed him of all his possessions, his reaction is absolutely heartless: "Mi fermai su due piedi, squadrandolo. Era vestito da città, col cappello di feltro e tutto. Fissavo il cappello di feltro. Dunque non era vero che Deliliers gli avesse portato via ogni cosa – riflettevo –; dunque un po' esagerava"

(282). (I stopped in my tracks and stood, eyeing him up and down. He was dressed in his city clothes, with his felt hat and everything. I stared at the felt hat. So it wasn't exactly true that Deliliers had taken all his things – I reflected – there was an element of exaggeration [85].)

It is in the following two chapters (13–14) that the parallel between the protagonist's situation and Fadigati's is made most clear. The campaign led by the Italian press against the Jews finally explodes and reaches a feverish pitch. The protagonist is now face to face with his imminent exclusion from Italian society; "Ricordo quei primi giorni come un incubo" (283; I remember those first days as a nightmare [86]), he says. No longer able to tolerate either Signora Lavezzoli's anti-Semitic speeches or his father's pathetic attempts to enumerate "i 'meriti patriottici'" (284; the patriotic merits [87]) of Italian Jews, he chooses isolation. "Sempre solo, e invaso di rabbia, addirittura di odio ... ormai non mi facevo più vedere sulla spiaggia" (283–4; Always on my own, seething with anger, even with hatred ... I was not even prepared to show my face on the beach [86–7]), he recalls, and only momentarily on his return to Ferrara is he able to escape "quell'atroce senso di esclusione che [lo] aveva tormentato nei giorni scorsi" (285; that atrocious feeling of exclusion that had tormented [him] in the last days [88]). The sense of relief is short lived. As soon as he runs into Nino Bottecchiari in front of the Caffè della Borsa, he realizes that the local party officials seated at the outdoor tables are staring at him. Their conversation stops, and they exchange knowing looks: in Fascist, Aryan Italy he has become a pariah.

The implicit juxtaposition of the Jew's plight and Fadigati's reaches its climax in the ensuing conversation with Nino Bottecchiari. First, the protagonist discovers (after insisting that he be told if this is the case) that in a letter written from Paris by Deliliers, full of condescending remarks about his former university companions, he has been called a "dirty Jew." Then Nino, the formerly enlightened Socialist, reveals that he has decided to accept a position in the Fascist bureaucracy. To lessen the blow, Nino tries to reassure him that, in his opinion, the persecution of Jews in Italy will never amount to much anyway – "tutto finirà nella solita bolla di sapone" (291; it will all burst like a soap bubble in the end [97]) – given the inconclusive national temperament of the Italians, whom he considers "troppo buffoni" (292; too buffoonish [97]) to undertake anything as serious as what the Germans are doing. The ambiguity of this statement only dawns on Nino once he has finished speaking and the young Jew is left seething: "Mentre parlava, riuscìi appena a mascherare il fastidio che mi davano le sue parole, e il tono, in ispecie, il tono deluso della sua voce. 'Tutto finirà nella solita bolla di sapone.' Si poteva essere più goffi, più insensibili, più ottusamente *goìm* di così? " (291). (While he was speaking, I barely managed to mask the annoyance his words provoked in me, and the tone especially, the disappointed tone of his voice. "It will all burst like a soap bubble in the end," he had said. Could you be any clumsier, more insensitive, more obtusely *goyische* than that? [97].)

Most ironically, the protagonist's incredulous reaction to Nino's words echoes exactly Fadigati's incredulous reaction to his own cold suggestion that the doctor report the theft of his belongings by Deliliers to the police, as if the Jew were unaware that he is in no position to do so:

> "Perché non lo denuncia?," buttai lì, freddamente.
>
> Mi fissò anche lui.
>
> "Denunciarlo!" borbottò sorpreso. Nei suoi occhi balenò a un tratto un lampo di scherno.
>
> "Denunciarlo?," ripeté, e mi guardava come si guarda un estraneo un po' ridicolo. "Ma le pare possibile?" (81)

> "Why not report him to the police?" I suggested, coldly.
>
> He stared back at me at me. "Report him?" he stammered in surprise.
>
> In his eyes there suddenly gleamed a flash of scorn.
>
> "Report him?" he repeated, and looked at me as one looks at a clueless, slightly ridiculous stranger. "Do you even think that's a possibility?" (85)

The protagonist speaks to Fadigati as a heterosexual, while Nino speaks to the protagonist as a Gentile. Fadigati reacts as a homosexual – "Denunciarlo? ... Ma le pare possibile?" ("Report him?" ... "Do you even think that's a possibility?") – while the narrator reacts as a Jew – "Si poteva essere più goffi, più insensibili, più ottusamente *goìm* di così?" (Could you be any clumsier, more insensitive, more obtusely *goyische* than that?). And yet, in these chapters, the narrator, as he thinks back, makes no direct reference whatsoever to Fadigati.

Fadigati reappears in the next chapter, which begins simply with the two words "Rividi Fadigati" (296; I saw Fadigati again [102]). It is the following November, and the two run into each other late one night in the dark streets of Ferrara. The protagonist learns of Fadigati's newest misfortunes: dismissed by the hospital, deserted by his private patients, he now lives in total isolation. And yet he is still able to extend a hand to his young Jewish friend, to acknowledge the plight of the Jews, and to express his solidarity: "In questi giorni, mi creda, ho pensato tante volte a lei e ai suoi" (300; In these times, believe me, I've many times thought about you and your family [107]). The protagonist, on the other hand, is completely incapable of offering any comfort to Fadigati. When Fadigati says, "Dopo ciò che è accaduto l'estate scorsa non mi riesce più di tollerarmi. ... Non c'è più niente da fare, per me, senta!" (300–1), (After all that happened last summer, I can't bear myself any longer. ... There's nothing to be done for me, don't you see? [107–8]), the protagonist remains characteristically silent and in his mind judges Fadigati more harshly and more explicitly than ever before: "Tacqui. Pensavo a Deliliers e a Fadigati: uno carnefice e l'altro vittima. La vittima al solito perdonava, consentiva al carnefice" (101). (I kept silent. I thought of Deliliers and of Fadigati: one, the executioner, the other, the victim. The victim as usual forgave and gave his consent to the executioner [108].)

Their leave-taking is equally indicative of their respective positions vis-à-vis each other; the protagonist is anxious to leave, Fadigati to linger: "Non appena fummo dinanzi al portone di casa, tirai fuori di tasca la chiave e aprii. ... Varcai la soglia. E poiché lui, sempre sorridendo a tenendo levato il braccio in segno di saluto, non si decideva ad andarsene ..., cominciai a chiudere il portone" (301). (As soon as we had reached the entrance to my house, I took the keys from my pocket and opened the door. ... I crossed the threshold. And since smiling and holding up his arm in salutation, he still had not made up his mind to go away ..., I began to shut the double door [108–9].) In order to avoid being rude, the protagonist adds, "Mi telefona?" (301; Will you phone me? [109]). Two days later, Fadigati does call, and the narrator betrays the unease and irritation he felt as his mother handed him the telephone: "Mi alzai, sbuffando. Ma un segreto batticuore mi aveva già avvertito di chi poteva trattarsi" (302). (I got up with a sigh of annoyance. But a secret quickening of the pulse had already warned me who it might be [110].) The conversation is full of awkward silences, as the protagonist grapples with Fadigati's desperation and his own conflicting feelings of guilt and shame. Reluctant to let his parents know with whom he is speaking, he answers in monosyllables, hoping to end the conversation as soon as possible, but to no avail: "Ma niente. Pareva che non gli riuscisse di staccarsi dall'apparecchio" (305). (But no luck.

It seemed as though he was unable to detach himself from the receiver [113–14].) The conversation ends with their tentative agreement to meet the following Saturday and, weather permitting, to take the tram to Pontelagoscuro, to look at the Po River, almost overflowing after the recent rains.

The next chapter begins with a return to the narrator's curious, contradictory ways: "Piovve tutto sabato e domenica: anche per questo motivo, forse, scordai la promessa di Fadigati. Non mi telefonò e nemmeno io gli telefonai: ma per pura dimenticanza, ripeto, non già di proposito" (306). (It rained all Saturday and all Sunday. Perhaps also for that reason I forgot Fadigati's promise. He did not phone me, nor did I call him: but only out of forgetfulness, I would like to stress, not from any deliberate decision [115].) While "anche" (also) and "forse" (perhaps) indicate the possibility of reasons other than the weather for the narrator's memory lapse, "per pura dimenticanza, ripeto, non già di proposito" (but only out of forgetfulness, not from any deliberate decision) closes the door, immediately, on any exploration of these reasons. The denial of his sense of guilt does not, however, result in its disappearance, merely in its symbolic transformation within the same paragraph, as the narrator goes on to describe the view from his window the very afternoon that Fadigati was to take his life by drowning himself in the waters of the Po:

> La pioggia torrenziale sembrava accanirsi particolarmente contro il pioppo, i due olmi, il castagno, ai quali veniva via via strappando le ultime foglie. Soltanto la nera magnolia, al centro, intatta e gocciolante in modo incredibile, godeva visibilmente dei rovesci d'acqua che la investivano. (306)

> The torrential rain seemed to mount a particular assault on the poplar, the two elms, and the chestnut tree, from which it gradually tore the last leaves. Only the black magnolia, at the centre, intact and dripping in the most exuberant manner, seemed to visibly enjoy the downpour that was battering it. (115)

The pleasure that the narrator attributes to the personified magnolia tree as it submits to the "abuse" of the torrential waters evokes the masochism so frequently attributed to Fadigati by the narrator. In the moments of his greatest humiliation at the hands of Deliliers, the narrator imagines Fadigati's eyes to have been "pieni di un'acre soddisfazione, di una infantile, inesplicabile, cieca allegria" (248; filled with a bitter satisfaction, with a childish, inexplicable blind joy [40]) or says "di nuovo vidi brillare negli occhi di Fadigati la luce assurda ma inequivocabile di una interna felicità" (249; once again I saw shining in Fadigati's eyes the absurd but unmistakable light of an interior joy [43]). Even Fadigati's account of the theft of his possessions seems to be filled with joy: "Terminò con uno strano grido, quasi esaltato. Come se, da ultimo, l'enumerazione degli oggetti rubati da Deliliers avesse avuto l'effetto di tramutare il suo strazio in un senso, più forte, di orgoglio e di piacere"(281). (He ended with a strange cry, almost of exultation. As though, finally, listing the objects stolen by Deliliers had had the effect of transforming his torment into a still more powerful sense of pride and pleasure [84].)

The rest of the chapter describes the anxiety that plagues the protagonist the day after the missed appointment: he scolds his sister too harshly for her errors in a Latin translation, promises to take her to the movies, and then goes without her. At the box office a sense of shame overcomes him, as he finds himself asking for a seat not in the balcony but at ground level, where Fadigati normally sat. Once he establishes that Fadigati is not in the theatre, he rushes to his house but finds only darkness. He then goes to a phone booth to call, but there is no answer. The crescendo of events and his mounting anxiety are obviously an indication of his suspicion that something has happened.

The remaining pages of the novel recreate a tightly woven series of events that focus on the Jewish question, on the protagonist's father's continuing attempts to believe that nothing will happen to the Jews, while he himself is filled only with hopelessness and rage at the situation and at his father for being so blind to what is happening. The climax occurs when, after having made another vain attempt to call Fadigati that morning, he picks up the newspaper only to find his worst fears confirmed in an article "il quale non parlava affatto di suicidio, s'intende, ma, secondo lo stile dei tempi, soltanto di disgrazia" (314; which did not at all speak of suicide, it should be understood, but, according to the style of the times, only of misfortune [125]):

> NOTO PROFESSIONISTA FERRARESE
> ANNEGATO NELLE ACQUE DEL PO
> PRESSO PONTELAGOSCURO. (314)

> WELL-KNOWN FERRARESE PROFESSIONAL DROWNED IN THE WATERS OF THE PO NEAR PONTELAGOSCURO. (124)

As the narrator brings his story to a close, he finally allows himself to express (in parentheses) some compassion for Fadigati, in commenting on the euphemistic newspaper description of his suicide: "A nessuno era lecito sopprimersi in quegli anni: nemmeno ai vecchi disonorati e senza più ragione alcuna di restare al mondo" (314; It was not acceptable for anyone, in those days, to kill themselves: not even for [a dishonoured old man] who had no reason whatsoever to remain on the earth [125]).

Having examined the nature of the Mann connection and Bassani's use of it to create a story (Fadigati's) that is effectively a projection of the Jew's own situation and of its possibly masochistic elements, it now remains to establish how all this might be germane to the themes and outlines of the family romance. This connection is suggested in a scene in which the narrator is recalling his return to Ferrara from Riccione after the summer holidays and just before the passage of the Race Laws. Not surprisingly, it turns out to be as painful as the days spent on the beach, during which the campaign against the Jews in the Italian press had reached a frenzied peak. Ferrara is no longer the protective cocoon it had once been, and the young protagonist is no longer at home in it: "Mi sentivo tagliato fuori, irrimediabilmente un intruso" (290; I felt set apart, irremediably an intruder [95]). In search of solace, he bicycles to a hilltop from which the cityscape and the Jewish cemetery can be embraced by the eye:

> Guardavo al campo sottostante, in cui erano sepolti i nostri morti. ... Quand'ecco, guardando ... al vasto paesaggio urbano che mi si mostrava di lassù in tutta la sua estensione, mi sentii d'un tratto penetrare da una gran dolcezza, da una pace e da una gratitudine tenerissime. ... Mi era bastato recuperare *l'antico volto materno* della mia città, riaverlo ancora una volta tutto per me, perché quell'atroce senso di esclusione che mi aveva tormentato nei giorni scorsi cadesse all'istante. Il futuro di persecuzioni e di massacri che forse ci attendeva (fin da bambino ne avevo continuamente sentito parlare come di un'eventualità per noi ebrei sempre possibile) non mi faceva più paura. (284–5; emphasis added)

> I looked around at the cemetery below, in which our dead were buried. ... Then suddenly, watching ... the vast urban landscape which displayed itself to me at that height in all its breadth, I was struck by a great sweetness, by a feeling of peace and the tenderest gratitude. ... It was enough

> for me to recover the *ancient, maternal visage* of my home town to reclaim it once again all for myself, for that atrocious feeling of exclusion that had tormented me in the last days to fall away instantly. The future of persecution and massacres that perhaps awaited us – since childhood I had heard them spoken of as an always possible eventuality for us Jews – no longer made me afraid.) (88–9; emphasis added)

Significantly, the *volto materno* (maternal visage) is an image employed in relation to Fadigati as well, in a scene on the train from Ferrara to Bologna in which he pulls out a photo of his mother:

> Come l'aveva adorata – sospirava –, la sua povera mamma!
>
> Intelligente, bella, colta, pia: in lei si assommavano tutte le virtù. Una mattina, anzi, e per la commozione gli occhi gli si inumidirono, estrasse dal portafoglio una fotografia che circolò di mano in mano. Si trattava di un piccolo ovale sbiadito. Ritraeva una donna in abito ottocentesco, di mezza età dall'espressione soave, senza dubbio, ma nel complesso piuttosto insignificante. (242)

> How he had adored her – he sighed – his poor mother!
>
> Intelligent, cultured, beautiful, pious: she was the sum of all the virtues. One morning, even, and his eyes grew watery with the emotion, he brought out from his wallet, a photograph which he passed around the circle of hands. It was a small faded oval, portraying a middle-aged woman in nineteenth-century dress: of gentle expression, certainly, but generally rather undistinguished. (34)

The *volto materno* (maternal visage), complete with its soothing effect and its capacity to erase feelings of exclusion, evokes the completely imaginary sense of oneness that the infant can experience in the exclusivity of the narcissistic pre-Oedipal relation with the mother, where each offers the other a perfect satisfaction of desire. While this relation is extremely important and constitutive of the child's emerging identity as a subject, it is a stifling one and if unmediated leaves no room for growth and independence.[42]

In the Freudian paradigm, it is the Oedipal crisis that provides this mediation: it forces the male child to recognize the difference between himself and his mother, and to embrace the "sameness" that connects him instead to the father. By making this identification and relinquishing the bond with the mother, he accomplishes the passage from "nature" to "culture," but the memory of the maternal connection remains lodged in the unconscious, leaving behind a sense of nostalgia and loss – exile – that is a permanent facet of the human condition. This sense of loss and incompleteness provides the basis for much constructive action in the world: indeed, the acknowledgment of "difference" from the mother is the very motor of culture and society. Where this recognition of difference, this recognition of one's "exile" from this early paradise, fails to take place, paralysis of the will sets in.

We know that the young protagonist cannot identify with those Jews like his own father, who is overjoyed when he hears that the chief of police has reassured the head of the Jewish community that there will be no racial legislation in Italy. Interestingly, he compares his father's reaction to that of to a young schoolboy suddenly re-admitted to the classroom after a temporary banishment for bad behaviour, indicating how inadequate he finds the older man at this difficult time and emphasizing that as a result his own sense of solitude has become even more acute: "Dal mio esilio non sarei mai tornato, io. Mai più" (313). (From *my* exile, I would never return. Never [124].)

His solitude is so great because he cannot express his anger and indignation to anyone but Fadigati, the only person who is sympathetic and with whom we see him discuss these sentiments. Paradoxically, however, the closer their destinies draw them to each other, the more he persists in denying any "kinship" and, in fact, in harshly condemning Fadigati. So fraught with discomfort is the possibility of acknowledging any identification for the narrator that at several crucial moments in the story he gratuitously calls attention to his own heterosexual erotic experiences, clearly to dispel any doubts in the reader as to which side of the divide he is on and to reduce his own "homosexual panic." It is important to underline that I am not suggesting that the narrator is himself a homosexual, but simply that his own sense of masculinity is not strong. The reasons for this will become clear in the last of the first-person novels, *Dietro la porta* (*Behind the Door*), in which he evokes the influence of anti-Semitic images of Jewish masculinity and sexuality, and in particular the Weiningerian image of the feminized Jew, on his own sense of himself as a male. In any case, the narrator's own as yet unacknowledged conflicts, in addition to his feelings of guilt, make it impossible for him to express any real compassion for Fadigati, even twenty-two years later.

Perhaps the single most indicative passage in this direction, which lends most credence to this reading, is to be found in chapter 12 when the protagonist learns from Fadigati of his definitive humiliation at the hands of Deliliers. The protagonist overhears his parents talking about a scandal concerning Fadigati and wants to know more about it (note the primal image "dietro la porta" [behind the door], which returns as the title of the third novel): "Resistetti alla tentazione di scendere in tinello per mettermi a origliare dietro la porta che dava nel giardino" (278; I resisted the temptation to go down to the breakfast room and eavesdrop behind the door that gave on to the garden [80]). Though he has been told in advance that his partners will not be there, he sets out fully equipped for the tennis courts because he expects to find Fadigati there. As he is about to leave the house, his father stops him to ask, "'Dove vai?'" ("Where are you off to?"). The protagonist's response is simply: "'Non lo vedi?'" (278; "Can't you see?" [80]).

Between the question and the answer, however, there lies a very explicit allusion to the narrator/protagonist's first sexual experience, which at first reading appears somewhat arbitrary. However, its appearance at this point in the narration and in association with the primal image that precedes it ("behind the door") can only point to one thing: the emergence of the narrator's own sexual anxiety at a particularly compromising moment in the unfolding of his story. In fact, he is about to tell us of the first time he sought out Fadigati, voluntarily and knowing full well that they would be alone:

> Due estati prima, sempre a Riccione, ad una quindicina di giorni dall'aver trionfato nell'esame di maturità ero finito a letto (ed era stata la prima volta, in assoluto!) con una trentenne signora milanese, conoscente occasionale di mia madre. In dubbio se essere fiero o preoccupato della mia avventura, per due mesi buoni il papà non aveva perduto uno solo dei miei movimenti. Bastava che mi accingessi a uscire di casa, o magari mi allontanassi dalla tenda, che già mi sentivo i suoi occhi addosso. (278)

> Two summers before, as always at Riccione, a fortnight after having acquitted myself splendidly in the school graduating exams, I ended up in bed (and it was the first time ever!) with a thirty-year-old married woman from Milan who was an occasional acquaintance of my mother. Uncertain whether to be proud or worried by my adventure, for two whole months my father had ceaselessly watched my every movement. I had only to be leaving the house or even to move away from the beach tent, to feel his eyes glued to me. (80–1)

Another such allusion appears towards the end of the novel in the chapter that begins "Rividi Fadigati" (I saw Fadigati again [102]) and that tells us about their late-night encounter in the streets of Ferrara after months of no contact. Again, an apparently casual reference to the narrator's heterosexuality coincides with his recollection of a face to face meeting with the homosexual doctor: "Fu per istrada e di notte: una umida nebbiosa notte del novembre successivo, a metà circa del mese. Uscito dal postribolo di via Bomporto con i panni impregnati del solito odore ..." (296; It was on the streets and at night: a humid, misty night about halfway through the following November. Coming out of the brothel on Via Bomporto, with my clothes impregnated with the usual scent ... [102]).

The narrator's sexual unease in treating the subject of Fadigati is suggested also by his interpretation of both Fadigati's and Deliliers's feelings and motivations in their dealings with him. In several instances these interpretations lend themselves to being read as clear projections of his own conflicts. For example, in speculating on Deliliers's reasons for inviting him to go with him to Rimini to meet up with the two sisters, he attributes to Deliliers ulterior motives that may reflect his own unconscious wish to reaffirm his heterosexuality: "Non ci teneva soprattutto a far sapere in giro, per caso, servendosi di me, che lui con Fadigati non ci stava per vizio ma soltanto per pagarsi la villeggiatura, e che comunque gli preferiva sempre una ragazza?" (272; Wasn't he, primarily, using me to broadcast that he was with Fadigati, not because of any vice but only to have him pay for the holiday, and that anyway he always preferred girls? [72]). In this very same chapter, in reporting an awkward conversation with Fadigati about his sister Fanny, who is on the edge of puberty, the narrator interprets Fadigati's facial expressions in such a way as to suggest that his own unease is somehow related to an unresolved conflict dating back to puberty: "Scosse il capo in atto di malinconica deplorazione: come se misurasse dentro se stesso tutta la fatica e tutto il dolore a cui ogni essere umano deve andare incontro per crescere, per maturare" (273–4; He shook his head in melancholic disapproval, as though he was weighing up within himself all the trouble and pain it cost every human being to grow and become an adult [75]).

It is the young man's own sexual conflicts that bring him to distance himself from Fadigati. Insecure in his manhood, any identification with Fadigati is profoundly threatening to him. The narrator's obsession with Fadigati as masochistic victim and his justification of his distaste and contempt for this aspect of the doctor's personality resonates not only with obvious ancestral, historical anxieties but also with deeper, personal ones.

He and Fadigati share the refusal to recognize their "difference." The young man prefers to isolate himself rather than silently endure the indifference and offensive remarks of Nino or Signora Lavezzoli. To break the silence, to speak up as a Jew and defend himself does not appear to be an option since to do so would mean stepping out of the fantasized inner circle and taking one's place in the ghetto or, as it were, behind the barbed wire of the concentration camp:

> Pensavo anche al nostro, di ghetto, a via Mazzini, a via Vignatagliata, al vicolo-mozzo Torcicoda. In un futuro abbastanza vicino, loro, i *goìm*, ci avrebbero costretti a brulicare di nuovo là, per le anguste, tortuose viuzze di quel misero quartiere medioevale da cui in fin dei conti non eravamo venuti fuori che da settanta, ottanta anni. Ammassati l'uno sull'altro dietro i cancelli come tante bestie impaurite, non ne saremmo evasi mai più. (291)

> I thought of our own ghetto. In a near enough future, they, the *goyim*, would once more have forced us to swarm there, in the narrow, twisting lanes of that wretched medieval quarter from which, when all was reckoned up, we had emerged only some seventy or eighty years ago. Piled one on top of the other like so many frightened beasts, we would never again manage to escape. (96)

By the same token, Dr Fadigati prefers to tolerate in silence the insults of Ferrara's citizens rather than acknowledge his "difference." As long as he turns a deaf ear and fails to react, he deludes himself into believing that he can avoid the isolation that eventually descends on him anyway; now he believes that he has been wearing a mask of bourgeois respectability to which, according to the keepers of that respectability, he no longer has a right:

> Ci crede che certe volte non sopporto di farmi la barba davanti allo specchio? Potessi almeno vestirmi in un altro modo! Tuttavia mi vede, lei, senza questo cappello ... questo pastrano ... questi occhiali da tipo per bene? E d'altra parte, messo su così mi sento talmente ridicolo, grottesco, assurdo! (300–1)

> Would you believe that I can't even bear to shave in front of the mirror. [If] I could at least dress in a different fashion! All the same, could you

> imagine me without this hat. ... this overcoat. ... these glasses, this uniform of respectability? And yet, dressed up like this, I feel so ridiculous, grotesque, absurd! (108)

To see this novel as the story of a young Jewish man's gradual recognition of what he shares with an ageing homosexual in Fascist Italy is, as I hope to have demonstrated, nothing but wishful thinking. The young Jewish protagonist does not acknowledge their shared experience in 1938 and, as the older narrator – and this I believe is Bassani's point – still resists accepting it in 1958, twenty years and six million dead Jews later. His massive blind spot turns him, ironically, into one of Fadigati's persecutors – not an active one like Deliliers or Signora Lavezzoli but a "blameless bystander," reminiscent of the masses who stood by while millions of Jews (and others) were carried to their deaths in the ovens of the Third Reich. If this novel has anything to say at all, it is not so much that we can all become victims, but that we can all, unwittingly, also become persecutors without realizing it and without ever knowing why. This recognition does not entirely elude the narrator and is made quite clear at the very beginning of his account, as he reports the frequently heard comparisons of Fadigati's modern, comfortable, and spacious waiting room to the crowded and squalid spaces available in other doctors' offices. Shot through with images that recall concentration camp inmates and Dr Menghele, the notorious doctor of death who performed medical experiments on them, the narrator's words testify to the unspeakable horror that continues to haunt him and also to the fact that a doctor, too, can bring either healing or horror:

> Dove erano, da Fadigati – non si stancavano mai di ripetere –, le interminabili attese ammucchiati l'uno sull'altro come bestie, ... mentre, alla fioca luce di una lampadina da venti candele, l'occhio non aveva da posarsi, scorrendo lungo i tristi muri, che su qualche NON SPUTARE! di maiolica, qualche caricatura di professore universitario o di collega, per non parlare di altre immagini anche più melanconiche e iettatorie di pazienti sottoposti a enormi clisteri davanti a un intero collegio accademico, o di laparatomie a cui, sogghinando, provvedeva la Morte stessa travestita da chirurgo? E come poteva essere accaduto, come!, che si fosse sopportato fino allora un simile trattamento da Medio Evo? (217)

> At Fadigati's, they never tired of repeating, where was the interminable waiting, heaped on top of each other like animals, ... while in the feeble light of a twenty-watt bulb, the eye coursing over the sad walls had

> nothing to rest on but some majolica tile announcing DON'T SPIT, some caricature of a university professor or fellow doctor, not to speak of other more jinxed and doleful images of patients being subjected to horrendous enemas in front of an entire medical school, or of laparotomies at which, grinning, Death himself officiated dressed as a surgeon? And how on earth had they – until then – put up with such medieval treatment? (3–4)

A final note about the role of the train, which figures so prominently in this novel as the site of Fadigati's harassment. In Sander Gilman's *Freud, Race and Gender* a subchapter is specifically entitled "Trauma and Trains: The Testing Ground of Masculinity." In pointing out, as is well known, that "the image of the trauma of modern civilization was closely associated with the train at the turn of the century," he also specifies that "the world of the train and the meaning of trauma had a secondary context for Jews in the nineteenth century":

> It was one of the public spaces, defined by class and economic power, in which the Jew could purchase status. It was part of the image of the world of "modern life" that helped deform the psyche of the Jew. A ticket assured one of traveling among one's economic equals – but not as racial "equals." The association of trains and the trauma of confronting one's Jewish identity is a powerful topos at the turn of the century.[43]

Gilman goes on to discuss what he calls Freud's "train neurosis," as revealed by Freud himself in his self-analysis and in his dreams. His fear of missing trains is linked by Gilman to the desire for social mobility, and his fear of being on trains to the fear of confronting his difference, because "confrontations with anti-Semites took place on trains": "Missing the train meant remaining an Eastern Jew; making the train meant confronting his own Jewish difference. The unimpeded journey was not for Freud."[44] Gilman cites one incident in particular:

> In December 1883 Freud experienced a scene in a train travelling through Saxony in which he was called a "dirty Jew" when he attempted to open a window in the car. "My first opponent also turned anti-Semitic and declared: 'We Christians consider other people ...' Even a year ago I would have been speechless with agitation, but now I am different; I was not in the least frightened of that mob, asked the one to keep to himself his empty phrases which inspire no fear in me, and the other to step up and take what he deserved. I was quite ready to kill him, but he did

> not stand up." The trauma of this incident was powerful enough that it haunted the "Count Thun" dream, recorded in August 1898. The imagery of that dream takes place on a train and reflects "a piece of anti-Semitic provocation during a railway journey in the lovely Saxon countryside." Trains became part of the mental space associated with Jewishness and the trauma of that race. …
>
> The anti-Semitic incident on the train became a set-piece for the graphic sexual humour of the late nineteenth century. It was almost always a *male* Jew, in his masculinity as well as in his role as a Jew, who stood at the centre of the train joke. This masculinity was disqualified by this association in jokes told about Jews by non-Jews [while] in the Jewish joke books of the turn of the century this association became one in which the aggressiveness of the male Jew was played out and the train became a space in which the marginal Jew … had his revenge.[45]

By the time Bassani takes up the topos of the train, it is not only the place where the Jew "could be (and was) directly confronted by the meaning of his own Jewish identity,"[46] but it has also become the vehicle deporting Jews to the camps like human cattle. Bassani's condensation of the two significations suggests that the desire for social mobility is what led to the psychic deformation of the Jews, which in turn, in the case of some, led them to the camps. Bassani's next novel, *Il giardino dei Finzi-Contini,* focuses precisely on the lure of social mobility and its tragic consequences for the Jews.

4 *Il giardino dei Finzi-Contini*: A Jewish Family Romance

The narrator has made a little headway – he is able to speak of himself more openly – but he still needs to do so indirectly, this time through the account of his relationship with the Finzi-Continis, and in particular with Micòl Finzi-Contini, deported with the rest of her family to the camps in 1943, never to return. The events take place in the period immediately following the suicide of Fadigati; it is 1938, the Race Laws are in place, and the young Jew has isolated himself from all of his friends. The gates to the luxurious estate of the Finzi-Continis open just as he is on the the brink of manhood and still reeling from the discovery that Italian mainstream society, into which he expected to be fully integrated, has slammed its doors in his face. He finds himself officially expelled from the public library where he was researching his thesis and from the exclusive tennis club where he and the rest of Ferrara's young elite spent much of their leisure time. The proud and wealthy Finzi-Continis, self-styled aristocratic Jews known for keeping their distance from the rest of the the citizens of Ferrara, Jews and Gentiles alike, have uncharacteristically invited the young people barred from their usual haunts by the new discriminatory measures to play tennis on their own private courts. It is this extraordinary circumstance that provides the protagonist with an entry into what proves to be a magical world for him – until he is cast out of it by Micòl Finzi-Contini, with whom he has fallen in love.

If *Occhiali* is essentially a realistic novel, *Giardino* (the title tells us this immediately) is a symbolic novel: while maintaining a realistic dimension, it is essentially an in-depth examination of a state of mind that is merely suggested in the previous works. Symbols, imagery, recurring situations, and symmetries are what count most in this densely and elegantly codified novel, in which Bassani explicitly but artfully combines the family romance and the Garden of Eden as the master narratives through which he delves into the psyche of the protagonist. The resolution of the Oedipal crisis becomes a metaphor not only for the accession to manhood, and therefore the recognition of sexual difference, but also for the process of acceptance of racial and ethnic difference, as well as for the recognition of the existence of evil in the world.

We know from the previous novel that the protagonist is in limbo: he cannot share his own father's continuing denial of the gravity of the Race Laws and feels both pity and contempt for him. At the same time he is incapable of accepting his own marginalization and is therefore incapable of "moving on." When Fadigati wishes he could accept who he is without shame and suggests that the protagonist do the same, the young man reacts with horror, since in his mind it would mean accepting that he is "just a Jew." So, too, in this next novel, the protagonist cannot bear to listen to his family's litany of complaints about the Race Laws as they sit around the table at the grim Passover meal. Immediately after dinner, he escapes to the Finzi-Continis, where this atmosphere of degradation has not penetrated, where there is no talk of "discriminazioni," "meriti patriottici," "certificati d'anzianità," or "quarti di sangue" (479; discrimination, patriotic awards of merit, certificates of ancestry, or proportions of Jewish blood [156]) and where the very same Passover sweets seem to taste completely different: "I dolcetti, i così chiamati *zucarìn*, ... all'incirca uguali a quelli che avevo assaggiato di malavoglia mezz'ora avanti, a casa ... mi parvero subito molto migliori, molto più gustosi" (488; The sweets, called *zucarìn*, ... almost the same as the ones I had just tasted at home, half an hour before ... immediately seemed far better, much tastier [164]).

Bassani explicitly casts the protagonist's relationship with the Finzi-Continis in that phase of the family romance in which the child, dissatisfied with his own parents, fantasizes that he is really the offspring of more satisfactory ones, sometimes, as Freud says, of aristocratic origin:

> At about the period I have mentioned, then, the child's imagination becomes engaged in the task of getting free from the parents of whom he now has such a low opinion and of replacing them by others, occupying, as a rule, a higher social status. He will make use in this connection of any opportune coincidences from his actual experience, such as his becoming acquainted with the Lord of the manor or some landed proprietor if he lives in the country or with some member of the aristocracy if he lives in

> town. Chance occurrences of this kind arouse the child's envy, which finds expression in a fantasy in which both his parents are replaced by others of better birth. ... This stage is reached at a time at which the child is still in ignorance of the sexual determinants of procreation.[1]

In fact, just as he is unable to accept the regime's hostility to the Jews and the difference between himself as a Jew and the Gentile world in which he lives, so too he will be unable to embrace the difference between himself and Micòl and the reality of her sexuality: this is the parallel that Bassani creates and reinforces symbolically over and over again throughout the narrative. While in *Gli occhiali d'oro* the protagonist is forever circling around the truth about his failure to defend either Fadigati or himself and struggling with his guilt, here the obsessive preoccupation is his failure to abandon his passive adoration of Micòl and declare his feelings to her at an opportune moment of particular physical closeness during one of their forays into the garden. As he remembers it, this missed opportunity remains the turning point in their relationship, after which things were never the same between them. The narrator recreates all these events in detail and recalls all the self-recriminations of the time, but again hesitates to draw the obvious conclusions about his own behaviour. His only comment is: "E dimenticavo di chiedermi l'essenziale: se in quel momento supremo, unico, irrevocabile – un momento che, forse, aveva deciso della mia e della sua vita –, io fossi stato davvero in grado di tentare un gesto, una parola qualsiasi" (419; But I was forgetting to ask myself the crucial question: whether in that supreme, unique, irrevocable moment – a moment that, perhaps, had shaped both my life and hers – I was really ready to risk any act or word at all [103]). In order to save Fadigati, he would have had to be able to reach out to him without feeling threatened by Fadigati's homosexuality. So, too, the truth he would have had to embrace about Micòl in order to kiss her – and perhaps to save her – was the truth of her womanhood, of her sexual difference.

Before her rejection of him, Micòl takes it upon herself to guide the narrator through the garden. Created by culture and hubris, it is a garden that defies the laws of nature. Its trees and plants are imported from different continents and different climates but coexist in apparent harmony. Immediately she notices his ignorance in matters of botany: he does not know the difference between one tree and another – "Non sapevo sul serio distinguere un olmo da un tiglio" (407; I seriously couldn't distinguish an elm from a [linden] tree [91]) – and it is she who instructs him in the distinctions. Significantly in the first chapter, the narrator, looking back years later, names all the trees in the garden that no longer exists, a sure sign of his having been finally inducted into the world of "difference":

> Tutti gli alberi di grosso fusto, tigli, olmi, faggi, pioppi, platani, ippocastani, pini, abeti, larici, cedri del Libano, cipressi, querce, lecci, e perfino palme ed eucalipti, fatti piantare a centinaia da Josette Artom, durante gli ultimi anni di guerra sono stati abbattuti per ricavarne legna da ardere, e il terreno è già tornato da un pezzo come era una volta, quando Moisé Finzi-Contini lo acquistò dai Marchesi Avogli: uno dei tanti grandi orti compresi dentro le mura urbane. (326–7)

> All the broad-canopied trees, the lindens, elms, beeches, poplars, plane trees, horse chestnuts, pines, firs, larches, cedars of Lebanon, cypresses, oaks, holm oaks, and even the palm trees and eucalyptuses, planted in their hundreds by Josette Artom during the last two years of the First World War, were cut down for firewood, and for some time the land [has been in the same] state it was in when Moisè Finzi-Contini acquired it from the Marchesi of Avogli: one of the many great gardens ringed within the city walls. (18)

The entire spirit of his sojourn in the garden of the Finzi-Continis is clearly presented by the author as a metaphorical excursion into the fantasy world of pre-Oedipal narcissism, in which the comforting mirroring of the child by the mother shields the infant from the harsh realities of a hostile world. Having been cast out from the society that once accepted him as one of its own, he refuses to accept that his beloved Ferrara has lost its once maternal face (*volto materno*);[2] he thus joins the Finzi-Continis in the ghetto/paradise they have created to mirror the image of themselves they so desperately sought and that the Gentile world would never quite yield up to them. Following the Race Laws, they do indeed allow other Jews into their enclave, and they do abandon their own private Spanish synagogue to join the Italian synagogue as a gesture of solidarity; but there is no action on their part otherwise, and no discussion of the events of the day. The Finzi-Continis have created an Eden before the Fall, in which there is no "knowledge" and no awareness, even in the face of the most brutal political and social realities: passive resistance and denial are their weapons of choice in the struggle for the preservation of their image once the Race

Laws take effect. Victims of the mirage of upward mobility promised by the emancipation of the Jews in the new Italy, their decadent world ultimately symbolizes the protagonist's fantasies and everything that had to die, to be put to rest, and to be given up before he could become a man in a way that history demanded, and for which he was in no way prepared.

Fittingly, the Finzi-Contini residence, acquired by Moisé, the first of the Finzi-Continis to leave the ghetto and to create the enormous wealth of the family through the shrewd acquisition of farmland, reflects the heady optimism and nouveau riche tastes of one of the first Jews to be granted the freedom to enter mainstream Italian society and thus to enjoy the privilege of being both Italian and Jewish. A former Este Renaissance villa reminiscent of Ferrara's once prominent courtly society, its opulence, like that of the family tomb described later on, reflects their wish to belong not to the productive and progressive sectors of post-Unification society, nor even to the landed bourgeoisie, but to the nobility of the nation. In fact, the manor is surrounded by a wood "davanti al quale i rimanenti parchi privati cittadini, quello del duca Massari compreso ..., sbiadivano al rango di pettinati giardinetti borghesi" (390–1; beside which the remaining private parks, Duke Massari's included ... faded into so many neatly tended, bourgeois gardens [76]). Their children were privately schooled at home, the family occupied a separate section in the synagogue, Micòl and her brother Alberto even have their own private language, *finzi-continico*.[3] Their stately home and garden, their silent, faithful servants, their tennis court, and their private library are all part of an enclave that points to their hubris, to their refusal to embrace the reality of their outsider status, and to their paradoxical turning of this "outside" into an "inside," the ultimate refuge of the helpless, a sort of adaptation to circumstance that turns a disadvantage into an advantage. They have surrounded themselves with all the trappings of the Gentile aristocracy and continue to lead the undisturbed lives of leisure and disinterested cultural pursuit that might have been their lot had they really been born Renaissance Christian aristocrats.

By attaching himself to this family at this very difficult time, the young protagonist takes a detour into unreality, which also allows him to fulfil many contradictory fantasies of his own. Through the Finzi-Continis he too can be both Aryan and Jewish, both aristocratic and Jewish, both an outsider and insider, all at the same time: in this paradise no contradiction exists between the two; there are no choices to make.

Micòl's Venetian uncles represent a Sephardic Jewish aristocracy, while the Finzi-Continis themselves could be mistaken for British peers; and yet to the protagonist they appear, as a family, to blend seamlessly into each other:

> Fra loro non si assomigliavano. Alti, magri, calvi, con le lunghe facce pallide ombrate di barba, vestiti sempre o di blu o di nero, e abituati inoltre a mettere nella loro devozione una intensità, un ardore fanatico di cui il cognato e il nipote, bastava guardarli, non sarebbero mai stati capaci, i parenti veneziani sembravano appartenere a una civiltà completamente estranea ai golf e ai calzettoni color tabacco di Alberto, alle lane inglesi e alle tele gialline, da studioso e da nobile di campagna, del professor Ermanno. E tuttavia, pur così diversi come erano, io li sentivo fra loro profondamente solidali. (345)

> There was little resemblance between the two pairs. Tall, thin, bald, their long pale faces shadowed with beards, always dressed in blue or black, and besides imparting to their devotions an intensity, a fanatical ardour of which their brother-in-law and nephew, one could tell at a glance, would never have been capable, those Venetian relatives seemed to belong to a world that was utterly removed from Alberto, with his tobacco-colored jersey and long socks, and from Professor Ermanno's English knitwear and ochre linen, his air of a scholar and a country gentleman. All the same, however different they were, I sensed a deep kinship between them. (33–4)

Similarly, Micòl's blonde beauty, her skill at tennis, and her general aura of relaxed self-confidence make her more desirable – and further away from the ghetto – than any other Jewish girl could be at this time: "Micòl dall'aria così libera, sportiva, moderna (libera, soprattutto!), da far pensare che gli ultimi anni non li avesse passati che in giro per le mecche del tennis internazionale, Londra, Parigi, Costa Azzurra, Forest Hills" (431; This Micòl who had such an athletic, modern, free and easy air [above all free!], that she made you think she'd done nothing else for the last few years than swan around in the Meccas of international tennis: London, Paris, the Côte d'Azur, Forest Hills [113]). In a dream he sees her precisely in these terms and yet juxtaposes her typically Aryan looks with a symbol of Jewishness, as if the two were entirely compatible: "i capelli biondi e leggeri, striati di ciocche quasi canute, le iridi celesti, quasi scandinave, la pelle color del miele, e sul petto, balenando ogni tanto fuori dallo scollo della maglietta, il piccolo disco d'oro dello *sciaddài*" (431; the weightless blond hair, with streaks verging on white locks, the blue, almost Scandinavian irises, the honey-colored skin, and on her breastbone, every now and then leaping out from her T-shirt collar, the little golden disc of the *shaddai* [113]).

The narrative opens not in 1938 but in 1957, with a prologue matched at the end by an epilogue, which together create a frame for the actual recalled story. The two other novels in the first-person trilogy have no such frame, which immediately makes this story unique. Moreover, as the middle story framed by the other two, it becomes the centrepiece of the trilogy and indeed of the entire *Romanzo*. These multiple frames emphasize the fact that this is a recollection and that the state of mind of the present-day narrator is as important as the actual story he is telling.

The spectre of death haunts this account from the very beginning. The narrator and some friends have gone on a day trip outside of Rome and on their way back make an impromptu detour to visit a famous archaeological site, the Etruscan cemetery at Cerveteri. The friends have a daughter Giannina, a lively and curious child, who is the first to bring the Jews into the discussion, asking whether the Etruscans or the Jews are the more ancient people since in her history book they both appear at the very beginning, together with the Egyptians. Her father immediately refers her to the narrator: "'Provi a chiederlo a quel signore,' disse, accennando a me col pollice" (319; "Try asking that gentleman," he said, signalling towards me with his thumb [9]).

The rest of the prologue is a melancholy meditation on the passage of time and on the fall of great civilizations. The cemetery, built by the Etruscans after the Roman conquest when their dominance over the territory was but a memory, has several functions: for the narrator it acts as both a defence and a rhetorical device, permitting a gradual entry into a difficult subject matter. (In fact, Giannina also asks her father why old tombs are not as sad as new ones.) He tries to return to the distant past, to imagine the Etruscans visiting their dead, but their cone-shaped tombs immediately evoke instead "i *bunkers* di cui i soldati tedeschi hanno sparso invano l'Europa durante quest'ultima guerra" (321; the bunkers German soldiers vainly scattered about Europe during the last war [10]). They also resemble the "abitazioni-fortilizi dei viventi" (321; the fortress dwellings of the living [10]) (alluding to the Finzi-Contini estate).

Each of the tombs is pictured as a sort of drawing room where the departed, surrounded by the objects of daily life, received their descendants, who in turn could maintain the illusion that nothing had or ever would change: a kind of liminal space in which the dead are alive and the living are dead, and where, as in eternity (and as in the unconscious), past and present no longer exist. So too the Finzi-Contini estate is a funerary *locus amoenus*, its inhabitants the living dead. Similarly, the motivations the narrator attributes to the Etruscans when they visited their dead were actually his own when, as a "regular" at the Finzi-Contini tennis courts and then as a friend of the family, he was hoping to hold at bay the encroaching reality of the racist plague raging outside: "In quell'angolo di mondo difeso, riparato, privilegiato: almeno lì (e il loro pensiero, la loro pazzia, aleggiavano ancora, dopo venticinque secoli, attorno ai tumuli tonici, ricoperti d'erbe selvagge), almeno lì nulla sarebbe mai potuto cambiare" (321–2; In that corner of the world, so well defended, adorned, privileged, at least there [and one could still sense their idea, their madness, after twenty-five centuries, among the conical tombs covered with wild grass], there at least nothing could ever change [11]).

For the author, the Etruscan cemetery serves a completely different function than it does for the narrator, namely, a means of evoking metaphorically, through the reference to archaeology, the process of mental reconstruction about to take place. Like the Etruscans, the Finzi-Continis are now extinct; but with the exception of Alberto and another son who died as a child, they have no burial places, having been deported to the camps in Germany in 1943. All that remains of them lies in the minds of those who knew them, and if they are to live again in this novel, they must be exhumed. It is important to note that when the narrator arrives at the most important tomb, that of the noble Matuta family, "adorna fittamente di stucchi polichromi raffiguranti i cari, fidati oggetti della vita di tutti i giorni, zappe, funi, accette, forbici, vanghe, coltelli, archi, frecce, perfino cani da caccia e volatili di palude" (320; densely adorned with painted murals that portrayed the dear [reliable objects of everyday life], hoes, rakes, axes, scissors, spades, knives, bows, arrows, even hunting dogs and marsh birds [10]), he says that he tried to understand not the Matutas themselves but the later Etruscans who religiously visited their tombs:

> E intanto, deposta volentieri ogni residua velleità di filologico scrupolo, *io venivo tentando di figurarmi concretamente ciò che potesse significare per i tardi etruschi di Cerveteri, gli etruschi dei tempi posteriori alla conquista romana, la frequentazione assidua del loro cimitero suburbano*. (320; emphasis mine)

> And in the meantime, having willingly discarded any vestige of historical scruple, *I was trying to figure out exactly what the assiduous visits to their suburban cemetery might have meant to the late Etruscans of Cerveteri, the Etruscans of the era after the Roman conquest.* (10; emphasis mine)

Similarly, since the noble Matutas are figures for the Finzi-Continis, what the narrator will be trying to understand here are his own reasons for stubbornly continuing to visit the family in spite of Micòl's rejection of him:

> Per qual motivo mi ostinavo a ritornare ogni giorno in un luogo dove, lo sapevo, non avrei potuto raccogliere che umiliazioni e amarezza? Non saprei dirlo esattamente. Forse speravo in un miracolo, in un brusco cambiamento della situazione, o forse, magari, andavo proprio in cerca di umiliazioni e di amarezza ...[4] (524)

> What was it made me stubbornly return every day, to a place where, as I well knew, I'd be rewarded with nothing but humiliation and bitterness? I couldn't say with any clarity. Perhaps I was hoping for a miracle, for a sudden change in the state of affairs, or perhaps I was actually going in search of humiliations and bitterness ... (197)

Freud himself famously compared the process of mental reconstruction based on fragments of recovered memory to archaeology, when he told the Wolf-Man that "the psychoanalyst, like the archaeologist in his excavations, must uncover layer after layer of the patient's psyche, before coming to the deepest, most valuable treasures."[5] In *Civilization and Its Discontents* he even suggests the house as a suitable metaphor for the representation of psychic function since, he says, with its many rooms it provides a more accurate analogy for the temporal stratification of mental life than, for example, the city:[6]

> The work of construction, or, if it is preferred, of reconstruction, resembles to a great extent an archaeologist's excavation of some dwelling-place that has been destroyed and buried or of some ancient edifice. The two processes are in fact identical, except that the analyst works under better conditions and has more material at his command to assist him, since what he is dealing with is not something destroyed but something that is still alive – and perhaps for another reason as well. But just as the archaeologist builds up the walls of a building from the foundations that have

> remained standing, determines the number and position of the columns from depressions in the floor, and reconstructs the mural decorations and paintings from the remains found in the debris, so does the analyst proceed when he draws his inferences from fragments of memories, from the associations and from the behaviour of the subject of the analysis.[7]

The home of the Finzi-Continis represents, I believe, just such a house, a house of psyche, a spatial and temporal figure of the narrator's internal world.[8] In fact, the description of the ruins of the house is marked at the end by what seems to be a direct allusion to the "mural decorations and painting from the remains found in the debris" mentioned in the Freud passage cited above:

> Resterebbe la casa vera e propria. Senonché il grande, singolare edificio, assai danneggiato da un bombardamento del '44, è occupato ancora adesso da una cinquantina di famiglie di sfollati, ... i quali, allo scopo di scoraggiare ogni eventuale progetto di sfratto da parte della Soprintendenza ai Monumenti dell'Emilia e Romagna, sembra che abbiano avuto la bella idea di raschiare dalle pareti anche gli ultimi residui di pitture antiche. (327)

> Which leaves the house itself. Except that the huge, singular edifice, badly damaged by a bombardment in 1944, is still today occupied by fifty or so families of evacuees. ... And so as to discourage any future eviction plan of the Overseers of the Local Monuments of Emilia and Romagna, it seems they had the bright idea of scraping the last remnants of antique murals from the walls. (18)

The erasure of the frescoes is a figure for the narrator's own resistance to the process on which he is embarking. In fact, his description of the Finzi-Contini home as it stands today not only makes reference to the different styles and layers created at various times, which have accumulated on top of each other, but also alludes to its "repression," to the fact that it has been completely forgotten:

> sebbene essa incorpori tuttora quelle storiche rovine di un edificio cinquecentesco, un tempo residenza o "delizia" estense, che furono acquistate dal solito Moisè nel 1850, e che più tardi, dagli eredi, a forza di adattamenti e restauri successivi, vennero trasformate in una specie di maniero neo-gotico, all'inglese: ad onta di tanti superstiti motivi d'interesse, chi ne

> sa niente, mi domando, chi se ne ricorda più? La Guida del Touring non ne parla, e ciò giustifica i turisti di passaggio. Ma a Ferrara stessa, nemmeno i pochi ebrei rimasti a far parte della languente Comunità israelitica hanno l'aria di rammentarsene. (326)

> although this still incorporates the historic ruins of a sixteenth-century building, once an Este residence or extensive "pleasure dome," which were acquired, as usual, by the same Moisè in 1850, and later transformed by his heirs, through a series of adaptations and restorations, into an English manor-house in a neo-Gothic style: despite so many interesting features which still survive, who knows anything about it, I wonder, who even remembers it? The Touring Club Guide does not mention it, and this lets any passing tourists off the hook. But even in Ferrara itself, the few Jews left that make up the dwindling Jewish community have the air of having forgotten it. (17–18)

The house will be patiently brought to life, along with its inhabitants, as the narrator makes his way slowly from the gates, to the garden, into the manor itself. Here again, he shall progressively move from room to room, describing each one as he re-evokes his relationship with members of the family. His *iter* shall take him from Professor Ermanno's private library and study, to Alberto's cold and modern bedroom, to the warm family dining room, and finally, by way of the ornate elevator, into the intimacy of Micòl's own private enclave on the top floor. The minor characters he encounters, from the dog Jor to the elders of the family and the caretaker Perotti, serve as both guards and escorts, incarnating the defences the protagonist/narrator either carries with him unaware, or summons up when needed, or allows to come down in his telling of the story. The inhabitants and guests are not just "real people" but projections of different aspects of his personality, values, wishes, unconscious desires, weaknesses, possibilities, all of which combined stage the unresolved conflicts that have kept him in a state of paralysis.

However, this represents only one side of the coin: the other theme that emerges here is the loss of history, the radical foreclosure of a past, which is also symbolized by the erasure of the paintings on the walls of this once-glorious residence. The past to which Bassani refers is not simply a mythologized artistic and cultural past (perhaps the one to which the narrator is most attached) but also the richly textured social and economic context that formed the backdrop for the transformation of Jewish identity in the aftermath of Italian Unification and Jewish emancipation. The fact that the squatters who now occupy what remains of the house are described with such bitterness and disdain signals his own pride and the narcissistic wound about to be opened up, his contempt for the "grigio diluvio democratico" (grey democratic deluge) that D'Annunzio had deplored half a century earlier in *Il piacere* (1898) and that the narrator obviously shared with the Finzi-Continis. Extremely hostile to the present attempts of the lower classes to remedy their situation, the narrator is still closely identified with the conservative and even reactionary values of the agrarian bourgeoisie. This attitude puts into focus the fact that the narrator, at the time of this telling, is still under the spell of the Finzi-Continis and of what they represented. At the novel's end his father tells him very frankly and succinctly that what made Micòl and her world so enchanting was simply its snob appeal. And yet the narrator is still subject to this appeal many years later. Here, in this bitterness and refusal to let go of the past, we get the first glimpses of Bassani's characterization of him as Nietzche's "man of resentment." Times have changed, new social classes have become important players on the postwar political scene, and yet he remains "nailed" to the past, unable to move forward.

The first chapter is really more like a second prologue or an extension of the first. It begins in the Jewish cemetery, where the monumental tomb of the Finzi-Continis lies in a state of decay as it did even at the time of the narrator's childhood. Most interesting is the description of the tomb, which evokes not so much the object but the way it appears in the mind and the eye of the beholder, "trasformata in quell'alcunché di ricco e di meraviglioso in cui si trasmuta qualunque oggetto rimasto a lungo sommerso" (325; changed, as every long-submerged object is, into something rich and strange [17]), again an allusion to the entire world that is about to be resurrected here. From their tomb, the narrator associates to the home of the Finzi-Continis and to the self-imposed isolation of the family, the causes of which remain a mystery to him: "Chissà come nasce e perché una vocazione alla solitudine. Sta di fatto che lo stesso isolamento, la medesima separazione di cui i Finzi-Contini avevano circondato i loro defunti, circondava anche l'*altra* casa che essi possedevano, quella in fondo a corso Ercole I d'Este" (325). (Who knows from what and why a vocation for solitude is born. The fact remains that the same isolation, the very separateness with which the Finzi-Continis surrounded their deceased, also surrounded the *other* house they owned, the one at the end of Corso Ercole I d'Este" [17].) Like the Etruscans they are described as having two homes: their own and that of their ancestors, in other words as having, so to speak, one foot in the grave.

The following chapter brings to life the tensions existing within the Jewish community of Ferrara during the narrator's youth. The use of indirect free speech conveys very effectively the atmosphere of rivalry in the community, reproducing linguistically the conflict of values in society and focusing not so much on the family's motives for setting themselves apart as on the fantasies and resentments that are spawned by their bizarre behaviour. Here the narrator recalls his father's reactions to the Finzi-Contini's self-segregation. He remembers that, according to his father, Josette Artom, Micòl's grandmother worshipped the Italian monarchy and made no attempt to hide "la propria avversione all'ambiente ebraico ferrarese, per lei troppo ristretto – come diceva –, nonché, in sostanza, quantunque la cosa fosse parecchio grottesca, *il proprio fondamentale antisemitismo*" (329; her own aversion to Jewish social life in Ferrara [for her it was always too claustrophobic, as she'd say] nor to hide, however bizarre it may sound, *her fundamental antisemitism* [20]).

In 1933, when the majority of those Jews of Ferrara who have not yet officially become Fascists do so, the Finzi-Continis decide to set themselves apart even more, as a form of passive resistance or protest, by restoring the old Spanish synagogue for their private use and withdrawing from membership in the Italian synagogue that they had previously attended with the narrator's family. His father, unsympathetic to their anti-Fascist stance, accuses them of seeking in segregation a kind of aristocratic status that would set them apart from other Jews:

> Il professor Ermanno e la signora Olga tuttavia (lui un uomo di studi, lei una Herrera di Venezia, e cioè nata da famiglia sefardita ponentina *molto* buona, senza dubbio, però piuttosto dissestata, e d'altronde osservantissima), che razza di persone si erano ficcati in mente di essere diventati, anche essi? Dei veri nobili? (329–30)

> But as for Professor Ermanno and Signora Olga, all the same (he a studious man and she a Herrera of Venice, and thus born into a *very good* Western Sephardic family, without doubt most respectable but rather fallen in the world, and besides which highly orthodox), what kind of people did they mean to become? Real aristocrats? (20)

This passage illustrates the contradictions not only of the Finzi-Continis but also of more mainstream Jews, such as the father: although critical of the aristocratic pretensions of this family, his own discourse is saturated with evidence of his belief in "good" families and the intrinsic value of lineage. It is on the background of these contradictions and perceptions that the narrator gradually sets the stage for his actual entry into the world of the Finzi-Continis after the passage of the Race Laws, slowly establishing their place and significance in his fantasies. As a child, he first encountered their tombs in the cemetery, after which he heard his father speak of them as "aristocrats," deriding them and yet indirectly endorsing their values at the same time; he then had occasion to hear them spoken of with wonder and admiration by his literature teacher, Giulio Meldolesi, who tutored the children at home. Thoroughly enchanted by every minute he spent in the family's company (perhaps also because he himself was of peasant origin), the teacher was particularly fascinated – and impressed – by the letters written by the poet laureate of the New Italy, Giosuè Carducci, to Professor Ermanno's mother, letters that had been lovingly preserved and personally shown to him by the old man and that he hoped to be able to publish, if only he could work up the courage to ask for permission. Later, these same letters will be offered by Professor Ermanno to the protagonist for precisely the purposes desired by Meldolesi, and in fact the teacher's accounts of the afternoons spent in the company of the Finzi-Continis seem to prefigure the narrator's own now, so many years later: "Quei pomeriggi straordinari rappresentavano evidentemente per lui qualcosa di troppo prezioso perché non ne facesse materia anche con noi di continui discorsi e divagazioni" (337; Those extraordinary afternoons evidently represented for him something too precious to deprive himself of the chance to turn them into a series of little speeches and digressions for our benefit [27]). This chapter illustrates how powerful aristocratic models were in the cultural imagination, although the desire to be "Italian" was as strong in the Finzi-Continis as in the protagonist's father. The Carducci letters symbolize this profound aspiration to be "Italian" on the part of the Finzi-Continis as well, but as part of a cultural and social elite, which the protagonist, with his own literary bent and aspirations, shares much more than he does his own father's bourgeois outlook. (The fact that the narrator never takes up the offer to publish the letters suggests his difficult relationship to Italian culture in the aftermath of the Race Laws).

Adding to his fascination with them was the private horse-drawn carriage in which they arrived at his school once a year to take exams. Described as a symbol of female sexuality in this early chapter that deals with the middle school years, the carriage will return in later chapters as the vestige of both a historical and psychological past that is difficult to let go. A vehicle that will have lost its usefulness by the time the narrator has been admitted to the garden, its value is that of a fetishized and decadent "transitional object" whose obsolescence makes it all the more fascinating. Its coachman Perotti, the ever-present caretaker, grants the young boy permission to climb onto the side step to peer through the window. He remembers examining its interior, "tutto grigio, felpato, e in penombra" (entirely grey … sumptuosly padded and in semi-darkness), as "uno dei tanti avventurosi piaceri di cui sapevano esserci prodighe quelle meravigliose, adolescenti mattine di tarda primavera" (339–40; one of the many adventurous pleasures which abounded in those marvellous late spring mornings of our adolescence [29]).

The following chapter deals with the synagogue and is particularly important in situating the Finzi-Continis as "objects of desire" in the context of the narrator's adolescent conflicts with his father, while also, again, subtly delineating the complexities and contradictions of Jewish identity in the Ferrara of the time. When he finally enters their world in his early twenties, he will still be prey to lingering childhood fantasies about their superiority, nurtured by the memory of a few fleeting glimpses and brief encounters during which he was both fascinated and intimidated by the aura of self-confidence and mystery that seemed to emanate from them.

The scenes in the synagogue take place when he is still a boy, between the ages of ten and twelve, but just before he reaches the age of thirteen, when a boy becomes a man according to the Jewish religion. The image of the young boy with his head turned away from his own father towards the Finzi-Continis – "Per un verso o per l'altro stavo quasi sempre con la testa voltata" (345; My head was almost always turned to one side or the other [33]) – prefigures their role in the young man's impending "identity crisis." The father, clearly uncomfortable with a Judaism that is too apparent, sees the Finzi-Continis as paradoxically both anti-Semitic and too Jewish at the same time. The young boy, however, perceives his own father as insufficiently Jewish – he knows only a few words of Hebrew compared to Professor Ermanno's perfect command of the language and the prayers – and as too commonly middle class, having all the preoccupations of a "modern Jew" eager to assimilate: "Un'intuizione confusa, certo, ma sostanzialmente esatta, si accompagnava in me al dispetto e all'umiliazione altrettanto confusi però cocenti, di far parte della platea, della gente volgare da tenere alla larga" (345; A confused impression, admittedly, but still essentially true, joined in me with a feeling of scorn and humiliation, equally confused, but which stung nevertheless, that I belonged with the others, the congregation, the rabble to be kept at bay [34]). The Finzi-Continis seem to represent for him the coexistence of the best of both the Jewish and Gentile worlds, as illustrated again by this description of Professor Ermanno pronouncing the words of the Jewish blessing: "La sua voce era esile e cantilenante, intonatissima; la sua pronuncia ebraica, raddoppiando di frequente le consonanti, e con le zeta, le esse, e le acca molto più toscane che ferraresi, si sentiva filtrata attraverso la duplice distinzione della cultura e del ceto ..."[9] (347–8; His voice was thin and sing-song, [perfectly in tune]: his Hebrew pronunciation, often doubling up the consonants, and with the *z*'s, the *s*'s, and the *h*'s far more Tuscan than Ferrarese, seemed to have been filtered through the dual distinction of culture and class [36]).[10] The chapter ends with the offspring Micòl and Alberto seeming to beckon to him: "E mi sorridevano, mi ammicavano, ambedue curiosamente invitanti: specie Micòl" (348; And they smiled and winked at me, both of them strangely inviting, especially Micòl [36]).

Micòl is the centre of the next two highly symbolic chapters, which immediately cast her as the catalyst of our protagonist's eventual foray into the estate and into the labyrinths of his own soul. Here we see him as an immature and vain young boy who has just failed mathematics. It is 1929, and he is thirteen years old. Wounded to the quick and dreading his father's reaction, he rides his bicycle to the edges of the Finzi-Contini estate and is spotted by Micòl, who is standing on a ladder behind the wall, very much like a princess in her tower. He recognizes her immediately "per via dei capelli biondi, di quel biondo particolare striato di ciocche nordiche, da *fille aux cheveux de lin*, che non apparteneva che a lei" (354; because of those blond tresses, the distinctive blond streaked with Nordic flax in the style of *fille aux cheveux de lin* which could only have belonged to her [41]).

Micòl soon reveals to him that she knows about the failure and tries to tell him, just like a mother, that it is not as tragic as he feels it is, very wisely putting things into perspective for him; but he receives her message as one of contempt, not consolation: "Dopo tutto era abbastanza normale che un guaio del genere fosse capitato a un tipo come me, venuto al mondo da gente così comune, talmente 'assimilata': a un quasi-*goi*, insomma. Che diritto avevo di far tante storie?" (355–6). (After all, it was not so unheard of for such a misfortune to befall someone of my type, from such a common background, so 'assimilated' as to be almost, in fact, a *goy*. What right did I have to make such a fuss? [42].)

This chapter is notable for the number of "interferences" that characterize it. The most striking is the description of the grades posted on the wall at school, where he came face to face with his failing mark. The textual memory of this humiliation becomes a "branding" that recalls the numbers tattooed onto the arms of concentration camp inmates: "Il cinque rosso, unico numero in inchiostro rosso di una lunga filza di numeri in inchiostro nero, mi si impresse nell'anima con una violenza e col bruciore di un marchio infuocato" (351; The red five, the only number in red ink in a long row of black numerals, seared itself on my soul with the violence of a branding iron [38]). During the desperate bicycle ride after the discovery of this failure, he stops under a tree, "uno di quegli antichi alberi ... che di lì a una dozzina d'anni, nel gelido inverno di Stalingrado, sarebbero stati sacrificati per farne legna da stufe" (352; one of those old trees ... which, a dozen years later, in the frozen winter of Stalingrad, would be sacrificed for firewood [39]). And just after he hears someone calling to him, and just before he spots Micòl Finzi-Contini leaning over the wall, the process of recollection takes us to the present by describing the precise location of the episode, calling attention again to his fantasy of the Finzi-Continis as a defence – "baluardo quattrocentesco" (fifteenth-century fortifications) – against the terrible narcissistic injury represented by the emergence of the working classes at the time of narration and earlier by the Race Laws. Still a solitary place, it now has at the right "decine e decine di variopinte casette operaie ... a paragone delle quali, e delle ciminiere e dei capannoni che fanno loro da sfondo, il bruno, cespuglioso, selvaggio sperone semidiroccato del baluardo quattrocentesco appare di giorno in giorno più assurdo" (353–4; scores of variously coloured workers' cottages ... in comparison with which, and with the factory chimneys and warehouses that compose their background, the brown, scrubby, half-rocky spur of fifteenth-century fortifications looks day by day ever more absurd [41]).

The chapter ends with Micòl's invitation to him to climb over the wall and join her in her garden, while the following one recreates the narrator's ultimate failure to accept the invitation. This is an important episode because an encounter that could not have lasted more than half an hour is described in such minute detail as to occupy an entire chapter. Moreover, it focuses not so much on what happened as on the protagonist's fears and fantasies about what might have happened. He is revealed to have been an immature thirteen-year-old, spoiled and petulant, ignorant of the facts of life but almost terrified of something intuitively understood about sexuality. As an adult recalling his hesitancy of that time, attributed partly to a fear of heights, he is characterized again as still not fully aware even now of what prevented him from accepting Micòl's invitation: "Comunque, non era tanto per questo motivo che ancora esitavo. A trattenermi era una ripugnanza diversa da quella puramente fisica delle vertigini: analoga ma diversa, e più forte" (359). (However, it was not so much for that reason that I still hesitated. Holding me back was a different repugnance than the purely physical one of vertigo: analogous, but different, and stronger at that [46].)

In order to conceal his fears, the protagonist insists that the real reason he cannot climb the wall is because of his expensive bicycle, which he cannot leave unattended at the foot of the wall. Micòl, resourceful as always, suggests that he store it in a subterranean room hidden under a nearby conical mound, one of many in the area, in which the defenders of Ferrara's walls used to hide their weapons. The nature of his fears, then as now, is reflected in the sexually charged description of the mound – "Era una sorta di fessura verticale, tagliata al vivo nella coltre d'erba che rivestiva compatta il monticello: così stretta da non consentire il passaggio a più di una persona per volta" (362; It was a kind of vertical crack, cut directly into the mantle of grass with which the mound was thickly clad, and too narrow to permit the entry of more than one person at a time [49]) – and is confirmed by Micòl's own embarassment as she urges him to enter it with his bicycle: "'Va giù tu,' bisbigliò, e sorrideva debolmente, imbarazzata. 'Preferisco aspettarti qua sopra'" (362). ("You go on down," she whispered, smiling weakly, embarrassed. "I'd prefer to wait up here" [49].)

The narrator overcomes his fear of the dark and of the unknown to enter the room and here begins to fantasize about what might have happened had Micòl accompanied him. He knows about long kisses from the movies but not about what follows, except that it frightens him: "Meno male che mi ero salvato. … E se vice-versa fosse accaduto? – pensavo –. Sarebbe stato davvero così terribile, se fosse accaduto? (364). (It was just as well I'd been saved. … And if the other things had happened, if they had, would that really have been so terrible? [50–1].)

At this point his fantasies, as he remembers them, centre around the possibility of remaining in the underground room, hidden from everyone including his own family and completely dependent on Micòl, who would bring him food and anything else he needed: "E ogni giorno ci saremmo baciati, al buio: perché io ero il suo uomo, e lei la mia donna" (365; And every day we would have kissed, in the dark, because I was her man, and she was my woman [51]). At night he might leave, but only to look at his parents' home and to imagine himself almost an orphan; to imagine his room having been turned into a parlour and his father turning the key in the door unaware that his son is spying from afar, "e non gli passa nemmeno per la testa che io sono vivo e sto osservandolo ..., proprio come se io, suo figlio maggiore, non sia mai esistito" (365–6; and it wouldn't even cross his mind I was alive and watching him ..., just as though I, his eldest child, had never existed [52]). These are very significant words in terms of the family romance: he completely wishes away his father and imagines himself in an exclusive relationship with a motherly, nurturing Micòl.

When the narrator emerges from the underground room, minus the bicycle, he finds that the bubble has burst; Micòl in the meantime has been spotted and called to order by Perotti the caretaker. She is now back on her ladder behind the wall: access to the garden is denied as a result of the narrator's initial reluctance. Section 1 of the novel closes on a note that reinforces the centrality of Micòl: "E il suo ultimo sguardo, prima che scomparisse di là dal muro (uno sguardo accompagnato da un ammicco sorridente, proprio come quando, al Tempio, mi spiava da sotto il *talèd* paterno), era stato per me" (366; And the last look she gave, before disappearing behind the wall – a look accompanied with a smile and a wink, just as when, at the synagogue, she spied me from under the paternal *tallit* – had been for me [52]).

One very subtle reference in this chapter, but perhaps even more significant because of its subtlety, may provide a clue as to what is going on in the narrator's unconscious as he tells his story. In remembering the "erbose montagnole coniche" (361; grassy, cone-shaped hillocks [48]) outside the wall, he associates them consciously to the Etruscan tombs of the prologue: "A vederle, assomigliano un po' ai *montarozzi* etruschi della campagna romana; in scala molto minore, s'intende" (361; At first sight, they look a bit like the Etruscan *montarozzi* of the Roman countryside, though obviously on a much smaller scale [48]). If one considers that he arrives at the Finzi-Continis by way of the Etruscan tombs, with the help of Giannina, the little girl whose association of the Jews to the Etruscans "coaxes" the narrator into telling his story, then the Etruscan tombs become stand-ins for the *montagnola conica* (cone-shaped hillock) with all its sexual connotation as noted above: Eros and Thanatos perhaps, but more likely a suggestion of the narrator's own sexual (and psychic) sterility prefigured in his adolescent fears of Micòl, which prevented him from accepting her invitation.

Part 2 of the novel begins precisely with an indirect reiteration of that failure, contrasted with the eventual entry into the estate: "La volta che mi riuscì di passarci davvero, di là dal muro di cinta di Barchetto del Duca, e di spingermi fra gli alberi e le radure della gran selva privata fino a raggiungere la *magna domus* e il campo di tennis, fu qualcosa come una decina d'anni più tardi" (367; When I actually managed to pass beyond, beyond the wall surrounding the Barchetto del Duca, and make my way between the trees and clearings of the great private wood as far as the *magna domus* itself and the tennis court was something like ten years later [55]).

The protagonist receives the first phone call from Alberto Finzi-Contini, Micòl's brother. Recalling a chance encounter at the train station where Alberto had snubbed him, he thanks him but remains noncommital. At this point, however, his father enters into the equation. This chapter, which marks the protagonist's decision to enter the world of the Finzi-Continis, is devoted to a lengthy discussion of the disagreement between father and son over which stance to adopt in the face of the current situation. Although the narrator never explicitly states that he looked to his father for an example that the older man was unable to set, it is clear that not only is the father unable to offer a model of action and decision in these new and difficult circumstances, but he actually looks to his son for support and guidance: "Con la mamma e con Fanny non era il caso che si confidasse: erano donne. Con Ernesto nemmeno: troppo *putìn*. Con chi doveva parlare allora? Possibile che non capissi che era proprio di me che lui aveva bisogno?" (369). (It wasn't possible for him to confide in Mamma and in Fanny: they were women. Nor could he do so in Ernesto – too *putìn*. So then who could he talk to? Was it possible I couldn't understand it was me he needed? [57].) The father continues to attempt to minimize the gravity of the situation by comparing Mussolini favourably to Hitler: "Secondo lui io vedevo troppo nero, ero troppo catastrofico" (372; According to him I took everything too grimly, I was too extreme [59]). He urges his son to stop isolating himself and to return to the tennis club (the protagonist has not yet received the official letter excluding him), and insists that the president of the club is, after all, relatively harmless. The narrator recalls his father's tone of voice: "Dicendo 'assai blandamente fascista' la voce di mio padre ebbe un tremito, un piccolo tremito di timidezza" (54; And in saying "harmless enough Fascist" my father's voice trembled, a little tremor of timidity [60]).

The rest of the discussion concerns the Finzi-Continis, whom the father accuses not only of being pleased with the advent of the Race Laws, since it justifies their policy of isolation, but also of harbouring a certain nostalgia for the ghetto. He is clearly not in favour of having his son accept their invitation, and of course the son promptly does so, though to this day obviously unaware of his motivations since the decision is reported in the form of a Freudian negation: "Era un martedì. Non saprei dire come mai di lì a pochi giorni, il sabato di quella stessa settimana, mi risolvessi a fare proprio il contrario di ciò che mio padre desiderava. Escluderei che c'entrasse il solito meccanismo di contraddizione e disubbidienza tipico dei figli"(375). (That was a Tuesday. I can't explain how, a few days later, on the Saturday, I decided to do exactly the opposite of what my father wanted. I'd deny that it had to do with the typical filial mechanism of contradiction and disobedience [62].)

The other catalysts for his decision to accept Alberto's invitation are the arrival of the formal letter accepting his "resignation" from the tennis club and a phone call from Micòl herself. The resulting conversation, "una normale, ironica e divagante chiacchierata" (376; a normal, ironic, rambling chat [63]), suggests that the climate in the garden will be one of denial as well; but curiously, though the narrator is intolerant both of his father's attempt to minimize the reality of the Race Laws and of his friend Nino Bottecchiari's failure to acknowledge them in the previous novel, Micòl's reticence is noted but fails to provoke anger:

> Aveva ripetuto l'invito del fratello ..., però senza insistere, e senza affatto accennare, a differenza di lui, alla lettera del marchese Barbicinti. Non accennò a niente altro che al puro piacere di rivedersi dopo tanto tempo, e di godere assieme, in barba a tutti i divieti, quanto di bello restava da godere della stagione. (378)

> She had repeated her brother's invitation ..., but without insisting, and without the slightest mention, in contrast to him, of the Marchese

> Barbicinti's letter. She mentioned nothing but the real pleasure of seeing each other again after such a long time and of enjoying together, [in defiance of all prohibitions], what good times were still possible while the season lasted. (65)

We do learn that she is writing her thesis on the poetry of Emily Dickinson and remembers her aborted attempt to smuggle him into the garden ten years earlier, but she cannot remember why he never did enter. He attributes all the responsibility to the caretaker Perotti and to the guard dog Jor, and does not mention his initial refusal to climb the wall or his motivations either to Micòl at the time or to the reader now twenty years later.

The following chapter takes place entirely on the threshold of the garden. When the protagonist arrives at the gates of the estate, he immediately discovers that he is not alone and that others, both Jews and Gentiles, have been invited as well. The others include the Jewish Bruno Lattes – "sempre più simile, di carnagione scura come era, a un giovane negro vibrante e apprensivo" (380; because of his ever swarthier skin, like a vibrant, nervous young black [67]) – and his Gentile girlfriend, Adriana Trentini. He and Bruno exchange "l'inevitabile occhiata di ebraica connivenza che, mezzo ansioso e mezzo disgustato, già prevedevo" (380; the inevitable quick glance of Jewish complicity which, partly in anxiety and partly in distaste, I had already foreseen [67]).

Adriana is furious: a doubles tournament she and Bruno were about to win at the club was abruptly cut short because, under the circumstances, it was unfitting to have a Jew as a winner. Her outrage is not at the Race Laws but at the hypocrisy of officials who she feels ought to have prevented Bruno from registering in the first place, instead of using the pretext of "fading daylight" to interrupt their game. Bruno attributes the decision to local Fascist thugs' intimidation of the club authorities; in neither case are the Race Laws themselves criticized directly. Here the protagonist first sees another of the guests who will soon play a very important role in his psychic development. Giampiero Malnate, a Gentile and Alberto's friend from Milan, "un tipo più anziano, sui venticinque, con pipa fra i denti, calzoni lunghi di lino bianco e giacca di fustagno marrone" (379; older, around twenty-five, with a pipe between his teeth, long white linen trousers, and a brown corduroy jacket [66]). He works as a chemist in one of the new rubber factories in the area and will provide an outsider's perspective on Ferrara as the protagonist gets to know him.

The following chapter presents the illusory, paradisiacal aspect of the garden as it appears to the narrator before reality sets in. It is a brief chapter, but full of portent:

> Per dieci o dodici giorni il tempo si mantenne perfetto, fermo in quella specie di magica sospensione, di immobilità dolcemente vitrea e luminosa che è particolare di certi nostri autunni. Nel giardino faceva caldo: appena meno che se si fosse d'estate. Chi ne aveva voglia poteva tirare avanti col tennis fino alle cinque e mezzo e oltre. ... A quell'ora, naturalmente, sul campo non ci si vedeva quasi più. Però la luce ..., quest'ultima luce invitava a insistere in palleggi non importa se ormai pressoché ciechi. Il giorno non era finito, valeva la pena di giocare ancora un poco. (387)

> For ten or twelve days the weather remained perfect, held in that state of magical suspension, of glassy, luminous, soft immobility which is the special gift of some of our autumns. In the garden it was hot, just slightly less than if it was summer. Whoever wanted to could go on playing until half past five and even later. ... At that hour, naturally, you could hardly see a thing. And yet ..., that last light tempted you to keep on playing, regardless of whether you were all but blind. The day was still not over; surely it was worth playing on just a little longer. (73)

These last lines of course indicate that the narrator is well aware that both he and the Finzi-Continis were "playing" during the time that their lives were connected and that their play was "blind." The continuing illusion that one can be both Italian and Jewish is also suggested by the magnificent tray of hors d'oeuvres offered to the guests with tea, on which *prosciutto* (ham) and kosher delicacies coexist peacefully, at least for the time being:

> Era stracolmo, il vassoio: di pannini imburrati all'acciuga, al salmone affumicato, al caviale, al fegato d'oca, al prosciutto di maiale; di piccoli *vol-au-vents* ripieni di battuto di pollo misto a besciamella; di minuscoli *buricchi* usciti certo dal prestigioso negozietto *cascèr* che la signora Betsabea, la celebre signora Betsabea (Da Fano) conduceva da decenni in via Mazzini a delizia e gloria dell'intera cittadinanza. (391)

> The tray was overflowing: rolls of anchovy spread, smoked salmon, caviare, pâté de foie gras, pork prosciutto; with little vol-au-vents filled with a sauce of chicken and béchamel; with tiny *buricchi*, which must have

> come from the prestigious little kosher shop which Signora Betsabea, the famous Signora Betsabea (Da Fano) had run for decades in Via Mazzini to the pride and delight of the entire citizenry. (76)

Significantly, Micòl, "non senza ostentazione di anticonformismo religioso, sceglieva tra quelli al prosciutto di maiale" (392; not without a show of religious nonconformism, ... chose from among those with pork prosciutto [77]).

This chapter is both decadent and prophetic, depicting the pretensions and contradictions of an elegant and privileged Jewish world on the brink of catastrophe. Micòl waxes on endlessly about her favourite drink, German *Skiwasser*, which she and Alberto discovered on a skiing trip to Austria in 1934. She has since altered it by adding grapes to create an Italian, even Ferrarese, version of it, in an eerie and ironic allusion to the German-Italian alliance and to the particularly violent form it was to take in Ferrara: "Rappresentava, l'uva, il particolare contributo dell'Italia alla santa e nobile causa dello *Skiwasser*, ovvero di esso, più esattamente, la particolare 'variante italiana, per non dire ferrarese, per non dire ... eccetera, eccetera'" (392; The grapes stood for Italy's special contribution to the holy, noble cause of *Skiwasser*, or rather of this, to put it more precisely, special "Italian variant, not to mention Ferrarese, not to mention ... etc. etc." [78]).

The elders of the family, and in particular Micòl's father, are the focus of the following chapter, in which the narrator describes the first of two encounters with him. At first Professor Ermanno would seem a more appropriate father figure than the narrator's own father, and indeed the old man initiates their conversation by quoting Dante as a sign of their common literary interest. However, their exchange proves to be entirely one-sided and focused on the professor's concerns. We learn that as a young man he had wanted to write a history of the Venetian Jews but was distracted by two other projects: the compilation of the Jewish tombstone inscriptions at the Lido and the study of other sixteenth-century documents pertaining to the Venetian Jewish community, of which he gave an account but "senza azzardare in proposito nessuna interpretazione" (401; without venturing on any interpretation with respect to them [86]). Symbolically his work is sterile, and the narrator now reflects ironically on his narcissism: "Parlavo, e il professor Ermanno, più che mai curvo, stava ad ascoltarmi in silenzio. A che cosa pensava? Al numero di 'illustrazioni' universitarie di cui si era fregiato l'ebraismo italiano dall'Unità ai nostri giorni? Era probabile"

(402). (I talked on, and Professor Ermanno, more hunched than ever, stood and listened to me in silence. What was he thinking about? About the number of illustrious university "figures" which Italian Jewry had supplied from the Unification to the present time? Probably [87].) The narrator then reports, with an almost mocking tone, the professor's reference to the unpublished Carducci letters in his possession, revealed to the protagonist by his teacher Meldolesi several years earlier: the professor spoke about them in a whisper, looking around to make sure there were no eavesdroppers, "né più né meno che se dovesse mettermi a parte di un segreto di Stato" (402; as if he were letting me into something no less than a state secret [87]). When Ermanno offers the letters to him for his thesis, the protagonist lies, pretending not to know about them, and claims to have already committed to a topic. His last words actually indicate agreement with his father's belief that the Finzi-Continis were not terribly affected by the advent of the Race Laws: "Ma aveva ragione mio padre. In fondo non sembrava granché addolorato, di questo. Tutt'altro" (404). (My father had been right. He didn't finally seem all that distressed by this fact. Quite the reverse [88].) They hold no conversation whatsoever about politics. The professor appears to be entirely absorbed by the past: in fact, he and his wife were betrothed in the Jewish cemetery at the Lido, and in encouraging the young narrator to visit it, he reveals the source of his fascination with it: "Lo troverai tale e quale come era trentacinque anni fa: uguale identico" (401; You'll find it just as it was thirty-five years ago, exactly the same [86]).

Unlike her father, Micòl does not believe in preserving the past. One day while she and the narrator are strolling in the garden, a sudden, violent rainstorm forces them to take refuge in the garage: "Faceva freddo. Battendo i denti, guardavamo entrambi dinanzi a noi. L'incantesimo a cui fino allora era stata sospesa la stagione si era rotto irreparabilmente" (415). (It was cold. Our teeth chattering, we both looked around us. The enchantment which had till then held the season in suspense had been irreparably broken [97].) Together with discarded objects from the past and the family automobile, the garage houses the old carriage in which Micòl and Alberto were driven to the public school for their exams as children and that had been described in great detail earlier on. In search of warmth, the protagonist and Micòl climb into it. In the following passage, drawn from an earlier episode, the narrator immediately associates the carriage with Perotti the caretaker, who had opened the gates of the estate to the young people outside on the day of his first visit:

> Era proprio lui, il vecchio Perotti, giardiniere, cocchiere, *chauffeur*, portinaio, tutto, come aveva detto Micòl: niente affatto mutato nel complesso dai tempi del *Guarini*, quando, assiso in serpa, aspettava impassibile che l'antro buio e minaccioso dal quale, impavidi, col sorriso sulle labbra, i suoi "signorini" erano stati inghiottiti, si decidesse una buona volta a restituirli, non meno sereni e sicuri di sé, alla vettura tutta cristalli, vernici, nichelature, stoffe felpate, legni squisiti – simili davvero a una teca preziosa –, della cui conservazione e guida soltanto lui era responsabile. (385)

> It was him in person, old Perotti – gardener, coachman, *chauffeur*, doorman, the whole lot and more, just as Micòl had described him. He had not changed in the least since my time at the Guarini when, enthroned on the box-seat, he waited impassively till the school's dark and menacing cave mouth, which had swallowed up his little fearless smiling "charges," finally decided to restore them, no less serene and self-confident, to the vehicle made of glass, varnish, nickel-plating, padded material, fine planished hardwoods – exactly like a precious [shrine] – whose conservation and conveyance were entirely his responsibility. (71)

We learn that the carriage is still Perotti's pet project, as he constantly works to keep it in shape despite its obsolescence. It is important to note that before the carriage scene, the narrator remembers an earlier conversation in which he and Micòl reminisced jokingly about their first private encounter years ago. Micòl confessed her adolescent crush on him, from their days in synagogue, while he recalled his own refusal to climb the wall to join her in the garden. Micòl revealed that because of his blue eyes, which she had noticed in synagogue whenever he turned around, she had secretly nicknamed him Celestino (blue eyes), to which he stammered, "*Che fece per viltade il gran rifiuto* ..." (413), quoting Dante's reference to Pope Celestine's famous refusal of the papacy.

The second refusal will be more subtle, since an invitation is never extended explicitly, at least not in words. Micòl climbs into the carriage and motions to the protagonist by patting on the seat next to her. He climbs in, but as soon as he finds himself close to her in this enclosed space, his voice betrays his nervousness. What he feels is described as a form of castration anxiety: "Lo sportello si chiuse da solo con uno schiocco secco e preciso da tagliola. ... 'Come la tenete bene,' dissi, senza riuscire a padroneggiare un'improvvisa emozione che mi si riflettè in un lieve tremito della voce. 'Sembra ancora nuova'" (416). (The carriage door closed on its own, with the dry, precise click of a trap ... "How well you keep it," I said, unable to suppress the sudden emotion, which registered in my voice as a slight tremor. "It still seems new" [98].)

Micòl senses his inability to come forward and moves away from him in frustration, expressing her anger at his idealization of the carriage and especially at his insistence that it seems almost brand new: "Non dire stupidaggini, per favore!"(417; Do me a favour and don't talk drivel! [99]).

As he tells his story years later, he is still in the process of trying to understand why he was unable to overcome a paralysis that made it impossible for him to kiss her and thus declare his feelings for her when the perfect occasion presented itself. This failure to come forward on that rainy day in 1938, which may well have determined the course of their lives and is now enshrined in words, scenes, images, and symbols fraught with meaning, is not to be confused with a mere momentary failure of nerve:

> Parlarle, baciarla: era allora, quando tutto ancora poteva succedere – non cessavo di ripetermi –, che avrei dovuto farlo! E dimenticavo di chiedermi l'essenziale: se in quel momento supremo, unico, irrevocabile – un momento che, forse, aveva deciso della mia e della sua vita –, io fossi stato davvero in grado di tentare un gesto, una parola qualsiasi. (419)

> To have spoken to her, to have kissed her: it was then, – I couldn't stop telling myself – then, when everything was still possible, that I should have done it! But I was forgetting to ask myself the crucial question: whether in that supreme, unique, irrevocable moment – a moment that, perhaps, had shaped both my life and hers – I was really ready to risk any act or word at all. (103)

The answer to his question is provided cryptically, of course, by Micòl herself, for such is her role in his life, both temptress (Eve) and guide (Beatrice).[11] Shortly after she has squirmed into a corner of the carriage, suddenly appearing to feel cold and as if privy to a superior knowledge about him and about life in general, Micòl launches into a complicated speech to cover up the awkwardness of the situation and at the same time to express her annoyance at his boyish behaviour. She uses the carriage and his anachronistic admiration for it as the way to convey her lesson. The carriage is old, a "penoso rottame"(417; a ghastly old wreck [99]), and all of Perotti's efforts to keep it in shape by constantly polishing, revarnishing, and so on are a waste of time; for in the light of day its shabby, time-worn appearance is clear to all. She then compares the carriage to an old canoe leaning against the wall that has also outlived its usefulness and points out how, in contrast to the carriage, it has graciously acknowledged its obsolescence:

> Guarda invece là il sandolino, e ammira, ti prego, con quanta onestà, dignità e coraggio morale, lui ha saputo trarre dalla propria assoluta perdita di funzione tutte le conseguenze che doveva. Anche le cose muoiono, caro mio. E dunque, se anche loro devono morire, tant'è, meglio lasciarle andare. C'è molto più stile, oltre tutto, ti sembra? (417–18)

> Consider the canoe, and admire how honestly, with what dignity and moral courage, it's faced up to the full consequences of its utter uselessness, as it needed to. Even things, even they have to die, my friend. And so, if even they have to die, it's just as well to let them go. Above all, there's far more style in that, wouldn't you say? (100)

This speech constitutes the very nerve centre of the novel. Both carriage and canoe belong to another time, are "in exile," so to speak, but the manly canoe accepts its fate with all the consequences it entails. The feminine carriage, on the other hand, hangs on to a fantasized past and function that no longer pertain, much as the Finzi-Continis, perhaps, hang on anachronistically to the aristocratic past they have created for themselves; by extension, some Jews hang on to an idea of themselves and their Jewishness that leads them to take refuge in study and in the passive cultivation of their illustrious history (see Prof. Ermanno's obsessions) instead of fighting back in the present, much as the protagonist himself is still mired in a mother-identified, "feminized" boyhood and fails to relate as a man to both Micòl and the events of the day. What follows is a bitter meditation on the folly of hanging on to the past, on the need to acknowledge obsolescence with manly courage, which in the context of this particular scene seems to provide a lesson in sexual difference: the feminine carriage is contrasted with the masculine canoe. But in the larger context, all those who hang onto the past (for example, Micòl's own father, as well as the narrator's father) are associated with a feminized passivity. The past is also associated with the illusion of sameness: for Professor Ermanno the illusion derives from being segregated from the Other, the third term that breaks the narcissistic illusion (as in the ghetto perhaps). For the narrator's father, the illusion of sameness stems from believing that Jews and Gentiles are the same, that one can be a Jewish Italian rather than an Italian Jew. The past to which he clings is more recent than the ghetto past but equally illusory. The manly thing to do would be to abandon pre-Oedipal narcissism and embrace difference, whether sexual or ethnic.

It is significant that the narrator describes his feeling when sitting in the carriage with Micòl as one of suffocation, evoking the stifling nature of the narcissistic pre-Oedipal mother-child relation: "Pareva davvero di trovarsi dentro un salottino: un piccolo salotto soffocante" (416; It truly seemed as if we were in a small drawing room, a cramped and suffocating one [98]). His perceptions are not the same as hers, however. What is stifling to him is an occasion for intimacy to her: she has outgrown him, just as the events of the day have left him behind in terms of what they now demand of him. As Micòl is about to launch into the carriage/canoe speech after expressing her exasperation at his idealization of the carriage, she suddenly appears much older to him: "Pareva di colpo invecchiata di dieci anni" (417; Suddenly she seemed to have grown ten years older [99]). She then proceeds to expound her lesson about sexual difference and the serene, manly acceptance of exile as opposed to the clingy refusal to let go of childish things.

The reasons for the narrator's inability to kiss Micòl at that time, that is, to acknowledge the sexual difference between them, are soon made explicit in a dream. Before narrating his dream, he recalls a telephone conversation with Micòl during which she described her room to him, and in particular her precious and large collection of Venetian glass objects, which she referred to as "làttimi":

> "Làttimi?" domandai. "Che roba è? Da mangiare?"
>
> "Ma no, no," piagnucolò, inorridendo al solito della mia ignoranza. "Sono vetri. Bicchieri, calici, ampolle, ampolline, scatolucce: cosette, in genere scarti d'antiquariato." (423)

> "*Làttimi*?" I asked. "What are they? Something to eat?"
>
> "No. Not at all," she protested petulantly, appalled as usual by my ignorance. "They're things made with milky glass: normal glasses, champagne glasses, ampoules, dainty vases, little boxes: stuff you might find in antique dealers' shops." (107)

The dream seizes on the similarity between *làttimi* and *latticini* (milk products). First he describes the sense of bewilderment and unease he remembers feeling in the dream at finding her to be a fully grown woman and no longer the blonde child he remembered; then they are suddenly again in the famous carriage with Perotti and his wife as chaperones of sorts and, in the next sequence in Micòl's room, which is full of "roba da mangiare" (432; things to eat [114]):

> Giacché i làttimi non erano affatto gli oggetti di vetro di cui Micòl mi aveva raccontato, ma, appunto come io avevo supposto, formaggi, piccole, stillanti forme di cacio biancastro, a foggia di bottiglia. Ridendo, Micòl insisteva perché io provassi ad assaggiarne uno, dei suoi formaggi. Ed ecco si alzava sulle punte dei piedi, ecco stava per toccare col teso indice della mano destra uno tra quelli collocati più in alto (quelli lassù erano i migliori – mi spiegava –, i più freschi), ma io no, non accettavo assolutamente, angosciato, oltre che dalla presenza del cane, dalla consapevolezza che fuori, mentre così discutevamo, la marea lagunare stava rapidamente montando. Se tardavo ancora un poco, l'acqua alta mi avrebbe bloccato, mi avrebbe impedito di uscire dalla sua camera senza farmi notare. (432–3)

> Only the *làttimi* were not at all the glass objects that Micòl had told me about, but, just as I'd supposed, cheeses – little round driplets of off-white cheeses, shaped like bottles. Laughing, Micòl insisted that I try one of them, one of her cheeses. At this she stood on tiptoe, and was about to touch with the stretched-out index finger of her right hand one of those which had been set on the topmost shelf – those were the best ones, she explained to me, the freshest. But not at all, I wasn't going to have one – I felt anxious not only because of the dog's presence but also because I realized that outside, whilst we were arguing, the lake tide was rapidly rising. If I were to delay any further, the high water would have locked me in, would have stopped me being able to leave her room unnoticed. (114)

Exile from the garden and the need to leave the mother-child dyad of pre-Oedipal narcissism are again intertwined in this symbolically charged dream, in which Micòl has obviously become a maternal Eve tempting the protagonist with her milk-derived products. And yet he resists, aware that he must leave the garden before the tide rises, although he is unable to do so: a very clear depiction of his dilemma, as well as a clear warning that the garden will soon become the site of his undoing if he does not grow up quickly, become aware of the real dangers facing him and other Jews, and decide on a manly course of action.[12] Not coincidentally in this very same chapter, in his account of an awkward telephone conversation with Micòl's latently homosexual brother Alberto, the narrator recalls having gratuitously and mysteriously invented a visit to a local brothel as an immediate means of distancing himself from the danger of identification with Alberto, much as he did vis-à-vis Fadigati in *Gli occhiali d'oro*: "'Pensa,' soggiunsi a questo punto, inventando di sana pianta, e chissà quale demone mi aveva a un tratto suggerito di raccontare una storia del genere, 'prima di tornare in stazione ho trovato perfino il tempo di dare un'occhiatina in via dell'Oca'" (435; "Just imagine," I added at this point, inventing the whole thing – who knows what devil had suddenly prompted me to tell a story of this kind, "before going to the station I even had time to have a quick look around the Via dell'Oca" [117]).

Their relationship finally reaches a crisis one evening when Micòl has taken to her bed with the flu and the protagonist decides to pay her a visit. An elaborate description of the ancient elevator that takes him up to Micòl's top floor room foreshadows the ensuing scene. Operated by Perotti, who takes care of its shiny wooden interior as lovingly and as obsessively as he does the decrepit old carriage, the elevator gives off a familiar, musty odour the protagonist recognizes from the episode in the garage. It immediately casts a sort of spell as "un immovativato senso di calma, di tranquillità fatalistica, di distacco addirittura ironico" (499; a motiveless sense of calm, of resigned fatalism, even of ironic distance) came over him, surely a sign of the Freudian "uncanny":

> Perotti era tornato a chiudersi in un silenzio gravido di tutti i significati possibili. Ma fu qui che ricordai e compresi. Perotti taceva non già perché disapprovasse, come a un certo punto m'era passato per la testa, che Micòl mi ricevesse in camera sua, bensì perché l'opportunità che gli si offriva di manovrare l'ascensore (un'opportunità forse rara), lo colmava di una soddisfazione tanto più intensa quanto più intima, più segreta. (500)

> Perotti had closed himself once again in a silence open to all kinds of interpretation. But it was then I remembered and understood. Perotti was keeping silent not because he disapproved, as at a certain point I'd conjectured, that Micòl was receiving me in her room, but rather because of the opportunity offered him to operate the lift (perhaps rare enough) which filled him with a satisfaction as intense as it was private and intimate. (175–6)

The elevator is associated with the old carriage by its musty smell and as such functions as both a sexual symbol and another symbol of the past so carefully guarded by Perotti and that must be left behind. In fact, in the next scene the young man literally enacts the Freudian belief that every boy wishes to sleep with his mother. When he opens the door to Micòl's room, he perceives her to be receiving him with a luminous, maternal smile "pieno di tenerezza e di perdono" (501; full of forgiving warmth [177]). Then he climbs onto her bed in an attempt to embrace her, only to find himself summarily rejected and humiliated. Micòl's words and actions signal both that the family romance is playing itself out and that the Oedipal resolution is imminent. She tells him that as a child, especially in synagogue, she felt sorry for him: "È assurdo, lo so: eppure a guardarti, provavo la stessa pena che se tu fossi stato orfano, privo di padre e di madre" (511; It's stupid, I know, and yet, I felt the same kind of sorrow as if you'd been an orphan, without a father and a mother [185]). While he is in the bathroom washing his face after the aborted attempt to seduce her, he hears her pick up the telephone and later begins to suspect the presence of a third party between them: "L'indomani soltanto, ripensando a tutto, mi sarei ricordato di quando ero chiuso nel bagno e l'avevo sentita parlare al telefono" (513; Only the day after, going over it all, would I remember when, closed in the bathroom, I'd heard her talking on the telephone [187]).

But all is not lost. In literature, whenever a hero is captivated or captured by a beautiful woman and drawn into her lair, he is in fact being waylaid on his journey to another destination and distracted from his real mission, like Ulysses and his men by Circe, Aeneas by Dido, and Rinaldo by Armida in Tasso's *Gerusalemme Liberata*. So too the protagonist's attraction to the world of the Finzi-Continis and to Micòl is a *battuta d'arresto* (setback), in this case an illusory escape from a difficult place and a difficult time in the life of a young protected Jewish male having to negotiate his entry into manhood at a time when the society for which he seemed naturally destined has just turned its back on him.[13]

Having adopted the Finzi-Continis as his own family, the narrator finds that, sadly, this golden Jewish ghetto offers no positive male role models either. Unable to identify with his own father's passivity in the face of persecution, he is equally stymied by the attitudes of the Jewish men he finds here. Micòl's father is an old man preoccupied with Jewish genealogy and cemeteries: death and the past. It is he who has created this artificial atmosphere and he who has condemned his own family to death. Interestingly, the narrator remembers the professor's limp handshake: "Sentii la sua mano piccola e grassa infilarsi quasi inerte nella mia e immediatamente ritrarsi" (440; I felt his small, plump hand rest inertly in my own and then as quickly withdraw [122]). And when he recalls his first visit to the professor's study, he remembers, but almost forgets, to tell us about the enormous portrait of the professor's mother that hangs on the wall and the professor's extreme, humourless reverence towards this life-sized likeness, "incombente come una pala d'altare dalla parete dietro il tavolo" (473; weighing on the wall behind the table like an altarpiece [151]): "Il ritratto della madre fu l'unica cosa, fra le innumerevoli presenti nello studio, di cui il professor Ermanno non sorridesse; né quella mattina, né mai (474; His mother's portrait was the only thing, among that host of objects in the study, which Professor Ermanno did not joke about – not that morning, not ever [151]).

His son Alberto is the inheritor of this legacy. A sickly young man who withers away in the face of his family's denial of his illness, he is a lifeless latent homosexual, doomed to live out his sterile destiny as the carrier of his family's defective male gene. When asked, Alberto describes Professor Ermanno's docility towards a Fascist official who comes to the garden to complain about the apparent establishment of an unofficial tennis club for Jews; he compares his father to the famous cowardly priest in Manzoni's *Promessi sposi*: "Non gli restava che comportarsi come Don Abbondio. Inchinarsi e mormorare: 'Disposto sempre all'obbedienza'" (522). (There was nothing left for him but to behave like Don Abbondio. To bow and murmur: "Your obedient servant" [196]). These remarks are preceded by a rhetorical question, "Che cosa vuoi che rispondesse?" (522; What could he say? [196]), signalling the son's inability to even imagine any other kind of reaction.

All of these characters are more symbolic than real, actors in the hero's own dilemma of identity at this difficult time. The only viable role model in this doomed paradise is, perhaps not surprisingly, a Gentile, Alberto's college friend Giuseppe Malnate. An anti-Fascist who works as an engineer in a local factory and belongs to the outlawed Communist Party, Malnate offers the model of an active, engaged masculinity that contrasts sharply with the passive demeanour of the Jewish men in the protagonist's entourage: "Conversando, discutendo, spesso litigando (odiandoci e insieme amandoci, insomma, fin dal primo momento), fu così che potemmo conoscerci a fondo, e passare molto presto al tu" (451–2; Talking, disputing, often arguing – in short hating and loving each other, from the first moment, it was thus that we got to know each other deeply, and we very quickly adopted the *tu* form of address [132]). Though somewhat put off by Malnate's size and "manly earnestness" in matters of politics, the protagonist finds himself increasingly drawn to him and recalls wanting his approval at all costs; as a result, he unconsciously begins to model himself on this Gentile: "Credo che l'adozione anche da parte mia della pipa risalga proprio a quell'epoca" (452; I think that the adoption also on my part of smoking a pipe goes back precisely to that period [132]).

In a desperate attempt to remain connected to Micòl after she tells him to stay away, the protagonist seeks out Malnate, and the arguments of the past give way to a new compatibility: "Fra noi due, fuori di casa Finzi-Contini ... , ogni ragione di contrasto era destinata a cadere" (535; Between us, away from the Finzi-Contini house ... , all reasons for conflict were destined to fall away [166]). They even visit a local brothel together (though Malnate abstains) and continue the political conversations meant to lead the way to manly militancy for the passive, bookish, sheltered protagonist attempting to come to grips with a world gone mad.

Appropriately, it is Malnate who gives our hero the impetus to work his way out of his Oedipal impasse. One day, on the basis of a few elements, the narrator concludes, or rather fantasizes, that Malnate is Micòl's lover. This belated suspicion, experienced as certainty by the young man, finally leads him to accept that he must withdraw. As the make-believe universe of the Finzi-Continis begins to fade away, the protagonist gradually mends fences with his own family and particularly with his own father, who suddenly appears to him a wise old man. Returning home late one night, he sees his father in bed and is struck by how the whiteness of everything, from his silver hair to the white sheets, "si accordasse alla serenità sorprendente, straordinaria, all'inedita espressione di bontà piena di sagezza che gli illuminava gli occhi chiari" (560; was in keeping with the surprising and extraordinary serenity, the unexpectedly benign expression, full of wisdom that lit up his bright eyes [231]).

Although this remains unsaid in the novel, the point at which he re-embraces his own family coincides with his realization that he must find a "third way": not his father's way, desperately clinging to the post-Risorgimento idea of Jewish integration and acceptance in spite of all the evidence to the contrary; not the Finzi-Contini way, creating one's own artificial reality to avoid the narcissistic injury of exclusion and marginality; but Malnate's way, a Gentile's way. He relinquishes Micòl, takes his place next to Malnate, the one active male figure in his family romance gone awry, and accepts that the only way to be a Jew and a man at this time in history is to join the Resistance and to fight. Though this is never said explicitly, one reference to Bassani's anti-Fascist activity appears when the narrator compares the mornings spent working on his thesis, with Professor Ermanno in the next room, to his time in prison:

> Qualche anno più tardi, durante la primavera del '43, in carcere, le frasi che avrei scambiato con un ignoto vicino di cella ... sarebbero state di questo tipo: dette così, soprattutto per il bisogno di sentire la propria voce, di sentirsi vivi. (476)

> Some years later, during the spring of '43, in jail, the phrases that I would exchange with an unknown neighbouring cellmate ... would be of this kind: spoken in just this way, above all from the need to hear your own voice, to sense that you are alive. (153)

By refusing to bring the relationship between Micòl and Malnate into the "real world," so to speak – all we know is what the narrator knows to be true and, more importantly, what he imagines to be true – Bassani emphasizes that its importance exists at the level of fantasy, as the protagonist's way of working through the fears that have driven him into the narcissistic passivity of the garden of soon-to-be-horrors. The "maternal face" of Ferrara, as of the garden and of Micòl, is an illusion: the world is not made in our image and must be dealt with as such. It is Malnate who indicates the way out for our protagonist by pointing out that Ferrara is not only the stifling bourgeois cocoon that the protagonist and Alberto know, "una specie di tomba o di carcere" (457; a kind of tomb, or jail [137]), but also much more if one is prepared to cease looking in the mirror and engage with the larger world. While recognizing the special position of the Jews, Malnate points out that they are not the only persecuted minority in Fascist Italy and that Ferrara has an active group of anti-Fascists, not only from the working classes but also from the bourgeoisie, who are risking their lives by standing up for their principles; "solamente dei ciechi e dei sordi, oppure degli aridi, avrebbero potuto ignorarli o misconoscerli" (457–9; only the deaf and blind, or rather the sterile, could ignore or misconstrue them [138]).

Once the protagonist has reconciled with his father and decided to stay away permanently from the Finzi-Continis, everything around him begins to look different. He sees everything "imparzialmente" (indiscriminately), that is to say, no longer as a narcissistic projection of his internal world but as a separate reality:

Nelle sere immediatamente successive insistetti a vagabondare a casa lungo le strade della città, notando tutto, attirato imparzialmente da tutto: dai titoli dei giornali ... ; dalle fotografie dei film e degli avanspettacoli esposte di fianco agli ingressi dei cinema; dai conciliaboli degli ubriachi ... ; dalle targhe delle automobili ... ; dai tipi diversi delle persone. (570)

In the evenings that immediately followed, I kept on wandering haphazardly along the city streets, noticing everything, indiscriminately drawn by everything: by the headlines of newspapers ... by the film photographs and announcement posters stuck up beside the cinema entrances; by the chatting clusters of drunks ... by the number plates of the cars ... by the various kinds of people. (240)

At the end of the story, he rides his bicycle one night "senza sapere nemmeno io perché" (571; without knowing even myself why [241]), until he finally comes to the wall that he had refused to climb over at Micòl's invitation many years before. On his way, he sees many couples in sexual attitudes very clearly in the moonlight. He is no longer "imagining" sexuality but facing it:

C'era una magnifica luna piena: così chiara e luminosa nel cielo perfettamente sereno da rendere superfluo l'uso del fanale. ... Sdraiati nell'erba, mi si scoprivano sempre nuovi amanti. Alcuni si agitavano uno sull'altro mezzi nudi. Altri, già divisi, erano rimasti vicini, tenendosi per mano. Altri ancora, abbracciati ma immobili, sembrava che dormissero. Contai via via più di trenta coppie. ... Mi sentivo, ed ero, una specie di strano fantasma trascorrente: pieno di vita e morte insieme, di passione e di pietà. (571)

There was a magnificent full moon: so clear and bright, in the perfectly serene sky, as to render the front light unnecessary. ... I kept on passing new lovers stretched out on the grass. Some were half-naked, one moving on top of the other. Others, already disentangled, remained close, holding each other by the hand. Others still, embraced but motionless, seemed to be asleep. Along the way I counted more than thirty couples. ... I felt like, and was, a kind of strange, driven ghost: full both of life and death, of passion and compassion. (241)

The protagonist finally arrives at the wall surrounding the Finzi-Contini estate. The wall looks smaller, and he climbs over it easily. He sees the ladder that Micòl had been standing on the first time, and he also sees the dog, Jor. The dog recognizes him and turns back, no longer creating obstacles, no longer acting as guard dog. He is not sure why he has climbed over the wall or what he is looking for, but again he sees everything more clearly than ever: "Tutto appariva chiaro, netto, come in rilievo, in luce meglio che non di giorno" (574; Everything looked bright and clear-cut, as though in relief, even more so than by day [243]). He stops in front of the hut that the tennis crowd would use to change in and stares at it. Here the truth finally dawns on him, or so he imagines, as the hut suddenly becomes in his mind the secret refuge where Malnate and Micòl would carry on their nightly trysts, long after he was fast asleep:

> Ma sì – continuavo quietamente a ragionare in una sorta di svelto bisbiglio interno –. Ma certo. Lui veniva in giro con me soltanto per far tardi, e poi, dopo avermi per così dire infilato nel letto, via a pieni pedali da lei, che già stava aspettandolo in giardino … …
>
> Ero lucido, sereno, tranquillo. Tutti i conti tornavano. Come in un gioco di pazienza ogni pezzo si incastrava al millimetro. (574–5)

> But of course – I calmly pursued this line of reasoning in a rapid internal whisper. It has to be. He would go wandering around with me only till it was late enough, and then, having so to speak tucked me up in bed, he would be on his way, pedalling at full speed round to her, already waiting for him in the garden … …
>
> I was lucid, calm and clear. Everything added up. As in a jigsaw puzzle, every piece fitted exactly. (244)

As the scales fall from his eyes and he finally "sees" Micòl's sexuality, Jor the guard dog disappears altogether:

> Tesi l'orecchio. Silenzio assoluto.
> E Jor? Dove era finito, Jor?
> Mossi qualche passo in punta di piedi verso la *Hütte.*
> "Jor!", chiamai, forte. (575)

> I listened out. Absolute silence.
> And Jor? Where had he got to?
> I took several steps on tiptoe towards the *Hütte.*
> "Jor!" I called out, loudly. (244)

Instead, the town clock chimes – chronological time, history, has returned – which reminds him that it is time to go home, to cease tormenting his father with his late hours, and to make peace with himself once and for all: "Sul serio. Per sempre" (For good. For ever after). "'Che bel romanzo'" ("What a great novel"), he says to himself ironically, "crollando il capo come davanti a un bambino incorreggibile" (576; shaking [his] head as if at an incorrigible child [245]). The family romance has come to an end.

In the last two paragraphs of the epilogue, we are told that Malnate died on the Russian front and that he never quite understood the Finzi-Contini's passivity in the face of the encroaching storm. And the unproffered kiss – the sign of difference – returns as the only thing that might have projected Micòl into the future (and perhaps saved her from death at the hands of the Nazis):

> Certo è che quasi presaga della prossima fine, sua e di tutti i suoi, Micòl ripeteva di continuo anche a Malnate che a lei del *suo* futuro democratico e sociale non gliene importava un fico, che il futuro, in sé, lei lo abborriva, ad esso preferendo di gran lunga *"le vierge, le vivace et le bel aujourd'hui,"* e il passato, ancora di più, "il caro, il dolce, il *pio* passato."
>
> E siccome queste, lo so, non erano che parole, le solite parole ingannevoli e disperate che soltanto un vero bacio avrebbe potuto impedirle di proferire, di esse, appunto, e non di altre, sia suggellato qui quel poco che il cuore ha saputo ricordare. (578)

> [Almost as if] with some presentiment of her own and her family's approaching end, Micòl would continually repeat even to Malnate that she didn't care a fig for *his* democratic and Socialist future, that for the future, in itself, she only harboured an abhorrence, far preferring to it *"le vierge, le vivace et le bel aujourd'hui,"* and preferring the past even more, "the dear, the sweet, the sacred past."
>
> And since these, I know, were only words, the usual desperate, deceptive words that only a true kiss would have been able to stop her saying, with these words and just these, the little that the heart has been able to recall will here be sealed. (250)

"Le solite parole ingannevoli" (the usual deceptive words) that the protagonist's passivity forced Micòl to speak are placed here at the novel's end as a reminder of her success and his failure: as a good "mother," she sent her son out into the world. During a conversation about books (before the actual scene in which the narrator attempts to seduce Micòl by climbing onto her bed), Micòl brings up a Herman Melville story, *Bartleby*, referring to the film version starring Spencer Tracy: "Si era messa a esaltare in Bartleby l' 'inalienabile diritto di ogni essere umano alla non-collaborazione,' cioè alla libertà" (505; She had begun to laud in Bartleby "the inalienable right of every human being not to collaborate," that is, to liberty [180]). Clearly, she is urging him to go out and fight. He should have been a man to her woman and drawn her out, helped her to face her "exile" as well as his own, but he was unable to do so. Just as "survivor's guilt" has motivated his telling the Fadigati story, so too this guilt may well be at the origin of the Finzi-Contini saga.

Who is Micòl? She is many things and many people, of course, as suggested by the many allusions that surround her person – Eve, Beatrice, Emily Dickinson.[14] She is also his "other half," and in this sense we may be dealing here with Bassani's positive and original appropriation of Otto Weininger's idea that every human being has a male and a female principle. From this perspective, it is possible to equate his failure to kiss her with his failure to embrace his feminine side, from which he draws his strength as a Jewish male. She is the only incarnation of health in this diseased environment, which she escapes at length when she goes to Venice, while the protagonist and her brother are unable to leave, limiting themselves to discussing a visit that never materializes. In Venice, where the Jews once flourished, she presumably "lives" a normal life for a young woman of her age.

Bassani's depiction of Micòl also recalls something that Nietzsche himself famously wrote about women in *The Gay Science*:

> Someone took a youth to a sage and said: "Look, he is being corrupted by women." The sage shook his head and smiled. "It is men," said he, "that corrupt women and all the failings of women should be atoned by and improved in men. For it is man who creates for himself the image of woman and woman who forms herself according to the image. ... All of humanity is innocent of its existence; but women are doubly innocent."[15]

This theory may explain why Micòl says the opposite of what she means: she needs to speak in ciphers, to disguise her real thoughts. In this connection, another possible reading of Micòl may be drawn from the effects of being a Jew raised in a Christian culture. The "real" Micòl presumably has desires of her own and also has no qualms about getting her hands bloodied by slaughtering a chicken; but the protagonist's literary imagination has drawn him very far away from the Jewish tradition in which women are anything but passive, desexualized, ethereal creatures devoid of bodily consistency and function. In fact Micòl's relationship with her father recalls "a pattern of nostalgic representations in modern Jewish literature … of the Jewish father whose compromised power and masculinity is supplemented by a strong, loyal daughter."[16] Moreover, the fact that Bassani casts her as "Beatrice" while calling her Micòl (Micòl is the wife of David and daughter of Saul, who urges her husband to leave in order to avoid being killed by her father) may be a way of signalling an aspect of the identity confusion caused by being a Jew schooled in a literature rooted in the New Testament. A recent study of the Jewish imagination points out the radical difference between Old and New Testament female figures:

> Le Nouveau Testament ne comporte aucune image de puissante matriarche, alors que l'histoire juive en contient de nombreuses, révérées et admirées, pour leur force de caractère, leur sagacité, leur intelligence et leurs actions décisives. Que l'on songe à Esther, Judith, Deborah ou Miriam, sans compter les quatres images cardinales de mères: Rachel, Sarah, Léa et Rébecca qui procrée la nation d'Israël. Ces femmes sont dépeintes comme des meneuses d'hommes capables de prendre des décisions et de suppléer aux déficiences de leurs époux. Leurs conseils sont recherchés et leurs avis sont suivis. Dans la tradition comme dans la pratique quotidienne, la femme juive possède un domaine en propre, le foyer, où elle s'affirme résolument comme la maîtresse des choses et où elle jouit d'une autorité réelle. Les femmes ne s'interdisent pas d'évoquer leurs désirs charnels. Ainsi on ne s'étonne pas de lire ces paroles de Sarah, épouse agée du vieux Abraham, qui dans un rire s'écrie: "A présent que je suis usée, pourrais-je avoir de la volupté, alors que mon seigneur est vieux?"
>
> Si l'on compare les exemples de la féminité juive aux femmes de la tradition chrétienne, on ne peut s'empêcher de relever le contraste. Les mères fortes et investies d'autorité n'existent pas dans les textes du christianisme. Les exemples proposés ne concernent que des épouses dociles et muettes, ou alors des vierges saintes, passives devant leur martyre ou des pucelles agressives, comme c'est le cas pour Jeanne d'Arc. Alors que les patriarches de l'ancien Testament peuplaient le monde de leur progéniture, Jésus n'a connu que des épouses vierges, saintes et posthumes.[17]

The New Testament contains no image of a powerful matriarch, while Jewish history includes many, revered and admired for their strength of

> character, sagaciousness, intelligence, and decisive actions. One need only to think of Esther, Judith, Deborah, or Miriam, without mentioning the four cardinal images of motherhood: Rachel, Sarah, Leah, and Rebecca, who procreate the nation of Israel. These women are depicted as leaders in their own right, able to make decisions and to compensate for their husbands' deficiencies. Their advice is sought and their recommendations followed. In the tradition as in daily practice, the Jewish woman possesses her own domain, the home, where she resolutely asserts herself as the dominant figure and where she enjoys a real authority. Women don't shy away from evoking their carnal desires. Thus, it is not surprising to read the following words from the older Sarah, wife of Abraham, who laughingly exclaims: "Now that I am worn out, how can I still be voluptuous, when my master is old?"
>
> When comparing these examples of Jewish femininity to those of the Christian tradition, the contrast is manifest. Strong and empowered women don't exist in the Christian scriptures. They portray only silent and docile wives, or saintly virgins, passive in their martyrdom, or aggressive young maidens, like Joan of Arc. While the patriarchs of the Old Testament populated the world with their offspring, Jesus only encountered virginal, pious, and posthumous wives.

A confirmation of this reading may be found in the description of Micòl, which makes reference to the *sciaddài* she wore around her neck. The symbol of Judaism, "il piccolo disco d'oro dello *sciaddài*" (the little golden disc of the *shaddài*) is described as close to the bosom and peeking out every so often from her sweater – it is there and not there, "sul petto, balenando ogni tanto fuori dallo scollo della maglietta" (431; on her breast perhaps, every now and then leaping out from her T-shirt collar [113]). In the biblical tradition the word *sciaddài* is also synonymous with "breasts" (particularly in the Song of Songs) and with the the name of God, who is also there and not there. Micòl in Hebrew means "she who is like God." The godliness and spirituality of human sexuality is strongly upheld by the Jewish tradition, as opposed to the Christian tradition, which has demonized the body and sexual instincts.[18] In the Talmud,

> par le biais de la dualité sémantique du mot *Chadai* (les Seins et le Nom), la vision érotique des seins derrière le voile est commentée par une analyse du rapport fini-infini. Le verset introduit le mot *Chadai* à partir duquel il n'est plus possible de penser l'érotique sans la transcendance et réciproquement.[19]

> by means of the semantic duality of the word *Shaddài* [Bosom and Name], the erotic vision of the breasts behind the veil is commented on by an analysis of the finite-infinite connection. The verse introduces the word *Shaddài* such that it is no longer possible to imagine the erotic without transcendence and vice versa.

The *sciaddài* appears again towards the end, in the scene in which the protagonist has finally entered Micòl's room, where he will be definitively rebuffed by her. The connection of the *sciaddài* to sexuality seems even stronger here, as it is mentioned just as he is about to climb onto her bed. Moreover, the sentence is followed by an ellipsis, suggesting that something here is not being said. Again, the *sciaddài* is described as close to the bosom: "In cima al petto, la medaglietta d'oro dello *sciaddài* scintillava sopra la lana della maglia ...[20] (501; Above her breasts the little gold medallion of the *shaddai* glinted over the wool [of the sweater] ... [177]).

From this perspective, the Dante intertext becomes a sign not only of the protagonist's identification with the Italian literary tradition but also of how it leads him astray: he mistakenly identifies Micòl with the *donna angelicata* (angelified woman) and hence with Christian contempt for the body as opposed to Judaism's celebration of sexuality.[21] In fact, it is on this note of contempt for the body and its instincts that the next novel, *Dietro la porta*, opens.

5 *Dietro la porta*: The Body in History

Ah! Seigneur! Donnez-moi la force et le courage de contempler mon coeur et mon corps sans dégoût!

– Baudelaire, epigraph to first edition of *Dietro la porta* (1964)

The third novel of the first-person trilogy, *Dietro la porta (Behind the Door)*, confirms the centrality of sexuality and gender in relationship to religious and ethnic (or racial) identity as a major theme in the *Romanzo di Ferrara*. Unlike the first two stories, both set in the crucial years 1936–8, this last story takes place in 1929–30. A tale of adolescent male rivalry, it delves into an earlier and thus more formative period of the narrator's life – the passage from middle school to the *liceo* – and as such provides the basis for a deeper understanding of the previous novels. Issues of class, race, and gender intertwine in a coming-of-age narrative that unfolds on the backdrop of a nation moving towards the marginalization of its Jewish population. It culminates in a brutal initiation to the realities of life as experienced by an overprotected, spoilt, and rather defenceless young Jew at the hands his wilier Gentile classmates, including his supposed "best friend." However, this novel is not only a tale of betrayal but also a story of passivity and impotence, the story of the protagonist's inability to react to the abuse of his classmates well before the final insult; as such this story is linked to the issue of his passivity in both earlier novels, as well as to the broader issue of the passivity of Italians, Jewish and not, in the face of Fascist oppression.

The search for understanding here is more pronounced than in the earlier novels; in fact the first edition of the novel stated this clearly in the first paragraph with a sentence that was removed from subsequent editions: "Se adesso ne scrivo, dunque, è soltanto nella speranza di capire e di far capire" (If I write about it now, therefore, it is only in the hope of understanding and of making others understand). Also, until this point the narrator has spoken of himself only obliquely through a series of mirrors that he has looked into: in the first case, this mirror is Fadigati; in the second, it is the different members of the Finzi-Contini family. Here his mirrors are two of his classmates, but he tells his story in a more direct and probing way, focusing on himself from the very beginning and alternating the account of events with his own analysis of his reactions at the time.

As in the earlier novels, Bassani here has woven a tale that is both realistic and symbolic. At one level, it tells the story summarized briefly in the previous paragraphs; at another level, it represents an internal conflict that is staged in realistic terms and that lies at the root of all the protagonist's misadventures in the novels of the first-person trilogy. In this reading of the novel, his antagonists are actually two doppelgängers, doubles of the narrator, in the persons of his two classmates Luciano Pulga and Carlo Cattolica. Luciano Pulga, though not a Jew, incarnates all the characteristics attributed by anti-Semitic propaganda to the Jew and internalized by the young protagonist, while Carlo Cattolica, as his name clearly indicates, functions as the protagonist's ego-ideal. They represent the two terms or poles of the identity conflict that is at the root of the narrator's problems.[1]

What is obviously missing here is the possibility of a positive male Jewish identification, and so the protagonist is doomed from the start since he must either identify with the negatively connoted ersatz Jew or the Catholic: conversion or self-hatred are the only two choices open to this unfortunate adolescent, given the models available. The title of the novel clearly refers to the Freudian primal scene invoked by the author in relation to the climax of the story, in which the young protagonist, hiding behind a closed door, hears his former best friend Pulga not only cast serious doubts on his virility but also speak of his mother in vulgar, explictly sexual terms in the presence of Cattolica and his cohorts. Both slurs are overtly linked to the Jewishness of the protagonist and his mother. The Oedipal configuration of the betrayal and insult, and the setting of the events in 1929 when Bassani would have been thirteen years old, the age at which a Jewish male is thought to become a "man," all point to the fact that this is a story of a failed attempt to accede to classic heterosexual manhood.

One might conclude that since the events begin in October 1929, well before the Fascist government was even thinking of passing the Race Laws, the story is in fact independent of events leading up to the

Holocaust. Such a conclusion is flawed because the adult narrator's account of his experiences always represents a reconstruction coloured by subsequent events, thus making the Holocaust, if it is not named, the elephant in the room. Moreover, 1929 was indeed an important year for the Fascist government, as well as for the Jews of Italy, since Mussolini made peace that year with the pope by signing the famous Lateran Pacts, regulating the relations between Italy and the Holy See. The most important part of these agreements was the Concordat. While the original formation of the nation rested on the defeat of the papal army and resulted in the pope's excommunication of the king, the government, and Parliament, the Concordat opened with the statement that the Catholic religion was to be the official and "sola religione dello stato" (exclusive religion of the state). The integration of the Jews had been favoured by the secular character of the Italian nation at the moment of its birth; Italy's rejection of this secular character for a religion of state can be said in retrospect to have marked the beginning of the official marginalization of the Jews.[2]

Coined by the press of the time, the term used to refer to the rift between the pope and the government was the papal "wound," while the Concordat was said to have "healed" this wound. The term is still in use today. A recent book on the subject, which points out that Italians experienced Catholicism as a form of national identity, is titled *La ferita sanata* (*The healing of the wound*).[3] Significantly, the first paragraph of *Dietro la porta* opens precisely with a reference to a wound inflicted upon the narrator at this time:

> Sono stato molte volte infelice, nella mia vita, da bambino, da ragazzo, da giovane, da uomo fatto; molte volte, se ci ripenso, ho toccato quel che si dice il fondo della disperazione. Ricordo tuttavia pochi periodi più neri, per me, dei mesi di scuola fra l'ottobre del 1929 e il giugno del '30, quando facevo la prima liceo. Gli anni trascorsi da allora non sono in fondo serviti a niente: non sono riusciti a medicare un dolore che è rimasto là come una ferita segreta, sanguinante in segreto. Guarirne? Liberarmene? Non so se sarà mai possibile. (581)

> I have been unhappy many times in my life, as a child, as a youth, as a young man, as an adult; many times, if I think back, I have touched what are called the depths of despair. And yet I remember few periods darker, for me, than the months of school between October of 1929 and June of 1930, my first year of *liceo*. The years that have passed since then have not

helped at all: they have not managed to heal a sorrow that has remained there like a secret wound, bleeding in secret. Get over it? Free myself of it? I don't know if it will ever be possible.

Though the narrator is clearly referring not to the Concordat but to a more personal wound, the author just as clearly links the gravity of this wound to the social and political climate of those specific years, to the wound inflicted upon the Jewish community when Catholicism became the official religion of state. At the same time, the narrator is characterized even more clearly than before by his *ressentiment*, his "resentment," as he states very emphatically that he is as traumatized now as he was when the events first took place some thirty-five or so years earlier. Bassani in fact perceived the Concordat as an affront to the Jews. In a speech given in 1961 he cites the Albertine Statute of 1848, the Piedmontese monarchy's constitution, which also declared the Catholic religion to be the official religion of state:

> La comunità israelitica di Ferrara, nel cui seno sono nato e cresciuto, era una piccola città dentro la città: così conformista e normale, anche essa, da fornire all'amministrazione comunale, per dodici lunghi anni, nientemeno che il podestà. È possible essere più conformisti, più normali, più fedeli? Eravamo così conformisti, così normali, così beatamente normali, da sentirci allargare il petto di fierezza e di commozione se le maggiori autorità cittadine accettavano di intervenire alla solenne celebrazione della ricorrenza dello Statuto che si teneva ogni anno nella sinagoga di rito italiano (la celebrazione di quello Statuto albertino, badate bene, che dichiarava religione dello Stato la religione cattolica, relegando le altre confessioni al rango di "tollerate"). Era, ogni anno, uno spettacolo grottesco: funebre, a ripensarci adesso, dopo Auschwitz e Buchenwald.[4]

> The Jewish community of Ferrara, where I was born and raised, was a small city within the city: so conformist and normal, it too, that for twelve long years it even provided the administration of the town with the mayor. Is it possible to be more conformist, more normal, more faithful? We were so conformist, so normal, so blissfully normal, that we felt our chests swell with pride and emotion if the higher city authorities accepted to participate in the solemn celebration of the anniversary of the "Statuto" that took place every year in the Italian synagogue (the celebration of that same Statuto albertino – take note – which declared the Catholic religion as religion of state, relegating all other confessions to the rank of "tolerated").

> It was, every year, a grotesque spectacle: thinking back, after Auschwitz and Buchenwald, I would even say funereal.

The events recalled in this novel begin just after the fateful summer marked by the failure in mathematics and his first face-to-face encounter with Micòl Finzi-Contini, during which he refused her invitation to climb over the wall into her garden. The sexual fears and fantasies alluded to in the description of that missed opportunity suggest the same reluctance to embrace the unknown that we find here in his reaction to the move from middle school to the *liceo*. This passage into the next phase of his life is described as a very difficult one for him, generating no excitement or anticipation but only fear and resentment. He is leaving a protective cocoon for a more impersonal and competitive environment that he does not feel prepared to confront. In the following passage the lexical choices clearly indicate that the anxiety plaguing the protagonist has atavistic roots and has perhaps been brought to the surface not only by the impending changes in his life but also by the recent legislation. With little effort it is possible to read the passage as the thinly veiled protest of a particularly insecure Jew reluctant to leave the ghetto, unsure of what awaits him in the broader world:

> Fin dai primi giorni mi ero sentito spaesato, profondamente a disagio. Non mi piaceva l'aula dove ci avevano messi, posta al termine di un tetro corridoio lontano da quello, allegro e familiare. ... Non mi piacevano i nuovi insegnanti, dai modi distaccati e ironici che scoraggiavano ogni confidenza, ogni considerazione di carattere personale. ... Non mi piacevano i nuovi compagni provenienti dalla quinta A ai quali noi della B eravamo stati aggiunti, diversissimi da noi, mi pareva, forse più bravi, più belli, appartenenti a famiglie forse migliori delle nostre: estranei, insomma, irrimediabilmente. E non riuscivo né a comprendere né a giustificare a questo proposito il comportamento di molti dei *nostri*, che, a differenza di me, avevano subito cercato di fare comunella con *loro*, ripagati, lo vedevo costernato, di uguale simpatia, di pari disinvolta arrendevolezza. ... La mia fedeltà, ... la mia assurda fedeltà avrebbe preteso che una linea di demarcazione invisibile continuasse a separare anche al liceo i superstiti delle due vecchie quinte, di modo che noi della B fossimo protetti e garantiti per sempre da ogni tradimento, da ogni contaminazione. (581–2)

> I felt profoundly ill at ease from the very beginning, completely lost. I didn't like the classroom to which we had been assigned, at the end of a

> grim corridor, far from the gay, familiar one. ... I didn't like the new teachers, with their ironic, detached manner, which discouraged any familiarity, any personal consideration. ... I didn't like my new classmates, who came from the A section of the fifth year of the middle school, to which we of the B section had been joined. They were different from us, it seemed to me – brighter perhaps, better-looking, generally from better families than ours: irreducibly alien, in other words. And I couldn't understand or justify, on this account, the behaviour of many of *us*, who, unlike me, had immediately tried to make friends with *them*, rewarded – as I saw in consternation – with the same friendliness and with similarly casual acceptance. ... My loyalty, ... my absurd loyalty demanded that an invisible line of demarcation continue to separate, even in the *liceo*, the survivors of the two old fifth sections, so that we from B would be protected and guaranteed forever against all betrayal, all contamination.

The narrator's anxiety is aggravated by the fact that he is about to lose his best friend, Otello Forti, who is leaving Ferrara to continue his schooling away from home. Otello Forti is described in the very physical terms in which the protagonist experienced him, almost as a comforting maternal presence rather than as a peer or rival. Deprived of "la presenza massiccia, un po' opaca, del suo corpo ... avevo provato il dolore persistente, l'irrimediabile senso di vuoto dei vedovi" (582–3; the massive, somewhat opaque presence of his body, so much bigger and heavier than mine ... I had felt the persistent grief, the irreparable sense of emptiness that widowers feel). His pride is also hurt because of his recent failure in mathematics. When the time comes to scramble for the best seats in the class, the protagonist remains aloof from the manly competition between the two groups (A and B, referred to again as "us" and "them"), significantly choosing to remain on the threshold of the classroom and to sit with the girls in the last row. The reference to this positioning is repeated a few pages later: "No, no, meglio la solitudine del posto che avevo scelto, in fondo alla fila delle donne" (587; No, no, better the solitude of the place I had chosen, at the end of the girls' row).

His attitude to the others is one of snobbish contempt and haughtiness, which covers up a profound sense of insecurity. He insists on the one card he feels he can play in the new climate of rivalry – class superiority – and looks down upon his classmates, whose last names clearly evoke "famiglie piccolo-borghesi di merciai, di salumieri, di legatori di libri, di impiegati del Comune, di mediatori di piazza, eccetera" (584–5; petty bourgeois families of tradesmen, grocers, bookbinders, town clerks, cattle dealers, and so on).

His teacher, however, does not accept his choice of seating, since in his previous school he was one of the best students, and forces him to sit closer to the front, next to the undisputed golden boy of the classroom, Carlo Cattolica, his logical deskmate from the perspective of academic achievement. Cattolica's name alone makes it very explicit what he comes to represent in the fantasies of our protagonist – the image of perfect integration, the ego-ideal. He sees him again in his mind, after so many years: "Rivedo della faccia di Cattolica il profilo netto, esatto, inciso minutamente alla mia destra come quello di una medaglia" (593; I can still see the sharp profile of Cattolica's face on my right, engraved with the same exquisite precision as a profile on a medallion). It is interesting that, as in the case of the Finzi-Continis before he actually comes to know them, he has already had occasion to be fascinated by Cattolica, by the self-assurance and determination with which he once saw him moving through a crowd. At first their relations are cool but cordial, with Cattolica appearing to maintain an intimidating distance from his closest rival for scholastic merit but without betraying any open hostility. However, when the members of the A group close ranks to help each other during class exams with Cattolica at their head, totally excluding the young Jew, all pretense of courtesy falls away: "E caduta la maschera, sconvolto dall'agitazione faziosa, l'irreprensibile viso di Cattolica mi si mostrava in tutta la sua odiosa realtà. Nudo finalmente. Eppure, nonostante che lo esecrassi, lo ammiravo e lo invidiavo" (595). (And once the mask had fallen, Cattolica's irreproachable face, disfigured by factional agitation, was visible to me in all its hateful reality. Naked, at last. And yet, though I loathed him, I admired and envied him.)

Again, the terms used to describe their relations – from "schiere rivali *ab antiquo*" (the two opposing squads *ab antiquo*) to the description of the outward cordiality masking hatred and contempt – can easily be transposed to descriptions of the relations between Jews and Gentiles. What the protagonist admired so much in Cattolica was not, he tells us, his academic prowess as much as everything else, every way in which he felt inferior to him: Cattolica's height, his disdain for sport (suggesting sexual maturity without the need to sublimate), his firm aspiration to a career as a surgeon, his seeming self-sufficiency, and his possession of an official girlfriend, signified by the ring on his finger. The protagonist, in contrast, is stocky, needy, unsure of what he wants to study later on, and has no experience at all with the opposite sex: "Forse per diventare uomini, o almeno per acquistare quel minimo di sicurezza in sé stessi indispensabile a passare per tali, un anello così andava bene, poteva aiutare molto" (596–7; Perhaps to become a man, or at least to gain that minimum self-confidence indispensable to passing for a man, such a ring was right, it could be a great help).

Clearly, the protagonist is concerned with manhood and feels very confused about what it entails, what signals precisely that it has been achieved. Cattolica, an object of both hatred and admiration, represents perfect manhood incarnate in his eyes. This belief is emphasized at the end of this chapter when the protagonist sees Cattolica leaving home one evening in the company of the two classmates who act as his henchmen, Boldini and Grassi, but heading in a different direction from them. As if mesmerized by the sudden appearance of his idol, the protagonist is powerless to stop himself from following him, driven by the compulsion to know where he is going. The sudden realization that Cattolica is heading to the home of his girlfriend is accompanied by a reaction that clearly indicates a struggle with Oedipal issues: "Ma l'idea che lui, dopo una operosa giornata di studio … potesse concedersi anche il premio del bacio serale alla fidanzata, mi era riuscita improvvisamente intollerabile" (598; But the idea that, after a hard day's work studying … he could also grant himself the reward of the evening kiss from his girlfriend suddenly seemed to me intolerable).

The reappearance of Otello in the next chapter confirms that the protagonist is in danger of regressing since he hopes to reconnect with his old friend in order to escape his emotional confusion. Otello is in town from boarding school, having been sent there as a result of his failure in public school, but he is no longer the same. He has grown up both physically and emotionally – in a word, he has left home – and tells the protagonist that he has little patience for his still childish ways: "La sventura aveva fatto di lui un uomo; e un uomo deve badare al sodo" (600; Adversity had made a man of him; and a man has to stick to hard facts).

After the rift with Otello, we hear about an encounter with Cattolica outside the confines of the school. Here the narrator invokes a faulty memory as to when it took place – "Non potrei affermar con sicurezza" (602; I couldn't say with certainty) – when it is obvious that he remembers it very well (the same technique is used in *Gli occhiali d'oro* when describing the first encounter with Fadigati). The setting, symbolically, is a church, which the protagonist enters for the first time without explaining why but telling us that previously he had always stayed outside of this church on the threshold. He is immediately drawn to a group of statues he had seen once before in another church, in the company of his Catholic aunt Malvina. The statues depict the immediate aftermath of the death of Christ, foreshadowing his own eventual betrayal at the hands of his Gentile classmates and organized by his idol, Cattolica. In fact, just as he is about to leave, he catches sight of Cattolica nearby in prayer – "offrendo a me che lo osservavo lo stesso profilo minuziosamente inciso, indecifrabile, che mi offriva ogni giorno a scuola" (offering to me who observed him the same finely chiseled, inscrutable profile he turned to me every day in school) – and is assailed by painful longings: "Perché non eravamo amici? – mi chiedevo torturato –. Perché non *potevamo* diventare amici?" (604). (Why weren't we friends? I asked myself in torment. Why *couldn't* we become friends?) In his mind, he dismisses lack of intelligence as well as religious difference as possible reasons. When Cattolica sees him and expresses surprise at his presence in the church, the protagonist immediately tries to impress him with his own Catholic credentials, mentioning his aunt Malvina and the childhood visits to another church in her company. This conversation, their first alone, "mi emozionava, stimolava la mia parlantina, il mio bisogno di confidenza" (605; excited me, stimulated my talkativeness, my need for intimacy), he tells us. Cattolica, however, uses the opportunity to humiliate him by asking a series of impertinent, condescending questions about Jewish religious beliefs and customs, questions designed to point out their inferiority to Catholic dogma and rituals. Yet even this is interpreted as a sign of goodwill: "E io a rispondergli punto per punto più che di buon grado, sentendo a un tratto dentro di me che la sua curiosità generica, volgare, per non dire insolente, anziché offendermi mi piaceva, mi liberava" (605; And I answered him, point by point, more than willingly, and feeling suddenly that his generic, vulgar, not to say insolent curiosity, instead of offending me, pleased me and liberated me). Finally, in an awkward attempt to lay the groundwork for a friendship, the protagonist points out that the surname Cattolica, as a place name, indicates that Cattolica may himself have Jewish ancestry. The suggestion is immediately rejected by Cattolica, who becomes defensive and answers in such a way as to end any possibility of dialogue. The protagonist has dared to put himself on the same footing as his classmate, only to be summarily put in his place. With much irony, the narrator recalls how he nonetheless took advantage of this episode to appear to be basking in Cattolica's friendship in the eyes of the other students as they approached their school, making sure that they walked side by side "come due buoni e affezionati amici" (606; like two close, affectionate friends).

What takes place next has been carefully anticipated by the earlier sequence of events: the move to the *liceo*, the feeling of exclusion, the estrangement from Otello, the failed attempt at *rapprochement* with Cattolica. The external props of the protagonist's ego and sense of belonging having been withdrawn; he is left to fall back on his own internal resources: it is at this moment of extreme vulnerability that a new boy appears. He turns up suddenly, seemingly out of nowhere, on the threshold of the classroom, occupying the same position as the protagonist on the first day of school and appearing to feel very much the same way as he did: self-conscious and disoriented. The new boy arrives in an environment perceived as hostile, is anxious to find his "place," approaches someone and is rejected, only to take refuge among the girls:

> Chi era? Un nuovo compagno evidentemente, anche se non portava sotto il braccio un solo libro. Comunque, mentre sostava incerto poco di qua dalla soglia a cercarsi con lo sguardo azzurrino, d'un azzurro intenso e freddo da ghiacciaio d'alta montagna, un posto disponibile, fui subito respinto dal suo fisico di piccolo trampoliere secco di gamba e adunco di naso, e al tempo stesso comosso dalla sua ansia di trovarsi un nido. Lo guardavo. … Esile, con un magro pomo d'adamo che gli tremava mezzo strozzato poco più su del colletto della camicia bianca, ricominciò a cercare in giro con gli occhi, per finire, poi, in fondo alla fila delle donne, proprio nel banco rimasto vuoto dove da principio avevo voluto esiliarmi io. … Piccole gocce di sudore gli imperlavano la pelle lungo l'orlo sinuoso, un po' rientrante, del labbro superiore. E questo particolare delle goccioline di sudore (l'avevo notato in un lampo, quando lui, quasi sfiorandomi, mi era passato vicino), mi aveva dato di nuovo un vago senso di ribrezzo. (607–8)

> Who was he? A new classmate, obviously, even if he had no books under his arm. Anyway, as he stood hesitantly just inside the door seeking an empty place with his bluish gaze, the intense, cold blue of an Alpine glacier, I was immediately repelled by his physique, like a little wading bird's, with his thin legs, his beaklike nose, and at the same time I was moved by his anxiety to find a nest. I [watched] him. … Thin, with a scrawny Adam's apple, which trembled, half-choked just above the collar of his white shirt, he began looking around again, his gaze finally settling at the back of the

> girls' row, at the very desk, now vacant, where at first I had wished to exile myself. ... Little drops of sweat beaded his skin above the sinuous, slightly receding edge of his upper lip. And this detail, the little drops of sweat (I noticed it in a flash when he passed by, almost grazing me), again gave me a vague feeling of revulsion.

This one paragraph encapsulates the entire experience of the protagonist in the first three chapters of the novel, suggesting that we are in the presence of a doppelgänger. Moreover, the cold gaze, the hook nose, and the anxious disposition – all characteristics attributed to Jews in the anti-Semitic literature of the period[5] – confirm he is not just the embodiment of the protagonist's general insecurities but the embodiment of the protagonist's internal image of himself as a Jew, the incarnation of the monster of Jewish self-hatred. He is described as physically small and fragile, notwithstanding the protagonist's own stocky build (*tarchiato*) and athletic constitution. His unpleasant surname (Pulga, suggesting the Italian *pulce* [flea]), the mixture of repulsion and attraction he elicits in the protagonist, the ways in which the protagonist will later attempt to break free of him all point to Pulga as the internal obstacle the protagonist must overcome as he struggles with his place in the world as a Jew, with his budding sexuality, and with his need to "become a man" in a hostile social environment. However, in spite of the repulsion the narrator claims to have felt, he will also be drawn to Pulga as if attracted by a magnetic force beyond his control (the same is true of his reactions to Cattolica, as when he is powerless to stop himself from following him). This attraction first manifests itself when the class laughs at the new student because he has no school supplies with which to do his work. The protagonist comes to his rescue without being asked, "non soltanto offrendo il foglio protocollo indispensabile perché anche a lui fosse concesso di fare il compito in classe, ma aderendo immediatamente all'invito di Guzzo a trasferirmi là, nell'ultimo banco, per dar modo al 'signor Pulga Luciano' di servirsi del mio dizionario" (608; not only offering him the regulation paper necessary so that he too be allowed to do his written work but also accepting willingly Guzzo's invitation to move there, to the last desk, so that 'Signor Pulga, Luciano' could use my dictionary).

Once seated next to Pulga, the protagonist experiences a "sensazione curiosa che mi accompagnò durante tutta quella prima ora e mezzo trascorsa a fianco a fianco con lui" (608; curious sensation that remained with me all through that first hour and a half spent side by side with him). The realization that Pulga is copying his work word for word – clearly a sign of his function as a double – fills him with "un sentimento complesso e invischiante, misto di piacere e di ripugnanza" (609; a complex, entangling sentiment, mixed with pleasure and repugnance) against which, the narrator tells us, he is helpless to defend himself.

We are also told that Pulga has "una chiacchiera scorrevole e suasiva, molto bolognese, da viaggiatore di commercio" (608; a glib, persuasive manner of speaking, very Bolognese, like a travelling salesman's), which immediately evokes the figure of the wandering Jew and the association of the eastern European Jew with the itinerant peddlar.[6] Moreover, we find out later that his father is a "medico condotto" (village doctor), another itinerant figure (the protagonist's father is also a doctor), and the family has therefore moved around considerably, so that Pulga has been to many different schools, always a stranger. Now they are living temporarily in a third-class inn of ill repute on the outskirts of town. Pulga interrogates his new friend and discovers that although their fathers share a profession, the protagonist's life is a far more comfortable one: "Ed era chiaro che mi invidiava, senza dubbio, invidiava l'ordine, la sicurezza economica, la borghese stabilità della mia famiglia, ma che nello stesso tempo un po' mi disprezzava" (612; And it was obvious that he envied me, no doubt, he envied the order, the economic security, the middle class stability of my family, but at the same time he also felt some contempt for me).

Pulga accompanies the protagonist home after school and suggests that he ask the teacher to allow him to abandon Cattolica as a deskmate and to move permanently to the seat next to him; but the young protagonist hesitates. Pulga points out that although Cattolica is undoubtedly very smart, there is nothing likeable about him. While the protagonist concedes that he and Cattolica are not exactly the best of friends, and that he has no one with whom to do his homework after school, he is not quite ready to give in, still hanging on to the idea of a connection with the golden boy of the class: "Con Cattolica non è che andassi granché d'accordo. Ma stavamo assieme da più di due mesi, ormai e piantarlo adesso ... Dopo tutto eravamo un tandem abbastanza affiatato" (613). (Not that Cattolica and I got along so well. Still, we had been together for more than two months now, and to drop him at this point ... After all, we were a pretty well-matched pair.)

Pulga, however, is persistent and when they reach the home of the protagonist, he shows no sign of wanting to leave and actually forces his way into the building. The protagonist not only does not resist but is led almost mechanically to invite him into his world, again as if driven by a superior force: "Le labbra mi si mossero da sole. Dissi: 'Vuoi tornare a fare i compiti con me, oggi?'" (614; My lips moved by themselves. I said: "Do you want to come back to do homework with me, today?").

The following chapter begins with a very telling sentence: "Mia madre fu ben felice che io avessi trovato un nuovo amico" (615; My mother was very happy that I had found a new friend). This is the first time in this trilogy of novels that we will get a real glimpse of the protagonist's relationship with his mother. When Otello Forti was his best friend, they always studied after school at Otello's home, and his own mother, he tells us, was jealous (615; gelosa). Now, happy that her son has finally found Pulga with whom to study at home, "i suoi occhi marroni lo accarezzavano con espressione materna" (615; her brown eyes caressed him with a maternal expression). She also shows great interest in the plight of his family, and as a result Pulga's father, taking advantage of the fact that they are both doctors, pays a visit to the protagonist's father. However, Dr Pulga immediately discredits himself by gossiping and speaking ill of his Bologna associates, thus foreshadowing the perfidious behaviour of his son.

In spite of this, and in spite of his continuing feeling of repulsion towards Pulga, the narrator admits that his own sense of superiority vis-à-vis the newcomer allowed him to replicate Cattolica's attitude towards others: "Ma per il resto debbo confessare che, specie da principio, la sua umiltà di profugo, la sua totale sottomissione di inferiore e di protetto, mi davano un senso di appagamento quasi inebriante" (618; But otherwise I must confess that, especially at the beginning, his refugee humility, his total submission as an inferior and a protégé, gave me an almost intoxicating satisfaction). The use of the term *profugo* meaning "refugee" in this context is particularly striking since it again associates Pulga with the eastern European Jews who fled the pogroms in their Russian and Polish villages at the end of the nineteenth century and who became symbols of the wandering Jew, Ahasuerus. Many of their more integrated or assimilated brethren in Germany and Western Europe in general viewed them as inferior and as a source of embarrassment. In *Gli occhiali d'oro* the narrator describes very vividly his fear that he and the other Italians who had just been stripped of their civil rights would be returned to this supressed – and repugnant – aspect of their heritage:

> E mentre Nino pieno di disagio taceva, io sentivo nascere dentro me stesso con indicibile ripugnanza l'antico, atavico odio dell'ebreo nei confronti di tutto ciò che fosse cristiano, cattolico, insomma *goi. Goi, goìm*: che vergogna, che umiliazione, che ribrezzo, a esprimersi così! Eppure ci riuscivo già – mi dicevo – : diventato simile a un qualsiasi ebreo dell'Europa orientale che non fosse mai vissuto fuori dal proprio ghetto. (291)

> And while Nino remained in a most uneasy silence, I felt in me, with inexpressible repugnance, the first inklings of the Jew's ancient, atavistic hatred for everything that was Christian and Catholic, in a word "goyish." *Goy, goyim*: what a sense of shame, what a humiliation, what [disgust, to be expressing myself like this]: and yet I had already managed this – I told myself – become exactly like any Jew whatsoever from eastern Europe who had never lived outside his own ghetto. (96)

Pulga, in keeping with this portrait of the ghetto or shtetl Jew as a hater of Christians, incites the protagonist to give in to his hatred of Cattolica by flattering his classmate and allowing him to feel superior intellectually, socially, and culturally: "Sicuro di farmi piacere, tutte le occasioni gli tornavano buone per parlare male di Cattolica" (620; Certain that he would be pleasing me, he used every possible opportunity to bad-mouth Cattolica). However, Pulga is wily enough to refrain from having recourse to racial stereotypes that might offend the protagonist and stops short of reminding him of "le virtù matematiche della razza" (621; the mathematical virtues of the race). The young Jew is not yet ready to acknowledge such sentiments: "Finsi comunque di non capire, e lasciai cadere il discorso" (622; In any event, I pretended not to understand, and let the subject drop). But Pulga's persistent attempts to ingratiate himself finally pay off. When Pulga is late one afternoon for their study session, the anxiety of the young protagonist mounts gradually as he waits at the window, until it reaches a feverish pitch and the narrator recognizes that Pulga had become indispensable to him: "Ed ecco, lì sotto, mentre il cuore, folle di battiti precipitati – folle di una gioia mista come al solito di contrarietà –, mi balzava duramente in gola, riconobbi a un tratto Luciano, proprio lui, che in quel preciso istante infilava rapido il portone" (622–3; And there below, my heart beating madly – mad with a joy mixed, as usual, with irritation – and leaping up to my throat, I suddenly recognized Luciano, yes him, at that precise moment, coming in rapidly through the front door).

In the next chapter things begin to get ugly. The friendship is still based on Pulga's willingness to flatter, entertain, and thus draw in the young protagonist, who continues to let his defences down, until one evening he urges Pulga to spend the night due to a heavy rainstorm. Pulga refuses but complains about how cold and humid his own home is. Instead of changing the subject, the protagonist casually asks if this is because they do not have central heating. Almost immediately he realizes he has gone too far: "Sentii a un tratto che stavamo scivolando verso una intimità dalla quale fino allora ci eravamo tenuti lontani, una intimità che *dovevo* a ogni costo rifiutare" (625–6; Suddenly I felt that we were slipping towards an intimacy that, until then, we had kept well away from: an intimacy I *had* to refuse at all costs).

It is the protagonist who makes the advances here, if we may term them as such, both by suggesting Pulga spend the night and by accepting to enter Pulga's private space with the question about central heating. The slippery slope that he senses they are on leads to a series of other verbal intimacies. At first Pulga refers to his own father as a "testardo di un cretino" (626; stubborn idiot) whose stubbornness had caused all attempts at improving the heating situation to fail. The insult to the father is shocking to the young Jew and leads to further and more grave accusations in which Pulga describes his father as avaricious and violent, and his mother as masochistic: "Cosa credi, che siano soltanto gli uomini a fare schifo? Anche le donne, sta' tranquillo, anche le donne!" (627). (What do you think, that only men are disgusting? Women too, don't worry, women too!)

From here Pulga steers the conversation to the Albergo Tripoli, the hotel of ill repute where he and his family stayed when they first arrived in Ferrara, describing in great detail the sexual activities that took place there. To the protagonist's surprise, he is told that they involved not only prostitutes and promiscuous young women but also the occasional "'gallinona' di quarant'anni, madre, forse già nonna, e trasudante peccato da tutti i pori della faccia di cuoio. Erano 'consorti' di ingegneri, di avvocati, di dottori: ... Dame della migliore società, insomma, che come niente, la sera stessa, sarebbero state capaci di mostrarsi dall'alto del loro palco del Teatro Comunale" (627). ("old hen" of forty: a mother, perhaps already a grandmother, exuding sin from every pore of her leathery face. They were the "consorts" of engineers, lawyers, doctors ... Ladies of the best society, in other words, who, like nothing, would show up that same evening in their boxes at the Teatro Comunale.) At this crucial point the protagonist's mother interrupts by coming into the room to urge Pulga to stay for dinner so as to avoid the rain. The protagonist watches their conversation from a distance: "Seguivo i movimenti delle loro labbra, ma la maggior parte delle parole non le capivo, non le udivo" (628; I followed the movements of their lips, but most of their words I didn't understand, I didn't hear). If Pulga is his double, then this last comment suggests that what is going on here has to do with the protagonist's struggle to keep at bay his own increasing awareness of his mother as a sexual being.

As the story unfolds, an increasing number of the traits attributed to the Jews by the culture of anti-Semitism come to flesh out the portrait of Pulga: "Appariva più pallido del solito, con gli scuri occhi blu profondamente cerchiati d'ombra nel piccolo viso ossuto, e con sopra, in luce, la radice del naso ricurvo e la fronte a bauletto" (625; He appeared paler than usual: with his dark blue eyes surrounded by deep shadows in his small, bony face, and above, in the light, the base of his nose crooked and his forehead protruding). Elsewhere, the narrator speaks of "le sue orecchie grandi, pallide e trasparenti come membrane, un po' da vecchio" (688; his big ears, pale and transparent as membranes, a bit like an old man's). In the remaining chapters, in addition to the devious, cunning personality, the parasitic, leech-like neediness, the hook nose, the large ears, the sallow complexion, the premature aging, the hollow eyes, the overenthusiastic and frequent masturbation, and the obsession with sex and pornographic images, the association of Jews with beasts and disease will emerge.[7] The only exception in this portrait is his colouring: Jews were thought of as swarthy, whereas Pulga is described as blonde and blue-eyed. These are, however, traits that he shares with the protagonist, confirming his role as the "eastern Jew" in the protagonist, as the shadow that cannot be expunged.

If Pulga represents the protagonist's emerging sexual awareness, it is an awareness polluted by the images of sordid voraciousness that formed part of the repertoire of anti-Semitic stereotypes. The protagonist cannot separate his own burgeoning instincts from these repugnant associations since the two are inextricably intertwined in his mind. As a result, he has tried to sublimate them through sport (which Cattolica holds in contempt) and through intellectual pursuits. But the urges are too strong and are now breaking through, with Pulga as the ever-present agent of his awakening and the Albergo Tripoli, functioning as a brothel at this point, as its site: "Certe notti nella stanza adiacente si succedevano una dopo l'altra perfino cinque coppie" (629; On some nights, in the adjacent room, as many as five couples followed one after the other), according to Pulga, who spent much of the night peering through a keyhole at their activities. Here again, the protagonist's fantasies, breaking into consciousness, are being staged:

> Una volta, per esempio – seguitò –, di sopra alla spalliera del letto aveva veduto sporgere una schiena. Era di una donna, e andava su e giù,"*hop-là, hop-là*," né più né meno che se stesse seduta sulla groppa di un cavallo al trotto. Un'altra volta i due passeggiavano in giro per la stanza nudi, di modo che venendo ogni tanto a tiro del buco della serratura gli mostravano "il davanti e il didietro." Un'altra volta ancora una coppia, invece che sul letto, aveva preferito venire a far l'amore per terra, proprio vicino alla porta. E se quella volta là, sebbene torcesse disperatamente l'occhio in basso, lui non era riuscito a vedere un fico secco, in compenso aveva potuto *ascoltare*: il che forse era stato anche meglio. (629–30)

> Once, for example, he went on, he had seen a back rising above the headboard. It belonged to a woman, and it went up and down, "pa-pum, pa-pum" no more and no less than if she were seated on the back of a trotting horse. Another time the two of them walked around the room naked, so that every so often, through the keyhole, he would catch a glimpse of "their front and their behind." Another time a couple, instead of on the bed, had preferred to make love on the floor, right near the door. And if that time, though he desperately tried to twist his eyes downward, he saw nothing at all, to make up for it he had been able to *listen*: which, perhaps, had been even better.

During the next few days, Luciano continues to subject the protagonist to these conversations, without the protagonist being able to stop him: "Ero debole, passivo, impotente a reagire; e lui ne approfittava" (630; I was weak, passive, incapable of reacting; and he took advantage of this). Pulga also brings literature into the conversation, from the simply erotic to the frankly pornographic, mentioning also Otto Weininger's notorious *Sex and Character* (630), which of course associates the Jew with women.[8] Finally, Pulga raises the topics of masturbation and circumcision, expressing amazement that his Jewish friend has never masturbated (at sixteen!) and wondering if this might not be the result of a diminished "sensibilità sessuale" (631; sexual sensitivity) caused by circumcision. The protagonist's answers to Pulga's questions reveal a remarkable innocence about his own sexuality. The inevitable comparison of male members is next, leading Pulga to declare, with surprise, that there appears to be very little difference between a circumcised and an intact penis, clearly the expression of the protagonist's own curiosity about this and his continuing obsession with sexual matters:

> Arrivammo così fino a Pasqua, con la sensazione continua da parte mia di venire sospinto a grado a grado verso qualcosa di ignoto e di minaccioso, ma senza che niente di preciso accadesse mai. Luciano parlava, parlava. La sua voce mi teneva fermo dentro le sue spire basse e ronzanti. (632)

> We went on like this until Easter, with the constant sensation, on my part, of being little by little carried along towards something unknown and threatening, but without anything specific ever happening. Luciano talked and talked, on and on. His voice held me firmly in the grip of its deep, buzzing coils.

At this point the narrator returns to an image that recalls his first encounter with Micòl in *Il giardino dei Finzi-Contini*, the image of the underground room where Micòl urged him to hide his bicycle so that he might climb over the wall to join her. The underground tunnel (*budello sotterraneo*) she points out to him is an ancient arms stash once used by the defenders of Ferrara. It becomes the site of his truncated sexual fantasies, behind which he senses a danger that he cannot describe more precisely other than to say that once in the tunnel, away from Micòl, his fear of the dark gave way to relief, to the feeling that he had escaped "un gran pericolo, [il] pericolo maggiore al quale un ragazzo della mia età … potesse andare incontro" (363; some great danger, the greatest danger a boy of my age … might ever meet up with [49–50]).

Here, the image of the underground tunnel returns, accompanied by the connection to a new, more complete awareness of his mother and by the allusion to a possible dream:

> Ho pochi ricordi precisi di quel periodo. Vivevo come dentro una galleria sotterranea: senza scorgerne il termine, ma temendo di trovarmici a un tratto a faccia a faccia. Rammento il senso di complicità abbietta che suscitava in me ogni ingresso di mia madre nella stanza. E rammento anche un pomeriggio durante le vacanze di Pasqua, un pomeriggio magari non vero, forse soltanto sognato. (632)

> I have few precise memories of that period. I lived as if in an underground tunnel: without being able to see its end but afraid that I would suddenly

> find myself face to face with it. I remember the feeling of abject complicity that came over me each time my mother appeared in the room. And I also remember one afternoon during Easter vacation, perhaps not a real afternoon but one I only dreamed.

The "dream" is very significant, as it depicts a soccer match, an activity that contributes to sexual sublimation. Pulga is on the sidelines, "troppo esile, troppo mingherlino, in squadra nessuno lo vorrebbe" (633; too slight, too thin, nobody would want him on a team), but he smirks at the protagonist from afar, threatening to return him to his (their) sexual obsessions as soon as the game is over: "E so perché resta. Per me. Dopo la fine della partita pretenderà di montare sulla canna della mia bicicletta e di pilotarmi poi fino in via Garibaldi, all'angolo tra via Garibaldi e via Colomba, di dove potremo spiare con tutta comodità la gente che entra ed esce dai portoni chiodati dei bordelli" (633). (And I know why he is staying. For me. After the end of the game, he'll want to climb onto the handlebars of my bike and guide me to Via Garibaldi, to the corner of Via Garibaldi and Via Colomba, from where we will be able to easily spy on the people going in and out of the big nail-studded doors of the brothels.) Sublimation is no longer very effective as a defence against sexual feelings; as they are about to finish the game, the protagonist injures a knee, and although he knows that it is nothing serious, he nonetheless gives in to a sudden desire to lie on the ground as if immobilized: "le membra indolenzite a poco a poco invase da uno straordinario senso di benessere" (633; my aching limbs slowly pervaded by an extraordinary sensation of well-being). He opens his eyes to find Luciano standing there, suddenly transformed from the small, puny boy he appeared to be at the beginning of the match to an overwhelming presence: "Dritto in silenzio accanto a me (è enorme, visto dal basso, gigantesco: e mi squadra freddamente da capo a piedi, come se fossi una cosa), non è rimasto che Luciano" (633; Erect, in silence, beside me [enormous, seen from below, gigantic, looking me up and down, from head to toe, as if I were an object], only Luciano remained).

This dream clearly indicates that the protagonist's attempts to defend himself against his own overwhelming sexual urges are failing him. The next line of defence is illness, a bad case of tonsillitis that covers, barely masked, for a bad case of castration anxiety, itself described not without a significant amount of irony on the part of Bassani, particularly as regards the role of his doctor father, who favours immediate removal of the infected tonsils. His uncle, also a doctor, disagrees, so his mother finally calls in Dr Fadigati, the best specialist in town:

> Incidere? Non incidere? …
> Circa la cura, anche lui come lo zio riteneva che per ora, a caldo, un "taglietto" poteva riuscire pericoloso. Bisognava attendere. Verso il settimo o l'ottavo giorno avremmo visto meglio se convenisse approfittare dell'occasione (a questo punto il dottore, che già mi sorrideva bonario e rassicurante, allungò una mano a carezzarmi una guancia), e portar via finalmente "tutto quanto." (634–5)

> To operate? Not to operate? …
> As for the cure, he too, like my uncle, felt that for now "cutting" could turn out to be dangerous. It was necessary to wait. Around the seventh or eighth day we would have a better idea whether or not to take advantage of the opportunity (at this point the doctor, who was already smiling at me kindly and reassuringly, stretched out a hand to caress my cheek) to finally remove "the whole thing."

In his sickbed, the protagonist reviews the events of the past few months, and the cause of the tonsillitis becomes clear: he finds himself obsessed by thoughts of the afternoon in which he and Pulga unbuttoned their trousers, and by how small his own penis was compared to Pulga's: "Non avrei mai supposto che un magrolino del genere nascondesse nei calzoni una *cosa* talmente sproporzionata: un che di gonfio, bianco, ma soprattutto enorme" (636; I would never have thought that a skinny kid like him could hide in his pants such a disproportionate *thing*: swollen, white, but above all enormous). His disgust at the whole thing and at his own obsessive thoughts, which keep returning to the spectacle of Pulga's huge member, overwhelms him, and only by staying away from school, and therefore from Pulga, can he hope to avoid succumbing to it.

Castration anxiety, for this Jewish boy, is accompanied by disgust because his perception of his own urges and fears at yielding to them is tainted by the anti-Semitic images he associates with Jewish sexuality. Overcoming castration anxiety by withdrawing one's erotic investment with the mother for an identification with the father, and by extension through the bloodline with all the forefathers, implies identification with the complex of images of the eastern Jew. This is exactly how the protagonist feels one afternoon shortly after his illness when, sidelined by his father's injunction to avoid sweating, he watches the boys play soccer: "un reietto, un debole, un meschino: degno in tutto e per tutto di fare il paio con un Luciano Pulga" (638; an outcast, a weakling, a wretch: in all aspects worthy of being paired up with a Luciano Pulga).

At this point, when the protagonist has reached the lowest point in his self-esteem and has thought at length about the possibility of breaking off all contact with Pulga, Cattolica turns up unexpectedly and casually at his side, a clear indication that the protagonist is thinking of moving back to the other enemy camp. Note how, just like Pulga, Cattolica suddenly appears out of the blue, summoned by the protagonist himself like another possible double: "Non ero solo, però. … Anche Cattolica, invece che filare subito a casa come al solito, si era fermato a guardare. … Ma a un tratto mi venne vicino, e, cosa straordinaria, infilò un braccio sotto il mio" (638). (I was not alone, however. … Cattolica, too, instead of going right home as usual, had stopped to watch. … Suddenly, however, he came over to me, and – an extraordinary thing – he slipped his arm under mine.) They begin to converse, and Cattolica is unusually friendly and interested, to the point of inviting him to his home to join his afternoon study sessions with Boldini and Grassi. This, of course, means abandoning Pulga, which Cattolica urges him to do; the protagonist contemplates this reluctantly, if only because joining Cattolica and his acolytes will also involve giving up something of his own reality, indeed accepting to have it treated as if it were unworthy of any consideration: "Inoltre era altrettanto ovvio e pacifico che fra casa sua e casa mia era casa *sua*, la *sua* camera, il *suo* tavolo, che anche io *dovevo* preferire. … Anche Luciano era un'entità astratta, trascurabile, un argomento increscioso e imbarazzante sul quale non valeva la pena di spendere una sola parola" (640–1). (Moreover, it was just as obvious and indisputable, that between his house and mine, it was *his* house, *his* room, *his* table that I, too, *had* to prefer. … Luciano, also, was an abstract entity, negligible, a painful and embarrassing topic not worth spending a single word on.)

The protagonist refuses this first approach, clearly struggling with a sense of divided loyalties, and finally proposes a compromise: that he be allowed to come with Pulga, that is to say, if we accept a symbolic reading of this novel, without being forced to renounce his Jewishness. When Cattolica refuses, the protagonist, humiliated by Cattolica's demands, attempts to defend Pulga, reminding him that Pulga does not have the bubonic plague (the Jews were accused of having brought the Black Death to Europe). At the same time, he realizes his defence is only half-hearted: "Ma aveva ragione lui – non potei fare a meno di pensare mentre ancora stavo parlando –. La peste Luciano ce l'aveva davvero, e ormai, a forza di stargli vicino, me l'ero presa anch'io" (642). (But he was the one who was right, I couldn't help thinking, even as I was speaking – Luciano really did have the plague, and now I too, having been around him so much, had caught it.)

On the verge of tears, he nonetheless holds his ground: "Scusa, sai, ma o tutti e due, o nessuno" (642; I'm sorry, you know, but it's both of us or no one). The next time they see each other, Cattolica refuses to be discouraged – it is now his turn to "seduce" the young Jew, who is suspicious but still open to his advances: "Senza mai accennare allo strano colloquio che avevamo avuto, faceva di tutto, non potevo non accorgermene, perché l'invisibile barriera che fino allora ci aveva divisi fosse tolta di mezzo" (643; Without ever mentioning the strange conversation we had had, he did everything he could, I couldn't help noticing, so that the invisible barrier that up to then had separated us be removed.) If we accept that Cattolica's perceived actions are actually the workings of the protagonist's own mind, then we see that he himself is trying somehow to overlook what he knows to be Cattolica's anti-Semitism, because Cattolica still represents for him "la perfe[zione] ... alla quale mi sforzavo di uniformarmi"(643; the perfect[ion] ... that I tried to model myself on). And just as the growing "intimacy" with Pulga is represented by "talking," which would signify an inner dialogue with this "double," so here too the *rapprochement* with Cattolica is marked by their fervent conversations: "Parlavamo, anzi, non facevamo che parlare" (643; We talked, indeed we did nothing but talk). These conversations are so frequent and intense that the usually perfect Cattolica is even caught off guard one day by the Latin teacher, unable to answer a question because of lack of attention. The teacher even threatens to send him to sit at the back next to Pulga. This would be a case of irony on the part of Bassani, were it not a way of indicating the equivalency between them as doubles. And although Cattolica and the protagonist do not go so far as to be seen alone together after school, their growing alliance is nurtured in the evening by long telephone conversations. The protagonist does not remember most of them because they were largely a pretext, merely a means of examining each other from a distance: "Continuavamo a studiarci, a sfiorarci l'un l'altro, protendendo in avanscoperta cauti tentacoli" (646; We continued studying each other, barely touching each other, extending cautious tentacles in reconnaissance). He does, however, remember Cattolica criticizing even his own constant companions, Boldini and Grassi, as if to suggest that he and the protagonist shared qualities that placed them "su un piano diverso e superiore" (647; on a different and superior plane). The protagonist is not convinced and is even more distrustful after having heard him express contempt for his best friends; he counters this by praising Pulga.

Here the protagonist is clearly weighing the two possible alternatives in his dilemma of identification, trying to see if he can combine them instead of having to make a difficult choice. At this point Cattolica reveals to him that Pulga has been speaking ill of him behind his back. And although the protagonist is hurt by this discovery of Pulga's treachery, he is also relieved: "Ecco l'occasione per liberarmi di Luciano – pensai in un lampo –. Eccola, finalmente!" (650). (Here is the opportunity to get rid of Luciano, I thought in a flash. Here it is, finally!)

It is significant that the thought of finally being free of Luciano and of what he represents seems to liberate the protagonist's emerging sexuality from its previous sordid associations. Suddenly the narrator uses sensual images from the natural world to evoke his awakening instincts, and he manages to brush off his mother with no difficulty whatsoever when she asks him with whom he has been speaking:

> Invece di risponderle, le sfiorai la guancia con un bacio e le augurai la buona notte.
>
> In camera mia faceva molto caldo. Appena entrato chiusi la porta a chiave e andai a spalancare la finestra. Era una bella notte stellata, senza luna ma chiarissima. Giù nel giardino le forme degli alberi si stagliavano nette: qui la magnolia, più in là l'abete, e laggiù, nell'angolo opposto, dove terminavano i tre archi del portico d'ingresso, il tiglio. Fra aiuola e aiuola il bianco latteo della ghiaia, e nel mezzo dello spiazzo anche più chiaro che si apriva davanti alla scura cavità del portico, un punto nero, immobile: forse una pietra, o magari Filomena, la tartaruga centenaria di casa, di cui la mamma, a cena, aveva gioiosamente annunciato l'uscita dal letargo invernale. ...
>
> Ero completamente nudo. Su dal giardino veniva un profumo intenso di piante, di erba. Convinto più che mai che Cattolica non avesse mentito, pensavo a Luciano. ... Ma certo! Ero stato ben cieco a non vedere per tanto tempo che Luciano era un traditore! (650–1)

> Instead of answering her, I grazed her cheek with a kiss and wished her good night.
>
> It was very hot in my room. As soon as I was inside, I locked the door and went to throw open the window. It was a beautiful starry night, with no moon but very bright. Down in the garden the outlines of the trees were clearly visible: here the magnolia, further away the fir, and down

> there, in the opposite corner where the three arches of the portico came to an end, the linden. Between one flower bed and another, the milky white of the gravel; and in the centre of the clearing, even whiter, which opened before the dark cavity of the portico, a black, motionless dot: a stone, perhaps, or maybe Filomena, the ancient family tortoise whose emergence from hibernation Mamma had announced gaily at supper. ...
>
> I was completely naked. An intense perfume, of plants, of grass wafted up from the garden. More convinced than ever that Cattolica hadn't lied, I was thinking of Luciano. ... Of course! I said to myself. ... I had been really blind, not to see for so long that Luciano was a traitor!

The protagonist even succeeds in imagining himself at the height of his powers in a fantasy of physical aggression, in which he is fighting back and beating his betrayer. This scene foreshadows what he will not be able to do at the end:

> Vedevo la scena: io rosso, gli occhi fuori della testa, i pugni alzati a picchiare; lui, il piccolo miserabile, l'ignobile piccolo malandrino, mentre, contorcendosi ai miei piedi, cercava di proteggersi la faccia livida, tumefatta; e gli altri, in silenzio, a fare cerchio attorno. Infierivo, lo massacravo di bòtte, e Luciano non si difendeva. Si limitava a ripararsi il viso con le mani di cui mostrava i ripugnanti palmi callosi, senza neanche piangere. Le pigliava e basta. (651–2)

> I could visualize the scene: myself, flushed, eyes bulging, fists ready to attack; and him, the little wretch, the ignoble little rascal, writhing at my feet while trying to protect his bruised, swollen face; the others, in silence, in a circle around us. I was beating him ferociously, and Luciano wasn't defending himself; he was simply protecting his face with his hands, of which I could see the repugnant calloused palms, and he wasn't even crying. He just took the blows and that was it.

In the light of day, however, he returns to a more usual and measured attitude: "Il mio ruolo di giustiziere mi apparve subito assurdo" (My role of executioner seemed immediately absurd to me). In fact, when he sees Pulga, he is overcome by "un oscuro senso di colpa e di paura" (an obscure sense of guilt and of fear), but at the same time Pulga does not loom as large in his mind as before: "Mi pareva più piccolo che mai, debole, misero nei suoi calzoncini di vigogna grigia, nelle sue secche gambette da fenicottero" (652; He seemed smaller to me than ever, weak, wretched in his gray flannel shorts, with his little flamingo legs). However, in what shall become a leitmotif, the young Jew cannot face up to Pulga, quite literally: "Ma la sua fronte verticale un po' sporgente, sede di tanta malizia, quella non osavo quasi guardargliela" (652; But that high, slightly domed forehead, the seat of so much malice, that brow, I could hardly bring myself to look at).

Cattolica also begins to change appearance in his eyes. Previously, he had always gazed at him in profile, idealizing him, but now he faces him head on (something he is not able to do with Pulga) and begins to see him as the inquisitor he is becoming: "Pallido, magro, mi scrutava coi suoi occhi neri, ardenti di fanatismo in fondo alle orbite come quelli di un monaco medievale. Capivo bene che a muoverlo era solo la voglia di umiliarmi. Ma adesso avevo bisogno di lui. Nessun altro, all'infuori di lui, avrebbe potuto aiutarmi" (652–3). (Pale, thin, he scrutinized me, his black eyes glowing fanatically in their sockets like those of a medieval monk. I understood that he was motivated only by the wish to humiliate me; but now I needed him. No one except him could help me now.) This description seems to suggest that only by identifying with the Catholic enemy could he free himself from the hold Pulga still had on him.

Eventually, Cattolica sets up the confrontation necessary "perché gli occhi mi si aprissero" (658; to open my eyes). It takes place at the home of Cattolica, the protagonist lurking behind a door where he can hear what Pulga has to say without being seen. Just before Pulga is slated to arrive, the protagonist looks out the window and sees some young boys playing. He suddenly yearns to be "con quei ragazzetti che in cima alla Mura stavano rincorrendo un pallone" (660; with those little boys who, on top of the bastions, were chasing a ball). When he nervously asks whether Cattolica is certain Pulga will turn up, Cattolica replies in such a way as to anticipate the Aryan race policy on the horizon, associating Pulga with common anti-Semitic stereotypes, such as the mongrel: [9]

> Sai certi cani bastardi che basta fargli un fischio e subito accorrono, trottando e scodinzolando? Da autentico meteco, Pulga è proprio così. Smania d'intrufolarsi, capisci?, e mica tanto perché abbia bisogno di qualcosa. È soltanto questione di carattere. Io, vedi, sarà perché non sono un bastardo e nemmeno un meteco, e le mescolanze non posso soffrirle, mi fanno venire una specie di pelle d'oca, io non sto bene che a casa mia, mentre al contrario c'è al mondo gente che a casa propria non ci si può vedere. (660–1)

> You know certain mongrels that you just have to whistle at and they come up to you right away, trotting and wagging their tails? Like a real mongrel, Pulga is just like that. Dying to worm his way in, you understand? And not so much because he needs something. It's just a question of character. Look, maybe it's because I'm not a bastard and not a mongrel either, and I can't stand mixed races, they give me goose bumps, I'm only happy in my own home, whereas, on the contrary, in this world there are people who can't stand to be in their own homes.

While they are waiting for Pulga to show up, the protagonist becomes increasingly anxious at the prospect of what he imagines will be a direct confrontation: "Era stata proprio questa prospettiva a stringermi a mano a mano lo stomaco in una morsa d'angoscia sempre più opprimente" (661; It was just this prospect that had gradually tied my stomach in increasingly oppressive and anguishing knots). When told that Cattolica's plan is not to have him face to face with Pulga but to eavesdrop unseen from behind the door of the next room, he is overcome with joy, quite literally: "Non vederlo, Luciano, poter evitare di guardargli la faccia mentre Cattolica lo faceva discorrere! Travolto da un senso improvviso di euforia mi staccai dalla finestra" (661–2). (Not to see him, Luciano, to be able to avoid looking him in the face while Cattolica made him talk! Overcome by a sudden feeling of euphoria, I moved away from the window.) However, Cattolica and his companions do urge him, once the protagonist has overheard the offensive remarks, to burst into the room and give Pulga a good beating. They even move the furniture to create a boxing ring of sorts and offer him some tips on how to strike effectively. Cattolica warns him that if he does not assert himself immediately, Pulga will eventually find a way back into his life and nothing will have been accomplished.

As soon as Pulga rings the bell, the protagonist hides in the adjacent bedroom in order to overhear the conversation from behind the connecting door, a clear reference back to Pulga himself eavesdropping on the sexual activity in the room next door at the Hotel Tripoli. Here again, we see the protagonist next to a Christ figure, this time a crucifix on the wall over the beds.

The figure is described as effeminate, blonde, and blue eyed, clearly a reflection of our protagonist about to be betrayed by his own Judas and then crucified by the local Romans. As he awaits his fate, the room suddenly takes on a different aspect and becomes a hiding place reminiscent of the room in Florence where Carlo Levi hid from the Nazis while writing *Christ Stopped at Eboli* (1945):[10] "La stanza che mi nascondeva si era configurata d'un tratto come un luogo infinitamente più segreto, più remoto, e perfino più tenebroso, di quanto non fosse in realtà: un punto perduto in grembo a uno spazio immenso, vasto come l'oceano" (666; The room that hid me suddenly assumed the guise of an infinitely more secret, more remote, even more sinister place than it was in reality: a dot, lost in the midst of an immense space, as vast as the ocean).

Not wanting to appear too obvious and clearly enjoying the thought of his rival squirming on tenterhooks in the next room, Cattolica steers the conversation over a number of topics before leading Pulga to the trap. Again here we find an allusion to *Christ Stopped at Eboli.* In the Levi memoir much space is dedicated to explaining the peasants' primitive belief that humans are part of the animal world and are indeed part beast, part human. Here, in a discussion of their philosophy class, a similar belief is expressed by Pulga and rejected by Cattolica, who objects that to believe in the transmigration of souls one would have to throw Catholicism out the window. Luciano nonetheless goes on to identify their teachers and classmates with different animals. Most of the portraits are unflattering, but Cattolica emerges as the descendant of an eagle, while Pulga sees himself as a dog; Pulga also identifies as a parasite, more precisely, a germ (*un microbo*), but of the unobtrusive sort, in keeping with anti-Semitic characterizations of the Jews as invisible parasites and carriers of disease, such as syphilis or tuberculosis: "Una volta trovato un posticino tranquillo, stanno lì quieti quieti a succhiare per venti, trenta, quarant'anni, e in fin dei conti non dànno fastidio a nessuno" (670; Once they find a quiet little place, they stay there quietly, quietly sucking for twenty, thirty, forty years, and in the final analysis don't bother anyone). Cattolica is not content to stop there, however, and asks what kind of animal the protagonist would be; to this Pulga answers, "un altro cane," making, however, a very clear distinction between himself and the protagonist by identifying himself with stereotypical images of the eastern Jew and his friend with characteristics that suggest the more assimilated or integrated Jew:

> Con questa differenza – continuò –: che mentre lui era stato, ci avrebbe scommesso sopra, uno di quei "cagnuzzi" di piccola taglia e di nessun prezzo, sempre in giro per le strade alla ricerca di robuccia equivoca da "nasare," stronzetti, pisciatine, eccetera, io al contrario dovevo essere stato uno di quei "cagnoni" di razza tutt'altro che pura, però incrociati abbastanza bene, ai quali riesce sempre facile trovare la famiglia dove

> sistemarsi. Insomma, un cane grosso ma non grossissimo, bello ma non bellissimo, forte ma nón fortissimo, coraggioso ma non coraggiosissimo: uno di quelli che quando gli capita di imbattersi in un bastardino "tipo Pulga" ... va spesso a finire che è proprio il bastardino a portarselo dove vuole. E non è neanche detto che il naso sotto la coda debba sempre tenercelo il "bel cagnone." Anzi! (671)

> With this difference – he added –; that while he had been, he was ready to bet on it, one of those "pooches," small and of no value, always wandering the streets in search of disgusting stuff to 'sniff' at, turds, pee puddles, etc., I, on the other hand, must have been one of those "big dogs," not at all pure-breds but still a fairly good cross-breed, the kind that always easily finds a family to take it in. All told, a big dog but not very big, good-looking but not too good-looking, strong but not too strong: the sort that when it runs into a little mongrel "of the Pulga type," ... it often ends up that it's the mongrel who leads him wherever it chooses. And it's not necessarily always the "big dog" that keeps its nose under the other's tail. Quite the opposite!

At this point the conversation turns in earnest to the protagonist. Everything that Pulga says is the truth: he says that the protagonist is "complicato e sospettoso" (672; complicated and suspicious), that what he wanted from Cattolica was not so much to be his friend but to be asked by Cattolica himself to join his group of acolytes – "Desiderava *soprattutto* che tu lo invitassi" (673; He wanted *above all* that he be invited) – and that he really did not like the protagonist, "ma non tanto perché gli fossi antipatico, oppure perché mi fossi comportato male nei suoi riguardi" (673; but not so much because he found me unpleasant or because I had behaved badly towards him). The reasons are objective, Pulga claims, the most important being the protagonist's "incredibile, assurda vanità da bambino dell'asilo" (674; incredible, absurd vanity, like that of a kindergarten child). (This characteristic, of course, has already been pointed out in *Il giardino dei Finzi-Contini*, when the narrator refers to himself at the time of his first encounter with Micòl as having been very spoiled and vain.) Not only had he shown Pulga around his twenty-room home with a nouveau riche attitude of superiority, the protagonist also boasted about his religion as a "faccenda privata, di famiglia" (a private, family affair), a type of exclusive club, as if he were bragging about "il conto in banca di mio nonno buonanima, facoltoso negoziante di tessuti all'ingrosso" (675; the bank account of my dead grandfather, bless his soul, the wealthy cloth wholesaler). The reference to Judaism as something private that excludes others, as a "family affair," is another way of evoking the sentiment of exclusivity that the narrator pointed out in the previous novel as well, when describing his first encounters with Micòl at the synagogue, and that also pervades the sense of Italian Judaism in that novel.

The next accusation concerns the protagonist's attitude towards Pulga himself. Pulga admits to having profitted academically from their friendship but nonetheless says that the protagonist never really considered him a friend but used him to inflate his own ego, like "una semplice macchina da lodi, da far funzionare con la stessa disinvoltura con cui uno, girando una manopola, mette in andare la doccia del bagno" (675; a simple flattery machine, to be turned on as casually as you might the bathroom shower). This comment echoes a sentiment expressed by the narrator earlier on, in which he admits that he was able to overcome the repugnance he felt towards Pulga precisely because of the feelings of superiority that Pulga engendered in him.

Thus far Pulga has said nothing that the narrator himself has not said, including the remarks that Pulga makes about the protagonist's mother, with the exception of the sexual innuendo – "come donna ti garantisco che ne vale la pena" (676; as women go, I guarantee that she's worth the trouble) – and the connection of these innuendoes to the stereotype of the *belle juive*: "magari un po' 'sfasciata' come sono sempre le donne ebree, ma però con una bocca tale, con certi occhioni '*marron*,' e con certe occhiate, specialmente ..."[11] (676; maybe a little "flabby" like all Jewish women, but with a mouth, with certain brown eyes and certain looks, especially ..."). This confirms Pulga's role as the incarnation of the protagonist's own sexual conflict: his sexuality and sexual awareness emerge so firmly and intimately embedded in shameful Jewish stereotypes as to cause him to wish to suppress them.

Pulga's remarks about the mother's behaviour are in fact echoes of what the narrator himself has already pointed out, that his mother used Pulga to keep her son at home, that at five o'clock she always arrived with a tray full of snacks that could feed a family for two days:

> Ma questo era ancora niente. Perché a parte l'aria che aveva sempre, "la maledetta," mentre ti riempiva la tazza o ti metteva il piatto dei pasticcini sotto il naso ..., dopo, accomiatandosi, non mancava mai di lanciare attraverso la fessura della porta un bel sorriso accompagnato da un'occhiata "mezzo materna e mezzo assassina." (676)

> But that was nothing! Because apart from her manner, "the damn woman," when she filled your cup or held the plate of cookies under your nose ..., afterwards, saying goodbye, as she was closing the door, she never forgot to give you a beautiful smile accompanied by a look that was "half motherly and half teasing."

Here Pulga voices what may also be the protagonist's own emerging thoughts and fears about his own mother, in language that is certainly disrespectful but not far from what are stereotypes of male adolescent ways of speaking to each other about women:

> Certo è che l'estate al mare ... , una donna così doveva combinarne di tutti i colori al marito. ... Con quella bocca larga, "ingorda," con quegli occhi languidi mezzo nascosti dai capelli (il petto lo aveva un po' basso, d'accordo, ma la "carrozzeria" meritava forse un viaggio apposta), impossibile che, presentandosi l'occasione, se la lasciasse scappare. (677)

> No question, in the summer, at the shore ..., a woman like that must be up to all sorts of things her husband isn't aware of. With that wide, "voracious" mouth, with those languid eyes half hidden by her hair (her breasts were a bit sagging, okay, but the "rest of the body" was worth a special trip), it was impossible that when an opportunity arose, she would let it slip by.

In *Gli occhiali d'oro* the narrator does in fact tell us that his own first sexual experience had taken place during the summer while on holiday in Riccione, with an older married woman who was a friend of his mother's – all the more reason for him to wonder, in retrospect, whether his own mother might not have been guilty of a similar transgression.

After this, Pulga turns to the most sensitive topic, the protagonist's own repressed sexuality and visible castration anxiety. The narrator himself has already described his reactions similarly, except for the interpretation of his "shock" at the size of Pulga's penis as a sign of his impending turn to homosexuality, again a stereotype long in vogue and further consolidated by the case of Oscar Weininger:

> Ebbene ero talmente impallidito a vedergli il suo, di cazzo, e poi, nei giorni successivi, la mia maniera di comportarmi era talmente cambiata (di colpo ero diventato ruvido, sgarbato, gli occhi mi sfuggivano da tutte le parti: come se mi facesse schifo, non so, o rabbia, o paura), che lui era stato indotto a pensare il peggio. Ma sì. Ero di sicuro un "finocchio," sia pure

> allo stato potenziale: un "busone" in attesa soltanto di "saltare il fosso," e tuttavia ignaro (questo, il tragico!) della bella carriera che mi stava davanti, inevitabile ...[12] (677–8)

> Well, I had gone so pale, on seeing it, and then, in the days after that, my behaviour had changed so much (I had suddenly become rude, abrupt, I couldn't look him in the eye: as if he disgusted me or, I don't know, made me angry or afraid) that he had been led to think the worst. Of course. I was surely a "fag," though still only with the potential to become one; a "fairy" just waiting to to "cross over" and yet unaware (that was the tragedy!) of the fine career ahead of me, unavoidable ...

The inevitable aftermath of this fateful scene begins at the dinner table that evening. The members of his family no longer look the same to him: "Li scrutai uno dopo l'altro tutti quanti come se fossero degli estranei" (679; I examined them one by one as if they were strangers). His father has become the image of slovenly ineptitude in his eyes, while his mother has become a harlot:

> Era mio padre – mi domandavo – quel povero vecchio che in giacca di pigiama e pantofole finiva di vuotare una scodella di minestra? ... E possibile che io, anche io, fossi figlio di quell'uomo mediocre, annoiato e noioso, incapace soprattutto in casa di tenersi su, di darsi un contegno, e di quella donna così volgare, e che proprio a quell'unione, a quell'unione fisica, dovessi la mia esistenza? (679)

> Was that poor old man, who in his pajama jacket and slippers was finishing a bowl of soup, my father? I asked myself ... And was it possible that I, I too, was the son of that mediocre man, bored and boring, unable, especially at home, to put up a good face, and of that woman, so vulgar, and that actually I owed my existence to that union, to that physical union?

That night, when she appears in his room to see if he is sleeping, we see the protagonist struggling with two images of his mother – the sexualized woman and the angel of the hearth:

> La sentivo lì accanto, alta e silenziosa sopra il mio corpo disteso, e avrei voluto alzarmi, insultarla, picchiarla, cacciarla via. Ma ecco leggera, fresca e leggera come mai, la sua mano scendere attraverso il buio a toccarmi la

fronte e posarvisi. Bastò questo. Non mi ci volle altro perché di lì a poco, di nuovo solo, fossi sommerso ancora una volta dal mio vecchio, riparatore sonno di bambino. (681)

I sensed her near the bed, tall and silent over my outstretched body, and I would have wanted to get up, insult her, hit her, drive her away. Instead, light, cool and light as ever, her hand came down through the darkness to touch my forehead and stay there. That was enough. Alone again, I didn't need anything else to soon be immersed once more in my old, restorative childhood sleep.

The next day in school the protagonist feels estranged from Cattolica and his crew, as well as from Pulga. He asks his teacher to change his place in the classroom, to allow him to occupy Pulga's seat in the back, in the same row as the girls. When the teacher asks where Pulga is supposed to sit, he suggests that he move to his own vacated seat next to Cattolica. The two alternatives in his search for identity as a man are equally unsatisfactory. Cattolica, the idealized image of an untainted virility (the temptation of conversion?) is clearly an enemy, while Pulga is his own sexuality, which repulses him. He is, quite literally, relegated to "no-man's-land," to the last row with the girls: forever to remain in limbo, on the threshold, still mother-identified, unable to embrace his own adult sexuality without at the same time embracing the images of abjection and degradation that his Jewishness brings to it.

Pulga is, of course, still there, ready to resume their friendship, but the protagonist wants only to be rid of him and to isolate himself completely: "Per tornare alla totale solitudine dell'autunno precedente mi restava da compiere un ultimo passo: rompere con Luciano" (683; To return to the total solitude of the past autumn, I still had to take one final step: I had to break with Luciano). And when the protagonist sees Pulga – "Mi fissava negli occhi pallido come un cadavere" (684; He stared into my eyes, pale as a corpse) – he turns his back on him. The story then comes full circle with a return to Otello Forti, his childhood friend who comes back from boarding school and seeks him out. With the protagonist's new sexual awareness, Otello too is no longer a suitable companion: "Se a Natale mi era sembrato tanto più alto e adulto di me, adesso appariva piccolo, una specie di bambino" (687; If at Christmas he had seemed so much taller, so much more adult than me, now he looked small, like a child). He invites Otello to ride on his bicycle home with him, as they used to do before, but thinks of Pulga:

"Anche se mi fossi sforzato di tornare a frequentare Otello come quando eravamo alle elementari e al ginnasio, in fondo al suo odore buono, onesto, avrei sempre ritrovato l'altro, quel disgustoso e opprimente tanfo di brillantina" (687–8; And yet I knew that even if I started seeing Otello like when we were in elementary or secondary school, under his good, honest odour I would always find the other, that disgusting and oppressive smell of brilliantine). Otello represents innocence, Eden before the Fall, while Pulga represents Jewish male adulthood, forever intertwined with and tainted by images – and odours – of filth and degradation, such as *foetor judaicus*,[13] the characteristic odour Jews were supposed to emanate.

When he returns home, the protagonist's mother is sitting in the garden. He sees her under the magnolia tree as if from afar – "Non era più che una macchia chiara, lontana" (689; She was no more than a bright spot, far-off in the distance) – indicating the separation that is taking place. He goes up to his room, she calls to him, and he opens the window. She is now the image of feminine sensuality, immersed in nature, but it is not a quiet pastoral scene, rather a more primitive and libidinous one:

> Al centro del suo reame, del suo teatro, circondata dalla sue "sante bestie," la barboncina Lulù, i due gatti persiani color fumo, la tartaruga Filomena, mi guardava e sorrideva. Stava ricamando l'orlo di un lenzuolo o di una tovaglia. L'ago le scintillava in grembo. Il giardino fiammeggiava attorno, rigoglioso come una piccola giungla. (690)

> At the centre of her realm, of her theatre, surrounded by her "sainted creatures," Lulù the poodle, the two smoke-coloured Persian cats, Filomena the tortoise, she was looking at me and smiling. She was embroidering the hem of a sheet or a tablecloth. The needle was glistening in her lap. The garden was afire around her, blazing like a little jungle.

The final realization takes place when he passes a photograph in the living room, of himself and his mother:

> E mentre mi stringeva appassionatamente al seno, rivolgeva in direzione dell'obbiettivo un sorriso gioioso, intensamente felice. ... La fotografia era stata scattata da mio padre nel corso di una delle sue brevi licenze dal fronte. ... Ma soltanto qualche minuto fa, guardandola, avevo compreso

il reale significato di quel sorriso della mamma, sposa da appena tre anni: ciò che prometteva, ciò che offriva, e *a chi* ...[14] (690–1)

And as she hugged me passionately to her bosom, she directed a smile to the camera, a smile full of joy, intensely happy. ... The photograph had been taken by my father during one of his brief leaves from the front. ... But only a few minutes before, looking at it, had I understood the real meaning of that smile of Mamma's, married barely three years then: what it promised, what it offered, and *to whom* ...

The last chapter serves as a sort of epilogue. It begins with a reference to the "wound" of the opening chapter, which has now become a "festering ulcer": "L'ulcera aveva preso a suppurare in segreto, lenta, torpida, immedicabile ..."[15] (692; The ulcer had begun to fester in secret, slow, sluggish, incurable ...). The setting is the seashore at Cesenatico, a month and a half after the end of the school year, where the protagonist and his family have come to spend the summer. Unable to sleep, he has risen early and is lying alone on the beach; he finally manages to doze off, when suddenly Luciano appears out of nowhere:

All'improvviso me lo vidi davanti.

Stava lì, in piedi, spiando il mio risveglio, il piccolo corpo bianco e scheletrico, totalmente glabro, reso ancora più esile dal rigonfio abnorme del sesso sotto le braghette grige. E intanto mi sorrideva. (692–3)

All of a sudden I saw him in front of me.

He was there, on his feet, watching me wake up, his little body white and skeletal, completely hairless, made to look even more slight by the abnormal bulge of his sex under his gray trunks. And he was smiling.

It turns out that Pulga has come by train, found the protagonist's home, and changed in his room with the permission of his mother. He announces that his family will be leaving Ferrara since his father has finally found a permanent post in Bologna and that he has come to talk to him, hoping to clear up any misunderstandings that may have divided them. The protagonist is happy to hear that he is leaving – "Aveva detto che lui e i suoi stavano per lasciare Ferrara, che non ci saremmo visti mai più. Bene" (695). (He said that he and his family were about to leave Ferrara, that we would never see each other again.

Good.) – and refuses to ask him any questions about what happened, in spite of Pulga's apparent willingness to discuss their past relationship. Pulga senses that the protagonist is hiding his true feelings: "Eppure sento che mi nascondi delle cose ... che non mi dici *tutta* la verità" (695; And yet I feel you're hiding things from me ... that you're not telling me the *whole* truth). The protagonist's silence leads Pulga to change the subject. He asks whether "durante quel mese e più qualche bella signora non si fosse per caso assunta l'incarico di ... di sverginarmi" (695; during that month or more some beautiful lady hadn't perhaps taken on the task of ... of deflowering me). The protagonist comments that he had expected Pulga to get around to this topic and had in fact thought of it as soon as he saw him leaning over him, but that he had not expected "il tono che la sua voce avrebbe assunto, cauto, stranamente ansioso" (695; the tone his voice would take on: cautious, strangely anxious). He replies that he is spending all of his time swimming with a group of boys and that in any case his acne would have prevented him from being taken into consideration by any members of the opposite sex. Pulga persists nonetheless, telling him that he has come across a prostitute in Ferrara who would certainly agree to a threesome, but the protagonist declares that he is not interested. The protagonist then suggests that they go out in the rowboat, and when they are one hundred metres from the shore, he spots his mother arriving at the beach with his younger sister. His mother has become even smaller than she was when he spotted her in the garden: "Tra poco, quando fosse uscita dal capanno indossando il suo bel Jantzen blu, non sarebbe stata che un punto appena distinguibile" (697; In a little while, when she came out of the cabin wearing her pretty blue Jantzen, she would be nothing but a barely distinguishable dot). Once they are out far enough, the protagonist jumps into the water. Pulga, who does not know how to swim, panics at the sudden motion of the boat. Then, full of admiration at his friend's ease and skill in the water, particularly at his mastery of the crawl, he says that he has never seen that stroke before, even at a recent swimming meet. The protagonist replies that it is a Hawaiian stroke, which he taught himself with no instruction. The conversation finally comes to a halt – the water is calm, and Pulga seems to have forgotten him; but the protagonist, contemplating his visitor, suddenly feels cold in spite of the heat: "Mi sentivo a disagio, improvvisamente ai margini, in qualche modo escluso, e appunto per questo invidioso, e gretto, e meschino ..."[16] (698; I felt uncomfortable, suddenly on the margins, somehow excluded, and because of this envious, mean, and petty ...).

He contemplates the possibility of facing the truth, of actually accepting Pulga's invitation to talk about what had taken place, but suddenly stops in his tracks:

> Senonché, nel momento stesso in cui, dinanzi a quel gramo dorso nudo, remoto, a un tratto, inattingibile nella sua solitudine, mi abbandonavo a questi pensieri, già allora qualcosa doveva pur dirmi che se Luciano Pulga era in grado di accettare il confronto della verità, io no. Duro a capire, inchiodato per nascita a un destino di separazione e di livore, la porta dietro la quale ancora una volta mi nascondevo inutile che pensassi di spalancarla. Non ci sarei riuscito, niente da fare. Né adesso, né mai. (698–9)

> But, at the very moment I was lost in these thoughts, looking at that wretched, naked back, remote, suddenly unattainable in its solitude, already then something must have been telling me that while he, Luciano Pulga, was able to confront the truth, I was not. Slow to understand, nailed by birth to a fate of separation and resentment, it was pointless for me to think of throwing open the door behind which I was hiding yet again. I would never be able to do it, no way. Not now, not ever.

The story ends on this note. The protagonist is destined to remain "by birth," because he is a Jew, forever "behind the door," forever unable to fully integrate his own sexuality, symbolized by the sudden appearance of Pulga with his oversized member, because of the associations that it brings to mind. While he may think about all sorts of possible sexual outlets – those mentioned by Pulga – he finally resorts to his usual way of dealing with these feelings: sublimation through sport, here swimming. He has put so much effort into it that he has been able to master a particularly difficult stroke, the crawl, on his own. He has managed to tame his overwhelming sexual feelings, to keep them somewhat at bay, but the price he pays is one of exclusion, of feeling that this will only increase his solitude and resentment. His conflict will remain forever unresolved, always to come between him and a life fully embraced. He and his body – and the Jew is always associated with bodily function – will forever remain estranged from each other.

This boat scene, in particular the moment in which the protagonist jumps into the water and Pulga panics at the motion of the boat because he cannot swim, seems to be an allusion to Artur Dinter's 1917 anti-Semitic bestseller *Die Sünde wider das Blut* (The Sin against the Blood) which was to sell more than 260,000 copies by 1934 and which vividly set forth the stereotypes of the racial perceptions of his time. Such an allusion confirms Pulga as the internalized self-hating Jew that the protagonist carries around with him, his doppelgänger. Required reading among Nazis in the 1920s, Dinter's book was meant as a warning about the Jewish plot to pollute the Aryan race by seducing its women. Robertson describes the scene:

> Here the hero's various liaisons leave him with two sons: Hermann is fair-haired, manly and German, while Heinrich is Jewish, dark, cowardly, mercenary, shameless and sexually precocious. One day, out boating, Heinrich falls into the water, and, as he cannot swim, Hermann jumps in to save him, but the terrified Heinrich clings to his would-be rescuer in a feminine gesture which is destructive, for he drags his half-brother down and both are drowned.[17]

A recent article by Marilena Renda[18] has correctly identified the characterization of Pulga as fraught with anti-Semitic stereotypes and has connected it to the influence of Weininger in Italy; yet her study still sees something "unresolved" in this novel and sides with Roberto Cotroneo's thesis about the "ambiguity" of Bassani, ostensibly demonstrated by the fact that the protagonist at times seems to defend Pulga against Cattolica's accusations. If Pulga represents the incarnation of "Jewish self-hatred," why does the protagonist at times appear to take his side "a testimonianza dell'ambiguità che è il *quid* della scrittura di Bassani"[19] (as a mark of Bassani's signature ambiguity)? The ambiguity immediately dissolves, at least as far as this particular episode is concerned, if we understand Pulga and Cattolica as the terms of a conflict experienced by an adolescent looking for a way to come to terms with his own sexuality, which, to his mind, presents itself saturated with anti-Semitic associations. "È alla cronaca di un Bildung bloccata che ci fa assistere Bassani"[20] (Bassani presents the chronicle of a stalled Bildung), Renda correctly states, but fails to understand, the specifically Jewish character of the protagonist's dilemma: identify as a Catholic male and betray one's origins or identify as a Jewish male and embrace the arsenal of repulsive images that, in his mind, taint his burgeoning sexuality. This is not a novel about the universal experience of the loss of innocence on the background of anti-Semitism, but instead a novel about the difficulty of sexual maturation as a Jew when Jewish males and their sexuality are associated with so much degradation and abjection.

The ending, in which the narrator returns to the "wound" mentioned at the beginning and affirms his inability to engage in dialogue with Pulga (which might be the way to heal the "wound"), frames the entire story as one of a "man of resentment" nailed to his suffering like Jesus to the cross. At the same time, it is clearly a story of the betrayal of the Italian Jews at the hands of the Catholic church and of the price paid by Italian Jews for their "assimilation" into a heavily Christian society: self-hatred. The first paragraph of *Dietro la porta* explicitly confronts the now very fashionable questions of memory and trauma, long before they enjoyed their current popularity, by having the narrator declare openly that he is unable to let go of his resentment. I quote the following passage once again, as it is vital for our understanding:

> Sono stato molte volte infelice, nella mia vita, da bambino, da ragazzo, da giovane, da uomo fatto; molte volte, se ci ripenso, ho toccato quel che si dice il fondo della disperazione. Ricordo tuttavia pochi periodi più neri, per me, dei mesi di scuola fra l'ottobre del 1929 e il giugno del '30, quando facevo la prima liceo. Gli anni trascorsi da allora non sono in fondo serviti a niente: non sono riusciti a medicare un dolore che è rimasto là come una ferita segreta, sanguinante in segreto. Guarirne? Liberarmene? Non so se sarà mai possibile. (581)

> I have been unhappy many times in my life, as a child, as a youth, as a young man, as an adult; many times, if I think back, I have touched what are called the depths of despair. And yet I remember few periods darker, for me, than the months of school between October of 1929 and June of 1930, my first year of *liceo*. The years that have passed since then have not helped at all: they have not managed to heal a sorrow that has remained there like a secret wound, bleeding in secret. Get over it? Free myself of it? I don't know if it will ever be possible.

Should we remember? How? Can we remember without sacrificing the capacity to move forward? Is it possible to forget? Is it better to forget? Is it possible to move forward without forgetting? One of the most controversial positions in the debate on this issue was that taken by Holocaust survivor and intellectual Hans Meyer, who wrote under the name of Jean Améry. An assimilated Austrian Jew who had moved to Belgium in 1938, he was nonetheless captured in 1943 and subsequently interned at Auschwitz-Monowitz at the same time as Primo Levi. After his release, he abandoned his German identity, so traumatized was he by his imprisonment, including the torture he had suffered at the hands of his former compatriots. Améry makes explicit reference to Nietzsche's concept of *ressentiment* in his writing. In a book translated as *At the Mind's Limits: Contemplations by a Survivor on Auschwitz and its Realities* (1980) and first published in 1966 in German, he describes and reflects upon his internment. One of the essays, entitled precisely "Resentments," takes issue with Nietzsche's position that resentment must be overcome. While agreeing with Nietzsche that *ressentiment* "nails every one of us onto the cross of his ruined past" and "blocks the exit to the genuine human condition: the future,"[21] he defends his right to hang on to it, for forgetting would be tantamount to the total repression of desire for real vengeance. Améry later entered into a polemic with Primo Levi, whose more conciliatory position he could not share.[22]

If we are to take Améry at his word, the after-effects of Auschwitz are more corrosive for its victims than the experience of torture itself. He acknowledges that he has become a Nietzschean "man of resentment" and that it is true that resentment freezes one in the past and blocks the way to the future; yet he does not want to let go of it.[23] Whether Bassani was aware of Améry's work at this early date, I do not know. However, it is important to remember that *Behind the Door* was being written on the eve of the sensational Auschwitz Trials (1963–4), in which perpetrators of the massacres that took place at Auschwitz were put on public trial. The trials dominated the press for many months and were notable because they inaugurated wide-scale public reflection among Germans on the Holocaust.[24] In the period leading up to the trials, which began in Frankfurt on 20 December 1963, many members of the public, uncomfortable with what was to come, asked how long the Germans would be considered responsible for what had happened.[25] Améry's essays were written in response to this question, and I would like to suggest that perhaps certain aspects of this novel of Bassani's were also provoked by German public reaction to the trials, in particular the sentiment that enough time had passed for the guilty to be absolved.

There are two factors that lead me to think this may be the case. The first is the fact that the discussion about the protagonist that takes place in Cattolica's home is in fact staged like a trial itself: the prosecutor Cattolica questions the witness Pulga, who "testifies" against the young Jew and brings up everything of which he is "guilty." The second is the centrality of the image of the crucifixion, which appears not only during this episode, in which the eavesdropping protagonist is pictured under a crucifix on the wall and compares his own beating heart to the bleeding one on the figure of Jesus, but also in an earlier scene that foreshadows it: I am referring to the one in which the young protagonist finds himself in a local church where he encounters Cattolica. Before he sees Cattolica, the protagonist catches sight of a group of statues depicting the body of Christ surrounded by his followers after the crucifixion; note how much space is devoted to the lead-up and eventual focus on the subject of the statues:

> La chiesa appariva deserta. Avevo percorso passo passo la navata laterale destra, naso all'aria come un turista, ma la luce del sole che penetrava attraverso gli ampi finestroni superiori mi impediva di distinguere chiaramente le grandi tele barocche poste sopra gli altari. Raggiunto il transetto, immerso anche questo nella semioscurità, ero passato alla navata sinistra, inondata di luce. E qui la mia attenzione era stata subito attratta da una specie di strano assembramento di persone immobili e silenziose, raccolte in gruppo di fianco alla seconda delle due minori porte d'ingresso.
>
> Chi erano? Come avevo potuto rendermi conto non appena ero arrivato a distanza sufficiente, non si trattava di persone vive, bensì di statue: di statue di legno dipinto, scolpite a grandezza naturale. Erano per l'appunto quei famosi *Pianzùn d'la Rosa* davanti ai quali da bambino (non lì al Gesù, ma nella chiesa della Rosa di via Armari, di dove evidentemente erano stati rimossi più tardi) mi aveva condotto tante volte la zia Malvina, l'unica zia cattolica che possedevo. Guardavo anche adesso la scena atrocissima: il corpo livido e misero del Cristo morto, disteso sulla nuda terra, con attorno, impietriti in muti gesti, in mute smorfie, in lacrime che non avrebbero mai avuto né termine né sfogo di grida, i parenti e gli amici accorsi: la Madonna, San Giovanni, Giuseppe d'Arimatea, Simone, la Maddalena, due pie donne. (602–3)

> The church seemed deserted. I walked slowly down the right lateral nave, nose in the air like a tourist; but the sunlight coming in through the broad upper windows prevented me from distinguishing clearly the large baroque canvases placed over the altars. Having reached the transept, immersed in semidarkness, I moved to the left nave, which was bathed in light. And here my attention was immediately attracted by a sort of strange gathering of people, immobile and silent, standing together in a group beside the second of the two smaller entrances.
>
> Who were they? As I was able to realize as soon as I came close enough, they were not living people but statues: painted wooden statues, life-sized. They were, in fact, the famous *Pianzùn d'la Rosa*, which my Aunt

> Malvina (the only Catholic aunt I had), had taken me to see many times (not there, however, in the Gesù, but in the Chiesa della Rosa on Via Armari, from which they had evidently been removed subsequently). I looked once more at the atrocious scene: the livid, wretched body of the dead Christ, lying on the bare earth, and around it, frozen in mute gestures, in mute grimaces, in tears that would never end or find an outlet in screams, the relatives and friends who had come running: the Madonna, St John, Joseph of Arimathea, Simon, the Magdalene, two pious women.

In *Gli occhiali d'oro*, a scene takes place on the beaches of Riccione, in which Signora Lavezzoli, holding court under her umbrella, quotes an article from the *Civiltà Cattolica* by Father Gemelli that suggests that the racial persecutions to which the Jews are now subjected are simply the logical outcome of their responsibility for the death of Christ:

> Tema dell'articolo era la "vecchissima e vessatissima *question juive.*" Secondo il Padre Gemelli – riferiva la signora –, le ricorrenti persecuzioni, di cui gli "israeliti" venivano fatti oggetto in ogni parte del mondo da quasi duemila anni, non potevano essere spiegate altro che come segni dell'ira celeste. E l'articolo si chiudeva con la seguente domanda: è lecito al cristiano, anche se il suo cuore repugna, si capisce, da ogni idea di violenza, avanzare un giudizio su eventi storici attraverso i quali manifestamente si esprima la volontà di Dio? (270)

> The theme of the article was the "ancient and vexed *question juive.*" According to Padre Gemelli – the signora continued – the recurrent persecutions to which the "Israelites" had been subjected everywhere in the world for almost two thousand years could not be explained other than as a sign of celestial ire. And the article concluded with the following question: is it permitted for a Christian, even if his heart recoils, as one can understand, from every idea of violence, to venture a judgement on historic events through which the will of God is so clearly manifest? (69)

What Bassani seems to be saying in *Dietro la porta*, echoing in a sense Améry's position, is that if the Jews were still being held responsible for the crucifixion of Christ two thousand years after the fact, then they have the right to hang on to their own resentments a mere twenty years after an event that has traumatized all Jews, not only those who have been through the worst. In fact, in an interview about this novel, in which he was asked whether it contained a response to a so-called "crisis of the novel," Bassani responded very laconically that no, it had no such intention: "No. Il mio romanzo *Dietro la porta* … non intende dare nessuna risposta all'attuale stato di crisi del romanzo italiano e europeo, come dice Lei. Nessuna."[26] (No. My novel *Behind the Door* … doesn't intend to provide any kind of answer to the current state of crisis of the Italian and European novel, as you say. None whatsoever.)

His failure to elaborate was, I believe, more eloquent than any further statement could have been.

6 *L'airone*: A Case of Mistaken Identity

The years passed. Life on the outer surface of consciousness continued. This was a life without a dark dimension, life built on a kind of fraud. We knew that something warm and precious in us had been lost on the path to self-forgetfulness. It was something we could not deny. Parents, images from our childhood, tribal incantations, whether in the form of customs or of ancestral faith. Without them, what are we? We are hollow, floating on the outermost layer of consciousness. I have said, "We knew." But this was a late knowledge, a belated fright. We were already in the domain from which there is no retreat, and any return seemed like withdrawal from a surrounded front.

So deep was our oblivion that when the day came, and we were roused from slumber, astonishment struck us a stunning blow: how far we had traveled from ourselves! As though we had not been born in Jewish homes, and everything that we had endured was merely twilight, its source no longer attainable. We spoke of the recent past from an alien distance, as if the thing did not concern us.

Just as our oblivion was profound, so our awakening from it was shocking. We woke up dazed, astonished, full of thirst and the desire to restore to ourselves everything we had lost in that dreadful desert of oblivion and self-alienation. Only now did it seem clear for the first time to what vast distance we had exiled ourselves, as though we had been imprisoned for all those years by unknown enemies, who had forbidden us any contact with our own secrets.

– Appelfeld, "The Awakening," 151–2

Bassani's last novel is the relatively little-known *L'airone*. Written in the third person, it is radically different not only from the novels of the first-person trilogy but from the stories that preceded it as well. While the first-person trilogy is about the difficult act of remembering, this novel deals with forgetting and the price exacted by it. *L'airone* tells the story of the last day of the protagonist's life, the day Edgardo Limentani undergoes what some critics have called a "conversion to death,"[1] which culminates in the decision to commit suicide. Limentani is a sort of "Jewish Prince," and I adopt this term not in its North American colloquial usage[2] but as a reference to the intertext that I believe forms the backbone of the novel and provides one of the keys to its interpretation, Giuseppe Tomasi di Lampedusa's *Il gattopardo*.

It is a well-known fact that Bassani was responsible for the publication of *Il gattopardo* in 1958 after Elio Vittorini and other representatives of the Italian Left had rejected the Sicilian novel because it did not mirror their own cultural politics of the moment: Lampedusa's pessimistic take on the Risorgimento, as well as its implied critique of post-Resistance triumphalism, did not sit well with the official optimism of left-wing intellectuals. His refusal to share their belief in what Micòl at the end of the *Giardino* sarcastically calls the "futuro democratico e sociale" (578) of the nation did not seem quite as jarring, however, to Bassani, who was also out-of-step with the official forward-march tempo of the politically correct. As a Jew who had spent the years since the war trying to keep alive and to come to terms with a past that most everyone else was trying to suppress, Bassani saw in Lampedusa's novel not only a good story and a work of art but also a reflection of some of his own feelings about what had been hastily swept under the rug in the rush to consensus after 1945. Moreover, Lampedusa's reflections on the failure of the new Italy to provide the social justice it had promised could not have been more relevant for the Jews, for whom emancipation had provided the same mirage of equality and the rights of full citizenship.[3]

It might be objected that the story of a proud and haughty prince coming face to face with the decline of his power and prestige in Risorgimento Sicily could not possibly have anything to do with that of a Jewish survivor in post–World War II Ferrara, and the objection would be correct. That is precisely the point. Set in 1947, Bassani's novel not only makes explicit Lampedusa's implicit critique of postwar Italy, it also uses the *Gattopardo* as an intertext through which it evokes the enduring "false consciousness" of some sectors of the Italian Jewish bourgeoisie as they struggle with the rapidly changing social and political landscape now that the Fascists have been defeated and the Communists loom large on the horizon.[4] Even in the face of what he witnessed in Ferrara under the Fascists and during the Repubblica di

Salò, the novel's central character, Edgardo Limentani, prefers to think of himself as a sort of modern-day Prince Fabrizio, a feudal landowner besieged by the demands of his labourers and fearful of an uprising, rather than as the shell-shocked Jew that he is, still reeling from the atrocities and humiliations of the recent past.

This dogged refusal to admit and absorb the enormity of what he and other Jews have been through prevents him from engaging in the mourning process that might make it possible to go on. Depressed and desperate to shake off the feeling of unease and confinement that plagues him, Limentani decides to go hunting for the first time since the passing of the Race Laws in 1938. There are many ironies in this decision. The first is that Jews, as every one except Edgardo Limentani seems to know, are not hunters.[5] But Limentani has strayed so far from his Jewish roots and identified so closely with the Italian landed classes that he sees a hunting expedition as a perfectly fitting way to enjoy some fresh air and escape the stifling atmosphere of his home and Ferrara.[6] The second irony, of course, is that he himself still feels like a hunted animal. The hunter turning into the hunted is a literary topos, but Bassani uses it in a very particular way, as a means of representing his repressed protagonist's internal life. Unconsciously, Limentani is setting out to enact his real feelings. The hunter will become the hunted as Limentani unwittingly re-enacts the trauma of his flight from Italy to Switzerland to escape the Nazi hunt for Jews. At the day's end he will take his own life after refusing to shoot any birds and recognizing himself in the struggling heron that his guide's precise aim brings down. But his suicide will take place only after he finally confronts, symbolically, a representative of his Fascist tormentors. We will see in this symbolic confrontation an allusion to Nietzsche's view that men of resentment can only express their desire for vengeance in symbolic ways, but this is not the only Nietzschean echo in this novel. In the first aphorism of part 3 of *Beyond Good and Evil*, the German philosopher refers to psychology as the "great hunt" and the psychological landscape as a primeval forest:

> The human soul and its limits, the range of human experiences reached so far, the heights, depths and distances of these experiences, the whole history of the soul *so far* and its yet unexhausted possibilities – that is the predestined hunting ground for a born psychologist and lover of the "great hunt." But how often he has to say to himself in despair: "One hunter! alas, only a single one! and look at this huge forest, this primeval

> forest!" And then he wishes he had a few hundred helpers and good, well-trained hounds that he could drive into the history of the human soul to round up *his* game.[7]

Bassani has been on the "great hunt" all through the *Romanzo*, searching for the truth about himself. In this novel, he finally brings the protagonist – one of the many "parts" of him represented in the *Romanzo* – face to face with the mirror image of his soul, the wounded heron. *L'airone* uses a third person very much like the one used by Lampedusa: a third-person narrator perched on his character's shoulder, seeing right into his thoughts and reporting them for the most part using free indirect speech. No mediations and no mediators are needed because in this novel Bassani has finally succeeded in bridging the distance between past and present, between the young man and the adult writer, between who he was then and who he is now: he has arrived at the final "unmasking," to use a Nietzschean term. Limentani's suicide is the necessary defeat of Bassani's own worst tendencies in the postwar period, as he tries to come to terms with the past and resituate himself as both an Italian and a Jew without falling prey to a paralysing *ressentiment*; and yet he wishes to achieve all of this without denying himself as a Jew, without forgetting. The novel was conceived in a state of depression brought on by the suicide of two Jewish Ferrara friends – "una malattia mortale" (a life-threatening disease) – which he claims is reflected in the catatonic *école du regard* tone of the narration. When he reached the end of the novel, Bassani experienced a catharsis that brought him "back to life."[8] When he says that Limentani has to die in order to return to life,[9] he is using, I believe, the Nietzschean concept of "overcoming," according to which "all things can be turned back upon themselves": "The consequence of such a turning back is no mere formal negation but a simultaneous annulling and uplifting, a sublimation, whereby the original self is both retained and yet transformed into something new."[10]

Edgardo Limentani's tale opens at the crack of dawn in his bedroom, as he prepares to set out on his day trip. In the first chapter we learn that he managed to escape the persecution and round-up of Jews in his native Ferrara. We learn that his economic survival was engineered through his timely marriage to a Gentile woman of the lower classes, thanks to which he was able to hang on to his property, in spite of the Race Laws, by transferring it to her. As for his physical survival, he and his family fled to Switzerland in 1943 when Ferrara was under Salò and spent a year and a half there. He now lives with his wife, his daughter, and his mother in his family home. It is his mother who has set out his hunting clothes for him the night before. He sleeps alone in the small bedroom that was his before his marriage (like Pino Barilari) while his wife sleeps alone in the master bedroom next to his. Like Lampedusa's Prince, he is forty-five years old. A member of the landed bourgeoisie and owner of a large estate called La Montina, reminiscent of the Prince's Donnafugata, he is shaken by the recent turn of events, more specifically the rise to popularity of the Communists and the changed climate at La Montina. Once received there as a quasi-feudal lord, he was faced with an uprising of the labourers demanding a greater share of the crop and better working conditions during his last visit, the first since 1938. His former sense of security is definitely a thing of the past, but he attributes this exclusively to his loss of power and prestige as a landowner, with little or no acknowledgment of what he has been through as a Jew. Just as the Prince fears on his way to Donnafugata that the deference to which he is accustomed will no longer be his due, so Limentani is nervous about setting out into the countryside in the current climate of hostility to the landowning classes:

> Prima della guerra – ricordava – , un signore di Ferrara poteva, la domenica, andare a sparare le sue due fucilate dalle parti di Codigoro o di Comacchio essendo sicuro al mille per mille della buona accoglienza e del rispetto generali. ... Ma al giorno d'oggi? ... I tempi dei sorrisi, delle scappellate, degli inchini, erano finiti. Per tutti: ex perseguitati politici e razziali compresi. (708)

> Before the war, he remembered, a gentleman from Ferrara, on Sunday, could go and shoot off his gun somewhere around Codigoro or Comacchio, one hundred per cent sure of a pleasant welcome and general respect. ... But nowadays? ... The days of smiles, of doffed hats, of bows, were over. For everyone: including former victims of political and racial persecution. (8–9)

Limentani sees himself as a relic of the past, incapable of adapting, like the Prince, or perhaps unwilling to do so. And just as the Prince compares himself to his cousin Malvica, whose aristocratic convictions remain unshaken by the recent turn of events in Sicily, so Edgardo compares himself to his cousin Ulderico, who, in terms of the *Gattopardo*, is perhaps more like the turncoat nephew Tancredi, the man for all seasons and all regimes. Ulderico also married a Gentile woman of a lower class but well before the Race Laws. Unlike Limentani, he had joined the Fascist party when it seemed opportune and now was completely assimilated and living with his large family in Codigoro, just outside Ferrara.

Before setting out on his trip, Limentani stops momentarily in the ground floor apartment of the building caretakers, who have been his family's faithful servants for over forty years. At first their small, familiar dwelling seems to provide a warm, womb-like refuge from the cold and hostile world: "Oh, se avesse potuto nonostante tutto restare là, al caldo della portineria, nascosto ai suoi di casa e a chiunque altro fino a sera! In cambio avrebbe dato qualsiasi cosa" (724; Oh, if he could have stayed there, despite everything, in the warmth of the concierge's lodge, hidden from his family and from everyone else, until evening! He would have given anything in exchange [26]). However, after the ritual niceties, the elderly couple immediately seek his counsel and intervention in a family dispute centred around their daughter's shiftless husband, an unemployed Communist whom they suspect of beating her. Limentani immediately casts this marital relationship in a sadomasochistic light, remembering "la faccia di lui, livida di rancore a stento contenuto, e quella di lei … con quei suoi occhi da vittima predestinata e forse consenziente" (724; Romeo's face, livid with ill-repressed bitterness, and hers … with those eyes, like the eyes of a foreordained victim, perhaps a willing one [26]). At this point his perception of his physical surroundings changes drastically: "E adesso anche la cucina dei Manzoli era diventata di colpo inabitabile: un posto anche questo da cui bisognava sloggiare. E subito" (725). (And now the Manzoli kitchen, too, had abruptly become uninhabitable: this, too, a place from which he had to clear out. And at once [27].)

From womb-like haven to "posto da cui bisognava sloggiare. E subito" (a place from which he had to clear out. And at once). This choice of words, totally inappropriate in the context of the caretaker's apartment, seems slightly enigmatic at first, but then it becomes clear that this perception is an interference, a residue of the time of persecution when the Jews of Ferrara were being hunted down for deportation. Though Limentani and his family were fortunate enough to have been able to escape to Switzerland, to have *sloggiato* (cleared out) perhaps just in the nick of time, the choice of words betrays the fact that this is a trauma that has not been worked through: it still haunts him and is being suppressed in the attempt to normalize. Not coincidentally, the words are conjured up by the image of a "consenting victim," a recurring motif that signals the presence of the haunting question about the possible passivity of the Jews in the face of their persecution. In *Gli occhiali d'oro* the protagonist constantly sees Fadigati as Deliliers's "consenting victim," while in *Dietro la porta* he finally focuses on himself, as he repeatedly wonders why he was so anxious to cozy up to his haughty rival Cattolica and so unable to resist the abuse of his "false friend" Pulga. Later, when Limentani imagines himself attempting to speak to Irma's husband, the Communist, as the caretakers have asked him to do, "si sentiva invadere da una sorta di disgusto. Di disgusto misto a paura" (725). (he felt a kind of disgust. Disgust mixed with fear [27]). This feeling too, given its intensity, can only be a residue displaced from the original object of his fear and loathing, the Fascists, to the Communists, who ostensibly represent the current threat to his well-being.

The extent to which his anger and revulsion vis-à-vis the Fascist collaborators has been suppressed is revealed when he makes a brief stop at the local inn in Codigoro. Fittingly, Limentani suffers from constipation and goes there in search of a place to relieve himself, having suddenly felt the call of nature. The innkeeper, Gino Bellagamba, had not very long ago been a Fascist thug, whose "occhiate minacciose e sprezzanti" (728; menacing and and contemptuous glances [30]) Limentani remembers having been subjected to in Ferrara in '38 and '39 as a Jew and a non-Fascist. Nonetheless, he is quick to rationalize away his lingering anger and the difficulty of confronting Bellagamba today, as if the atrocities of the recent past had never taken place:

> Però, a conti fatti, erano davvero tanto peggio i fascisti di prima del '43 in confronto ai comunisti di adesso? ... Quanto a Bellagamba, magari era vero, come sosteneva la Nives, che dopo il periodo badogliano si fosse messo con quelli di Salò. Possibilissimo. Ad ogni modo se perfino i comunisti, che oggi erano i padroni assoluti di Codigoro, lo lasciavano stare e prosperare, per quale motivo avrebbe dovuto essere lui, proprio lui, a fare adesso delle storie? (729)

> However, when you came right down to it, were they really so much worse, those Fascists before '43, than the communists now? ... As for Bellagamba, it may be true, as Nives insisted, that after the Badoglio period he joined up with the Salò crowd. Quite possible. In any case, if even the communists, who today were the undisputed masters of Codigoro, left him alone and allowed him to prosper, why should he, Edgardo Limentani, of all people, make any fuss? (31)

When he knocks at the door of the inn at five in the morning and Bellagamba asks, "Chi è!" (Who's there?), Limentani's answer expresses the ultimate irony: "'Amici,' rispose piano" (771; "Friend," he answered softly [32]).

Bellagamba treats him with the utmost cordiality and deference befitting the difference in their social status, but at the same time he seems anxious to establish a certain complicity that makes Limentani uneasy. The Jew has his limits and allows no undue familiarity, but he denies his right to any anger: "Lui non ce l'aveva con nessuna persona al mondo, e con Bellagamba meno che meno" (731; He bore no grudge against anyone in the world, and least of all against Bellagamba [33]). However, when he finds himself face to face with Bellagamba in the closed space of his office, what the mind denies, the body speaks: "Col senso più che mai di trovarsi fuori del mondo, non sapeva da che parte incominciare. Prendere qualcosa nemmeno pensarci. Lo stomaco se lo sentiva chiuso come un pugno" (732). (With the sensation, stronger than ever, of being outside the world, he didn't know how to begin. To ask for something to drink was out of the question. He felt his stomach clenched like a fist [35].)

As he makes his way up the stairs, he is struck by the renovations the inn has undergone. Rather than focusing on his real status, a nervous Jew on his way to the enemy's toilet, reminiscent of Joyce's Leopold Bloom who is also afflicted by constipation and seen sitting on a toilet,[11] Limentani contrasts Bellagamba's newly found prosperity with his own situation as a landowner-in-distress à la Fabrizio Salina, incapable of adjusting to changing times and to changing methods of agriculture. He remembers having read an article in the *Giornale di Emilia* about the banks refusing to give credit to "relitti del passato" (relics of the past) and immediately recognizes himself as fitting into that category, in other words as "un sopravvissuto" (734).

The irony of course is that Limentani is indeed a survivor (the literal translation of *un sopravvissuto*), not of his agrarian, aristocratic past but of another past as lengthy as the Prince's: as a Jew. Once he is sitting on the toilet, his body speaks the repressed emotions: "Ma niente, ancora una volta, niente: il ventre non voleva saperne di vuotarglisi. Nonostante ogni sforzo sentiva che neanche adesso ce l'avrebbe fatta" (735). (But nothing, again, nothing happened: his abdomen would have no part of emptying itself for him. Despite every effort, he felt he wouldn't make it this time either [38].)

The toilet paper in the bathroom consists of cut-up newspaper bearing fragments of old headlines and articles. One of them details the continuing bloody persecutions of the Jews in Poland. In spite of all that he has been through, Limentani has difficulty believing it: "Possibile? Il tono dell'articolo gli sembrava eccessivamente enfatico. Chi l'aveva scritto certo esagerava. Alla base, però, qualcosa di vero doveva pur esserci. Diamine – sogghignò –, non potevano mica essere tutte balle!"(736). (Was it possible? The article's tone seemed excessively vehement. The man who had written it was undoubtedly exaggerating. But at the bottom of it, nevertheless, there must be some truth. My God, he grimaced, it couldn't be all lies! [39].)

As he is leaving the inn, he notices that Bellagamba "assomigliava abbastanza al Mussolini degli ultimi anni" (740; bore a certain resemblance to Mussolini in his last years [44]). He also notices that Bellagamba is becoming increasingly solicitous, provoking or at least patronizing him, but instead of standing his ground, he rationalizes away his unease and denies the reality of the situation: "Se non capiva male, voleva soltanto rassicurarlo, confermargli che non c'era nessun bisogno che continuasse a darsi pena per delle ombre, pure e semplici" (742; Unless he was mistaken, Bellagamba wanted only to reassure him, to prove to him that there was no need to go on suffering because of mere shadows [46–7]). As a result, by the time they make their way together to the café in the central piazza, they appear to have become old friends: "Attraversarono la piazza camminando a fianco a fianco come due vecchi amici: ... e, proprio come succede spesso fra amici, senza scambiare una sola parola" (743; They crossed the square, walking side by side like two old friends: ... and, as often happens in fact among old friends, without exchanging a single word [48]). This particular remark recalls a similar scene in *Dietro la porta,* in which the protagonist and his Gentile classmate Carlo Cattolica walk together towards school "come due buoni e affezionati amici" (606; like close, affectionate friends) in spite of their rivalry and in spite of the fact that Cattolica has just insulted him.

Their false intimacy reaches its climax when Bellagamba tries to discourage Limentani from continuing on his hunting expedition by offering to prepare a bed for him at the inn: "Si volse a guardarlo. Al solito gli strizzava l'occhio, ma questa volta tutto rosso in viso come se stesse offrendogli qualcosa di eccezionale, per non dire di proibito" (745). (He turned to look at the man. Bellagamba was winking, as usual: but this time, his face all flushed, as if he were offering him something exceptional, not to say forbidden [49].) Bellagamba's wink to Limentani recalls Pino Barilari's conspiratorial wink to Sciagura at the trial in "Una notte del '43," when he claims to have been sleeping and therefore not to have witnessed the shootings in the square. In both cases, victims are conspiring with their persecutors to deny the past.

When they reach the café, Limentani decides to call, but to no avail, his cousin Ulderico, with whom he has entered into contact recently for the first time in fifteen years. The barman dials the number for him and asks who he should say is on the telephone. Limentani's self-loathing is so great that he finds he can barely bring himself to pronounce his own name. The repulsion he felt when confronted with the image of his caretaker's daughter as consenting victim finally finds its true object: "'Limentani,' rispose non senza sforzo, vincendo a fatica quella specie di stupore mescolato d'imbarazzo e di ripugnanza che tornava a dargli il suono del proprio cognome" (746; "Limentani," he answered, not without some effort, overcoming with difficulty that kind of amazement, mingled with embarrassment and repugnance, which the sound of his own name again aroused in him [51]). The association between his self-loathing and his name, an identifiably Jewish one, signals his self-hatred as a Jew. Appelfeld describes the will to forget as "a latent protest against suffering and fate, and certainly against its immediate cause, our being Jewish":

> Everything that had happened to us had only happened as a consequence of that. This recognition soon degenerated to its ugliest and most painful phase. At the lowest point the victim took on the malevolence of the evildoer: something wicked lurked within us. The inability to submit a full accounting to oneself and the will to forget fused mysteriously and turned into abysmal loathing. Not loathing for the murderer who had committed the crime but loathing for ourselves. The victim, in his weakness of spirit, took on the wickedness of the evildoer and attributed it to himself. Anything that was Jewish or seemed Jewish appeared feeble, ugly, harmful. Loathing is full of bitterness, but loathing for oneself is the most grievous thing of all.[12]

Unable to reach his cousin, Limentani leaves Codigoro to continue to the area where he had arranged to be met by a guide. This is a particularly interesting aspect of the story since it seems to evoke the flight to safety during the worst days of the Repubblica di Salò. Almost all the Jews who fled to Switzerland employed guides, known as *passatori*. Some were Resistance fighters, some were smugglers, others were professional guides specialized in clandestine border crossings. Not all these crossings went well; in fact, many did not, for the guides could not all be trusted.[13] There is no reference to this aspect of the escape in the novel, but the trauma of this flight seems to lurk behind the meeting of Limentani and his guide. As soon as he sees him, Limentani immediately tries to ascertain whether or not he is a Communist but manages only to learn that he had been a partisan (*partigiano*) before the liberation. Unlike the Fascist Bellagamba, the guide is taciturn, and this makes Limentani extremely uncomfortable; again he imagines that he is being looked at with derision, projecting his own self-hatred onto his companion: "Ma quella vaga aria di scherno che gli circolava attorno agli zigomi ossuti non era forse più eloquente e deprimente di qualsiasi discorso?" (761; But the vaguely contemptuous expression that played over Gavino's bony cheeks: wasn't it, perhaps, far more eloquent, and depressing, than any words? [70]). When he and the guide finally settle into the boat from which they will be shooting ducks and other birds, Limentani offers the guide a rifle. At first he refuses, claiming that as a guide his only job is to go around with the boat "a raccogliere morti e feriti" (767; to collect the dead and the wounded [77]), but he then relents.

The fact that the phrase "morti e feriti" (the dead and the wounded) is part of the narrator's reported speech and not attributed directly to the guide suggests that the hunting episode we are about to witness is one in which the birds exist also as metaphors, as stand-ins for the victims of Nazi-Fascist violence. In fact, almost immediately they spot the heron of the novel's title, with which Limentani will identify. This particular moment recalls a very similar and famous hunting scene from *Il gattopardo*, in which the Prince identifies with a hare struggling in vain to escape the trap into which it has stepped.[14] Famous as it is, however, the hare scene represents but a passing moment in the Lampedusa novel. Here the description of the heron, and indeed of the whole hunting episode, is long and detailed; it attempts to render Limentani's perception of this mass shooting scene, as well as its effect on him, as it slowly transports him from the present to the time of persecution:

> Per più di un'ora rimase così, seduto col fucile in mano a guardare gli uccelli arrivargli sopra la testa. Non sparava. Non tentò di farlo nemmeno una volta. A sparare, ad abbattere uno dopo l'altro gli uccelli che gli capitano a tiro, era soltanto Gavino, da dietro il suo cespuglio. *Pam-pam. Pam-pam-pam. Pam-pam-pam-pam. Pam-pam-pam-pam-pam.* A serie di due, di tre, di quattro, perfino di cinque spari successivi, era raro che le sue

fucilate fallissero il bersaglio. E le bestie, fulminate o ferite, a piombare giù nell'acqua con sordi tonfi.

... Il numero degli uccelli abbattuti da Gavino era salito in breve a una trentina. ... lui nel frattempo non faceva niente. Stava lì a guardare e basta.

Era un po' sempre come se stesse sognando. ...

... Come può accadere soltanto negli incubi, in un attimo ... lui era riuscito a vedere tutto, a notare tutto, e a tutto pensare, nel mentre, tranne che a imbracciare la Krupp e premere il grilletto.

Niente più gli appariva come reale. ... Lui stesso ... col fucile in mano come Gavino, però inerte, incapace di un solo gesto ... Vero e non vero, visto e immaginato, vicino e lontano: tutte le cose si mescolavano, si confondevano fra di loro. Perfino il tempo normale, quello dei minuti e delle ore, non c'era più, non contava più. (772–4)

For more than an hour he stayed like that: sitting with the gun in his hand, watching the birds arrive over his head. He didn't shoot. He didn't even try it once. The only one shooting, knocking down, one after the other, the birds that came within his range, was Gavino, from behind his thicket. *Bang-bang. Bang-bang-bang. Bang-bang-bang-bang. Bang-bang-bang-bang-bang.* In series of two, of three, of four, and even of five successive explosions, his shots rarely missed their mark. And the birds, killed or wounded, plunged into the water with dull thuds.

... Rapidly, in other words, the number of birds Gavino shot rose to about thirty. ... he, meanwhile, did nothing. He just sat there watching, and that was all. It was, always, a bit as if he were dreaming.

... As sometimes happens in nightmares, in an instant ... he had managed to see everything: and to think of everything, in the meanwhile, except of grasping his Krupp and pressing the trigger.

... Real and unreal; seen and imagined; near and far: all things became mixed and confused among themselves. Even normal time, the time of minutes and hours, no longer existed, counted for nothing. (83–5)

Limentani has gradually shifted from chronological to psychological time, to the time in which he has remained frozen, the time of persecution. When the heron suddenly reappears, wounded and agonizing, Limentani is mesmerized. His identification with the crippled bird, as it hovers between life and death for an entire chapter, is total:

Credeva che fosse morto e che la cagna si sarebbe avventata a raccoglierlo. Invece no. Appena riemerso, fu pronto a drizzarsi su quei suoi trampoli di gambe, cominciando a muovere in qua e in là la testina minuscola. "Dov'è che mi trovo?", aveva l'aria di chiedersi. "E cosa mi è successo?" ...

Lo guardava pieno di ansia, immedesimandosi totalmente. Anche a lui sfuggiva il perché di tante cose. Per quale motivo Gavino aveva sparato? E perché non si alzava in piedi, adesso, e non tirava un altro colpo, quello di grazia? Non era questa la regola? ... Si sentiva la testa confusa, sbalordita, affollata di domande che non ricevevano risposta. ...

... E benché ferito, benché indebolito dal sangue perduto, ... a un dato momento aveva pensato che gli convenisse comunque e subito "cambiare zona." ... Nascondersi là dentro, intanto, in attesa della notte ormai vicina. E dopo, dopo stare a vedere. ... E la terraferma a portata di gamba avrebbe significato una possibilità ulteriore di fuga, forse addirittura di salvezza, o magari, se non proprio la salvezza definitiva, la garanzia quasi sicura di farcela a resistere vivo per lo meno fino a domani.

... Ma come si illudeva! – gli venne all'improvviso da dirsi – . Si illudeva a un punto tale ... , era chiaro, povero stupido, che se a pensare di sparargli non gli fosse sembrato a lui, di star sparando in un certo senso a se stesso, gli avrebbe tirato immediatamente. E così se non altro sarebbe finita. (776–80)

He thought it was dead, and that the dog would burst out and collect it. But no: as soon as it surfaced, it pulled itself up on its stilt legs, moving here and there, in jerks, its minuscule head. "Where am I?" it seemed to be wondering. "And what's happened to me?"

... He looked at it, full of anxiety, identifying with it completely. For him, too, the reason of many things was obscure. Why had Gavino fired? And why didn't he stand up now, and fire a second shot, the *coup de grâce*? Wasn't this the rule? ... His head felt befuddled, stunned: crammed with questions that received no answer. ...

... and, though wounded, though weakened by loss of blood, ... at a certain moment it had thought that it was wise still, immediately, to "move on." ... To hide in there, for the present, waiting for night, which was now near; and afterwards, afterwards it would see what could be done. ... And having the mainland within walking distance would mean a further opportunity to escape, perhaps even salvation, or perhaps, if not definitive salvation, the almost certain guarantee of staying alive at least until tomorrow.

... But how mistaken it was, he suddenly said to himself, it fooled itself to such a degree ... , obviously, poor stupid animal, that if he hadn't felt that shooting at it would seem, to him, shooting in a sense at himself, he would have fired at once. Then, at least, it would be all over. (87–91)

It is clear that the hunting scene functions for Limentani at a subliminal level as a re-enactment of the hazards of his own flight to safety in the days of persecution. The thoughts of escape and hiding, of waiting for nightfall to try to reach safety, all hark back to the passage over the border from Italy to Switzerland at the mercy of mountain guides and in danger of capture at any moment. It is also clear that he sees his inability to participate in the hunt here not as a rejection of a violent activity but as a symbol of his own passivity in the face of persecution and violence. It is a moment of epiphany; looking at the heron, he seems to be looking into a mirror and seeing himself for the first time for who he has become: from hunter he has turned into the hunted.

Appropriately, on the way back to Codigoro Limentani begins to feel as if he is being pursued: "Prendeva le curve facendo fischiare le gomme sull'asfalto: esattamente come se Gavino, la cagna, e tutto quello che i due gli ricordavano, venissero a distanza ravvicinata, addirittura lo tallonassero" (782; He took the curves, making the tires scream against the asphalt, exactly as if Gavino, the dog, and everything the two of them reminded him of were following him closely, were even at his heels [96]). In the trunk of his car he is carrying the game, "un carico imbarazzante e schifoso" (827; an embarrassing and disgusting cargo [96]). As he enters Codigoro, "l'impressione che continuava a provare di essere inseguito, assurda, se ne rendeva ben conto, ma non per questo meno reale" (783; the impression he continued to feel of being pursued, absurd, he knew, but not for that less real [97]) intensifies, perhaps because he is on his way back to Bellagamba's inn. In fact, as he approaches his destination, "non poteva fare a meno di meravigliarsi sentendo nei confronti di un simile ambiente, che in circostanze normali avrebbe affrontato di malavoglia, oppresso, al solito, dal timore di brutti incontri, un'attrazione così intensa, così irresistibile" (783–4; he couldn't help being amazed, since an atmosphere of this sort which, in normal circumstances, he would have faced reluctantly, oppressed, as usual, by the fear of unpleasant encounters, now had for him an intense, irresistible attraction [98]).

Limentani pulls up to the inn as if in a trance, unaware of what he is about to do. Slowly the purpose of this return takes shape: here he will unload the game as if confronting Bellagamba, finally, with the evidence of his past activities, the corpses of the hapless victims of his violence: "Mentre faceva manovra gli venne in mente Bellagamba. Forse Bellagamba la selvaggina avrebbe accettato di prenderla lui. … Scaricare le bestie morte dal bagagliaio, e poi portarle dentro (la luce del neon avrebbe reso l'operazione ancora più facile), diventava un lavoro da niente" (784). (As he was parking, he thought of Bellagamba. Perhaps Bellagamba would agree to take the dead birds. ... To unload the game from the trunk, and carry it inside [the light of the neon would make the operation even easier], became then a trifling task [98].)

Of course none of this is clear to Limentani, and he sits down at a table and discusses the meal he is about to order calmly with his host. However, he perceives Bellagamba differently this time, seeing in his eyes "l'ansia, chissà perché, di un animale che fiuta il pericolo" (786; the anxiety, for some reason, of an animal that scents danger" [101]). During the meal, Limentani is tormented again by the thought of his passivity during the hunt: "Un colpo solo, lui, nonostante la doppietta che aveva in mano, non era mai riuscito a trovare la forza di tirarlo" (789; Despite the gun in his hand, he hadn't been able to find in himself the strength to fire a single shot [104]). Finally, when Bellagamba comes to ask whether the meal was satisfactory, Limentani works up the courage to confront him, in a manner of speaking of course:

> Inghiottì. Si asciugò le labbra col tovagliolo.
> "Perfetto," rispose.
> Non sapeva da che parte incominciare.
> "Senta," disse alla fine. "Ho il bagaglio della macchina carica di bestie. Le vuole lei?" (789–90)

> He swallowed, then wiped his lips with his napkin.
> "Fine," he answered.
> He didn't know how to begin.
> "Listen," he said finally, "the trunk of my car is full of birds. Do you want them?" (105)

Unaware of what is going on, Bellagamba brings up the possibility of having the heron stuffed and embalmed, even suggesting the name of a taxidermist in town that regularly performs this service for hunters. He then proceeds to ask Limentani about his car – he had asked about it earlier, offering to buy it from him. At first Limentani, whose mind is clearly elsewhere, does not react, but then he remembers: "La macchina, certo. Come no. Invece che vendergliela, sarebbe stato quasi meglio regalargliela. Insieme con tutti gli uccelli che aveva in corpo" (792). (His car, of course. Instead of selling it to him, it would almost have been better to give it to him. Along with all the birds in its body [108].)

When Limentani leaves the inn after having spent a few hours asleep in one of the rooms, he decides to pay a visit to his cousin but changes his mind. He is aware that the sexual dreams he had while asleep and the fantasies he has about his cousin's wife all point to a state of mind bordering on delirium, a delirium that began when he first set out on his hunting trip and that is now bringing him close to a definitive understanding of the falsity of his position, of his life, of his decisions, and of the persona he has adopted: "Con una lucidità repentina si sorprese a chiedersi: ma lui, lui stesso, vestito da caccia, col berretto di pelo in testa, a quell'ora, sotto quei portici, ma lui chi era, veramente?" (822; With a sudden lucidity, he surprised himself by wondering: he, he himself, in his hunting clothes, with the fur cap on his head, at that hour, under those arcades, who was he, who, really? [143–4]). His feelings of exclusion and entrapment are total. Everything he sees is perceived in terms of his sense of being "shut out" or "shut in": he imagines that the heron must have felt like him, cornered, "chiuso da ogni parte, senza la minima possibilità di sortita" (823; hemmed in on all sides, without the slightest possibility of escape [145]). He sees a man and a woman gesticulating to each other from afar and feels like a lone spectator: "Gli sembrava di assistere dal margine di una piazza sterminata a una rappresentazione di burattini fatta solo per lui" (824; He seemed to watch, from the edge of an endless square, a puppet show being put on for him alone [146]). The sight of a group of card players in a café provokes him to ask, "Come mai lì, chiusi in quella stanza, dietro la lastra della finestra, apparivano talmente estranei e irraggiungibili? … Gli pareva di trovarsi davanti a un quadro in cornice. Impossibile entrarci dentro. Non c'era posto, spazio sufficiente" (827). (Why, there, shut in that room, beyond the window, why did they seem to him so alien, so unapproachable? … He felt as if he were standing before a picture in a frame. It was impossible to enter. There was no place, no room for him [149–50].) Even the thought of his daughter inspires only "il consueto, amaro senso di estraneità, quasi di repulsione, che gli aveva sempre impedito di considerarla sua, di volerle bene" (843; the usual, bitter sense of foreignness, almost of revulsion, which had always prevented him from considering her his own, from loving her [167]).

The idea of suicide, which has been subliminally taking shape in his mind all day, finally crystallizes when he stops in front of the window of the taxidermist mentioned to him by Bellagamba. Faced with a wide array of embalmed birds and animals, instead of finding them repulsive as he usually does, he suddenly sees them as occupying an enviable position:

> Di là dal vetro il silenzio, l'immobilità assoluta, la pace.
>
> Guardava ad una ad una le bestie imbalsamate, magnifiche tutte nella loro morte, più vive che se fossero vive. ... di una vita che non correva più nessun rischio di deteriorarsi, tirati a lucido, ma soprattutto diventati di gran lunga più belli di quando respiravano e il sangue correva veloce nelle loro vene, lui solo, forse – pensava – , era in grado di *capirla* davvero la perfezione di quella loro bellezza finale e non deperibile, di apprezzarla sino in fondo. (834–5)

> Beyond the glass: silence, absolute stillness, peace.
>
> One by one, he looked at the stuffed animals, magnificent, all of them, in their death, more alive than if they were alive. ... with a life that no longer ran any risk of deteriorating; polished to a high gloss; but made beautiful, above all, surely more beautiful, and by a great deal, than when they were breathing and the blood ran swiftly through their veins: only he, perhaps, he thought, was able really to *understand* it, the perfection of this beauty of theirs, final and imperishable, to appreciate it fully. (157–9)

In the *Gattopardo*, the Prince, an amateur astronomer, is similarly struck by the beauty of the stars. Reliable and eternal, regular in their movements, the stars attract him precisely because they offer a refuge from the chaos and unpredictability of life. It is to the mathematical calculation of the transit of the stars that the Prince turns when seeking solace and escape from confrontation with his passivity and with the inevitability of the demise of his class and his own family. In the *Gattopardo* there is also an embalmed animal, the family dog Bendicò, who ends up in a heap of dust when, in the very last scene of the novel, the eldest daughter Concetta decides abruptly to throw away his carcass, finally letting go of the past. Lampedusa's stars and embalmed domestic animal become embalmed hunted animals in the Bassani novel and offer the same comfort; the Prince becomes a hunted Jew who decides to put an end forever to the torture that his life has become. Once Limentani makes the decision to shoot himself, he feels an immense peace come over him, and his bitterness disappears, dissolved by the prospect of finally joining the dead. The embalmed animals are a symbol not unlike Pino Barilari's paralysis in "Una notte del '43"; just as his physical paralysis is the figural representation of Pino's spiritual reality – emotional paralysis – so here the embalmed animals are the figural representation of Limentani's spiritual reality – that of the hunted animal frozen in time.

The novel's protagonist, Edgardo Limentani, shares much with other Jewish males portrayed by Bassani. He is characterized very much as a man suffering from arrested development, symbolized by the fact that he lives with his mother, that he sleeps alone in his childhood room, that it is she who laid out his hunting clothes for him, and that it is in her room that the novel closes: it is as if by taking his own life he is finally separating from her in the only way he can – or perhaps returning to the womb. Even his face – "le labbra grosse, sporgenti, un po' da donna" (706; the heavy, protruding lips, slightly womanish [6]) – bears the mark of his incomplete masculinity. His marriage is a sham; in fact, as he watches his wife sleep before leaving the house, the wedding band on her finger is barely visible: "Il cerchietto d'oro della fede quasi non si distingueva" (713; The narrow gold wedding ring could hardly be discerned [13]). Limentani only married when desperate to find a way to hang on to his property, suggesting that under different circumstances he would have never married at all, that he would have remained forever a bachelor. The years of his attempt at playing the role of husband, "i tempi in cui, faticosamente quanto volenterosamente, aveva tentato di fare il marito, il buon marito" (the times when, laboriously, though willingly, he had tried to act the husband, the good husband) had been "gli anni peggiori della sua vita" (765; the worst years of his life [75]). We are told that before the Race Laws he and Ulderico often shared women, women of the Gentile lower classes, until Ulderico converted, married, and left Ferrara. Although it would seem that Ulderico represents the capacity for seamless adaptation, or assimilation, this too is clearly Limentani's perception: when Limentani decided to marry Nives, Ulderico did everything in his power to dissuade him, though to no avail.

Like earlier protagonists, Limentani's idea of himself is very much tied up with his class consciousness, which permeates all of his thoughts: "Come era meschino e antipatico anche il suo viso, come era assurdo! Sua madre aveva sempre sostenuto, naturalmente compiacendosene, che assomigliava a quello dell'ex-re Umberto. Poteva darsi" (706). (How base and disagreeable his face was, too, he said to himself, how absurd it was! His mother had always insisted, naturally pleased by the fact, that it resembled the face of the former King Umberto. Perhaps [6].) His contempt for his wife is total and more bound to her lower class origins than anything else. While recognizing that he had married her out of opportunism, he nonetheless sees her as a bird of prey, the usurper of his wealth and his social status; he resents the airs she now puts on, as he sees her "recitare con compunzione la sua parte di dama della più eletta società cittadina" (714; demurely play her role as lady of the highest society of the city [14]).

As in previous works, primal images abound along with those of exclusion. However, they assume particularly interesting dimensions here and are couched in otherwise enigmatic behaviours, particularly in relation to the cousin Ulderico, whom Limentani has not seen for years. When he calls Ulderico's home from the bar in Codigoro, the maid answers the phone and promises to get someone to talk to him, but he is left hanging for a long time. He hears all the noises of the family and is left to imagine what he cannot see:

> Tratteneva il fiato, non faceva il minimo movimento. Gli sembrava di essere anche lui a casa Cavaglieri, nascosto dietro qualche porta a origliare, a spiare.
>
> ... Che baccano – si diceva – , che baraonda. Alla larga, per carità.
>
> E tuttavia, sebbene le labbra gli si piegassero da sole in una smorfia di disapprovazione e di insofferenza ... tuttavia non poteva fare a meno di continuare a star lì, il ricevitore incollato all'orecchio, teso ad ascoltare voci e rumori con una specie di ansiosa, combattuta avidità. (748)

> He held his breath, he didn't make the slightest movement. He felt that he too was in the Cavaglieri house, hidden behind some door, eavesdropping, spying.
>
> ... What a racket, he said to himself, what chaos. He would keep out of it, all right.
>
> And yet, though his lips curved instinctively in a grimace of disapproval and intolerance ... , still he couldn't help but stay there, the receiver glued to his ear, tensely listening to the voices and sounds with a kind of anxious, torn greediness. (53–4)

When Limentani returns to Codigoro after the hunt, he accepts Bellagamba's offer of a room to rest in before the return to Ferrara. Here he has a clearly primal dream about the very inn in which he is staying:

> L'albergo era pieno di gente. Benché lungo le scale non ci fosse anima viva, fuori da ogni camera rispondente sui due corridoi del primo piano,

> davanti a ogni porta, si vedevano esposte l'una a fianco dell'altra in ordine perfetto, alcune illuminate da obliqui raggi solari, due paia di scarpe: un paio da uomo e un paio da donna. Quante scarpe, mio Dio! Però non c'era da meravigliarsene. Anche a non aver fatto caso a tutte quelle scarpe in fila, era chiaro lo stesso che il ristorante del pianterreno serviva soprattutto a coprire ciò che accadeva lì di sopra, al primo piano come al secondo. (802–3)

> The hotel was full of people. Although there wasn't a living soul along the stairs, outside of each room on the two corridors of the second floor, at each door, you could see, one beside the other, in perfect order and, some of them, illuminated by oblique rays of sunshine, two pairs of shoes: a man's pair and a woman's pair. How many shoes there were, my God! However, it was nothing to be amazed at. Even if one ignored all those lined-up shoes, it was still clear that the restaurant on the ground floor served chiefly to mask what happened up here, on the second floor and on the third. (119–20)

Limentani then dreams of a sexual encounter with a prostitute, spied in Bellagamba's dining room, a "donna in *tailleur* scuro" (799; woman in a dark suit [115]) who recalls the woman in a brown suit who in the *Gattopardo* comes as a vision to the Prince on his deathbed to escort him out of this life. The Prince's woman in a dark suit is beautiful, while here she is a vulgar prostitute, even more deformed by Limentani's perception of her as "una specie di bestia" (800; a kind of animal [116]) sent by Bellagamba. All he can think of is how to get rid of her, and here again he compares himself to Ulderico, so much more at ease with sexuality and with degraded sexuality than Limentani, even in their youth: "mentre lui, al contrario, era sempre stato timido, incerto, riguardoso, e bisognoso ogni volta di un'eternità, questo il punto, prima di arrivare ai famosi fatti" (800; whereas he, on the contrary, had always been shy, hesitant, reluctant, respectful, and requiring long hours, each time, this was the point, before getting down to the famous business [116–17]). Again he recalls youthful escapades with Ulderico and remembers his own reluctance and lack of sexual desire as opposed to Ulderico's virile enthusiasm; he attributes this hesitance to "una paura, quella delle malattie veneree" (805; the fear of venereal disease [123]).

When Limentani awakens, he decides to return to the café in the main square, but before that he thinks about the pros and cons of taking his automobile and projects his own primal fantasies on to Bellagamba:

> Era anche vero, però, che se fosse andato a piedi gli sarebbe poi toccato tornare indietro, rivedere per forza Bellagamba. Immaginava la scena. Lui reduce dalla piazza, e là, ad aspettarlo, profilandosi al momento giusto dietro i vetri appannati della porta d'ingresso del *Bosco Elìceo,* la faccia come smagrata, stravolta dalla solita smania di spiare, di indovinare, di sapere ...[15] (809)

> But it was also true, however, that if he went on foot, he would then have to see Bellagamba again afterwards. He could imagine the scene. Himself, coming back from the square, and there, waiting for him, appearing at the right moment behind the steaming panes of the *Bosco Elìceo*'s front door, the face of Bellagamba, distraught, as if thinned, by his usual mania for spying, guessing, knowing ... (127–8)

He then thinks about going to visit Ulderico, and even this seemingly benign fantasy takes on a primal colouring, with clearly regressive connotations in which Limentani becomes the bachelor uncle who spends the night in a room with one of the children:

> Si figurava intanto a casa Cavaglieri: calda, piena di luce, e con tutti i sei ragazzi, maschi e femmine, dai più piccoli ai più grandi, a fare corona rumorosa attorno al papà e alla mamma già abbastanza maturi, si capisce, eppure in qualche modo ancora giovani, sulla breccia. E non riusciva a comprendere come mai la prospettiva di essere ricevuto in mezzo a quella inevitabile baraonda invece che respingerlo lo attirasse, lo riempisse a sorpresa di desiderio e di speranza. (809–10)

> He imagined, at the same time, the Cavaglieri house: warm, filled with light, and with them, husband and wife – already middle-aged, to be sure, and yet somehow still young, still active – and with all six children, boys and girls, from the youngest to the older ones, making a noisy circle around their Papa and Mamma. And he couldn't understand why, now, the prospect of being received there, in the midst of that inevitable racket, instead of repelling him, attracted him, filled him with desire and hope. (128)

After imagining this scene, he decides to call Ulderico's house once again, and this time his cousin's wife, Cesarina, anwers. Ulderico is not at home, and when she invites Limentani for a cup of tea, he immediately sexualizes the invitation and reacts to her as a young man who cannot face the thought of his mother as a sexual being:

> Gli era bastato sentire nel ricevitore quel suo "sìii" strascicato e miagolante. Doveva essere grande, grassa, calma: tutta l'opposto della Nives. Una di quelle belle donne verso i quaranta, insomma, dalle quali era stato talmente turbato che ancora adesso, alla sua età, ogni qualvolta ne incontrava una per la strada preferiva fingere anche con se stesso di non essersene accorto, di non averla nemmeno veduta. (819)

> He had only had to hear, in the receiver, that "yeeess" of hers, drawled and whining. She must be large, heavy, calm: the very opposite of Nives. One of those handsome women of about forty, in other words, who had always upset him to such a degree that even now, at his age, whenever he encountered one on the street, he preferred to pretend, even to himself, that he hadn't noticed her, that he hadn't seen her at all. (140)

In the family romance mould, Limentani imagines that Cesarina has betrayed Ulderico with every man in town, and for a moment he entertains the idea of taking up the offer to drop by, given that as young men he and his cousin "avevano l'abitudine di andare insieme anche a donne e spesso di scambiarsele" (821; had been accustomed to go whoring about together, and often, to trading their women [142]). As he approaches the door, he recalls these sexual escapades more explicitly, then immediately looks at his expensive watch, and realizes that he is beginning to lose his mind. The movement from a degraded adolescent kind of sexuality to a sign of his social status, and then to an existential question about his identity indicates that these are all somehow mysteriously linked:

> D'un tratto, trovandosi sotto gli occhi il quadrante dell'orologio, il minuscolo, calmo volto rotondo e familiare, incorniciato d'oro, del suo Vacheron-Constantin, d'un tratto fu penetrato dalla certezza di stare delirando. ... Con una lucidità repentina si sorprese a chiedersi: ma lui, lui stesso, vestito da caccia, col berretto di pelo in testa, a quell'ora, sotto quei portici, ma lui chi era, veramente? (822)

> Suddenly, seeing the dial of his watch beneath his eyes, the minuscule, calm, round, familiar, gold-framed face of his Vacheron-Constantin, suddenly he was overcome with the harsh certitude that he was raving. ... With a sudden lucidity, he surprised himself by wondering: he, he himself,

> in his hunting clothes, with the fur cap on his head, at that hour, under those arcades, who was he, who, really? (143–4)

At home, as he plots every move of his impending suicide and thinks about the aftermath, he takes comfort in the fact that he will be buried in the Jewish cemetery, since his business manager has seen to it that his dues to the community are paid: "Lo stesso presidente della Comunità, quel Cohen, che fino dall'epoca del suo matrimonio gli aveva tolto il saluto per non più restituirglielo, si sarebbe trovato con le mani legate" (847; The president of the community himself, that Cohen, who had cut him off after his marriage to Nives, and had never spoken to him since, would find his hands tied [172]). In the last chapter we are told that his daughter has left his mother "un pensierino di Natale" (853; a little Christmas wish [178]), another detail that signals how far the lamb has strayed from the flock, just like the heron:

> Lo vide sorvolare adagio … , e quindi sospendersi a perpendicolo sopra le loro teste: fermo, in pratica, e perdendo via via un po' di quota. Ad attirarlo a questo punto erano di sicuro i richiami. Ma prima? Fino a poco fa, insomma? Che buffa bestia! Valeva la pena di chiedersi che cosa lo avesse indotto a volare tanto a lungo così, contro vento o quasi, che cosa fosse venuto a cercare talmente lontano dalle rive, nel mezzo della valle. (769–70)

> He saw it fly slowly … and then hover, perpendicularly, over their heads: motionless, practically speaking, and gradually losing altitude. It was drawn to this point by the decoys, surely. But before? This far? What a funny animal! It was natural to wonder what had made it fly so long, against the wind or almost, what it had come hunting for, so far from the shore, in the midst of the valley. (80)

The novel closes, emblematically, in his mother's bedroom, where Limentani has come to say goodnight as always. The usual small talk is followed by the usual leave-taking, only this time it is the last one. It is significant that Bassani has chosen to close the story in the room of the protagonist's mother: he is about to break out of his narcissistic isolation to join the embalmed animals in the taxidermist's window, no longer on the outside looking in. Among the dead he will truly be at home. Moreover, unlike Bendicò in the *Gattopardo*, who will end up in a heap of dust once his owner, Concetta, throws him out the window, the embalmed animals in the window are frozen in time, just like this "man of resentment."

7 *L'odore del fieno*: On Becoming What One Is*

L'odore del fieno (*The Smell of Hay*) is the collection of short pieces that Bassani placed at the end of the *Romanzo*. Written at different times and subjected to various rewrites, retitlings, and rearrangements over the years, the stories range from the fictional to the semi-fictional to the personal essay. Though less interesting individually than the novels and stories that precede them, these writings do, however, illuminate the previous works in small ways. Moreover, taken together, they allow us to catch a glimpse – if only a glimpse – of the man behind the author, since the "I" in all these pieces represents some version of Bassani himself, although he never removes the veil completely. The phrase "the smell of hay" appears in the tryptich entitled "Altre notizie su Bruno Lattes," where the smell of freshly cut hay in a field functions as sort of Proustian madeleine, bringing back to life significant moments in Bruno's past. As the title chosen for this collection of writings, the phrase seems to allude to the fact that each piece leads into the next by association. I will attempt, where possible, to highlight these associations in my account of their content and of what I believe to be their significance.

In the interview Bassani gave to Anna Dolfi in 1979, he says:

> Tutta l'ultima parte del *Romanzo di Ferrara* è anticipata, pur nella grande distanza temporale, da *Dietro la porta*, tutta la parte ultima della mia opera tenta di far coincidere un passato faticosamente e criticamente recuperato, attraverso la distanza ed il tempo, con la realtà dello scrittore attuale.[1]

> The whole final section of the *Romance of Ferrara* is foreshadowed, despite the great temporal distance, by *Behind the Door*. The last part of my oeuvre

> is an attempt to make a past that has been critically and arduously recovered, across time and distance, coincide with the reality of the contemporary writer.

The first two pieces would seem at first to belie this claim, paired together, as they are, under the fanciful title "Due fiabe" ("Two Fables"); however, they are based on what Bassani considers his two most important achievements in terms of the story he is telling in the *Romanzo*. The first piece is partly based on a true story,[2] but its basis in reality is completely secondary to its function as a sign of Bassani himself having overcome the shame associated with his ghetto roots. It brings out of the closet the eastern Jew, clearly reminiscent of the ghetto Jew the protagonist was so fearful of resembling or being identified with as a result of the Race Laws. He is the ancestor or relative who represents the reality that integration had supposedly erased. Sander Gilman describes the meaning of the eastern Jew in the Western imaginary:

> The Western European (read: Christian or secularized Christian) mind needed to create a mental structure through which to cope with the movement of the Eastern Jews. Here was a class of individuals readily recognizable not only through their dress and appearance, but also through their language and rhetoric. This was the Other *par excellence*, the reification of the anti-Semitic caricature of the Jew in the West. Indeed, they were living proof of one of the basic tenets of late-nineteenth century popular thought. These Eastern Jews were clearly degenerate: one could sense it in their dirty, smelly, barbaric essence; one could hear it in their decayed mock-German and their crude, loud, boisterous love of argument. For the Western mind this was proof enough of all Jews as degenerate, as overt or covert forms of the Eastern Jew; the Westernized Jew, on the other hand, was presented with the fearful specter of that which he feared he had been – the Eastern Jew seemed to be the embodiment of the image of the Jew fossilized in the bedrock of Western myth.[3]

In this first story the eastern Jews are presented in an entirely positive light to signal the author's joyful acceptance of this aspect of the history of the Jewish people. They are a Ukrainian family, husband, wife, and son, who arrive in Ferrara in 1935 from Odessa. Refugees, one assumes, of the pogroms, they are received and sheltered by the Jewish community of Ferrara. The father soon becomes an assistant to the rabbi because of his perfect knowledge of Hebrew, as well as of religious customs and rituals. What is most striking about this family is the dignity with which they carry themselves, proud as they are of their identity as "wandering Jews." They are described here in great detail, with a focus on every aspect of their appearance that would previously have made the protagonist wince, at the very least:

> Padre e figlio ... possedevano facce dello stesso tipo: facce lunghe, ossute, emaciate, con zigomi salienti in cima ai quali brillavano, azzurri, i medesimi piccoli occhi obliqui, mugicchi. La madre al contrario era di bassa statura, grossa, rotonda: una specie di serva, o di contadina, con tanto di fazzolettone bianco annodato sotto la gola.
>
> Ma ciò che colpiva maggiormente gli astanti ... era l'innegabile dignità di tutti e tre, la naturale, commovente disinvoltura con cui, in cambio di qualche modesto servizio, sapevano restare ospiti. ... Dal semplice modo come ci stavano, al Tempio, tutti e tre silenziosi, composti, senza dar scandalo con particolari esibizionismi askenaziti (il padre conservando il caffetano, la barbetta stenta, biondiccia, nonché i pii riccioli dello stesso colore fuoruscenti dal cappello rotondo attorno alle orecchie; la madre il fazzolettone contadinesco; ma il figlio, lui, vestito correttamente all'occidentale, di panno grigio), sembravano preoccupati di una cosa sola: di rassicurare l'assemblea della loro ferma intenzione di andarsene il più presto possible. Domandavano di poter restare appena un poco, giusto il tempo necessario a riprendere fiato. Dopo essersi riposati, stessimo tranquilli, avrebbero subito ripreso le vie del vasto mondo. (859–60)

> Father and son ... had faces of the same type: long, bony, emaciated faces, with prominent cheekbones above which shone the same little slanted, blue, muzhik eyes. The mother, on the contrary, was short, heavy, rotund: a kind of servant or peasant woman, with a big white kerchief tied under her throat.
>
> But what most struck those present ... was the undeniable dignity of all three, the natural, touching ease with which, in exchange for some modest services, they knew how to remain guests. ... From the simple way in which the three of them sat in the temple, silent, poised, without calling attention to themselves by any display of Ashkenazi customs (the father, true, kept his caftan, his sparse, small, blonde beard, as well as, around his ears, the pious side curls of the same colour, emerging from under the round hat; the mother kept her peasant kerchief; but the son, he, was correctly dressed in Western style, in grey flannel), they seemed concerned with one thing only: reassuring the congregation of their firm intention to

> leave as soon as possible. They asked to be allowed to stay just a little, just long enough to catch their breath. After they had rested, we were not to worry, they would promptly resume their journey across the wide world.

As misfortune would have it, the three are made so comfortable that they do not leave and eventually they are deported along with other Ferrarese Jews to the camps in the winter of '43–'44. However, the narrator tells us, their presence has not been completely erased, "la loro trasmigrazione da oriente a occidente non fu vana" (860; their migration from East to West was not in vain). It was not in vain because it led to the birth of Yuri Rotstein, the child of the couple's son and of Egle Levi-Minzi.

Egle was a young woman of Ferrara whose parents had despaired of ever being able to find a suitable match for her, since she had refused every prospect that the community had managed to turn up. The narrator speculates that her reluctance to marry may have been partly due to an excessive, "virginal" attachment to her elderly parents, but another cause is also hinted at: she may have been attracted to a kind of virility that none of the young Jews presented to her as potential husbands seemed to possess:

> C'entrava anche, magari, la segreta suggestione esercitata su lei ai tempi folli della prima giovinezza – i tempi, occorre ricordarlo, del famigerato squadrismo padano, così simili per certi aspetti a questi nostri – da qualche violenta immagine che poi, negli anni successivi, le aveva impedito di volgersi a differenti tipi di maschilità …[4] (858)

> There was, perhaps, also some secret impression made on her in the tumultuous days of her early youth – the days, it should be recalled, of the infamous Fascist hooliganism in the Po Valley, so similar in some ways to our own times – by some violent image that then, in the following years, prevented her from being attracted to different types of masculinity …

"Differenti tipi di maschilità …" (different types of masculinity …) seems to be a coy allusion to the fact that Egle may have been put off by the more passive, possibly conflict-ridden, Jewish-Italian men of the sort that Bassani describes in the rest of the *Romanzo*. This important detail is followed by an ellipsis that lets us know again that more is intended than what is being said; it is also the only explicit reference to the fact that a meditation on Jewish masculinity in the age of emancipation underlies the *Romanzo*. Perhaps Egle is attracted to the

the young Ukrainian Jew because his identity has not been compromised by assimilationist aspirations. She can detect his free-flowing energy and vitality across the floor of the synagogue: "Guardava in su, dalla parte del matroneo, con magnifici occhi azzurri, ridenti, ammiccanti, selvaggi. Ebbene, perché non averlo appunto con quel giovane, un figlio? – si era detta a un tratto Egle Levi-Minzi come risvegliandosi da un lungo torpore –" (860–1). (He was looking upward, towards the women's section, with magnificent, laughing, sparkling, wild blue eyes. Well, why not have a son by that very young man? – Egle Levi-Minzi had asked herself abruptly, as if aroused from a long torpor.) The marriage takes place, and the result is a boy, Yuri Rotstein, as full of energy, judging from his eyes, as his father: "Alto, magro, ossuto, con celesti occhi obliqui, fiammeggianti al di sopra degli zigomi aguzzi, vive ancora adesso con la madre, solo insieme con lei, per sempre, nella loro grande casa di Ferrara" (861; Tall, thin, bony, with slanted blue eyes blazing above his sharp cheekbones, he still now lives with his mother, alone with her, forever, in their big house in Ferrara).

Yuri stands in sharp contrast to the only other child born in the context of the *Romanzo*, Lida's inept and slothful son Ireneo, the fruit of her ill-fated relationship with the cruel and conflicted David Camaioli in the short story "Lida Mantovani." Because his father and grandparents were deported to the camps, Yuri can be seen as the personification of life that ends and begins, of vitality and the life force, perhaps a symbol of the indomitable spirit of the Jewish people. It is no accident that he is the son of a "virile" Jewish male, one not saddled by the identity conflicts resulting from integration and assimilation. The Rotstein family stands in clear counterpoint to the Pulga family of *Behind the Door*, depicted as intrusive parasites, the incarnation of anti-Semitic images of the wandering Jew. Yuri also stands in counterpoint to Pulga himself: from disease to health, from the protagonist's internalized self-hating Jew to a symbol of a healthy integration and proud acknowledgment of a formerly "shameful" ancestry, the joyful acceptance of this heritage and history. The only somewhat dissonant note here is the fact that Yuri ends up with his mother, alone "forever"; now that he has entered the mainstream Christian world, he too may be unable to find a suitable male identity and therefore may remain forever mother identified. Alternatively, one might read this solitude as the author's desire to keep him out of the mainstream world, where he would inevitably face the conflicts of all Bassani's protagonists. I will address this question in the conclusion.

The second *fiaba* deals with the anti-Fascist underground and perhaps is not a coincidence, since the energized Bassani, liberated by the teachings of Croce from the impediments to action in his own background, was able to join the fight for freedom from Fascist and later Nazi oppression. The experience, only alluded to briefly in *Il giardino dei Finzi-Contini,* is elaborated here, but in a dream-like context, which serves to emphasize the spiritual nature of the Resistance experience for Bassani. The narrator of this story uses the "I" as opposed to the "we" of the previous "fable," signalling a further self-revelation. The story opens in the Albergo Tripoli, which here has a completely different connotation than in *Dietro la porta,* where it was a site of shame and degradation as the temporary residence of Pulga and his family. Just as Pulga and family have been replaced by the Rotstein family in the first of the two fables, in this story the Albergo Tripoli becomes a site of marginalization in a positive sense: that of the active Resistance fighter carrying clandestine literature and posing as a travelling salesman in search of a room for the night. As he prepares to sleep, the phrase *la vita è un sogno* (life is but a dream) repeatedly comes to his mind. The following part of the story describes a dream within a dream, in which the narrator sees himself having an out-of-body experience as a skeleton in a closet, which seems to symbolize the fear of exposure. In the next part of the dream he is out on the street, walking hurriedly towards the railway station, when he suddenly realizes he has left his suitcase, with the leaflets in the false bottom, in the hotel room. After a moment's hesitation he decides to continue on without the clandestine material, since he hears his train manoeuvring into the station and realizes it is too late to turn back. The story ends as he awakens and is only bitterly comforted by the knowledge that he was dreaming.

An anxiety dream that articulates the fear of capture that dogged the members of the Resistance, it also conveys the feeling of unreality that characterized the entire experience of living under the Nazi-Fascist threat: life has become a bad dream, indeed a nightmare. The reference to Calderòn de la Barca's famous play – perhaps also simply an allusion to the general literary and philosophical trope of life as a dream or an illusion – becomes more meaningful if we consider Bassani's choice of name for his travelling salesman: Buda. Agostino Buda was actually one of Bassani's co-conspirators in the Underground and apparently did transport leaflets to Sicily,[5] but in the context of this story the name evokes associations to the Buddhist belief that life is an illusion in comparison to the superior state of "wakefulness" or awareness that Buddhist practice aims to achieve. Although I have no evidence of Bassani ever turning to Buddhism, we know from his statements that he believed the only reality to be a spiritual one, in the idealist sense, consisting of the conscious moral experience of the individual. Moreover, he describes himself as possessed of a superior awareness and sense of moral purpose resulting from his conversion to Croce's *religione della libertà* (religion of freedom), in comparison to his more passive, Jewish compatriots who found no relief from the humiliation and bitterness of life under the Race Laws.[6]

The next three stories, grouped together under the title "Altre notizie su Bruno Lattes," return to fiction but seem to address the causes of passivity, at least in the case of the character whom Bassani uses as his alter ego. The only other story entirely devoted to Bruno is of course "Gli ultimi anni di Clelia Trotti," in which we see him grasping at straws as he attempts unsuccessfully to find meaning and purpose in a relationship with the Socialist schoolteacher many years his senior and who represents an ideal that is completely irrelevant at this point. Bassani eroticizes that relationship ever so subtly in order to allude to the source of Bruno's troubles, which here are unveiled in a realistic manner as opposed to the symbolic treatment reserved for them in the earlier story.

The three stories are connected by the theme of longing. In the first story we encounter Bruno at the burial site for his uncle Celio's funeral. Suddenly "un odore acuto di fieno tagliato sopraggiunse a rianimare il corteo oppresso dal caldo" (868; an acute odour of freshly mowed hay wafted over to revive the procession, oppressed by the heat). It is 1938, the year of the Race Laws. Completely self-absorbed, Bruno stands alongside his family members, contemplating all the ways in which he is ostensibly different from them: physically, morally, and otherwise. His desire to dissociate himself as completely as he can from what he considers to be their "Jewish" characteristics is an ironic reflection of his self-hatred, since he clearly does not know himself at all:

> Da quando i becchini avevano cominciato a adoperarsi per far entrare la bara nella fossa, e i suoi sguardi erano tornati a incrociarsi con quelli smarriti del padre, da quell'istante si era sentito riprendere dalla sorda rabbia che gli era abituale.
>
> Che cosa c'era di comune – tornava a domandarsi –, fra lui, da una parte, e suo padre coi relativi suoi parenti e affini dall'altra? … anche dal lato carattere nessuna somiglianza fra lui e *loro*, grazie a Dio, nemmeno la

> più piccola. Niente di instabile, di eccitabile, di morboso in lui, niente di così tipicamente ebraico. Il suo carattere era molto più vicino, così almeno gli sembrava, a quello forte e schietto di tanti suoi amici cattolici, e non per nulla la mamma, nata cattolica, cattolicissima, si chiamava Marchi. (869)

> As soon as the gravediggers began to lower the coffin into the grave, and his gaze had again met his father's bewildered eyes, from that instant he felt himself again overtaken by his usual silent anger.
>
> What was there in common – he asked himself again – between him, on the one hand, and his father with his various, assorted relatives, on the other? ... even when it came to character, there was no resemblance between him and *them*, thank God, not even the slightest. Nothing unstable, excitable, morbid in him, nothing so typically Jewish. His character – at least, so it seemed to him – was much closer to the strong and straightforward nature of so many of his Catholic friends, and it was no coincidence that his mother, born Catholic, very Catholic, bore the name Marchi.

As he watches the grave being filled in, Bruno's mind wanders, first to the couples making love on the grass, whom he knows he will pass and be tempted to look at during his evening bicycle ride, and then to a young sentinel on guard duty at a nearby arsenal whose humming he had heard earlier on during the burial; he wonders if he will be able to find him later on. As these thoughts run through his mind, the desire to befriend this guard begins to torment him: "Diventati amici, forse sarebbero andati al cinema, e più tardi, nonostante i propri diciott'anni nemmeno compiuti, più tardi a casino, magari" (871; If they became friends, maybe they would go to the movies together and later, even though he was not yet even eighteen, later to the brothel, perhaps). He feels bitterness and anger, and yet he realizes that this anger comes not from having been forced to attend this funeral "ma da assai più lontano, da lontanissimo: da un punto del passato perduto in fondo a una lontananza quasi infinita" (871; but from much farther back, very far back: from a moment in the past lost in the distance, the infinite distance).

The two thoughts – of the copulating lovers he will hesitate to look at and of the ambiguous attraction to the young man on guard duty – are joined together as a sign of his level of psychosexual development, which is explicitly connected in the text to his Jewish self-hatred and his inability to identify with his Jewish father. Towards the end of *Il giardino dei Finzi-Contini* the protagonist is finally able to look at the couples making love on the grass as he is about to complete the Oedipal passage. In *L'airone* Limentani remembers his youthful sharing of prostitutes with his cousin, clearly more a homosocial bonding ritual than a sexual experience with women.

Bruno is aware that his feelings are rooted in the past, and his mind turns to another funeral he attended long ago, his grandfather's in 1924 when he was nine years old. At that funeral he had hurt himself while running in the freshly cut grass, and no one had noticed at first, not even his mother; when she finally did notice, she scolded rather than comforted him. A series of olfactory and visual associations lead him slowly back to this and other earlier incidents in a Proustian series of recollections in which we see him trapped between his rage towards his father and his sense of having been neglected by his mother. The moments he remembers are all moments of longing: longing for his mother when he was left alone with his grandfather in 1918 at the age of three, because she had gone to join his father during a brief leave from his military duties; and then his longing for her attention at his grandfather's funeral.

The next story in this tryptich is also one of longing, but here the longing is sexualized. Set again in 1938, "il fatidico 1938" (875; the fateful 1938), the story opens on a note that ties it to the previous story. His mother's perceived neglect evolves into his Gentile girlfriend's indifference to him: "Alle domande rabbiose, insistenti, che Bruno Lattes rivolgeva all'Adriana Trentini, questa non rispondeva. 'Al diavolo!', pensò Bruno alla fine, esasperato. E distolse gli sguardi" (874). (Bruno Lattes's angry, insistent questions to Adriana Trentini received no answer. "To hell with her," Bruno thought finally, exasperated. He turned his eyes away.) We discover that Adriana's indifference has been present since the beginning of their relationship and may even have been its glue: "Per tre anni lui non aveva fatto altro che parlare. Invece lei, a rifletterci, era sempre rimasta zitta. … In realtà stava lì ad ascoltare in silenzio, minacciosa. Come un muro, non so, o un albero …"[7] (874). (For three years, he had done nothing but talk. Whereas she, come to think of it, had always sat there silently. … In reality, she sat there listening, in silence, threatening. Like a wall, or, I don't know, a tree … .) The rest of the story describes his self-imposed isolation in the wake of the Race Laws and his fruitless waiting around for Adriana to call. Their relationship has clearly been dealt its final blow by the discriminatory legislation, but he is unable to accept this; still in the throes of denial, he continues to fantasize about a possible reunion, deluding himself that the only obstacle would be another boyfriend, not the Race Laws: "Gli avrebbe telefonato, e lui, naturale, sarebbe subito accorso. … Rivederla, parlarle: questo l'essenziale. Bisognava soltanto trovare il modo …"[8] (876). (She would phone him and he, naturally, would run over immediately. … To see her again, to speak to her: this was the essential thing. He just had to find the way. …) Bruno avoids his father, as well as his usual haunts, and is drawn instead repeatedly to a site of marginalization and degradation: a small, seedy amusement park that has sprung up on the outskirts of town: "Per qual motivo non si stancava mai di tornarci, lassù, in quel deserto, in quello squallore? Che cos'era a riportarcelo? Non lo sapeva bene nemmeno lui" (877). (Why did he never tire of returning there, to that forsaken, sordid place? What was it that drew him there repeatedly? Even he really didn't know the answer.)

What keeps him returning there night after night is another cold woman, another *belle dame sans merci*, the girl in charge of the shooting gallery, to whom he is compulsively attracted. He tells himself that this cheap-looking, lower class girl and Adriana have nothing in common, but then he realizes that her eyes are "freddi, duri, cattivi" (cold, hard, mean); everything about her suggests to him "magagne segrete" (secret perversions) that fascinate him, and he is constantly trying to catch her elusive gaze. When he succeeds, he feels "un piacere amaro, una specie di gioia vendicativa" (a bitter pleasure, a kind of vindictive joy) because she too, like Adriana, is a wall: "'O bella!,' fece una volta con voce a un tratto tremante, strangolata, e intanto la ragazza ricaricava la carabina. 'Avete degli accumulatori?' Non fu degnato di risposta" (878). ("Hey, gorgeous!" he said once, in a suddenly trembling voice, almost choking, as the girl reloaded the rifle. "Do you have a generator?" She didn't deign to answer.)

One night she does briefly acknowledge him, but only just barely, and the next night she is gone forever. Her departure is experienced as an abandonment by Bruno, who is already feeling rejected by the Race Laws and by Adriana. In the final paragraph, suffering, abandonment, abject sexuality, and violence (she is, after all, the "rifle girl" ["la ragazza dei fucili"]) are conflated in a portrait of Bruno's sensibility that suggests a masochistic tendency to brood and to wallow, which renders impossible any active stance in the face of Nazi-Fascist persecution:

> E di colpo capì due cose: che soltanto a cominciare da quel momento avrebbe saputo ciò che davvero volesse dire la parola "sofferenza"; e che il ricordo della smorfia della ragazza dei fucili (una smorfia che la sera prima lo aveva riempito improvvisamente di felicità, di gelosia, e di un

> oscuro senso di abbiezione) gli sarebbe rimasto impresso dentro per molti anni a venire, chissà mai quanti. Come un piccolo marchio: minimo ma indelebile. (879)
>
> And suddenly he understood two things: that only from that moment on would he know what the word "suffering" really meant; and that the memory of the wry face that the rifle girl made at him (a face that the night before had suddenly filled him with happiness, jealousy, and an obscure sense of abjection) would stay impressed upon him for many years to come, who knows how many. Like a little brand: tiny, but indelible.

The "piccolo marchio: minimo ma indelebile" (little brand: tiny, but indelible) is not only clearly a stand-in for the branding of Jews and other concentration camp prisoners, it is also connected textually to the image of the swastika at the very end of the next and last story of the Bruno Lattes triptych.

In this third piece we see Bruno in the summer of 1939, at the height of his masochistic sloth, convinced that only by getting Adriana to make love with him one more time will he free himself from the yoke that still tethers him to her a full year after their break-up, a year that he has spent doing absolutely nothing, not reading, not studying, just brooding.

Determined to force her to see him, Bruno travels all the way to Abbazia, near Yugoslavia, where the Trentinis have gone for the summer. He is obsessed by thoughts of the imminent war and of Adriana all at the same time – "L'Adriana e la situazione internazionale: da quando si era messo in treno non aveva pensato ad altro" (882; Adriana and the international situation: since boarding the train, he had thought of nothing else) – Bassani's way of explicitly connecting sex to politics. Once he arrives, he waits passively at the pension for her to return his calls. He finally goes to their hotel and manages a lunch with the family, and eventually a day at the beach, but no time alone with Adriana, who is clearly avoiding him. Haunted by images of her Aryan body, he lies in wait again in his room for the summons to a private encounter that never comes. Finally she agrees to meet but then sends her younger brother in her stead. The boy arrives on a bicycle. On the bicycle there is a small blood-coloured banner to which Bruno turns in order to avoid the boy's gaze as he delivers the news. In the centre of the banner "un piccolo, inequivocabile segno nero: una svastica" (a small, unmistakable black sign: a swastika) catches his eye. Suddenly the boy appears to him like a bloodhound: "Gli aveva mostrato in un sorriso i denti forti e bianchissimi da cane giovane" (889; Smiling, he revealed to him his very white and strong teeth, like those of a young dog). Bruno is avoiding or denying reality but finds it in spite of himself: sex and politics.

And so ends the voyage into the psyche of Bruno Lattes. The text also clearly positions him alongside Dr Fadigati, particularly in the following paragraph in which, like Fadigati who watches his beloved and scornful Deliliers from afar on the beaches of Riccione, Bruno hungers after the body of the unattainable Aryan Adriana on the sands of Abbazia:

> Era grande, l'Adriana, abbronzata, pacifica, potente. Mentre lui, nervoso, magro-scheletrico, sbiadito di pelle, non poteva non fare la figura del tipo per tanti motivi sgradevole (pessimo nuotatore, fra l'altro!), da piantare quasi subito là, accoccolato nell'acqua a pochi metri dall'asciutto, in paziente attesa che lei, la *vamp* americana e ariana, dopo essersi allontanata a pigre bracciate verso il largo – e talmente, per giunta, da fargli perdere di vista la sua graziosa cuffia da bagno di gomma rossa –, si degnasse infine di restituirsi alla terra. (885)

> She was a big girl, Adriana, tanned, calm, powerful. Whereas he, nervous, thin as a rake, his skin pale, couldn't help looking like a loser (a terrible swimmer, among other things!), somebody to drop almost immediately, right there, crouched in the water a few yards from the beach, patiently waiting for the American and Aryan vamp to deign to return to land, after she had swum lazily out into the distance – so far that, on top of it all, he lost sight of her pretty, red, rubber bathing cap.

The parenthetical allusion to the fact that he is a poor swimmer also explicitly connects this episode to the concluding beach scene in *Dietro la porta*, in which Luciano Pulga, who has travelled to Riccione to seek out his former classmate after their falling-out, fails to engage him in a real conversation. In *Dietro la porta* the protagonist is a strong swimmer, but Pulga, the figure of his Jewish self-hatred, is characterized as an inferior non-swimmer, thin and pale like Bruno.

The next piece, entitled "Ravenna," is autobiographical and consists of a series of vignettes centred around the recollection of visits to this city, known for its intensely Fascist leanings. The vignettes are set between 1922 to 1943, a period that also marks the beginning and the end of the Fascist regime. They are subtly connected to the Bruno stories by the recurring image of airplanes, which both open and close the ensemble and which subtly suggest a hypersensibility that can be traced back to early childhood.

The first vignette tells of a family outing to Ravenna to watch an air show in honour of a fallen war pilot. The author remembers in particular the frightening noise of the fighter planes. The last vignette moves the narrative to 1943, shortly after Bassani's marriage, when he and his wife honeymooned in the area of Ravenna. He and his new wife are sailing at Marina di Ravenna when they catch sight of a group of fighter planes practising their formations: "E il loro rombo lacerante, quando sfrecciavano sulle nostre teste accostate, ci riempiva di un'allegria infantile, alla quale, in me, seguiva una segreta tristezza tutta intrisa d'addio" (897; And their piercing roar, when they zipped over our heads next to each other, filled us with a childish joy, followed, in me, by a secret sadness, all wrapped up with feelings of abandonment). This secret sadness is meant as a reference, I believe, to Bruno's feelings of rejection and frustration that are connected to airplanes and the perceived abandonment by his mother. In fact, in the Bruno stories we are told that at the age of nine Bruno saw a swarm of mosquitoes at his grandfather's funeral that reminded him of the fighter planes that he had seen as child of three from his grandfather's window, when he was left alone with him by his mother: longing and airplanes, frustrated desire, the urge to touch something out of reach and prohibited, cold, hard eyes:

> Gli aeroplani da caccia scendevano adagio adagio, uno dopo l'altro, nel cielo color di latte della sera, senza produrre il minimo rumore. Toccarli pareva facile. Sarebbe bastato, per toccarli, sporgere un braccio da una delle due finestre del tinello. Senonché c'era il nonno, purtroppo, lì dietro, che cenava da solo. … Se il nonno, capace come era di indovinare tutto, anche i pensieri più nascosti, avesse capito quello che lui avrebbe desiderato fare, non lo avrebbe sgridato, macché. Si sarebbe limitato a fissarlo coi suoi occhi duri e pungenti, di smalto celeste. E sarebbe stato molto peggio. (872)

> The fighter planes descended very slowly, one after the other, in the milky evening sky, without making the slightest noise. It seemed easy to touch them. It would have been enough, to touch them, to extend an arm through one of the two kitchen windows. Except that his grandfather, unfortunately, was there, behind him, eating alone. … If his grandfather, who was

> able to guess everything, even the most hidden thoughts, had understood what he wanted to do, the old man wouldn't have yelled at him, not at all. He would just have glared at him with his hard, piercing, pale blue enamel eyes. And that would have been much worse.

By introducing his marriage to the story, Bassani acknowledges the autobiographical nature of the character of Bruno Lattes and also gradually "reveals" himself. The story focuses on a series of small events that may have contributed to the formation of his own particular sensibility and attitudes under Fascism. In the first vignette the automobile trip to Ravenna is marked by a threatening gesture from peasant day labourers. Brandishing sickles, they insult the travellers driving by in their luxurious car: "Ma da quel preciso istante io *so* che i braccianti romagnoli ... ce l'hanno con noi perché possediamo una Fiat, una Fiat tipo due" (891; But from that precise moment on, I *know* that the Romagna day labourers ... have something against us because we own a Fiat, a Type Two Fiat). In the second vignette the author is about ten or eleven and recalls stopping in Ravenna on the way to the beach, where in the local piazza or bar the "squadristi del posto" (892; the local Fascist *squadristi*) were always highly visible. He recalls his father's attitude towards them, a mixture of pride and admiration on the one hand and repugnance on the other, and his observation that the young *squadristi* of Ferrara could not hold a candle to those of Ravenna, far more fearless and daring in their escapades – political, sexual, and recreational.

In the following vignette, which is perhaps the most arbitrary of the group and takes place after 1930, Bassani recalls he and his brother racing their bicycles to the beach against the rest of the family travelling in his father's car. At Sant'Apollinare in Classe the first to arrive would take refuge from the heat in a church: "E ogni volta il refrigerio dell'interno, la luce tra verde e celeste che lo pervadeva, ci apparivano i medesimi che sapevamo di ritrovare di lì a poco in riva al mare" (894; And each time the cool air of the interior, the blue-green light that pervaded it, seemed to us the same coolness and light we knew we would find very soon at the seashore). The interior of the church here appears to be a source of comfort and relief as opposed perhaps to its connotation in *Dietro la porta*, where it is the site of the protagonist's failed attempt to build a bridge between himself and Carlo Cattolica.

The next piece deals with the great variety of political opinion to be found in Ravenna, as represented by the different orientations of the families encountered on the beaches of Cesenatico, most of whom were from Ravenna. Fervent Catholics, anticlerical anarchists, moderate anti-Fascists, militant anti-Fascists all managed to coexist peacefully as they argued and frolicked together on the sands. Bassani may have included this image here because this iconoclasm made a lasting impression on him as a young adolescent. The social climate on the beach appears to have contrasted, though nowhere is this said explicitly, with the political climate of Ferrara, where the Fascists may have been less fervent than in Ravenna but where Fascist sentiment was more uniformly widespread. It also contrasts with Bassani's own description of the homogeneity and devotion to Fascism of the Jewish community of Ferrara in a speech he made in 1961.[9]

The second-to-last piece is a rather curious one, as it recalls an incident whose setting may have been a source of inspiration for *Il giardino dei Finzi-Contini*, or so it is made to appear retrospectively. In 1935 the author was invited with a group from Cesenatico to play tennis at the home of a certain Vezio Buscaroli, who promptly forgot that he had invited them. No surprise – he was known to be generally inept and self-absorbed, so much so that he did not notice that his voluptuous wife was cuckolding him regularly. The setting – "una bella casa in mezzo alla pineta con annesso campo di tennis" (895; a beautiful house in the middle of a pine forest with an adjacent tennis court) – and the image of young people on bicycles in tennis gear in front of the house are both snapshots from the famous novel. Buscaroli himself is described as an aspiring man of letters, who had already published a collection of poems, and as enjoying the sympathies of the local Fascist authorities, who were contemplating assigning him a writerly task within their ranks. When the group arrives, Buscaroli is sitting in a chaise longue in the shade, absorbed in a book. Not a tennis player himself, he had nonetheless issued this invitation enthusiastically only to have it slip his mind. It is his wife who saves the day with her effortless hospitality. This episode seems to be a veiled allusion to the author's own early writing vocation before his conversion to politics. The fact that Buscaroli is oblivious to his wife's betrayals parallels the situation in *Giardino*, in which the protagonist imagines at the end that he was being "betrayed" all along by Micòl and Malnate. Like the protagonist, Buscaroli is both politically and sexually naïve.

Bassani the present-day author will be explicitly mentioned in the first of the following two stories, grouped together under the title "Les neiges d'antan"; this choice of title signals a past that has been left very far behind, as in the famous line "mais où sont les neiges d'antan" from the fifteenth-century poem by Villon, "Ballade des dames du temps jadis."

Here Bassani speaks openly from the moment of narration as a successful writer who has left Ferrara and is now looking back at some of the male figures who had made such an impression on him in his youth. They are the same ones whom his father grudgingly admired in the Ravenna vignette:

> Loro, i giovanotti che andavano già a morose e a casino, e prossimi, alcuni, a entrare nel novero dei cosiddetti sfatti cittadini, stavano spesso raccolti a semicerchio intorno a qualche automobile straniera lasciata a fianco del marciapiede da una comitiva di turisti in transito. Assorti a valutarne pregi e difetti, mi bastava guardarli perché mi sentissi non soltanto diverso ma inferiore. (899)

> They, the young men who already had girlfriends or went to the brothel, some of them about to join the number of the so-called *sfatti*, the local degenerates, were often gathered in a semicircle around some foreign car left along the sidewalk by a group of tourists passing through. I had only to look at them intently weighing the car's merits and defects, to feel not only different but inferior.

One of his idols was Marco Giori, who intimidated him so badly that he never had the courage to greet him in the street. Now, many years later, as he passes through Ambrogio, a village near Ferrara, he happens upon father and son. Marco, who vowed to leave Ferrara as soon as possible, is now the spitting image of the older man, a prosperous farmer but a farmer nonetheless. He has clearly not left Ambrogio, let alone Ferrara, is dressed shabbily and has lost his aura along with his good looks. There is obviously some satisfaction for Bassani at seeing what thirty years have done to Giori and the extent to which he has come to resemble the father from whom he so wanted to distinguish himself. Here in the town square, in the face of a fallen idol, Bassani finally utters, "Ciao," the greeting that he has waited so long to feel worthy of proffering.

The second story concerns Mario Spisani, also known as Pelandra, another of the young men of the Giori ilk, who tried instead to change his ways by marrying, taking a respectable job as an insurance agent, and having children, only to disappear mysteriously ten years later after telling his wife he was going out to buy cigarettes. His story, however, is curiously intertwined with a parenthesis about the fictional Deliliers of *Gli occhiali d'oro*, "quel Deliliers, che esclusivo responsabile come era della morte del povero Fadigati, … a Porto Longone avrebbe dovuto stare, altro che all'estero a godersela con soldi e macchina!" (906; that Deliliers who, exclusively responsible as he was for the death of poor Fadigati, … should have been in the prison at Porto Longone, not abroad, enjoying himself, with money and cars!). Of Pelandra he says:

> Dai venti a venticinque – fino, ripeto, al '37 – lui che si sappia non ha mai detto no a niente. Puttaniere e bassettista di prima forza, consumatore notevole di cocaine, di ètere allo stato puro o, in mancanza, di qualsiasi intruglio possible, anche Pelandra, … come, più tardi, Eraldo Deliliers, … ne ha combinate di ogni colore. (905–6)

> Between the ages of twenty and twenty-five – until, I repeat, 1937 – as far as anyone knows, he never said no to anything. First-rate whoremonger and gambler, quite the user of cocaine, of unadulterated ether, or, in the absence of those, of any available concoction, Pelandra too … like, later, Eraldo Deliliers … was up to all sorts of evil tricks.

Not only does the story blur the distinction between fiction and memoir with the mention of Deliliers and Fadigati, it also uses the patently clichéd story of the man who goes out to buy cigarettes and disappears. It also emphasizes dates: the "decennio '30–40" (the decade 1930–1940) is characterized as the golden age that saw the rise of the local degenerates. As for Pelandra, however, "dal '38 al '48" (911; from 1938 to 1948) he did his best to turn the page, to be a good husband, father, and citizen: "Né ci fu mai una sola estate (escluse per forza quelle del '43, del '44 e del '45, trascorse nel piccolo fondo Pasetti, a Formignana), senza che l'agosto lo passassero in villegiatura coi bambini" (909; Nor was there a single summer [excluding, inevitably, those of 1943, 1944, and 1945, spent at the little Pasetti farm at Formignana] when they didn't spend August on holiday with the children).

The story of Pelandra's failed conversion from degenerate to upstanding citizen and family man is told to the narrator by a local photographer, Uller Tumaìni. Tumaìni's main attraction for the narrator is that he never changes – he is always the same and can always be found in his studio, out of sight and out of time: "Tutte le volte che torno a Ferrara e passo a salutarlo, è Uller Tumaìni, il fotografo, a ricordarmi queste cose" (910; Every time I return to Ferrara and drop by to say hello, it is Uller Tumaìni, the photographer, who reminds me of these things). Tumaìni is a sort of stand-in for the author himself as author, and when the narrator describes the feeling of being in the dark with him (Uller only turns on lights when absolutely necessary), he describes the two of them as out of time and out of life: "Noi qui, invisibili, come fuori del tempo, come morti. E là, richiamate ogni tanto dal *neon* sfolgorante della vetrina e dalle foto esposte, le ingenue, fidenti, inconsapevoli facce della vita, tutte scoperte e protese …"[10] (910–11). (We here, invisible, as if outside of time, as if dead. And there, attracted now and then by the neon light flashing in the window and the photographs on display, the naive, trusting, oblivious faces of life, all open and receptive. …) Tumaìni in a sense may be considered the positive counterpart of Pino Barilari. Pino is an emotional adolescent frozen in time by his traumatic sexual experience during the March on Rome, who now sits at his window watching and judging his fellow citizens, the paradoxical embodiment of their guilt. Pino Barilari looks at the world through his binoculars, Tumaìni through the lens of a camera. Tumaìni also makes a moral judgment about Pelandra that may be connected to something in Bassani's own life and is treated in the following story; he says that Pelandra's attempt at transformation from dissolute idler to responsible citizen, husband, and father was a mistake, a serious one, because it was unsustainable and eventually led to his abandonment of his family: "Mille volte meglio condurre doppia, tripla, magari quadrupla o quintupla vita, piuttosto che …[11] No, no. … Esistono certi valori, e la famiglia è uno di questi, davanti ai quali all'individuo non rimane che metter giù un po' di *gàliga* e sacrificarsi" (912). (A thousand times better to lead a double, or triple, or even quadruple or quintuple life, rather than … No, no … There are certain values, and the family is one of these, in the face of which there is nothing for the individual to do but swallow a bit of his pride and sacrifice himself.) The narrator comments: "Forse sono d'accordo, forse no. Forse sono d'accordo e in disaccordo insieme" (912). (Perhaps I agree with him, perhaps not. Perhaps I agree and disagree at the same time.)

The last scene of the story is a protracted, imagined reconstruction of Pelandra's last moments at home before leaving to buy the proverbial cigarettes. Clearly a pretext, the story of Pelandra is a story of betrayal and disappearance. One way to make sense of this story is to view it as part of a gradual approach to Bassani's own departure from Ferrara and eventually his own abandonment of his wife and family, which is explicitly alluded to in the first of the next group of stories, entitled "Tre apologhi."

Apologo usually refers to a parable, to a story told with a moral intention; it can also be a defence of something or someone, as in *apologia*. In fact, each of the three stories in this tryptich appears to allude to something about which Bassani feels, or at least has been made to feel, somewhat uneasy, if not downright guilty: having left his wife and children, having joined the Socialist Party after the end of the war, and having exaggerated his role in the Resistance. The first story takes place during a drive from Ferrara back to Rome, in which nothing much happens except that it is fraught with tension between Bassani and his wife, who argue about everything: which roads to take, whether to stop and where, whether to overnight somewhere, where to eat, and so on. At a certain point Bassani mentions that his choice to take the Tiberina over the Flaminia, after having initially decided the opposite, is seen by his wife Val as a sign of his flighty character and of his "sempre più debole attaccamento a lei e alla famiglia" (916; ever waning attachment to her and to the family). Moreover, what could have been called simply a "change of mind" is termed an "abandonment" of one plan for another.

Bassani explains that taking the Tiberina would allow them to stop at Sansepolcro, where he could get another look at Piero della Francesca's painting *Resurrection*. He also attributes his indecision and neurotic agitation to the fact that he is a small-town boy returning to the big city, characterized as an "alveare cementizio" (a cement beehive) that can only be reached by crossing "il mostruoso ponte sul Tevere (the monstrous bridge on the Tiber): "Giacché come è possible – farnetico dentro me stesso – per chiunque sia nato in una città di media grandezza della Val Padana, nella quale tuttora possegga casa propria e separata, rientrare a Roma senza angoscia?" (918; For how – I rave to myself – can anyone born in a medium-sized town of the Po Valley, and in which he still has a separate, independent home of his own, how can such a person re-enter Rome without anguish?)

At the end, he has calmed down, and he and Val enjoy a meal at a restaurant in Perugia, at which point he admits lucidly that the agitation and insistence on one road instead of another was really much ado about something quite different, something that is suggested but never made explicit: to be noted that the home in Ferrara is described as his own *separate* home, which he does not have in Rome either physically, since Rome is a "cement beehive" of apartments, or otherwise, for that matter, since he lives with his family. The famous Piero della Francesca painting *Resurrection* may also allude to his own desire for a rebirth of sorts, perhaps as a single man. Bassani abandoned his own family in 1958.[12]

The next *apologo* is set in Naples during the American occupation, where Bassani has travelled to meet other members of the Partito d'Azione (the Action Party), of which he was one of the original members. The story is really more about the atmosphere he finds there, an atmosphere of greed and lust, where the canned foods and cigarettes that have been made available to party activists by the Americans have become more important than anything else. Moreover, these supplies are hoarded and jealously guarded under lock and key at the home of the party member with whom he is staying. Forced to share his provisions with a guest whose presence also interferes with his sexual activities, his host does not always treat him courteously. Nonetheless, Bassani too partakes of the food and tells us that he quickly gained back the weight he had lost during the German occupation of Rome, when food was very scarce. Resistance heroes, courageous conspirators, former prisoners, and exiles are united in this story not so much by a common cause as by a common deprivation that they are now making up for rather indecorously. The story ends on a note of gluttony that describes his own nausea after gorging himself out of pure excess. This piece may have been written in response to criticisms he received after joining the Socialist Party in 1946 following the dissolution of the Action Party. To those who accused him of inconsistency, Bassani replied that though he was certainly a member of the bourgeoisie, he was not decadent and was well aware of his responsibilities.[13] This rather unflattering portrait of the members of the Action Party in the immediate postwar period may be Bassani's way of removing the party from its pedestal.

The last of the *apologhi* is of a completely different sort that deals with Bassani as a writer. A young journalist doing research for an article has invited him to look at a series of photographs, choose the one that "speaks" to him, and explain why. He chooses a photo of an old man, rather down at the heels, who has been arrested for falsely boasting in public that he was the recipient of a medal for bravery. As he begins to imagine the man's situation, he finds himself feeling guilty for transforming a real individual into a "personaggio di fantasia" (an imaginary character) in his mind:

L'operazione alla quale sto accingendomi, di mischiare il vero col falso, o, che è lo stesso, con l'immaginario, mi si preannuncia questa volta particolarmente arbitraria, empia. Ma che cosa importa? Oltre che intelligente ..., il signor Riccardo T. è senza dubbio persona gentile e comprensiva: più assai, in ogni caso, di tanti altri modelli presi dalla vita, ai quali, da quando scrivo novelle, racconti e romanzi, ho dovuto per forza rifarmi. (930)

The operation I'm about to undertake, of mixing the true with the false, or, and it amounts to the same, with the imaginary, seems to me this time particularly arbitrary, ungodly. But what does it matter? Not only is signor Riccardo T. intelligent ..., he is also undoubtedly a kind and understanding person: more so, in any case, than so many other models, taken from real life, that I have had no choice but to resort to since I started writing short stories and novels.

Bassani then sets about imagining the scene between the old man and the police officers who confront him about his false claims. The old man insists that it was all a joke, an attempt to salvage his dignity in the face of some passers-by who made disparaging remarks about his appearance. Having concluded this particular scenario, Bassani then sets about imagining how the old man might have explained his actions to someone like himself "(chi scrive, per esempio)" (me, a writer, for example):

"Se lei, professore, quella sera ... si fosse trovato nelle mie condizioni, forse che non l'avrebbe detta anche lei una piccola balla? E non la dirà, sia sincero, ogni qualvolta ne abbia bisogno ...[14] compreso ... compreso quando scrive ... quando" – e sogghigna – "compone? E poi, e poi: proprio da lei, autore fra l'altro degli *Occhiali d'oro* e di *Dietro la porta*, un poveraccio come me ha da sentirsi lesinare la comprensione?"

Lui quella disgraziata sera là – prosegue, con aria di colpo contrita – la balla l'aveva mollata un po' grossa, è vero: una balla che, ehm ... poteva fare a meno di ... anche per il riguardo dovuto ai molti che ... Indubbiamente.

Senonché di Medaglie d'Oro ce ne sono talmente tante, in giro – soggiunge ... ce ne sono talmente tante, in giro, con tutte le guerre in cui, a partire dalla Libia, la *nostra* Italia è andata a cacciarsi! Una più una meno, siamo giusti, che differenza fa? (933–4)

"Sir, if that evening ... you had found yourself in my circumstances, wouldn't you too perhaps have told a white lie? And, honestly, don't you

> tell one every time you need one … including … including when you write … when" – and he sneers – "you compose? Besides which, you, the author, among other things, of *The Gold-Rimmed Spectacles* and of *Behind the Door*, you, of all people, should understand a poor fellow like me, don't you think?"
>
> That infamous night – he continued, with a sudden air of contrition – the lie was a bit over the top, it's true: a lie that, hmm … he could have avoided telling … also out of consideration for the many who … Undoubtedly.
>
> Only, there are so many Medals of Bravery around, he adds … there are so many of them around, with all the wars, especially from Libya onward, that our dear Italy has gotten itself into! One medal more, one medal less, let's be honest, what difference does it really make?

The story ends on this note. Here Bassani is clearly coming out as an author and defending his right to mix truth and invention, perhaps answering accusations that have been directed at him. The story has a Pirandellian touch to it, with a character addressing an author as they both have to explain liberties they have taken with the facts. The story obviously contains an ironic dimension, with Bassani perhaps casting his own Resistance activities in a self-deprecating light, but it also rings of self-justification, as if he had been criticized for having painted himself as something of a "hero," just like the old man in question.

In the next and last piece, Bassani speaks openly about himself as a writer and about the long and laboured gestation and parturition of the *Storie ferraresi.* Many of the comments he makes here have been cited over and over by critics. Among the most significant is the one from which the title of the piece, "Laggiù, in fondo al corridoio," is drawn, in which he claims that the past is alive and can be recovered:

> Bisogna, tuttavia, se proprio si ha voglia di recuperarlo, percorrere una specie di corridoio ad ogni istante più lungo. Laggiù, in fondo al remoto, soleggiato punto di convergenza delle nere pareti del corridoio, sta la vita, vivida e palpitante come una volta, quando primamente si produsse. Eterna, allora? Eterna. E nondimeno sempre più lontana, sempre più sfuggente, sempre più restìa a lasciarsi di nuovo possedere. (939)

> However, if one really wishes to recover it, one must go down a kind of corridor that grows longer with every moment. There, at the very back, where its black walls converge into a distant, sun-drenched point, there will one find life, vivid and throbbing, as it once was, at the time of its first

incarnation. Eternal, then? Eternal. And yet always further away, always more fleeting, more resistant to any attempt to possess it once again.

This image of the long corridor sends the reader back in a circular fashion to the beginning of the *Romanzo*, to Lida Mantovani, the first of Bassani's many doubles, sitting at the end of a long corridor. Perhaps *L'odore del fieno* was added to the *Romanzo* because it was not fitting to end with the story of Alberto Limentani's suicide. It offers, without being explicit or fleshing out a complete portrait, a few veiled glimpses of the man who survived to tell the proverbial tale. A complex, brooding man, Bassani has overcome one of his worst characteristics (Jewish self-hatred) and has gained an awareness of other possible shortcomings. In "Les neiges d'antan," the tables have turned. He now looks at Marco Giori with pity and disdain and not through the filter of his own insecurities, as he contrasts the life of his former idol, who has turned into a poor copy of his father, to his own:

> Mi sono sposato, sono andato via da Ferrara, ho messo radici altrove, ho avuto dei figli, ho scritto e pubblicato dei libri: coi molteplici contraccolpi in bene e in male che da tutto cio è derivato. In ogni caso mi sono dato da fare, come dicono qui a Roma, lavorando, faticando, vivendo. (899)

> I married, I left Ferrara, I put down roots elsewhere, I had children, I wrote and published books: with the many consequences, for better and for worse, that have derived from all of this. In any case, I kept at it, as they say here in Rome, working, toiling, living.

In the Nietzschean world-view, *amor fati* (learning to love one's fate) means accepting those "intractable relatively permanent elements of one's identity" that have been identified and accepting that life will be a permanent struggle with these elements. Nor can one come to the bottom of oneself; there is always more to come.[15]

L'odore del fieno seems to be the sign of this acknowledgment and acceptance.

Conclusion

Previous criticism has read Bassani mostly in the context of Italian literature and culture, with some concessions to authors such as Proust, Hawthorne, and a few others, but only superficially. On the whole, Italian literature has had little frame of reference for understanding his writing on its own terms. Bassani is a genuinely cosmopolitan writer, deeply concerned with problems of Jewish identity and history, whose body of work is situated on the border between the Italian tradition and discourses of Jewishness in the period before World War II, as well as Jewish issues of the postwar period.

My own work, by attempting to decipher the unifying autobiographical palimpsest of his novels and short stories, has led me to uncover and reconstruct the extremely important, and largely ignored, intellectual "Jewish context" of his novels and short stories, without which, I maintain, they cannot truly be fully appreciated. It is the lack of awareness of this context that accounts for the many accusations of ambiguity still levelled at him, and which his own reticence has fuelled. To really grasp what Bassani is about, one must take into account broad cultural issues concerning the role of Jews in European society and culture between the late nineteenth century and World War II, coinciding with the years of his formation; these are the very same issues that I demonstrate that he engages with. His deep interest in the writings of Freud, Nietzsche, and Thomas Mann, as well as discourses of anti-Semitism in general, all subtly but tightly interwoven into his writing, derives from his interest in the place of Jews in Germanic society and cultural discourse, for obvious reasons. He also engages in a veiled manner with Jewish issues of concern to him in the postwar period – the Frankfurt Auschwitz Trials, alluded to in *Dietro la porta*, and the question of trauma, which runs through the entire *Romanzo* and reaches its climax with *L'airone*. Moreover, the difficulty of speaking out as a Jew in Italian society in the postwar period is thematized in the hesitancies and reticence of his first-person narrator.

What does it mean to be a Jew in a Gentile world? When the mask of *italianità* was torn from their faces abruptly and brutally by Mussolini's decision to embrace Hitler's racial policies, Italian Jews were left bereft and completely disarmed. In many cases, the siren song of emancipation had eroded much of their Jewishness, now reduced to the perfunctory observance of rituals and holidays. Images of the ghetto and of the pariah status of the eastern Jew, so disparagingly represented in Western culture as the wandering Jew, returned to haunt them. The enigma of their stunned passivity in the face of ostracism and persecution is the point of departure for Bassani's inquiry into the Jewish condition in a Gentile world.

The *Romanzo di Ferrara* is a richly and elegantly woven tapestry of literary, cultural, and historical allusion with a bright red thread running through it from beginning to end that poses the question, "Who am I"? From David Camaioli in the opening novella, "Lida Mantovani," about whom Lida asks, "Chi era, che cosa voleva?" ("Who was he, what did he want?") to Edgardo Limentani who witnesses the false persona he has cultivated all his life collapse before him when he recognizes himself in the agonizing heron, to Yuri Rotstein, the son of eastern Jews, who ends up with his mother "alone forever," Bassani creates a series of characters (not all Jews or male) who function as doubles and through whom he slowly and patiently unpacks the layers of a hypothetical Jewish male psyche. As he dons and removes these different masks – including Lida Mantovani, Ausilia Brondi, Elia Corcos, Geo Josz, Bruno Lattes, Dr Fadigati, the Finzi-Continis (all of them), and even Pino Barilari – he slowly evokes the internal obstacles that he believes provide the answer to what he sees as the burning question of Jewish passivity in the face of Nazi-Fascist persecution.

To give shape to the "rubble" that he has "excavated," he calls on three main "guides," so to speak, each of whom provides him with a different building block: Nietzsche, a way into the prehistory of contemporary Jewish male psychology; Freud, a framework for constructing the tortuous psychosexual development of the Jewish male in a non-Jewish world; and finally Thomas Mann, a mirror to look into.

In the stories that precede the first-person trilogy, the Jewish male character comes into progressively clearer focus, much as through the lens of a camera. In the first story, "Lida Mantovani," he is absent, a ghost-like figure recalled in flashbacks by the Gentile girl he used and spurned; her difficult relations with her mother mirror his own "off-stage" parental difficulties, which are alluded to repeatedly but never represented directly. In the second story, "La passeggiata prima di cena," Elia Corcos, a prominent doctor, is viewed through the double perspective of the Gentile sister-in-law who idolizes him from afar and of the Jewish community of Ferrara in the years immediately following Unification and the opening of the ghetto. Aloof and uneasy, Elia has broken with his father's religion and worships at the altar of science. However, fearful of striking out into the world, he refuses to embark on the illustrious career that would have required him to leave the comfortable cocoon of Ferrara and marries a lower class Gentile girl whom he views with contempt. Stuck on the threshold between two worlds, he is a victim of emancipation. In the third story, "Gli ultimi anni di Clelia Trotti," Bassani's declared alter ego Bruno Lattes makes his first appearance. A young university student faced with the shock of the Race Laws, Bruno has been spurned by his Aryan girlfriend and feels completely isolated. To fill the void, he flirts with the idea of becoming a Socialist by befriending a former activist schoolteacher now under house arrest. Though this can be read as a realistic story, Bassani casts it more as a quest narrative, complete with obstacles and guides. The final discovery that he has no potential as a Socialist and is simply a young overprotected and spoilt bourgeois in a hostile world underlines the emptiness of upper class Jewish identity as one of the reasons for the inability to react in the face of persecution. Moreover, the schoolteacher not coincidentally is an older woman, a mother figure who represents a movement that in Ferrara is "passé": though Bruno realizes that the "feminine past" is not a solution, he is unable to pass into the world of the "fathers," that is to commit to a combative stance. Condemned to remaining forever on the threshhold of manhood, on the outside looking in, Bruno ultimately flees to America where he becomes a university lecturer in Italian. In an interview, Bassani said that Bruno Lattes was a coward,[1] clearly someone he could have been himself had he not found his way to anti-Fascist militancy. The last two stories are focused on Holocaust issues, at least overtly. In the first, "Una lapide in via Mazzini," a survivor of Buchenwald returns to Ferrara after the war only to find that no one, not even the remaining Jews, wants to hear his story. While attempting to re-adapt to life in an epoch of "reconciliation," one day he finds himself face to face in the town square with a former Fascist spy and betrayer of Ferrara's Jews to the Nazis. In an epiphanic moment, he slaps the old Fascist across the face in full view of the citizenry, who react with shock at such a breach of good manners. He then disappears forever. Here a Jew finally assumes responsibility for his identity as a Jew and acts in its name, but then has to leave town. This is the only case in Bassani's entire corpus in which such an active stance is assumed by a Jewish male character. The last story, "Una notte del '43," recounts the circumstances surrounding a trial held in the immediate aftermath of the civil war, in which a Fascist thug and killer escapes condemnation because the only eyewitness to the mass execution he ordered in 1943 refuses to testify against him. The witness is the former town pharmacist, paralysed from the waist down as a result of a venereal disease contracted during a visit to a brothel with the accused during the March on Rome. He spends his time stationed at the window of his upstairs apartment looking out on the main square, while his wife carries on her own sexual activities that he pretends to know nothing about. When called upon to testify at the trial, he claims to have seen nothing, because he would have had to acknowledge at the same time his wife's infidelities, since she too was at the site of the killings, just returning home from a tryst. His impotence and paralysis, and condemnation to a life of observation, are literal figures of passivity and helplessness in the face of history. The convergence, climax, and figural representation in a Gentile character of psychological motifs previously attributed to Jewish characters (and this is the only story in which there is no male Jewish character) suggests that the pharmacist represents a spiritual sickness that afflicted both Jews and non-Jews in Bassani's eyes.

In *Gli occhiali d'oro,* the short novel that inaugurates the first-person trilogy, the sexual motif moves from the metaphorical to the literal. The narrator is a Jew who in 1957 tells the story of his highly fraught friendship with a homosexual physician in 1936–7, when both were facing exclusion from society, the doctor for having sacrificed respectability for an open affair with a young gigolo, the young Jew because of the imminent Race Laws. The most fascinating element of this story is its rewriting and "outing" of the famous Thomas Mann novella, *Death in Venice,* based on Bassani's intuition that its protagonist, Gustav von Aschenbach, represents a composite of Mann himself and of Gustav Mahler, a converted Jew struggling with his Jewishness in an increasingly anti-Semitic society, whom Mann both admired and with whom he clearly identified. Bassani transposes many elements of Mann's text to his own, but the most important is Mann's ambivalence towards Aschenbach, a sign of Mann's own struggle with his submerged homosexuality and of his ambivalence to Mahler as a Jew, notwithstanding his identification with his pariah status. The Bassani story focuses on his protagonist's inability to defend himself against the indifference and even overt anti-Semitism of his milieu, as well as on his ambivalence towards the similarly persecuted homosexual doctor for fear of being identified with him. The carefully crafted first-person narration reveals contradictions, memory lapses, ambiguities, and unconscious tensions, as well a residual denial of the protagonist's contribution to the doctor's isolation, which thematize both the difficulty of speaking as a Jew in postwar Italy's climate of reconciliation and reconstruction, and the barely repressed guilt that continues to plague him. Fadigati's story is also a metaphor, a way for the Jew to tell the "Jewish" story indirectly, for every aspect of Fadigati's *iter* in Ferrara society is reconstructed as a projection of the attempt of Jews to enter and "pass" in Christian society, revealing that the identification with Fadigati is very strong indeed. Bassani's story "outs" the Mann novella, as well as Mann's sexual proclivities, a full twenty-eight years before Anthony Heilbut's 1995 biography of Mann, *Eros and Literature*. It also establishes Bassani's own identification with Mann at the literary level.[2]

Set in the aftermath of the passage of the Race Laws, as well as of Dr Fadigati's suicide, *Il giardino dei Finzi-Contini* combines a literal elaboration of the family romance motif with the Jewish motif found in Thomas Mann's novella *Blood of the Walsungs*. Bassani also employs elements of the *Divine Comedy* in this story – for example, in the protagonist's idealization of Micòl – to signal the contradictions and pitfalls of being a Jew schooled in a Catholic culture, which he must overcome in order to free himself. The chaste obsession with Micòl represents both an escape from the difficult decisions facing the young protagonist as history encroaches and an idealization that reflects the protagonist's psychosexual immaturity. Both temptress and guide, Micòl (in the Old Testament the wife of David and daughter of Saul) is Beatrice and Eve all-in-one, Bassani's Jewish rewrite of the courtly ideal and of its ultimate sublimation in the Dantean figure. The grandiose isolation of the Finzi-Continis and their refusal to acknowledge what is going on in the outside world represent the Jews' denial of the reality of their imminent persecution and their dogged refusal to relinquish the status they had attained in Italian society after Unification. But again, this "garden" is not to be taken entirely realistically; the death of the Finzi-Continis also represents the death of an impossible fantasy: they and the garden are the projection of a state of a mind, the ultimate fantasy of acculturation without assimilation, a Garden of Eden where the burden of racial/religious difference need not be borne. Moreover, the archaeology motif on which the introduction to the novel is built alludes, I believe, to Freud's use of archaeology as a metaphor for the work of digging through the layers of the psyche. The Finzi-Contini mansion, through whose different rooms the protagonist progressively passes until he finally gains admittance, forcefully, to Micòl's private quarters, again symbolizes a mapping of the different aspects of the young man's psyche and of the "passages" he must traverse on the way to a semblance of maturity. In this novel, the recognition of sexual difference goes hand in hand with the acceptance of ethnic difference.

In *Dietro la porta* Bassani uses the Freudian primal scene image of the door quite explicitly, conflating it in the climax of the novel with a scene that recalls the betrayal of Christ to the Romans at the hands of a fellow Jew. The events take place in 1929, well before the Race Laws but, very significantly, in the year in which Mussolini signed the Concordat. Part of the Lateran Pacts that healed the rift with the Catholic church dating back to Unification, the Concordat declared Catholicism the official religion of state. This brought an end to the secularity of the nation, under which Jewish Italians had considered themselves full citizens for all intents and purposes. On the surface, the novel tells the story of the difficulties encountered by the young protagonist during the passage from middle school to the *liceo*, the period corresponding to adolescent manhood or puberty. The narrator here arrives at what he considers to be the root of his problem – the traumatic injury inflicted upon him by the verbal besmirching of his mother's body and of his own sexuality by a Catholic, socially inferior classmate as he listens behind a door. This betrayal – he had previously considered this boy his best friend – replays not only the betrayal of the Jews by Catholic and Fascist Italy but also the Judas Iscariot motif, the betrayal of a Jew to the Romans by another Jew, revealing the novel's secret: Pulga, the "best friend," though nominally Catholic, embodies all the contemporary anti-Semitic stereotypes with which the protagonist associates his burgeoning and uncontrollable adolescent sexual instincts. These instincts thus become hateful to him: at the bottom of his neuroses lies the hatred of his own Jewish masculinity. The novel echoes Otto Weininger's popular theories according to which Jews were a feminized and oversexualized race. My reading of this novel thus casts the characters of Pulga and Cattolica as the protagonist's doubles, representing the terms of a conflict that sees him having to choose between assimilation as represented by Carlo Cattolica and a reviled Jewish identity based on the worst stereotypes of anti-Semitic discourse as represented by Pulga (even though Pulga is not depicted as a Jew). In a sense, Pulga can be seen to represent the Jew whose self-hatred has led him to convert to Catholicism.

Self-hatred is the overriding emotion of the main character in Bassani's last novel. Written in the third person and set in the immediate aftermath of the war, *L'airone* focuses on Edgardo Limentani, who had escaped deportation by fleeing Ferrara just in the nick of time with his Gentile wife and family. The difficult and dangerous journey to Switzerland has left him with a bad case of what today would be called post-traumatic stress disorder. Combined with his self-loathing and a total sense of isolation and entrapment, his state of mind now sends him careening towards suicide. It is well known that Bassani was responsible for the publication of Lampedusa's *Gattopardo* (1957), which had been rejected by, among others, Elio Vittorini. Set in 1947, Bassani's novel not only makes explicit Lampedusa's implicit critique of post-war Italy, it also uses the *Gattopardo* as an intertext through which it evokes the enduring "false consciousness" of some sectors of the Italian Jewish bourgeoisie as they struggle with the rapidly changing social and political landscape now that the Fascists have been defeated and the Communists loom large on the horizon. Even in the face of what he witnessed in Ferrara under the Fascists and during the Repubblica di Salò, Limentani prefers to think of himself as a sort of modern-day Prince Fabrizio, a feudal landowner besieged by the demands and threats of his labourers, rather than as the shell-shocked Jew that he is, still reeling from the atrocities and humiliations of the recent past. Desperate to shake off the feeling of unease and confinement he is suffering from, Limentani decides to go hunting for the first time since the passing of the Race Laws in 1938. The hunter will become the hunted, and at the day's end Limentani will take his own life after refusing to shoot any birds and recognizing himself in the struggling heron that his guide's precise aim brings down. But his suicide will take place only after he finally confronts symbolically a representative of his Fascist tormentors. This novel is about the importance of acknowledgment, of mourning, and of working through – all stages that Limentani refuses to go through. The many examples of threshold and primal scene imagery indicate that he has remained psychologically unable to negotiate the Oedipal passage; it is this inability, marked by the fact that the last scene of the novel takes place in his mother's bedroom as Limentani says goodbye to her for the last time, that accounts for his passivity and denial.

The fictional and semifictional short pieces that make up *L'odore del fieno* appear to have been included by Bassani in the final version of the *Romanzo* in order to connect the "I," as he himself puts it, of the earlier fictional novels to the living "I." They allude, some very cryptically, to a number of significant events in his life: participation in anti-Fascist conspiracy, postwar anxieties, the decision to join the Socialist Party after the dissolution of the Action Party, leaving Ferrara for Rome in both the literal and metaphorical sense, returning to Ferrara as a visitor, marriage, separation, his literary career. The character of Bruno Lattes returns here as the connection between the fictional "I" and the living "I." The last piece is one in which he addresses the difficulties of writing the early *Storie ferraresi* and finally emerges as the persona he wishes to embody: the author. A number of things omitted from the novels and short stories are allowed to appear here. The most important and significant is the figure of the formerly reviled eastern Jew who, in the first of the stories, is embraced as a sign of the author's positive reintegration of his history as a Jew, the overcoming of his self-hatred. However, the author finds no resolution, and the reader is left with the feeling that the digging into the layers of his psyche is still a work in progress.

Bassani's use of the Nietzschean paradigm allows him to tell the story of a very specific Jewish "everyman," moving from self-ignorance to self-knowledge and in the process coming face to face with the enemy: his own internalized view of himself as a Jewish male in a Christian society. Jacob Golomb, a scholar who has studied in depth the influence of Nietzsche on the marginal Jews of the late-nineteenth-century Germanic world, has attempted to understand what it was that so appealed to them in the philosopher's teachings. His conclusion is that Nietzsche's call for personal authenticity and self-creation provided a way out of their dilemmas of identity. Caught between their own rejection of traditional Judaism and the refusal of the Gentile mainstream to fully accept them, they turned to Nietszsche to help them understand their own conflicts:

> The marginal Jews urgently felt the need to overcome their unbearable identity crisis and the conflict between their heritage and their present culture. Nietzsche excelled at describing their predicament. Although his analyses dealt with western ethics in general, they were specifically

> relevant to and valid for the *Grenzjuden,* who had become the main victims of the culture which they had been so instrumental in growing and fostering. … Under Nietzsche's guidance they tried to overcome both the traditions of their Jewish forefathers and their ultra-Germanism and self-hatred. They aspired to a harmonious synthesis between Berlin and Jerusalem, and to accept their marginality in an *amor-fati* manner not as their inevitable fate but as their own authentic, creative accomplishment.
>
> Nietzsche's attractiveness to them is rooted in his inspiring call to become a genuine free spirit and to search for one's *own* self and personal authenticity. …
>
> Nietzsche employs the metaphor of art and artistic creation. The search for authenticity is the wish to express one's indeterminacy by the spontaneous choice of one of many possible ways of life. The individual is akin to the artist who freely shapes his self as a work of art. To become what we are is not to live according to our so-called "innate nature," but rather to create ourselves freely. To that end we must know ourselves, in order to distinguish what we can change in ourselves and in the external circumstances which have shaped us from that which we have to accept as inevitable. This we must do in the heroic manner of *amor fati* and of "self-overcoming." The purpose of this self-overcoming is to attain maturity, authenticity and power. In this respect the will to power is of a piece with the quest for authenticity – it is the will to become the free author of one's own self.[3]

Golomb focuses in particular on the appeal Nietzsche held for the Jewish followers of Freud, whom he calls the "Jewish psychoanalysts":

> The Jewish psychoanalysts were especially attracted by Nietzsche's genealogical methods of "unmasking." … Following the death of the Father – the Jewish God – and the decline, in the typical Jewish family, of the authority of the father, who was responsible for bringing his sons to the schizoid state they were now in, the *Grenzjuden* sought to establish firm and authentic identities which would not draw their content from faith and tradition, but would derive it solely from the individual's own mental resources. Nietzsche encouraged this process by showing how psychologization could liberate the individual from dependence on mechanical internalizations, habits of thought and hereditary conventions.
>
> Nietzsche served as a model of penetrating self-analysis of an acute neurosis, and also demonstrated, before Freud, the therapy needed to overcome this neurosis. … Only those, like many of the marginal Jews,

> who had experienced and overcome such neuroses possessed an "inborn fastidiousness of taste with respect to psychological questions" (*Genealogy of Morality* Preface 3) and were able to "go inside." This ability to "go inside" and overcome states of negative pathos is regarded by Nietzsche as a major indicator of an individual's positive power – his ability to explicate the darkest recesses of his soul for the sake of health and vitality. Many of the creative *Grenzjuden* dared "go inside" and used such self-overcoming to produce masterpieces which were informed by this psychological enlightenment. Nietzsche served them as both guide to and monumental model of this creative process.[4]

When I first came across these passages, I could not help but think of the spiritual journey that Bassani evokes in the *Romanzo di Ferrara*. Mutatis mutandis, taking into consideration all the obvious differences between them, there is no question that a Jew such as Bassani in the face of the Race Laws confronted many of the same identity issues as German or Austrian Jewish intellectuals of Nietzsche's time seeking integration into and identification with a culture and society that refused them full acceptance. Of course, in his immediate quest for an alternative to what his own milieu was able to provide, Bassani turned to Croce, as he repeatedly states in his interviews; however, my contention is that in the telling of the story that unfolds in the *Romanzo di Ferrara*, he turned to Nietzsche for what Croce could not offer him: on the one hand, a means to understand and come to terms with his dilemma as a Jew, both before, during, and after the days of persecution; on the other, a model for his own creative masterpiece, the monumental narrative that functions as the objective correlative for this process of understanding and "overcoming." In fact, as he produced the works that constitute the *Romanzo*, there is every reason to believe that Bassani became increasingly aware of the shape it was taking and began consciously modelling it along Nietzschean (and Freudian) lines.

Nietszche's metaphors, like in a dream, assume literal embodiment in the *Romanzo*: "going inside" manifests as penetrating the many layers between the outer walls of Ferrara and the inside of Micòl's room, while "unmasking" consists of removing the many layers of culture and class (that he so admired in the voice of Ermanno Finzi-Contini) until Bassani reaches the damaged Jewish boy we find in *Dietro la porta*. The damaged parts of this boy are killed off in Alberto Limentani, who exacts Nietzsche's "symbolic vengeance" against the Fascist Bellagamba and goes on Nietzsche's "great hunt" for himself. Limentani's suicide is clearly a form of "self-overcoming."[5] The Jewish boy at the core of this cycle is subsequently recuperated and rehabilitated in the mysterious figure of Yuri Rotstein, the son of an eastern Jew, who ends up "alone forever" with his mother.

This mysterious Yuri takes us to the the heart of Bassani's "confession" and to the question of Bassani's purported "ambiguity" that I raised in the introduction in response to Roberto Cotroneo. Certainly (though Cotroneo does not take up this example) the fact that Yuri ends up alone forever with his mother in the house in Ferrara can be viewed in two ways: either as the inevitable fate of a Jewish male in a Christian world, destined to remain forever mother identified and excluded from the world of the (Gentile) "fathers," or, alternatively, as the expression of Bassani's attachment to the "difference" of Jewish manhood, which he now regards without shame through the lens of Jewish history, as opposed to viewing it negatively through the lens of anti-Semitic discourse. I believe this dual reading to be not, however, an undeciferable ambiguity but a very clear sign of ambivalence, Bassani's own residual ambivalence as a Jew who has recognized the non-normative nature of Jewish masculinity and both embraces it positively as part of his heritage and yet rejects it as undesirable in the face of political and historical realities. Warren Rosenberg summarizes the issues surrounding Jewish masculinity that form the backdrop of Bassani's treatment of it:

> Recent scholarship ... describes the ideal Jewish male during the Rabbinic/Diasporic period, from the destruction of the Temple in Jerusalem (70 CE) to the founding of the State of Israel, as a counter-image to the hegemonic Western masculine ideal of the warrior/knight. With no nation-state to defend, the ideal Jewish male became a biblical scholar, a congregant, and a loving husband and father who rejected violence. As Jews were subject to attacks and expulsions throughout the Diasporic period, a code ... evolved that located Jewish superiority in the refusal to share the aggressive values of their oppressors. ...
>
> The Enlightenment and the rise of nationalism, culminating in Zionism, undermined the ideal of the gentle, scholarly Jewish mensch, or good Jewish man. ... Even Sigmund Freud, in a famous passage in *The Interpretation of Dreams,* saw his own father's passivity in response to an anti-Semitic act "as unheroic conduct."
>
> ... The Holocaust, in addition to threatening the survival of all European Jews, exacerbated the tensions surrounding Jewish masculinity, as the

> very passivity that had characterised the ideal of Jewish manhood was now seen as contributing to its extinction. The post-World War II years were dominated by psychic and political responses to the Holocaust, culminating in the founding of the State of Israel in 1948.[6]

John Champagne, in a recent reading of *Giardino dei Finzi-Contini*[7] from the area of queer studies has attempted to use Bassani's ambivalence to claim the novel as "queer," in other words, as rejecting binary and prescriptive gender and sexual identities, and cites the following passage as ostensible proof of this position:

> Da Fadigati a venire a parlare dell'omosessualità in genere il passo era stato breve: Malnate, in materia, aveva delle idee molto semplici: da vero *goi* – pensavo tra me – . Per lui i pederasti erano soltanto dei "disgraziati," poveri "ossessi." … Io, al contrario, sostenevo che l'amore giustifica e santifica tutto, perfino la pederastia: di più, che l'amore, quando è puro, cioè totalmente disinteressato, è sempre anormale, asociale, eccetera: proprio come l'arte. (552)

> From Fadigati to a more general discussion of homosexuality was just a few steps. On this topic Malnate had very uncomplicated views – like a true *goy*, I thought to myself. For him, pederasts were nothing but "miserable wretches," "poor obsessives." … By contrast, I maintained that love justified and sanctified everything, even pederasty. I went further, saying that love, when it was pure, by which I meant totally disinterested, is always abnormal, asocial and so on: exactly like art. (223)

What the queer studies critic does not know is that in the interview with Camon cited earlier, Bassani speaks of Pulga in *Dietro la porta* as "il perfido, il maligno, l'omosessuale,"[8] putting to rest the notion that his attitude to homosexuality was devoid of any ambivalence. Nor does Champagne take into account the association of unsavoury characters, such as Sciagura and Pino Barilari, with homosexuality in "Una notte del 43." Moreover, one cannot overlook that the politically and heterosexually active Malnate, for all his shortcomings, is nonetheless the male with whom the protagonist of *Giardino* identifies in the symbolic, Oedipal resolution that brings to an end his relationship with Micòl.

Champagne's queer reading extends this supposed deconstruction of hierarchical identities to religious identities as well, seeing it as "an attempt to bring to crisis … a series of binaries, including … Christian/ Jew." Indeed. It is true that in *Dietro la porta,* the Jewish protagonist approaches Cattolica with the possibility that he may have Jewish ancestors, as his surname, being a place name, might lead one to believe. However, Cattolica rejects this outright, and the protagonist's attempt to resolve his identity conflict by not having to "choose" is thwarted. It is the complete failure of the utopian notion of nondifference that lay at the bottom of the Italian Jews' illusion of full belonging that is documented here and likened to the notion of sexual nondifference. Underneath the paradisiacal surface of the garden is a deadly dystopia for the Jews, and in fact Micòl dies as a result of the protagonist's inability to act on their sexual difference by kissing her.

Taken as whole, the *Romanzo di Ferrara* tells not one, not two, not three, but four stories. The first is that of the characters and places as figures of the world. The second is the symbolic story, the palimpsest that traces the unfolding of the family romance; this is the intimate story of the young protagonist who failed to kiss Micòl, who failed to reach out to Dr Fadigati, who failed to fight back when Pulga and Cattolica attacked him, and whose psychological state is prefigured by the series of characters and situations described in the stories that precede the first-person trilogy. The third story is that of the narrator, situated in postwar Italy, a traumatized Jew still trying to work through the residual guilt, reticence, and feeling of impotence and resentment that continue to haunt him as he ponders the past and the mysteries of his own soul, some of which will forever remain inaccessible to him. He still carries with him the sexual dilemmas of his youth. The fourth story is that of Bassani the writer, who has created all these characters in order to stage his own conflicts and the internal obstacles that he felt needed to be overcome for him to become a militant anti-Fascist in spite of his background and then to go on as a Jew in post-Holocaust Italian society. It is this fourth story, that of Bassani the writer, that I wish to explore in what follows.

A very interesting article by Fabio Girelli-Carasi, "Contemporary Jewish Memorialists in Italy," discusses the plethora of writings by and about Jewish Italians that began as a trickle in the seventies and then became a full-fledged publishing phenomenon. Citing the numerous Italian Jewish authors who failed to openly embrace their Jewishness in the early and mid-twentieth century – Saba, Svevo, Moravia, Ginzburg, Carlo Levi – Girelli-Carasi attributes the emergence of a Jewish voice, and the interest in it displayed by non-Jews in the last thirty or so years, to the beginnings of a discourse of diversity in Italy as a result of immigration, a discourse that up to that time had been made impossible by the Catholic church and the Communist Party. The presence of immigrants, however, brought to the fore the question of difference in such a massive way that it could no longer be ignored. What is most interesting about this article for our purposes is that it mentions Primo Levi as the only exception to the rule of silence and reticence seen in the previous generations of Jewish writers. Paradoxically, not only does the author fail to include Giorgio Bassani alongside Primo Levi, he actually goes so far as to say that "the exception of the Finzi-Contini, is really no exception at all, in that the work's literary form, the novel, corresponds to all the expectations of the Italian literary canons. In it, the Jewish text, lacking a context, becomes almost a pretext."[9] Even more striking is the fact that he actually fails to even *name* Bassani, identifying him simply by his most famous novel. Whether or not this omission is symptomatic of the extent to which Italian critical discourse has managed, for all sorts of reasons, to obliterate his message, or whether Bassani himself has contributed to this image of himself, it certainly raises the issue of his status as a Jewish writer.

In a book on aspects of Jewish writing in twentieth-century Italy, Luca De Angelis claims that all Jewish writers are, in a sense, Marranos:

> Ogni scrittore ebreo, in termini assoluti o relativi, è un marrano più o meno volontario, ed incarna l'uomo dell'intimità *tout court*. Nella coscienza dell'ebreo nascosto (e così pure dello scrittore) si sviluppa un'identità ambivalente, dimidiata in un aspetto ufficiale esteriore ed uno interiore criptoebraico, accentuata da un'elaboratissima e finissima cultura del segreto.[10]

> Every Jewish writer, in absolute or relative terms, is more or less voluntarily a Marrano and incarnates the man of intimacy tout court. In the conscience of the hidden Jew (and also of the writer) an ambivalent identity develops, divided into an official exterior aspect and an interior cripto-Jewish one, accentuated by a very elaborate and very refined culture of secrecy.

I cite this passage for two reasons: because of Bassani's own repeated allusions to secrets, confessions, and "concealed subjects," which was the starting point for my incursion into his work; and because the title of De Angelis's book, *Qualcosa di più intimo* (Something more intimate), is drawn from a passage in *Il giardino dei Finzi-Contini*:

Per quanto concerne me personalmente, nei miei rapporti con Alberto e Micòl, c'era stato da sempre qualcosa di più intimo. Le occhiate d'intesa, i cenni confidenziali, che fratello e sorella mi indirizzavano ogniqualvolta ci incontravamo nei pressi del *Guarini*, non alludevano che a questo, lo sapevo bene, riguardante noi e soltanto noi.

Qualcosa di più intimo. Che cosa propriamente?

Si capisce: in primo luogo eravamo ebrei, e ciò in ogni caso sarebbe stato più che sufficiente. ... A noi ragazzi non sarebbe occorso niente di più perché ritrovandoci altrove, e soprattutto in presenza di estranei, passasse subito nei nostri occhi l'ombra o il riso di una certa speciale complicità e connivenza. (341)

So far as I was personally concerned, in my relationship with Alberto and Micòl there was always something more intimate. The knowing looks, the confidential nods that brother and sister both directed towards me whenever we met in the grounds of the Guarini, were signs, I fully realized, of just this private understanding between us.

Something more intimate. But what exactly?

Certainly, to start off with, we were Jews, and this on its own would be more than enough. ... To us children this alone would be enough for us, meeting elsewhere, and above all in the presence of the uninitiated, to prompt the shadowy look or the smile of special complicity or connivance. (30)

The tone used by Bassani in the above passage is one of exclusivity, because the narrator is speaking of a time in which he idolized the Finzi-Continis, when the idea of belonging to a private "club" to which they also belonged was highly flattering to his vanity. However, this is not always the case in this novel; belonging to this club can also be experienced as a source of shame, as when the protagonist first sees Bruno Lattes at the gates of the Finzi-Contini estate: "Passò rapida tra me e lui l'inevitabile occhiata di ebraica connivenza che, mezzo ansioso e mezzo disgustato, già prevedevo"(380; Between the two of us passed the inevitable glance of Jewish complicity which, partly in anxiety and partly in distaste, I had already foreseen [67]).

In attempting to understand Bassani's attitude towards writing about Jewish matters for a primarily non-Jewish readership, De Angelis detects in his work a scepticism about the possibility of really being understood by non-Jews, a feeling of impotence and isolation, as if Bassani perceived the abyss between Jews and Gentiles as too great: so great that the issues that really mattered to him could not be of concern to non-Jews and perhaps were not even capable of attracting their interest. The result of this perception is a kind of reserve, a fear of disclosing intimate details that, if revealed, may be misunderstood completely. The idea of different understandings of what is important is alluded to in the passage that describes Micòl and Alberto's private language, *finzi-continico*, which they used to communicate even in the presence of outsiders. The tone in this passage is one of exclusivity, but what it masks is a fear of being misunderstood; a disadvantage has been made into an advantage, an "outside" has been made into an "inside":

> Parlavano entrambi nello stesso modo, spiccando le sillabe di certi vocaboli di cui essi soli sembravano conoscere il vero senso, il vero peso, e invece scivolando bizzarramente su quelle di altri, che uno avrebbe detto di importanza molto maggiore. Mettevano una sorta di puntiglio nell'esprimersi così. Questa particolare, inimitabile, tutta privata deformazione dell'italiano era la loro *vera* lingua. Le davano perfino un nome: il finzi-continico. (355)

> They both spoke in the same way, stressing the syllables of certain words of which only they seemed to know the true sense, the real weight, but then sliding bizarrely over other syllables which one might have thought had more importance. They made a point of expressing themselves this way. [This particular, inimitable, completely private deformation of Italian was their *true* language.] They even gave it a name: Finzi-Continish. (42)

The difference of perspective results also from a difference of knowledge. De Angelis cites a passage in which the narrator, speaking of the intricacies of the different subcultures in the Ferrara Jewish community, says that only he and his kind could understand these subtle, irrelevant, and yet no less real distinctions: "Gli altri, tutti gli altri, ... inutile pensare di erudirli in una materia talmente privata" (343; As for the others, all the others ... it was futile to think they might be instructed in such an occult zone of knowledge [32]).

The intricacies of Jewish masculinity may be considered as just such an "occult zone of knowledge." The sense that something is "concealed" in Bassani's writing has not escaped some of his readers, but it has, I believe, been misunderstood. Enzo Siciliano, one of Bassani's early critics, has gone so far as to suggest that his work constitutes a veiled *j'accuse*, veiled for fear of offending the "fathers": "Pone ai padri alcuni perché: Perché avete avuto rapporti con i cattolici? Perché con i fascisti? Perché non avete capito il male che vi facevate con le vostre stesse mani? La grande domanda sottintesa è: perché il vostro masochismo?"[11] (He asks the fathers a series of questions: Why did you keep up relations with the Catholics? Why with the Fascists? Why is it that you did not understand the harm you were inflicting upon yourselves with your own hands? The key underlying question being: Why this masochism of yours?) In a similar vein, more recently Piero Pieri has made a very detailed analysis of the early version of Bassani's short stories, the *Storie ferraresi* (1956), in an attempt to show that at first he was writing not as a Jew but as a militant anti-Fascist motivated by tremendous anger towards his fellow Jews for their complicity with the regime. Pieri claims that Bassani censored that anger in subsequent rewrites, driven by pity and compassion for his people.[12]

While Pieri's analysis of these early versions of the *Storie* is incisive, revealing, very useful for Bassani scholars, and seems to be motivated by the desire to recuperate a specific historical dimension of the short stories that he feels has been lost, it suffers from a rather perplexing and disturbing desire to isolate Bassani the Jew from Bassani the liberal intellectual and anti-Fascist, as if the two were mutually exclusive. He even claims that looking at Bassani from a Jewish perspective leads to a return to what he terms "piatti conformismi positivisti leganti vita e letteratura, biografia e narrazione" (positivistic platitudes linking life and literature, biography and narration) and a reduced understanding of its multiple and polemical dimensions. Pieri also suggests that elements in Bassani's work that reflect anything other than his original moral indignation and anger derive from "una pagina psichica rimossa" (a repressed psychic page) that was only activated by the humiliation of anti-Semitic legislation, and that the "sentimento di morte" (death sentiment) in Bassani's work is a motif that all writers share independently of their origin.

While what Pieri proposes about the "repressed psychic page" may be true, it is not independent of the protagonist's Jewishness. As for the obsession with death, I find it truly amazing that Pieri can claim that it is simply the same obsession shared by all writers. To Pieri, who wishes to obliterate Bassani's Jewishness, Bassani might have responded as his protagonist does when faced with Nino Bottecchiari's insensitivity in *Gli occhiali d'oro*: "Si poteva essere più goffi, più insensibili, più ottusamente *goìm* di così?" 291; Could you be any clumsier, more insensitive, more obtusely *goyische* than that? [97]). Moreover, regarding Enzo Siciliano's claim that Bassani had launched a "veiled" accusation at the "fathers," there is nothing hidden about the young protagonist's inability to tolerate his father's attitude of passivity and denial in the face of the Race Laws. Judging Bassani's work as an accusation would be tantamount to judging *Il gattopardo* (*The Leopard*), the novel that Bassani alone was willing to publish in the politically correct climate of postwar Italy, as an accusation launched by Lampedusa against his aristocratic ancestors. Bassani shared Lampedusa's outsider perspective and was subjected to similar criticism. Both authors were out of the step with the tempo of the times, both looked back instead of ahead, and both were merciless critics of contemporary pieties. Both spared neither the minorities to which they belonged nor those responsible for what had happened to them. Like *Il gattopardo*, the *Romanzo di Ferrara* (and especially *Il giardino dei Finzi-Contini*) is at once a monument to a lost world and a critique of it, not an accusation, unless one considers it an accusation against the Italian society that allowed its Jews to be persecuted.

What is veiled in Bassani's work is not his youthful anger at his father or at his fellow Jews, but the story he has constructed of his emotional and sexual difficulties as a specifically *Jewish* male living at a very particular time and in a very particular place, circumstances of which he took stock only after the Race Laws had forced him to. The use of an unreliable narrator, or at least a narrator who is only partly aware of what drives him, has many advantages, not the least of which is that he can tell his story without making it explicit. Such narration is "veiled" but invites readers to lift this veil, if they care enough to do so and have the necessary tools. It is indeed a very private and intimate Jewish story, and yet a part of the author wants it to be exposed. Clearly his affinity for Thomas Mann and his work was not only literary but also personal. In a review of one of Mann's stories, Bassani's portrait of him ("Mann e il mago") suggests that he was very attuned not only to Mann the author but also to Mann the human being, "al suo privato destino di intellettuale deluso e insidiato" (1022; to his private fate as a frustrated and trapped intellectual). Perhaps in *Death in Venice* Bassani saw also a muffled cry for recognition, Mann's desire to be known fully. In *Gli occhiali d'oro* Bassani takes up Mann's invitation by "outing" his story and its author. Fadigati's inexplicable capitulation to Deliliers, including the parading of his proclivities on the beaches of Riccione to the good citizens of Ferrara, can similarly be viewed as a cry for recognition, however misguided.

Bassani's response to Ferretti's famous accusation that he lacked a sense of history, in the Marxist sense,[13] suggests that Bassani felt the Jewish specificity of his work was being ignored: "L'accusa che io, a mia volta, muovo a Ferretti è quella di una mancanza totale di senso storico. Invece di *scendere sul mio terreno*, e leggere i miei testi, Ferretti applica, a me, schemi che non sono i miei."[14] (I, in turn, accuse Ferretti of completely lacking a sense of history. Instead of reading my texts *on their own terms,* Ferretti applies to me criteria that have nothing to do with me.) Nowhere does he say exactly what his own terms might be and of which history he is speaking. Elsewhere in the same interview, Bassani says, in response to another criticism, "Faccio quello che mi sento di fare, e vorrei che gli altri si rassegnassero a *prendermi per quello che sono*"[15] (I do what I feel like doing, and I would like others to resign themselves to *taking me for who I am*), echoing Nietzsche's "on becoming who one is." Here again, Bassani fails to specify what he means by "who I am": perhaps a Jew telling a Jewish story?

In connection to this sentiment – to the frustrated desire for recognition – one may understand a rather curious attack on Malnate that Bassani launches in the interview with Ferdinando Camon, which reproduces the Jewish twins' slur against the Gentile Beckrath in the first version of Thomas Mann's "Blood of the Walsungs." After explaining that all the male characters in *Giardino* are *rottami* (wrecks) and *fiacchi* (weak), Bassani goes on to single out Malnate for special consideration:

> Oltre a essere un rottame come tutti gli altri, Malnate ha un altro difetto: quello, cioè, di essere anche, in certa misura grottesco e comico. Egli dice di sognare un futuro "lombardo" e "comunista," mentre è legato invece a gretti e mediocri affetti domestici, e non sa dare a Micòl tutto quello che Micòl si aspetta.[16]
>
> In addition to being a wreck like all the others, Malnate has another fault: that of being also to a certain extent grotesque and comical. He says that he dreams of a "Lombard" and "Communist" future, when instead he is tied down by narrow and mediocre domestic affections, and cannot give Micòl everything that she expects.

Two things are striking here: the slippage from text to life, as if Micòl were a person with secret wishes to which he is privy; and the either/

or vision of family ties versus progressive political outlook, reflecting Bassani's own experience of having had to break away from his family and their limited perspective in order to embrace political militancy. Malnate is clearly the object of a residual resentment on the part of the Jew vis-à-vis the Gentile and, in this case, the Communist as well. In a conversation with Malnate, the protagonist says that art, "quando è pura, cioè totalmente disinteressata, dispiace a tutti i preti di tutte le religioni, compresa quella socialista" (552; when it's pure, and therefore useless, it displeases the priests of every religion, including Socialism [223]), raising the possibility that the Communist Malnate, whom the narrator is clearly accusing of provincialism at the very least, becomes in Bassani's interview a stand-in for the left-wing critics who denigrated Bassani's work when it first appeared: this would account for the slippage from text to life.

Bassani has become "who he is" but still refuses to name the Jewishness of his work. De Angelis is right. The conflicts have been identified and understood, but the reserve has not been entirely overcome: he who so brilliantly depicts the silence of the Jew and the homosexual in *Gli occhiali d'oro* ironically prefers silence to speaking up as a Jew in response to the failure of literary and ideological critics to understand him as such. The most eloquent of these silences is the one following another interviewer's question about *Dietro la porta*, which I have already mentioned and which bears repetition. Asked whether this novel constituted a response to a so-called "crisis of the novel" being debated in literary circles at the time, Bassani responded very laconically, and somewhat sarcastically: "No. Il mio romanzo *Dietro la porta* … non intende dare nessuna risposta all'attuale stato di crisi del romanzo italiano e europeo, come dice Lei. Nessuna."[17] (No. My novel *Behind the Door* … doesn't intend to provide any kind of answer to the current state of crisis of the Italian and European novel, as you say. None whatsoever.) Here again Bassani seems to be challenging the interviewer to give him an opening, to coax him into being more specific, but the invitation, if such it is, is never taken up and in all likelihood not even understood. The background of this novel, in which the young Jewish protagonist is put figuratively "on trial" by his Gentile classmates, was the famous Auschwitz Trial taking place in Frankfurt at the time, but nowhere did Bassani let on that this event was in any way significant, nor does it appear that anyone thought to ask him about it.

Certainly Bassani's reticence and the "deafness" of his entourage were largely due to the prevailing cultural climate, in which most

Italians, Jews and Gentiles alike, each for reasons of their own, did not wish to emphasize the differences between them. The Holocaust and memory had not yet become the objects of cultural exploitation and consumption that they are today. Gender studies, both Jewish and otherwise, are also relatively recent areas of inquiry. Any new light I may have shed on Bassani's work I owe to those who have opened up these areas, as well as to the insightful critics before me who have paved the way for this encounter with Bassani.

Notes

Introduction

1 Interview with Giorgio Bassani, "Il Punto," May 31, 1958, cited in Ferretti, *Letteratura e ideologia*, 64; English translation quoted in Kiernan, "Giorgio Bassani," 38.
2 My understanding of this concept in Nietzsche's work has been very much enhanced by D. Conway, "Regimens of Self-Overcoming: The Soul Turned Inside Out," in *Nietzsche and the Political*, 61–77. Nietzsche uses "overcoming" liberally; its most prominent use is in *Thus Spoke Zarathustra* book 2, ch. 12 entitled "On Self-Overcoming." He says: "And this secret did Life itself tell to me. 'Behold,' she said, 'I am that which must always overcome itself'" (Nietzsche, *Thus Spoke Zarathustra*, 99).
3 See, among others, Gilman, *Freud, Race and Gender*; Boyarin and Boyarin, *Jews and Other Differences*; Mosse, *The Image of Man*; Harrowitz and Hyams, *Jews and Gender*.
4 Dolfi, *Giorgio Bassani*, 121n14.
5 From the chapter entitled "Sexual Identity and Political Persecution," in Schneider, *Vengeance of the Victim*, 88–9.
6 Eskin, "Sex and Jewishness," 71.
7 Champagne, "Bassani's *The Garden of the Finzi-Continis*."
8 Kertesz-Vial, "Interview de Giorgio Bassani," PDF 12.
9 Eskin, "Sex and Jewishness," 74.
10 Bauman, *Modernity and the Holocaust*, 142.
11 "In risposta VI, *Di là dal cuore*," in Bassani, *Opere*, 1327.
12 Camon, *Il mestiere di scrittore*, 67.
13 Ibid., 63.
14 For the complete publishing history of all his works, see Paola Italia, "Notizie sui testi," in Bassani, *Opere*, 1763–95.

15 Cotroneo, "La ferita indicibile," introduction in Bassani, *Opere*, liii.
16 On his interviews, see Kertesz-Vial, "Giorgio Bassani, entrevues."
17 An interesting article about how the reader is seduced by Bassani's "teasing" of sorts is Imberty, "Il lettore e l'opera."
18 Kertesz-Vial, "Interview de Giorgio Bassani," PDF 6.
19 "In fondo la confessione dell'io nel *Romanzo di Ferrara* non ha potuto che essere limitata, ridotta nello spazio e nel tempo. L'autore vi si è confessato, attraverso l'io narrante che è un personaggio (una parte di lui), e attraverso gli altri protagonisti, che sono anche ovviamente parti di lui, forme del suo sentimento" (Dolfi, "Meritare il tempo," 177). (Ultimately, the confession of the "I" in the *Romanzo di Ferrara* had to be limited, reduced in time and space. The author's confession unfolds through the narrating "I,"who is also a character [a part of him], and through the other protagonists, who are obviously parts of him as well, expressions of his sentiment.)
20 In the same interview with Kertesz-Vial he claims to like the indirect, free style that connects him to Verga because it allows him to be and not be his characters at the same time: "Verga m'a toujours fasciné. En employant une méthode qui permet d'entrer dans la réalité, avec tous ses détails, sans vraiment y pénétrer. Pour faire de moi-même un personnage sans en être tout à fait un. Je ne peux pas dire tout jusqu'au bout sinon je n'écrirais pas ce que j'écris. J'ai moi aussi ma manière d'écrire indirectement sur moi-même" (Kertesz-Vial "Interview de Giorgio Bassani," PDF 10–11). (I was always fascinated by Verga, by his way of entering into reality, in all its details, without really penetrating it. It allowed me to turn myself into a character, but not completely. I must refrain from saying everything, otherwise I would not write what I write. I too have my method of writing indirectly about myself.)
21 Dolfi, "Bassani, la storia, l''Onticità' del tempo," in *Giorgio Bassani*, 178–9.
22 "In ogni caso non posso non ribadire, ancora una volta, che la seconda parte di *In rima e senza* … è stata dettata dal bisogno fondamentale di dire in versi tutto ciò che di me, nel *Romanzo di Ferrara*, non avevo detto esplicitamente" ("Un'intervista inedita [1991]," in Bassani, *Opere*, 1350; In any event, I must reiterate and confirm that the second part of *In rima e senza* … was dictated by the fundamental need to say in verse everything about myself that I had not explicitly stated in *The Romanzo di Ferrara*).
23 "J'ai écrit *Dietro la porta* pour donner une réalité au personnage qui dit 'je' depuis *Gli occhiali d'oro*. Le narrateur avait besoin de dire tout sur lui-même, de dire toute la vérité sur son passage de l'enfance à l'âge adulte. … J'aurais pu me mettre à nu seulement dans mes poésies, mais je voulais le faire à l'intérieur du *Roman de Ferrare*" (Kertesz-Vial, "Interview de

Giorgio Bassani," PDF 12). (I wrote *Behind the Door* to give a real dimension to the character saying "I" from *The Gold-Rimmed Spectacles* onward. The narrator needed to express everything about himself, to tell the whole truth about his passage from childhood to adulthood. ... I could have revealed myself only in my poetry, but I wanted to do it within *The Romanzo di Ferrara*.)

24 "Un'intervista inedita (1991)," in Bassani, *Opere*, 1348.

25 Guerriero, "Crocianesimo e antifascismo."

26 Ibid., 151.

27 "In risposta V," in Bassani, *Opere*, 1321.

28 A recent compilation of essays on the situation of Jews not only under Fascism but also since the Risorgimento is to be found in Zimmerman, *Jews in Italy*.

29 Frandini, *Giorgio Bassani e il fantasma*, 56.

30 As cited in Roveri, *Giorgio Bassani e l'antifascismo*, 75–6.

31 "Un'intervista inedita (1991)," in Bassani, *Opere*, 1341–2.

32 Kertesz-Vial, "Interview de Giorgio Bassani," PDF 5.

33 Bassani's almost complete silence in his writings on his political activities is pointed out also in Guerriero, "Crocianesimo e antifacismo," 150. On this aspect of his life, see Roveri, *Giorgio Bassani e l'antifascismo* and *Tra Micòl e il Partito d'Azione*.

34 "In risposta V," in Bassani, *Opere*, 1320.

35 Schneider, *Vengeance of the Victim*, 10.

36 Analogous sentiments are expressed by Paolo Vanelli ("Il cerchio spezzato," 75); however, he does not provide an analysis that substantiates this interpretation. Says Vanelli: "Riteniamo che *Il romanzo di Ferrara*, al di là di tutte le altre interpretazioni, sia soprattutto la storia dell'educazione sentimentale e civile dell'autore, o meglio la narrazione (artificiale e simulata) del percorso che lui ha compiuto per spezzare il cerchio inibente della sua città e del suo clan e raggiungere una emancipazione – intellettuale e psicologica – che potesse permettergli di ritornare a contatto con le sue radici e osservare se stesso, il suo clan e la sua città, con quella lucidità di pensiero che non esclude la commozione, ma la assume come accompagnamento e controcanto del tessuto narrativo. *Il romanzo di Ferrara*, insomma, scorre su due piani paralleli: quello testuale (ovvero il 'discorso formalizzato') narra storie private e collettive collocabili in uno spazio (Ferrara) e in un tempo (la prima metà del XX secolo) chiaramente connotati e il cui nucleo inventivo fondante – personaggi e vicende, spazi e tempi – è collegabile al mondo ferrarese (soprattutto al clan ebraico) nella prima metà del Novecento; quello metatestuale, che possiamo anche

definire come 'discorso informale,' è invece la storia della formazione dell'autore stesso che, dopo essersi più o meno velatamente rispecchiato in alcuni personaggi (*in primis*: Bruno Lattes), poi esce allo scoperto, diventa lui stesso protagonista, e ci racconta tra le linee quale sia stato il tortuoso percorso della sua anima e della sua mente, per approdare alla coscienza dei suoi doveri di uomo e di scrittore e per filtrare la somma degli affetti e dei sentimenti nella serenità di giudizio – storico, civile e morale – indispensabile per intraprendere la grandiosa architettura narrativa del *Romanzo di Ferrara*." (We believe that the *Romanzo di Ferrara*, above and beyond all other interpretations, is chiefly the story of the sentimental and civil education of the author, or better yet, the [artificial and simulated] narration of the path he had to take to break out of the inhibiting circle of his city and of his clan, in order to reach an emotional and psychological emancipation that would allow him to return to his roots and look back on himself, on his clan, and on his city with a lucidity of thought that does not exclude emotion but assumes it as accompaniment or counterpoint to the narrative fabric. In short, the *Romanzo di Ferrara* unfolds on two parallel levels: the first one, textual [the 'formalized discourse'], narrates private and collective stories set in a given space [Ferrara] and time [the first half of the twentieth century] with clear connotations and the founding creative nucleus of which – characters, events, spaces, times – can be connected to the world of Ferrara [especially the Jewish clan] in the first half of the twentieth century; the second one, metatextual, which we can also define as 'informal discourse,' is instead the story of the formation of the author himself, who after a series of more or less veiled identifications with several characters (Bruno Lattes first among them), comes out into the open, becomes himself the protagonist, and describes between the lines the tortuous path taken by his mind and soul to arrive at the consciousness of his duties as a man and a writer and to filter the sum of his affects and emotions through the serenity of judgment – historical, civil, and moral – indispensable to take on the grandiose narrative architecture of *The Romanzo di Ferrara*.)

37 Giorgio Bassani was born in Bologna in 1916 of upper middle class Jewish Ferrarese parents and was raised and schooled in Ferrara. His grandmother was Catholic, and his grandfather was a prominent surgeon in Ferrara. His own father was also a doctor but did not practise. The family was more than comfortable, and its members lived on their income as landowners. For a complete and detailed biography, see "Cronologia," in Bassani, *Opere*, lvix–xcvi.

38 Bernardini, "The Jews in Nineteenth-Century Italy," 292–310. This article provides an excellent overview of the issues confronted by Italian historians of this period, as well as a very extensive bibliography.

39 Vittorio Segre, "The Emancipation of the Jews in Italy," in *Paths of Emancipation*, ed. Ira Katznelson and Pierre Birnbaum (Princeton, NJ: Princeton University Press, 1995), 206–37, as cited in Bettin, "Jews in Italy," 345. This article also provides a review of the literature on the question of whether postemancipation Jewry integrated or assimilated. Also Molinari, *Ebrei in Italia*, 25–49.

40 Pavan, *Il podestà ebreo*, 10.

41 For a nuanced discussion of the attitude of the Jews to their marginalization, as well as of the reactions of Italians in general to this legislation and of the state of historical studies on this pivotal moment and its ramifications, see Alberto Cavaglion, "Postfazione," in Pavan, *Il podestà ebreo*, 271–88. Also, in English, Michelis, "The Holocaust in Italy," 439–62.

42 See Winter, "Notes on the Memory Boom," 54–73.

43 Schwarz, "The Reconstruction of Jewish Life," 369. See also Villa, "Il silenzio dei vivi," 139–50.

44 "In the 1940's and 1950's collective stories about the war focussed on heroic narratives of resistance to the Nazis and their allies. Even when such stories were true, they took on mythical proportions. … Why did this kind of idealising remembrance flourish? In part it appeared because intrepid chronicles of Resistance were more useful in the revival of the political culture of countries humiliated by occupation and collaboration." Winter, "Notes on the Memory Boom," 60.

45 For his reactions to the literary establishment of his times, see "In risposta III," in Bassani, *Opere*, 1215–19. Umberto Eco, who was part of Gruppo '63, has since famously recanted, claiming that in hindsight he would have been proud to consider Bassani "a fellow traveller" (Eco, postscript to *The Name of the Rose*, 61).

46 "For that matter, broad sectors of post-war Italian culture, ranging from the liberals to Marxists and Catholics, showed themselves largely unable, or unwilling, to address the problems posed by Judaism and the condition of the Jews in the West. After the war, the question arose about the reformulation of the conditions of the minority in the national state. In its failure to recognise how modern antisemitism was required to be interpreted in relation to the demands and autonomous cultural processes of those who identify and persecute the 'Jew,' the Italian intelligentsia, while condemning the phenomenon, was incapable of reacting against it.

Antisemitism was considered to be a reaction of society to the alleged antisocial behaviour of the Jews, a by-product of the minority's attachment to its cultural and religious peculiarities which did not allow full and complete assimilation. This testifies to serious underlying deficiencies of the Italian cultural system, which ultimately meant that the new republic was unable to reintegrate the Jews without, at the same time, rejecting them." Schwarz, "The Reconstruction of Jewish Life," 365.

47 "Un'intervista inedita (1991)," in Bassani, *Opere*, 1342.

48 "Il faut bien me comprendre, je suis différent des autres écrivains juifs qui se sont occupés des juifs. Pour la première fois, et c'est une de mes suprêmes vanités, j'en ai parlé autrement: … le judaïsme … est un trait fondamental de mon œuvre. Cependant, un de mes mérites en tant qu'écrivain est d'avoir été le premier à avoir parlé des juifs sans aucun 'cléricalisme' et sans les avoir placés en dehors de l'histoire, de la politique et de tout le reste … Je n'ai jamais accepté d'expliquer l'histoire des juifs italiens par l'Holocauste. C'est une manière d'envisager leur extermination qui ne me convainc pas" (Kertesz-Vial, "Interview de Giorgio Bassani," PDF 2). (It is important to understand that I am different from the other Jewish authors who have written about the Jewish experience. I am very proud of having been the first to have spoken about it differently: … Judaism … is a fundamental feature of my work. However, one of my merits, as a writer, is to have been the first to talk about the Jews with no 'clericalism,' and without placing them outside history, politics, and the like … I have never accepted the Holocaust as a means of explaining Jewish history. It's a way of considering their extermination that fails to convince me.)

49 Rinaldi, *Le biblioteche di Giorgio Bassani*, 166. See also Della Coletta, "La cultura del giardino," 138–63. Coletta cites a passage from *House of the Seven Gables* as the epigraph to her article: "It was a kind of Indian summer, with a mist in its balmiest sunshine, and decay and death in its gaudiest delight" (Hawthorne, *The House of the Seven Gables*, 107).

50 Hawthorne, *The House of the Seven Gables*, 3. Emphasis added.

51 Ibid., 4.

52 All quoted material in this paragraph is from Slavet, *Racial Fever*, 7.

53 De Stefanis rightly saw in Bassani the convergence of a Crocean sense of history and a sense of the individual himself as historically determined: "Si crea così un legame tra passato e futuro in quanto il passato diventa una forza attiva che ha avuto interventi determinanti nello svolgersi dei tempi successivi" (De Stefanis, *Bassani entro il cerchio*, 12; Thus a link is formed between the past and the future, inasmuch as the past becomes an active force having a determining impact on the subsequent unfolding of events).

De Stefanis concludes that all accusations of a failure to historicize, or of taking refuge in a decadent-intimistic perspective, are wide of the mark because the individual at the centre of his oeuvre is very much the conduit of his search for answers to historical questions: "Bassani cerca nell'enigma dell'individuo la risposta a certi eventi storici" (Ibid., 16; Bassani is searching, in the enigma of the individual, for the answer to certain historical events).

54 This dynamic is eloquently described also in Ferroni, "'Ma che sa il cuore?,'" 19.

55 It is Anna Dolfi who has said it best, I believe, applying to Bassani something that I think Bassani himself applies to his narrators as well (*Giorgio Bassani*, 105):

> Il fatto è, come avrebbe forse detto Lacan, che la storia (ove la si veda dal punto di vista dell'arte o della patologia) non è il passato, insomma non è il passato in se stesso, ma il passato come si è storicizzato nel presente, con i suoi vuoti, le sue *béances*, le ferite. Quel che conta della storia, ove la si veda ontologicamente, è quanto ne può ricostruire il soggetto: si tratta insomma *"moins de resouvenir que de reécrire l'histoire."* Una volta fissata una precisa cronologia, storia sarà allora ripercorrere l'impotenza, la malinconia che per effetto di fatti esterni si sono fatte storia interna dell'io, tracciare le variazioni di senso di alcune parole, individuare gli effetti, gli affetti provocati da quella che Freud aveva chiamato la *piété juive* ... , distinguere la verità dei fatti (intoccabile e spietata nella sua assolutezza) dalla storia che sui fatti si è lentamente costruita, più o meno consapevolmente, generando altra verità, altra storia. Generando anche il romanzo, verità probabile, giocata tutta sull'adeguazione delle parole alle cose, così come le costruzioni dell'analisi, soggette alla legge della *"moindre résistance,"* sì che il racconto si regge sulla verosimiglianza che permette di colmare le lacune e costruire un'opera che, più che storica in senso manzoniano, lo è in senso freudiano (malgrado le possibili resistenze) piuttosto. (The fact remains that history, as Lacan might have put it, when considered from the perspective of art or pathology, is not the past. In that sense, it is not to be understood as the past itself, but rather as the "historicization" of the past in the present, with its voids, its *béances* [gaps], its wounds. From an ontological perspective, what matters is the capacity of the subject to reconstruct history: in short, *"moins de resouvenir que de reécrire l'histoire"* [rewriting rather than remembering history]. Once a precise chronology is set, history then becomes retracing the impotence and the melancholy that, as a result of external facts, have become the internal history of the

subject, following the variations in meaning of certain words, identifying the effects and the affects resulting from what Freud called *piété juive* [Jewish piety] … , distinguishing between factual truth [as an untouchable and merciless absolute] and the history gradually built up around the facts, more or less consciously, generating other truths, other histories. Also generating the novel, that probable truth, which plays on adapting words to things, just like the construction of analysis, subject to the law of "*moindre résistance*" [least resistance], such that the story is built on plausibility, which allows certain gaps to be filled and the construction of a work, which becomes historical, understood less from a Manzonian perspective but rather [despite possible resistances] in a Freudian sense.)

56 The narrator mentions his brother Ernesto and his sister Fanny in both *Gli occhiali d'oro* and *Il giardino dei Finzi-Contini*. In this second novel, in the first chapter of part five, he refers to his brief friendship with the ill-fated Dr Fadigati and his failure in mathematics in June 1929. In the last novel of the first-person trilogy, *Dietro la porta*, this same failure in mathematics in June 1929 is mentioned in the first chapter.

57 Güntert, "La riflessione letteraria," 56. In an earlier article Güntert offers a more elaborate view of his ideas but focuses more on the moments in which the narrative, as in the short stories, takes on the hypocritical voice of the townspeople ("L'arte narrativa," 365–80).

58 See Dolfi, "Meritare il tempo," 17.

59 See n19.

60 In *Beyond Good and Evil*, ch. 2, par. 26, in speaking of the exceptional individual, one who seeks knowledge of the self, Nietzsche says, "And he would go down, and above all, he would 'go inside'" (Nietzsche, *Beyond Good and Evil*, 30).

61 In his autobiography *Ecce Homo*, par. 7, entitled "Why I am a Destiny," Nietzsche uses this term specifically when he says, "What defines me as, what sets me apart, is that I have unmasked Christian morality" (Nietzsche, *Ecce Homo*, 95).

62 The complex temporal perspective created by this is eloquently described in a recent contribution by Giulio Ferroni. According to Ferroni, in Bassani the "impulso a raccontare prende avvio da una spinta sentimentale, da un moto del 'cuore,' che aspira a cercare i segni delle vite portate via dal tempo: ma nel ritrovare il passato, quello della Ferrara e dell'Italia prima della guerra e della giovinezza dell'autore, lo proietta nel suo divenire, verso il futuro che gli è succeduto, di cui esso non sapeva, ma di cui sa ora il narratore; non mira a fissarlo nel suo immediato accadere, nella

momentanea emergenza del suo essere particolare, ma vi inserisce lo specchio del *dopo*, sia il *dopo* atroce e non narrato della *shoah*, sia il dopo del mondo che è uscito da quell'orrore e che oscilla ambiguamente tra ricordo e oblìo" (Ferroni, "'Ma che sa il cuore?'" 17–18; impetus for storytelling derives from a sentimental thrust, from an impulse of the "heart," which aspires to find signs of the lives taken away by time: however, in recovering the past, that of prewar Ferrara and Italy and of the author's youth, he projects it forward into what it is to become, towards the future that lay ahead, of which he was unaware at the time but of which the contemporary narrator is fully mindful; he does not attempt to fix the past in its immediate occurrence or in the momentary emergence of its specificities, but rather he reflects it in the mirror of *after*, both the atrocious and unnarrated *after* of the Holocaust and the *after* of the world that emerged from that horror and that oscillates ambiguously between remembering and forgetting).

63 For example, in *Gli occhiali d'oro* the narrator thinks he is speaking of how favourably the citizens of Ferrara viewed Fadigati's office as compared to those of other local physicians, but, unbeknowst to him, his unconscious conjures up an image of Dr Menghele, the "angel of death," and of the diabolical experiments he conducted on prisoners: "Dove erano, da Fadigati – non si stancavano mai di ripetere –, le interminabili attese ammucchiati l'uno sull'altro come bestie, … mentre, alla fioca luce di una lampadina da venti candele, l'occhio non aveva da posarsi, scorrendo lungo i tristi muri, che su qualche NON SPUTARE! di maiolica, qualche caricatura di professore universitario o di collega, per non parlare di altre immagini anche più melanconiche e iettatorie di pazienti sottoposti a enormi clisteri davanti a un intero collegio accademico, o di laparatomie a cui, sogghinando, provvedeva la Morte stessa travestita da chirurgo? E come poteva essere accaduto, come!, che si fosse sopportato fino allora un simile trattamento da Medio Evo? (Bassani, *Opere*, 217). (At Fadigati's, they never tired of repeating, where was the interminable waiting, heaped on top of each other like animals, … while in the feeble light of a twenty-watt bulb, the eye coursing over the sad walls had nothing to rest on but some majolica tile announcing DON'T SPIT, some caricature of a university professor or fellow doctor, not to speak of other more jinxed and doleful images of patients being subjected to horrendous enemas in front of an entire medical school, or of laparotomies at which, grinning, Death himself officiated dressed as a surgeon? And how on earth had they – until then – put up with such medieval treatment? [3–4].)

64 Kuspit, "A Mighty Metaphor," 142.

65 This famous quotation appears in *I promessi sposi* (The Betrothed) at the end of ch. 8.

66 Among the notes and comments to Guido Calogero's text, Bassani also expresses, in opposition to Croce's view, his doubts about the possibility of rationally accounting for history: "Ma la storia è sempre prodotto, risultato, della volontà umana? la storia non travolge spesso la volontà? … la storia non è qualche volta il segno di una irrazionalità irrefrenabile, il regno del dio cattivo?" (But is history always the product, the result of human will? Doesn't history often overpower will? … Is history not sometimes the sign of an uncontrollable irrationality, the reign of the evil god?) Says Guerriero, who quotes these passages: "La visione storica di Bassani è di matrice crociana ma problematica e consapevole dell'esistenza di una soglia di mistero di difficile penetrazione" ("Crocianesimo e antifascismo," 160; Bassani's historical perspective has Crocean roots, yet it is more problematic and aware of the existence of a threshold of mystery difficult to penetrate). Bassani's comments are written in his hand in the margin of Bassani's copy of Calogero's text, which was examined by Guerriero. The annotations are on pp. 96–100 of the Calogero text.

67 Kiernan, *Giorgio Bassani*, 32–42. Kiernan summarizes the critique of Bassani by Marxists in the fifties and sixties while presenting the argument that "the 'Ferrara cycle' is a project in secular Jewish historiography inseparable from its being an intimate and lyrical confessional 'novel of the interior'" (39). In Italy, this is the story of the loss of the promised land, which for Italian Jews was not Israel but the "paradise" of equality and acceptance that was post-Risorgimento Italy itself.

1. Jews and Gender

1 Pellegrini, "Whiteface Performances," 108, 109, 113.

2 Robertson, "Historicizing Weininger," 296–7.

3 For an excellent discussion of Weininger's theses in relation to Freud, see Sander Gilman, "The Construction of the Male Jew," in *Freud, Race and Gender*, 49–92.

4 Cavaglion, *Otto Weininger in Italia*.

5 Freud, *The Interpretation of Dreams*, 285–6.

6 Rosenberg, *Legacy of Rage*, 34.

7 See Breitman, "Lifting the Shadow of Anti-semitism," 101–17.

8 Boyarin, "Masada or Yavneh?" 306.

9 Boyarin, *Unheroic Conduct*, 212.

10 As an example of this in Bassani's work, in "La passeggiata prima di cena," set in the early post-emancipation period, Moisé, the father of protagonist

Elia Corcos and a ghetto dweller for most of his life, is represented as warm, human, and entirely at ease with himself, in contrast to his emotionally distant and clearly awkward and conflicted son, who has rejected his Judaism and embraced "science" but mistreats his wife and fails to realize his potential as a scientist.

11 See Neiger, "L'Ebreo marginale," in *Bassani e il mondo ebraico*, 7–28. Says Neiger: "Incapaci di raggiungere un'identità biculturale e di optare per la fedeltà alla propria eredità etnica o per l'integrazione nella collettività non ebraica, molti personaggi bassaniani lottano col loro dilemma, quello stesso in cui si è dibattuto il loro autore, che ha sublimato liricamente la propria esperienza esistenziale" (11; Unable to reach a bicultural identity and to choose between remaining faithful to their proper ethnic heritage or integrating into the non-Jewish community, many of Bassani's characters struggle with their dilemma, the same one Bassani himself wrestled with, lyrically sublimating his personal existential experience).

12 Dolfi, "Meritare il tempo," 179.

13 "Per ciò che mi riguarda, non ho ambizioni letterarie di tipo balzachiano. Non mi importa niente di dare un quadro generale della nostra società" ("In risposta I," in Bassani, *Opere*, 1173.) (As for me, I don't have Balzachian literary ambitions. I have no desire to create a general portrait of our society.)

14 "Affermo la certezza, per me, che l'io profondo è ineffabile. È effabile soltanto ciò che si dice, che si fa. Di qui lo scarso interesse che ho sempre avuto per la psicanalisi, le cui operazioni mi sembrano fondamentalmente arbitrarie" (cited in Camon, "Cosa c'insegna Bassani," 139). (I can declare with certainty that, for me, the deep self is ineffable. Only words and action are effable. Hence my scant interest for psychoanalysis, whose workings seem to me fundamentally arbitrary.)

15 "Intervista inedita a Giorgio Bassani," 623.

16 Kertesz-Vial, "Interview de Giorgio Bassani," PDF 1.

17 Freud, "Family Romances," 236. The short essay, written in 1908, first appeared in Otto Rank, *The Myth of the Birth of the Hero* (1909), transl. F. Robbins and Smith Ely Jelliffe, Nervous and Mental Disease Monograph Series 18 (New York: The Journal of Nervous and Mental Disease Publishing Co., 1914).

18 "In risposta V," in Bassani, *Opere*, 1321.

19 Ibid., 1320.

20 Robert, *Origins of the Novel*.

21 On this novel alone as a family romance, see Kertesz-Vial, "*Le jardin des Finzi-Contini*," 119–22. Although the author identifies the characteristics

of the family romance in this novel, she does not see it as a conscious appropriation.

22 "Quanto a me, io appartenevo, come ho già detto, a una famiglia privilegiata, fascista come tante altre … Ho trascorsa una delle adolescenze più felici che si possano immaginare, in una casa, bellissima, fra le mura della quale tutti si volevano molto bene: per cui non mi sono potuto rendere conto che abbastanza tardi degli abissi di ingiustizia che mi circondavano" ("In risposta VI," in Bassani, *Opere*, 1328). (As for me, I belonged – as I mentioned – to a privileged family, Fascist like so many others … My adolescence was one of the happiest imaginable, spent in a beautiful home, in which we all loved each other very much, which is why I only became aware quite late of the depths of injustice that surrounded me.)

23 Ascheim, "Nietzsche, Anti-semitism and the Holocaust," 6.

24 Santaniello, "Nietzsche and the Jews," 40.

25 For a survey of theories of *ressentiment* in social thought and its relation to the Holocaust, see Olick and Demetriou, "From Theodicy to *Ressentiment*."

26 Santaniello, *Nietzsche, God and the Jews*, 124.

27 See Cingari, *Benedetto Croce*, in particular in ch. 1 entitled "Il problema Nietzsche," 18.

28 "A quantum of force is just such a quantum of drive, will, action, in fact it is nothing but this driving, willing and acting, and only the seduction of language (and the fundamental errors of reason petrified within it), which construes and misconstrues all actions as conditional upon an agency, a 'subject,' can make it appear otherwise." Nietzsche, *On the Genealogy of Morality*, 28.

29 Ibid., 21.

30 Ibid., 29.

31 Jacob Neusser, "Emotions in the Talmud," *Tikkun* 1 (1986): 74–81, as quoted in Breitman, "Lifting the Shadow of Anti-Semitism," 116.

32 Nietzsche, *On the Genealogy of Morality*, 22–3.

33 Ibid., 30.

34 Nietzsche, *The Will to Power*, as quoted in Santaniello, "Nietzsche and the Jews," 40.

35 Nietzsche, *On the Genealogy of Morality*, 35.

36 Ibid., 22–3.

37 Golomb, "Nietzsche and the Marginal Jews," 171.

38 Lessing, as quoted by Golomb, "Nietzsche and the Marginal Jews," 171.

39 Golomb, "Nietzsche and the Marginal Jews," 168.

40 Yirmiyahu Yovel, a Nietzsche scholar, calls this Nietzsche's "non-contradictory ambivalence": "For modern Jews, after they go out of the

ghetto and become secularized, Nietzsche has far-reaching prospects, whereas the modern anti-Semite is analyzed as the genealogical cousin of the ancient Jewish priest, whose properties the anti-Semite has inherited, but on a lower level still, since he lacks the value-creating power which the Jewish priests have demonstrated, and since, in order to feel that he is somebody, he requires the fake security of mass culture and the 'togetherness' of a political movement. ... Nietzsche holds two rather univocal positions: against modern antisemitism and against priestly Judaism, which are linked by the same genealogical root, *ressentiment*. Nietzsche's ambivalence derives from the combination of these two positions, which look contradictory but are not so in effect. From a logical or systematic point of view there is no contradiction between rejecting both antisemitism and the moral message of ancient Judaism, yet this combination creates a strong psychological tension which ordinary people find hard to sustain" (Yovel, "Nietzsche and the Jews," 125–6).

41 A famous example of such discourse is Max Nordau's *Degeneration* (1892). On the subject see Pick, *Faces of Degeneration*.

42 "Gli anni ... non sono serviti a niente: non sono riusciti a medicare un dolore che è rimasto là come una ferita segreta, sanguinante in segreto. Guarirne? Liberarmene? Non so se sarà mai possibile" (581). (The years that have passed since then have not helped at all: they have not managed to heal a sorrow that has remained there like a secret wound, bleeding in secret. Get over it? Free myself of it? I don't know if it will ever be possible.)

43 A translation and commentary of this short text is included in Robertson, *The German-Jewish Dialogue*, 153–78.

44 G. Bassani, "Perché ho scritto *L'airone*," *La fiera letteraria*, November 14, 1968, as quoted in Dolfi, *Giorgio Bassani*, 85.

45 Mann, "The Blood of the Walsungs," 304. On this story, see Gilman, "Sibling Incest, Madness and the Jews," 134–55. Gilman's discussion hinges on the connection between incest, Jewish endogamy, and economic control in the anti-Semitic discourse of the period. See also Levenson, "Thomas Mann's *Wälsungenblut*."

46 Mann, "The Blood of the Walsungs," 318.

47 "Il giardino tradito," in Bassani, *Opere*, 1263.

48 As quoted in Camon, "Cosa c'insegna Bassani," 138.

49 On the "ghetto mentality" in Bassani, see the chapter entitled "La nostalgia del ghetto," in Neiger, *Bassani e il mondo ebraico*, 29–48.

50 Erlich, "Race and Incest in Mann's *Blood of the Walsungs*," 114.

2. *Dentro le mura*: Men of Resentment

1 As cited in the preface to Joyce, *Dubliners*, ix. A discussion of Joyce's influence on Bassani, with reference also to previous critical identifications of Joycean echoes, can be found in Moloney, "Giorgio Bassani, James Joyce."
2 Baldelli, "La riscrittura 'totale.'" Baldelli analyses several stories and feels that in "Lida Mantovani" the movement is from a lyrical realism to a more contingent and "ordinary" (*quotidiano*) realism (190).
3 See "Storia di Debora," in *Una città di pianura* (1940), now in Bassani, *Opere*, 1544–71. *Una citta di pianura* was first published under the pseudonym Giacomo Marchi by Arte Grafica A. Lucini and Co., Milan.
4 For a very detailed and interesting historical and sociological portrait of Ferrara's Jewish community in this period, see "Nascere a Ferrara nel 1893," in Pavan, *Il podestà ebreo*, 3–45.
5 On the two entrances as symbols of a double life, see Sergio Parussa's very acute observations relating *Gli occhiali d'oro* to Sophocles's *Philoctetes*, whose cave has two entrances, to Dr Jekyll's two entrances, one for him and the other for Mr Hyde, and to Nathaniel Hawthorne's *Rappacini's Daughter* (Parussa, "The Construction," 107–8).
6 Nietzsche, *Ecce Homo: How One Becomes What One is*, 22, as quoted in Golomb, *Nietzsche and Jewish Culture*, 7.
7 On epiphanic moments in Bassani's works and their possible derivation from epiphanic moments in James Joyce, see Moloney, "Giorgio Bassani, James Joyce."
8 Mendelsohn, review of *The Charterhouse of Parma*.
9 "In risposta IV," in Bassani, *Opere*, 1326.
10 "When presently the child comes to know of the various kinds of sexual relations between fathers and mothers and realizes that *pater semper incertus est* while the mother is *certissima*, the family romance undergoes a peculiar curtailment: it contents itself with exalting the child's father, but no longer casts any doubts on his maternal origin, which is regarded as something unalterable. The second (sexual) stage of the family romance is actuated by another motive as well, which is absent in the first (asexual) stage. The child, having learnt about sexual processes, tends to picture to himself erotic situations and relations, the motive force behind this being his desire to bring his mother (who is the subject of the most intense sexual curiosity) into situations of secret infidelity and into secret love-affairs. In this way the child's fantasies, which started by being, as it were, asexual, are brought up to the level of his later knowledge." Freud, "Family Romances," 238.

11 An essay by the writer Roberto Pazzi, commenting on the difficulty of writing about Ferrara after Bassani, speaks of Bassani himself as a sort of Farinata: "Il suo sguardo sulla città, sospeso e ambiguo com'è fra 'realistico e metafisico,' richiede pupille che vedano come Farinata degli Uberti nel canto X dell'*Inferno* dantesco" (He looks at the city through the same lens as Farinata degli Uberti in Dante's canto X of the *Inferno*, in an ambiguous suspension between the realistic and the metaphysical). He also uses the image of the telescope: "Bassani da lontano, rovesciando il cannocchiale, poteva porre fra sé e Ferrara quella distanza che sola sapeva trasfigurare la città" (Pazzi, "Lo sguardo di Farinata," 128–9; From far away, Bassani was able to turn the binocular upside down and put between himself and Ferrara the distance required to transfigure it).

12 Moloney, "Giorgio Bassani, James Joyce," 237.

13 Hayden, "Nietzsche's Secrets," 302–7.

3. *Gli occhiali d'oro*: Jews and Homosexuals Revisited

1 Bassani, "Laggiù in fondo al corridoio," *L'odore del fieno*, in *Opere*, 941–2.

2 Interview with Giorgio Bassani (1979), repr. in Dolfi, *Giorgio Bassani*, 175.

3 See Meyer, *Outsiders*; the treatment of the homosexual is studied in "Sodom," 143–265 and that of the Jew in "Shylock," 269–395.

4 See Neiger, "Storie di 'vite nascoste.'" Neiger focuses on the differences between the ways in which Fadigati and Aschenbach live their homosexuality but stops there. So, too, does Dominique Fernandez in his preface to the French edition of the Bassani text: "L'Allemand a écrit le drame de la dégradation, l'Italien celui du déclassement" (*Les Lunettes d'or*, 17; The German has written the drama of degradation, the Italian that of social decline).

5 Mann, *Death in Venice*, ed. Ritter, 33. All subsequent quotations from *Death in Venice* shall be from this edition.

6 Reed, *"Death in Venice": Making and Unmaking a Master*, 17.

7 Heilbut, *Thomas Mann*, 259; for a fuller account of critical avoidance of the homosexual motif, see 259–61. Heilbut's biography relies heavily on Mann's diaries, the most recent of which appeared in October 1995, and depicts him as a great "erotic writer": "Liberated by his diaries, he becomes no longer the magisterial titan, but a troubled, self-doubting artist attempting a spectacular form of literary transcendence" (x).

8 Bassani, *Opere*, 1022.

9 Ibid., 1023.

10 Ibid., 1194–5.

11 Actually it was not the world's first ghetto, but the first to go by that name; the first was in Frankfurt-am-Main, established in the 1460s, or perhaps in Prague, flourishing in 1262 but less tightly controlled.
12 Siporin, "A Map to the World's First Ghetto," 1.
13 Letter to Wolfgang Born, 18 March 1921, quoted in "Extracts from *Backgrounds and Contexts, Criticism*," in Mann, *Death in Venice*, trans. and ed. Koelb, 99.
14 Robertson, *The "Jewish Question,"* 161.
15 Franklin, *The Life of Mahler*, 34.
16 McGrath, "Mahler and the Vienna Nietzsche Society," 224.
17 Carr, *Mahler: A Biography*, 84–5.
18 Franklin, *The Life of Mahler*, 186.
19 "Hirschfield accepted that the symphony was cathartic and Dionysian in its effect on a mass audience, but thought that such an effect liberated only anarchic and irrational enthusiasm ('explosive forces which have been pent up in quiet bourgeois duties and professions'). At once tasteless and ironic in its confusion of high and low cultural elements, it seemed to him to represent 'a cult of trifles and details' in which individual details acquired importance at the expense of the noble unity that 'great symphonists' properly sought to master. He felt obliged to 'combat the Mahler principle because it contains a danger.'" Franklin, *The Life of Mahler*, 184–5.
20 Carr, *Mahler: A Biography*, 132–3.
21 Franklin, *The Life of Mahler*, 166. Mann's endorsement of this particular symphony suggests that he identified precisely with Mahler's titanic but ultimately unsuccessful effort to conform to dominant musical tastes, as well as to the dominant religion: "Interestingly, the Eighth Symphony would come to be regarded even by many of Mahler's admirers as his most dubious 'official magnum opus' (Adorno's estimation in 1960). The conception of his great choral symphony as a "gift to the nation" has fueled the suspicion of more than one generation of Mahler critics that here their composer most fully revealed his feet of clay. Goethe and pious Catholicism seemed to be whipped together into a heady mixture that represented the conservative, authoritarian German bandmaster in Mahler at his very worst." Franklin, *The Life of Mahler*, 159.
22 As quoted in Reed, *"Death in Venice,"* 109.
23 Unmistakable echoes of the negative reviews of Mahler's concerts cited earlier, and images of Mahler conducting his orchestra, can be found in the text of *Death in Venice*. Conflated with images of Jewish moneylenders, Jewish gesticulation, and the hypocritical obsequiousness associated with assimilated Jewry, these echoes appear in the description of the itinerant

musician who captures Aschenbach's attention in Venice and reveals to him the existence of the cholera:

> He was quite evidently not of Venetian origin, but rather of the Neapolitan comic type, half-pimp, half-actor, brutal and bold-faced, dangerous and entertaining. The actual words of his song were merely foolish, but in his presentation, with his grimaces and bodily movements, his way of winking suggestively and lasciviously licking the corner of his mouth, it had something indecent and vaguely offensive about it ... This suspect figure seemed to be carrying his own suspect atmosphere with him as well. For every time the refrain was repeated the singer would perform, with much grimacing and wagging of the hand ... a grotesque march round the scene, which brought him immediately below where Aschenbach sat ... Having completed his ballad he began to collect money ... Bowing and scraping, he crept from table to table, and a sly obsequious grin bared his prominent teeth, although the two furrows still stood threateningly between his red eyebrows. The spectacle of this alien being gathering in his livelihood was viewed with curiosity and not a little distaste; one threw coins with the tips of one's finger into the hat, which one took care not to touch ... His bowing and scraping amused the company and so he redoubled them ... [Outside] however, he suddenly discarded the mask of comic underdog, uncoiled like a spring to his full height, insolently stuck out his tongue at the hotel guests on the terrace and slipped away into the darkness. Mann, *Death in Venice*, 77.

24 Robertson, *The "Jewish Question,"* 220–1.
25 Heilbut, *Thomas Mann*, 206–7.
26 See Parussa, "The Construction," 106, for a fascinating take on other intertexts here and and how intertextuality functions in this novel: "In place of raw symbols in need of interpretation, the reader is invited to read another literary text, which in turn recalls another literary text, in an intertextual progression that enriches the meaning of the novel and, at the same time, provides the reader with an interpretation of the texts to which it refers and of the symbols they contain."
27 Furst, "The Potential Deceptiveness," 169.
28 Luke, "Thomas Mann's 'Iridescent Interweaving,'" 201.
29 Furst, "The Potential Deceptiveness," 169.
30 Reed, "The Art of Ambivalence," 177.
31 Cohen, "The Second Author of *Death in Venice*," 192.
32 Anna Dolfi speaks of a "coincidente consapevolezza dell'autore e del personaggio" (*Giorgio Bassani*, 36; coinciding awareness of the author and

the protagonist); according to Massimo Grillandi, the doctor's suicide "coincide con la presa di coscienza del giovane io narrante" (*Invito alla lettura di Bassani*, 69; coincides with the moment of realization of the young narrator). The Marxist critic Gian Carlo Ferretti says: "Attraverso le dolorose esperienze del dottor Fadigati l'intellettuale ebreo arriva ... a cogliere con umana pietà e al tempo stesso con estrema lucidità critica, tutta una serie di sottintesi morali della propria condizione" (*Letteratura e ideologia*, 49; Through the painful experiences of Dr Fadigati, the Jewish intellectual manages ... to tap into a whole series of moral implications regarding his own condition, doing so with merciful humanity and extreme lucidity all at once). See also Cicioni, "Insiders and Outsiders" and most recently Parussa, "The Construction," 105; although Parussa also considers that Fadigati and the young Jew are "brothers," he qualifies this by saying that "the picture that Bassani paints in *The Gold-Rimmed Spectacles* is not idyllic: the understanding between the two men is gradual, the symmetry of their solidarity imperfect" (105).

33 In a discussion of the difference between the film version, directed by Giuliano Monaldo, and the book, Bassani says of the narrator and Fadigati: "I due si trovano insieme e si capiscono perché sono diversi, eppure simili. Nel film non c'è niente di tutto questo. Dell'unione di questi due emarginati, che proprio dall'emarginazione traggono la forza di stare insieme, e che anzi sentono di essere uguali proprio perché diversamente perseguitati, nel film è stato evitato con ogni cura di dirne" ("Un'intervista inedita [1991]," in Bassani, *Opere*, 1346). (The two find themselves together and can relate, because they are different yet similar. In the film, there is none of this. The film deliberately and cautiously avoids the whole issue of the union of these two marginalized characters, who find in their marginalization the strength to stay together, and what's more, who feel like equals precisely because they are both persecuted, each in his own way.)

34 Brian Moloney, apropos of Bassani's first-person novels and of the fact that they present many unanswered questions, has written ("Tematica e tecnica," 494–5): "A tutte queste domande non c'è risposta. Ad alcune di esse, naturalmente, non può esserci risposta. Per altre, potrebbe esserci, e di tanto in tanto vi è qualche accenno ad esse. Ma inevitabilmente c'è un elemento che impedisce lo svolgimento di questi accenni, ed è questo elemento che aggiunge un'extra dimensione ai romanzi e li differenzia completamente dalle storie meno mature. Si tratta della presenza di un personaggio centrale che è un enigma per se stesso, che è incapace, o meglio non vuole esaminare più da vicino il travaglio del suo cuore e della sua mente. Questo personaggio è il narratore." (There is no answer to all

these questions. Some of them, naturally, cannot have answers. Others might, and every so often we find some hint to them. But inevitably there is an impeding element to the fulfilment of these clues, and it is this element that adds an extra dimension to the novels and sets them totally apart from the less mature stories: the presence of a central protagonist who is an enigma to himself, unable – unwilling – to examine more closely the travails of his heart and mind. This protagonist is the narrator.)

35 Cicioni, "Insiders and Outsiders," 103.

36 Chatman, *Story and Discourse*, 149.

37 Ibid., 148.

38 See De Stefanis, *Bassani entro il cerchio*, 75–86. De Stefanis's interpretation is more subtle than the others – "La storia del dottor Fadigati ... funge da suggestiva proiezione metaforica dell'io narrante, e solo alla fine scatterà il momento della rivelazione, quando, levato lo schermo, il narratore sarà costretto a vedere sé stesso" (78; The story of Dr Fadigati acts as a suggestive metaphoric projection of the narrating 'I', and only at the end will the moment of revelation come about, once the screen is lifted, as the narrator is forced to see himself) – but it persists in seeing the point of the story in the epiphany, minimizing the significance of the fact that it takes place only on the last page and confusing protagonist and narrator: "Tutto il racconto mira fin dall'inizio a quel momento finale di dolente attonita consapevolezza. Se l'identificazione avviene alla fine è perché solo allora il narratore è maturato alla presa di coscienza" (77). (The whole story tends from the beginning towards that final moment of painful, shocking awareness. If that identification only happens at the end, it is because only then is the narrator mature enough for such clarity.)

39 Suspension points in original.

40 Mann, *Death in Venice*, ed. Ritter, 24–5.

41 Suspension points in original.

42 Wright, *Feminism and Psychoanalysis*, 345–8.

43 Gilman, *Freud, Race and Gender*, 125.

44 Ibid., 126.

45 Ibid., 126–8.

46 Ibid., 128.

4. *Il giardino dei Finzi-Contini*: A Jewish Family Romance

1 Freud, "Family Romances," 157.

2 Cf. ch. 3, p. 95, where the protagonist, as he looks out at the Jewish cemetery, finds once more the "maternal face" of Ferrara.

3 The significance of this private language is discussed in the conclusion below, p. 255.
4 Suspension points in original.
5 "My recollections of Sigmund Freud," in *The Wolf-Man by the Wolf-Man*, ed. M. Gardiner (1971), 139, as quoted in Gay, *Freud: A Life for Our Time*, 171. On Freud and archaeology, see also Kuspit, "A Mighty Metaphor, 133–51 and Bowdler, "Freud and Archaeology," 419–38.
6 Freud describes Rome as a city in which layers and fragments of different moments in its history can be found next to each other in excavations, just as they are in the psyche. However, he goes on to say, there is no way to represent this fragmentation using the image of the city since it would involve reconstructing buildings from different eras on top of each other, in a way that is unimaginable. He therefore concludes that the archaeological model has severe limitations if one uses the city – Rome –: "If we want to represent historical sequence in spatial terms, we can only do it by juxtaposition in space. The same space cannot have two different contents." Freud, *Civilization and its Discontents*, 19.
7 S. Freud, *"Constructions in Analysis,"* (1937), in S. Freud, *The Standard Edition*, 23, 258, as quoted in Kuspit, *A Mighty Metaphor*, 138.
8 For a phenomenological analysis of the house as image, see Gaston Bachelard's classic *Poetics of Space*, 3–73. According to Bachelard, "It [is] reasonable to say 'we read a house,' or 'read a room,' since both room and house are psychological diagrams that guide writers and poets in their analysis of intimacy" (38). On the house and the psyche, see Shamir, *Inexpressible Privacy*, in particular ch. 2, "Divided Interiority in Three Antebellum Short Stories."
9 Suspension points in original.
10 A very recent essay re-emphasizes, in terms that recall the figure of Ermanno Finzi-Contini, the importance of voice in the characterization of Jewish men in the European imagination: "Whether his use of voice makes him too Jewish (like Jackie Mason) or, on the contrary, appropriates high culture in the kind of colonial mimicry described by Homi Bahba, such that the Jew's linguistic prowess becomes a feature of his characteristic identity passing, speech and pitch are implicated in the making of Jewish masculinity." Lefkowitz, "'Demand a Speaking Part!,'" 290.
11 On Micòl as Beatrice, see De Stefanis, *Bassani entro il cerchio*, 126–8; Woolf, "Micòl and Beatrice," 167–84.
12 Marilyn Schneider offers a different reading of this dream: "To the extent that Micòl and the narrator are equals, Micòl functions as her author's symbol of artistic inspiration; thus she remains chaste and mystified.

Her banishment of the narrator is required for her ideal image to be preserved intact. An erotically permeated dream offers an interesting variation on the theme of chastity. ... In the most surreal part of the dream the [*làttimi*] have changed into bottle-shaped oozing ('stillanti') small cheeses (the word *làttimi* evokes milk). A smiling Micòl invites her guest to taste one 'of the best ones,' but 'stared at' by Micòl's dog and 'anguished' about a rising tide of water surrounding the house, he declines. The explicit symbolization of sexual intercourse has Micòl (the threatening 'female' water) – in apt proximity to her bed – proposing sex (the oozing 'male' cheese); but the exposed and imperiled narrator, longing for the protection of an 'outside,' a non-Finzi-Continian space, refuses her offer. The dreamworld projection of a sexually available Micòl reins in its own desire *in order to protect the narrator*, whose creative 'oozing' must depend on his pen and not his penis." *Vengeance of the Victim*, 125.

13 A similar comparison is made in Marcus, "De Sica's *Garden of the Finzi-Continis*," 99–100.

14 On the many interpretations of Micòl, see Farnetti, "Il tema di Micòl," 111–16.

15 As quoted in Millen, "The Garden of Innocence?," 73–4. Millen goes on to say: "In classic Christian theology, man (the male) is guilty and woman is doubly guilty, having initiated the sin of disobedience against God in the Garden of Eden. For Nietzsche, however, in a quite marvelous reversal, 'All of humanity is innocent of its existence, but women are doubly innocent.' ... That is, women are not culpable for their corruption, rather, this quality develops in response to men, who desire women to be a certain way" (74).

16 Lefkowitz, "'Demand a Speaking Part!,'" 289.

17 Goldschlager and Lemaire, *L'imaginaire juif*, 127–8.

18 On this topic, see Boyarin, *Carnal Israel*. Boyarin asserts "the essential descriptive accuracy of the recurring Patristic notion that what divides Christians from rabbinic Jews is the discourse of the body and especially of sexuality" (2). He distinguishes rabbinic Judaism, the cultural formation of the Hebrew- and Aramaic-speaking Jews of Palestine and Babylonia, from Hellenistic Judaism, and says that "rabbinic Judaism invested significance in the body which in the other formations was invested in the soul. For rabbinic Jews the human being was defined as a body – animated, to be sure – by a soul – while for Hellenistic Jews and Christians the essence of a human being is a soul housed in a body" (5). Boyarin's study then explores the consequences of this view for Jewish sexuality, marriage, and the role of women. On the Christian side, see Peter Brown, *The Body and*

Society: Men, Women and Sexual Renunciation in Early Christianity (New York: Columbia University Press, 1987). According to Brown, "the division between Christianity and Judaism was sharpest in this. As the Rabbis chose to present it, sexuality was an enduring adjunct of the personality. ... Among the Christians, exactly the opposite occurred. Sexuality became a highly-charged symbolic marker precisely because its disappearance in the committed individual was considered possible, and because this disappearance was thought to register, more significantly than any other human transformation, the qualities necessary for leadership in the religious community" (as cited in Boyarin, *Carnal Israel*, 2–3).

19 Goldschlager and Lemaire, *L'imaginaire juif*, 138.

20 Suspension points in original.

21 Sergio Parussa points out that in *Gli occhiali d'oro* Fadigati alludes to Nathaniel Hawthorne's novella *Rappacini's Daughter*, in which a young Italian student falls in love with beautiful Beatrice only to find "the poisonous nature of her beauty." He cites the following passage of the novella: "And yet, strange to say, there came across him a sudden doubt, whether this intense interest on his part were not delusory – whether it were really of so deep and positive a nature as to justify him in now thrusting himself into an incalculable position – whether it were not merely the fantasy of a young man's brain, only slightly, or not at all, connected with his heart!" Parussa, "The Construction," 109. He gives her a potion to try to save her from the toxic fumes emanating from her father's garden, but she dies nonetheless. Clearly this is another intertext that points from *Gli occhiali d'oro* to *Il giardino dei Finzi-Contini*.

5. *Dietro la porta*: The Body in History

1 Bassani's portrait in particular of the relationship between the narrator and Pulga has drawn in a significant measure on the relationship of William Wilson to his namesake and double in the short story "William Wilson" by Edgar Allan Poe (1839).

2 "A quel punto venne a cadere uno degli argini fondamentali tale da impedire per molto tempo che sull'antigiudaismo cristiano, tutt'altro che assente tanto più in Italia, potessero innestarsi i contenuti del moderno antisemitismo pur essi presenti soprattutto in alcune correnti del fascismo" (Levi, "Gli ebrei e l'Italia contemporanea," 107; At that point one of the fundamental long-standing barriers to the conflation of modern anti-Semitism present in certain Fascist circles with more traditional Christian anti-Jewish sentiment, clearly pre-existing in Italy, came tumbling down).

3 Ricciotti, *La ferita sanata*. Says Ricciotti: "Quando ero bambino, io, romagnolo, sentivo alcuni adulti chiamare 'meridionali' i toscani; a nostra volta, come abitatori della sponda meridionale del Po, eravamo i 'terroni.' Però tutti, polentoni, terroni, 'lumbard,' siciliani abbiamo tenuto come patrimonio prezioso Virgilio, Orazio, Dante, Petrarca, Tasso, Ariosto, e tutti, fino a Manzoni, a Pirandello, a Carducci, a Pascoli, a Papini, a Prezzolini, a Montale; e ancora Giotto, Raffaello, Michelangelo, Leonardo, Bernini, e via via. Ma il maggior segno d'identità nazionale italiana è nella fede cristiana, nei suoi miti, nei suoi teologi, nei suoi educatori, nei suoi Santi. E nelle piccole cose: la parrocchia, l'oratorio, il servir messa, il mese di Maggio, la Prima comunione, la dolcezza dell'educazione materna alla preghiera. Questi miti e questi sentimenti entrarono in conflitto il 20 settembre 1870, e questo tormento impedì che, fatta l'Italia, fossero fatti gli Italiani" (4). (When I was a child, being from Romagna, I would hear certain adults qualify Tuscans as "southerners"; we, on the other hand, being from the southernmost bank of the Po valley, were referred to as "terroni," a derogatory term for southerners. However, all of us, northerners, southerners, "lumbard," Sicilians, have cherished the precious heritage of Virgil, Horace, Dante, Petrarch, Tasso, Ariosto, all the way to Manzoni, Pirandello, Carducci, Pascoli, Papini, Prezzolini, Montale; even Giotto, Raphael, Michelangelo, Leonardo, Bernini, and so on. Nonetheless, the strongest marker of national identity is the Christian faith, with its myths, its theologians, its educators, its saints. And also in the smaller things: the parish church, Sunday school, serving at mass, the month of May, first communion, the sweetness of motherly instruction of prayer. These myths and sentiments came into conflict on 20 September 1870, and this torment prevented Italians from fully embracing the new state that was being born.)

4 As quoted in Roveri, *Giorgio Bassani e l'antifascismo*, 76–7.

5 Gilman, *The Jew's Body*, 64–72, 169–93.

6 "The outsider symbolized physical and moral disorder, and popular German novels of the nineteenth century liked to contrast a settled bourgeois life to an unsteady, rootless existence. Here the Jews were a prime target, for unlike Gypsies or vagrants, they were a menacing presence as competitors and, more important in this period, an emancipated minority in the process of assimilation. Thus Gustav Freytag in his popular *Soll und Haben* (*Debit and Credit*, 1855) pitted a virtuous German merchant house, rooted in its locality, against a Jewish merchant house, always on the move, shifty and dishonest. Similarly, Friedrich Hacklander's *Handel und Wandel* (*Trade and Change*, 1850) derided frequent travel as leading to insanity, as

well as commercial speculation and risk-taking over against so-called honest work. … Typically enough, the legend of the "wandering Jew" which took its modern form in the seventeenth century, obtained a new lease on life. Gustav Doré, famous as an illustrator of the Bible, in 1852 made a woodcut of the wandering Jew with a red cross on his forehead, spindly legs and arms, huge nose and blowing hair, and staff in hand that popularized this image. … The Jew was now co-opted by anti-Semitic propaganda, whereas originally he had moved with some dignity." Mosse, *The Image of Man*, 57.

7 "The so-called Jewish nose, bent at the top, jutting hawk-like from the face, existed already as a caricature in the sixteenth century. … It became firmly established as a so-called Jewish trademark only by the mid-eighteenth century, however, and soon became a foil for the straight nose of Greek beauty. Winckelmann himself had not explicitly condemned the Jewish nose, which he described as similar to a hawk's nose. … Nevertheless, the Jewish nose … came to symbolize an untrustworthy, immoral and suspicious character. However, not only the nose, but his whole body identified the Jew … : the flat feet, the waddling gait (opposed to the manly stride), the neckless body, the big ears, and the swarthy color. Moreover, young Jews are an exception in nineteenth-century literature. Jews are usually pictured as worn and aged at a time when youth was highly prized. … Henri Baptiste Grégoire, the champion of Jewish emancipation during the French Revolution … held that Jews in general had sallow complexions, hooked noses, hollow eyes, and prominent chins, and that they aged prematurely. Moreover, Jews were chronic masturbators, testifying to a nervous disposition." Mosse, *The Image of Man*, 63–5.

8 For Weininger, "the Jew is sexually obsessed, but without true masculinity. … The Jew has more sexuality than the Gentile male, though his sexuality ('more lustful and sensual') is not under rational or ethical control." Robertson, "Historicizing Weininger," 24.

9 Houston Stewart Chamberlain, Richard Wagner's son-in-law, categorizes the Jews as "a mongrel race which always retains this mongrel character." *Foundations of the Nineteenth Century*, trans. John Lees (London: John Lane, 1910), 1:388–9; as cited in Gilman, *Difference and Pathology*, 30.

10 See Levi, *Cristo si è fermato a Eboli*: "Mi pareva di essere staccato da ogni cosa, da ogni luogo, remotissimo da ogni determinazione, perduto fuori del tempo, in un infinito altrove. Mi sentivo celato, ignoto agli uomini, nascosto come un germoglio sotto la scorza dell'albero" (198). (I felt detached from every earthly thing and place, lost in a no-man's land, far from time

and reality. I was hidden, like the shoot under the bark of a tree, beyond the reach of man [Levi, *Christ Stopped at Eboli*, 225].) The passage in question refers to Levi's state of mind after he fails to save a sick peasant in a remote farmhouse in the countryside. However, since the memoir was written while Levi was closed in a room that served as his hiding place and to which he refers explicitly at the beginning, it can legitimately be deduced that in this instance time of action and time of narration collapse to form a new time, the time of memory.

11 Suspension points in original.

12 Suspension points in original.

13 Sander Gilman points out that "the mephitic odor of difference had been one of the central markers of the Jew in the biology of race in late-nineteenth century Germany"; for a complete discussion of *foetor judaicus*, see Gilman, *Freud, Race and Gender*, 152–5; also Gilman, *The Jew's Body*, 204.

14 Suspension points in original.

15 Suspension points in original.

16 Suspension points in original.

17 Robertson, "Historicizing Weininger," 36.

18 Renda "Lo spazio vischioso," 127–42; also in Renda, *Bassani Giorgio*, 113–35.

19 Renda, "Lo spazio vischioso," 138.

20 Ibid., 137.

21 Améry, *At the Mind's Limits*, 68. For a discussion of *ressentiment* and of Améry, see Olick and Demetriou, "From Theodicy to *Ressentiment*, 74–95.

22 On this polemic, see the foreword by Alexander Stille to the Améry translation cited above. Also Wood, "The Victim's Resentments," 257–67; and more recently, Heidelberger-Leonard, *The Philosopher of Auschwitz*, 65–72.

23 "Levi, who tries to 'understand,' is, in Améry's eyes, a 'reconciler' – of course not to be confused with the emigrants Martin Buber and Victor Gollancz, whom Améry dismisses as Jews 'trembling with the pathos of forgiveness and reconciliation. …' To wish to understand everything, the self-confessed aim of Primo Levi, says Améry, dismissing the idea rather too briefly, means wishing to forgive everything. He himself favours resentment, the 'slave morality.'" Heidelberger-Leonard, *The Philospher of Auschwitz*, 137.

24 For a full account of these trials, see Pendas, *The Frankfurt Auschwitz Trial, 1963–65* and Wittmann, *Beyond Justice.*

25 Wittmann, *Beyond Justice*, 263.

26 "In risposta II," in Bassani, *Opere*, 1212.

6. *L'airone*: A Case of Mistaken Identity

1 Pampaloni, "L'airone," 285.

2 The term, used primarily in reference to Jewish women, is seen as an outgrowth of Jewish self-hatred; it is a derogatory stereotype of a subtype of Jewish-American female, implying materialistic and selfish tendencies attributed to a pampered or wealthy background.

3 See Bassani's "Prefazione al *Gattopardo*," in *Opere*, 1156–61; also "In risposta II," in Bassani, *Opere*, 1207–9.

4 "Il libro ha un'ottica diversa dagli altri miei libri, ma certo Limentani è della stessa razza dei Finzi-Contini: è anche lui testimone di un mondo finito, di un mondo aristocratico e borghese giunto alla sua estrema consunzione" (The book has a different perspective than my other novels, but Limentani is certainly of the same race as the Finzi-Continis: he too is witness of a lost world, an aristocratic and bourgeois world about to draw its last breath). Interview with Ferdinando Camon, as reproduced in Camon, *Il mestiere di scrittore*, quoted in Dolfi, *Giorgio Bassani*, 87n16.

5 Bassani himself describes the research he had to do in order to write the hunting scenes: "Siccome non sapevo nulla di caccia andai più volte nelle valli di Comacchio per documentarmi. Durante uno di questi sopralluoghi assistei all'uccisione di un airone. Un certo conte S. di Siena m'aveva promesso di tenermi nella botte accanto alla sua. Poi cambiò idea, non mi volle. Così mi accampai in un isolotto vicino, me ne stetti lì, mentre il conte dalla sua botte sparava, sparava. Fra l'altro colpì un airone. … Ed io che non sparavo un colpo, potei seguire la sua sorte, immedesimandomi in lui, fino a che venne ucciso" ("Perché ho scritto *L'airone*," *La fiera letteraria*, November 14, 1968, as quoted in Dolfi, *Giorgio Bassani*, 84–5). (Since I knew nothing about hunting, I went several times to the valleys of Comacchio to research the topic. During one of these forays, I witnessed the killing of a heron. A certain Count S. from Siena had promised to let me stay in the hide next to his. Then he changed his mind. So, I camped out on a nearby islet and stayed there, while the Count kept shooting from his hide. Among other birds he shot a heron. … Abstaining from shooting, I could follow the heron's fate, empathizing with it, until it was killed.)

6 "Edgardo Limentani cerca disperatamente di tornare al mondo uccidendo gli animali come fanno tutti quanti i borghesoni della sua città. Anche lui cerca di fare altrettanto, ma non gli serve più, allora uccide se stesso" ("In risposta VII," in Bassani, *Opere*, 1346). (Edgardo Limentani is desperately seeking to re-enter the world by killing animals, as all the good

bourgeois of his town are doing. He tries to imitate them, but it's no use, so he kills himself.)

7 As quoted in Cadello, "Psychology as the 'Great Hunt,'" 23.

8 Bassani, "Perché ho scritto *L'airone*," *La fiera letteraria*, November 14, 1968, as quoted in Dolfi, *Giorgio Bassani*, 78–9nn4–5, 82–3n11.

9 "La novità, l'originalità di Edgardo Limentani, sta soprattutto nel suo aver capito che l'unico modo, per lui, di sopravvivere, è quello di uccidersi" ("Un'intervista inedita [1991]," in Bassani, *Opere*, 1347; The novelty, the originality of Edgardo Limentani, lies in his having understood that the only way for him to survive is by killing himself).

10 Sedgwick, *Nietzsche: The Key Concepts*, 143.

11 In the fourth episode of the second chapter of *Ulysses*, entitled "Calypso," we see Bloom reading a prize-winning article in a magazine while sitting on the toilet. After he has finished reading it, he uses it as toilet paper, thus indicating his contempt for the article. Like Limentani, Bloom suffers from constipation, but this time he manages to empty his bowels, unlike Limentani who is unable to express his emotions.

12 Appelfeld, "The Awakening," 151.

13 Zuccotti, *The Italians and the Holocaust*, 234.

14 Tomasi di Lampedusa, *Il gattopardo*, 114.

15 Suspension points in original.

7. *L'odore del fieno*: On Becoming What One Is

*"Becoming What One Is" is drawn from the subtitle of Nietzsche's autobiography *Ecce Homo*: "*Wie man wird, was man ist*" (How one becomes what one is).

1 Dolfi, "Meritare il tempo," 177. In the same interview he says, "Il problema dell'*io*, il problema tra l'*io* narrante e l'*io* scrivente, non si è fermato al *Romanzo di Ferrara*, ma è continuato nelle poesie di questi ultimi anni. Il motivo vero di queste poesie è quello di continuare la confessione, di portarla avanti, di esaurirla, avendone il diritto, ormai" (177). (The problem of the 'I,' the problem between the narrating 'I' and the writing 'I,' is not exclusive to the *Romance of Ferrara* but is present throughout the poems of these last few years. The true motivation of these poems is to continue the confession, to bring it forward, to exhaust it, having finally earned the right to do so.)

2 See Fink, "Growing up Jewish in Ferrara," 203–10.

3 Gilman, "Heine, Nietzsche and the Idea of the Jew," 78–9.

4 Suspension points in original.

5 Roveri, *Giorgio Bassani e l'antifascismo*, 44–5.
6 See introduction above.
7 Suspension points in original.
8 Suspension points in original.
9 See chapter 5 on *Dietro la porta*, n3.
10 Suspension points in original.
11 Suspension points in original.
12 "Treasure Seized in Bassani Battle."
13 "Dopo il congresso in cui avviene la frattura nel Partito d'Azione, constatata la sconfitta di Parri e Lombardi, passa al Partito socialista. A chi lo accuserà di incoerenza rispetto alla sua origine borghese, risponderà: 'certo che sono di origine borghese: però, siccome non sono un borghese decadente ed ho il senso delle mie responsabilità, milito in un partito di sinistra.'" "Cronologia," in Bassani, *Opere*, LXXII–LXXIII. (After the congress where the schism takes place in the Partito d'Azione, given the defeat of Parri and of Lombardi, he moves to the Socialist Party. To the accusations of inconsistency with regards to his bourgeois origins, he will answer: "Clearly I am of bourgeois origin: however, given that I am not a decadent bourgeois and have a sense of responsibility, I actively support a leftist party.")
14 Suspension points in original throughout rest of paragraph and following paragraph.
15 Conway, *Nietzsche and the Political*, 71–2.

Conclusion

1 Unfortunately, I have not been able to locate again the source of this comment, but it has remained etched in my mind; I ask the reader's indulgence in mentioning it.
2 Eloquently described in Güntert, "La riflessione letteraria," 53–60.
3 Golomb, "Nietzsche and the Marginal Jews," 174–5, 165.
4 Ibid., 158.
5 See ch. 5, n7.
6 Rosenberg, "Jewish Masculinities," 350.
7 Champagne, "Bassani's *The Garden of the Finzi-Continis*"; see introduction, n7. For all its shortcomings – Champagne reads the novel completely out of context, not being familiar with any of Bassani's other works, and makes no mention whatsoever of the issues surrounding discourses of Jewish masculinity and anti-Semitic stereotypes of Jewish sexuality that form the backdrop of Bassani's self-analysis – the article does have the

merit of calling attention to the centrality of sex and gender in Bassani's work. Its argument, however, suffers not only from a lack of knowledge of the Bassani corpus and of surrounding issues, as well as intertexts, but also from the ideological bias that wishes to impose a label on Bassani. While Bassani is well aware of the non-normative nature of Jewish masculinity and of the fact that Jewishness and homosexuality share a discursive field, to say that he embraces homosexuality wholeheartedly along with the passive resistance of the Finzi-Continis to the Race Laws is to completely disregard his own spiritual journey and his struggle to break away from passivity, as well as much textual evidence.

8 Camon, "Cosa c'insegna Bassani," 66.

9 Girelli-Carasi, "Contemporary Jewish Memorialists in Italy," 218.

10 De Angelis, *Qualcosa di più intimo*, 16.

11 Siciliano, "L'anima contro la storia," in *Autobiografia letteraria*, 115.

12 Pieri, *Memoria e Giustizia*, 14–15.

13 Cited in Camon, "Cosa c'insegna Bassani," 64.

14 Camon, "Cosa c'insegna Bassani," 64.

15 Ibid., 67 (emphasis added).

16 Ibid., 62.

17 "In risposta II," in Bassani, *Opere*, 1212.

Bibliography

Améry, Jean. *At the Mind's Limits: Contemplations by a Survivor on Auschwitz and its Realities*. Translated by Sidney and Stella P. Rosenfeld. New York: Schocken Books, 1986.

Antognini, Roberta, and Rodica Blumenfeld, eds. *Poscritto a Giorgio Bassani: Saggi in memoria del decimo anniversario della morte*. Milan: LED, 2012.

Appelfeld, Aharon. "The Awakening." In *Holocaust Remembrance: The Shapes of Memory*, edited by Geoffrey H. Hartman, 149–52. Oxford: Blackwell, 1994.

Ascheim, Steven E. "Nietzsche, Anti-Semitism and the Holocaust." In *Nietzsche and Jewish Culture*, edited by Jacob Golomb, 3–20.

Bachelard, Gaston. *Poetics of Space*. Translated by Maria Jolas. Boston: Beacon Press, 1994.

Baldelli, Ignazio. "La riscrittura 'totale' di un'opera: Da *Le storie ferraresi* a *Dentro le mura*." *Lettere Italiane* 2 (1974): 180–97.

Bassani, Giorgio. *Behind the Door*. Translated by William Weaver. New York: Harcourt, Brace, Jovanovich, 1972.

———. *Five Stories of Ferrara*. Translated by William Weaver. New York: Harcourt, Brace, Jovanovich, 1971.

———. *The Garden of the Finzi-Continis*. Translated by Jamie McKendrick. London: Penguin, 2007.

———. *The Gold-Rimmed Spectacles*. Translated by Jamie McKendrick. London: Penguin, 2012.

———. *The Heron*. Translated by William Weaver. New York: Harcourt, Brace, Jovanovich, 1970.

———. *Opere* (1998). Edited by Roberto Cotroneo. Milan: Mondadori, 2009.

———. *The Smell of Hay*. Translated by William Weaver. New York: Harcourt, Brace, Jovanovich, 1975.

Bauman, Zygmunt. *Modernity and the Holocaust*. Ithaca, NY: Cornell University Press, 1989.

Bell, Duncan, ed. *Memory, Trauma and World Politics: Reflections on the Relationship Between Past and Present*. Basingstoke: Palgrave Macmillan, 2006.

Bernardini, Paolo. "The Jews in Nineteenth-Century Italy: Towards a Reappraisal." *Journal of Modern Italian Studies* 1, no. 2 (1996): 292–310. http://dx.doi.org/10.1080/13545719608454919.

Bettin, Cristina M. "Jews in Italy between Integration and Assimilation, 1861–1938." *European Legacy* 12, no. 3 (2007): 337–50. http://dx.doi.org/10.1080/10848770701287032.

Booth, Wayne. *The Rhetoric of Fiction*. Chicago: University of Chicago Press, 1961.

Bowdler, Sandra. "Freud and Archaeology." *Anthropological Forum* 7, no. 3 (1996): 419–38. http://dx.doi.org/10.1080/00664677.1996.9967466.

Boyarin, Daniel. *Carnal Israel: Reading Sex in Talmudic Culture*. Berkeley, Los Angeles: University of California Press, 1993.

———. "Masada or Yavneh? Gender and the Arts of Jewish Resistance." In Boyarin and Boyarin, *Jews and Other Differences*, 306–29.

———. *Unheroic Conduct: The Rise of Heterosexuality and the Invention of the Jewish Man*. Berkeley, Los Angeles, London: University of California Press, 1997.

Boyarin, Jonathan and Daniel Boyarin, eds. *Jews and Other Differences: The New Jewish Cultural Studies*. Minneapolis and London: University of Minnesota Press, 1993.

Breitman, Barbara. "Lifting the Shadow of Anti-Semitism: Jewish Masculinity in a New Light." In *A Mensch among Men: Explorations in Jewish Masculinity*, edited by Harry Brod, 101–17. Freedom, CA: The Crossing Press, 1988.

Cadello, James. "Psychology as the 'Great Hunt.'" In Golomb, Santaniello, and Lehrer, *Nietzsche and Depth Psychology*, 23–36.

Camon, Ferdinando. "Cosa c'insegna Bassani." In Gaeta, *Giorgio Bassani: Uno scrittore da ritrovare*, 137–40.

———. *Il mestiere di scrittore: Conversazioni critiche*. Milan: Garzanti, 1973.

Carr, Jonathan. *Mahler: A Biography*. Woodstock, NY & New York, NY: Overlook Press, 1997.

Cavaglion, Alberto. *Otto Weininger in Italia*. Rome: Carucci editore, 1982.

Champagne, John. "Bassani's *The Garden of the Finzi-Continis* and Italian 'queers.'" *CLC Web: Comparative Literature and Culture* 12, no. 1 (2010). Accessed May 25, 2011. http://docs.lib.purdue.edu/cgi/viewcontent.cgi?article=1574&context=clcweb.

Chatman, Seymour. *Story and Discourse: Narrative Structure in Fiction and Film.* Ithaca: Cornell University Press, 1978.

Cheyette, Bryan and Laura Marcus, eds. *Modernity, Culture and "the Jew."* Cambridge: Polity Press, 1998.

Cicioni, Mirna. "Insiders and Outsiders: Discourses of Oppression in Giorgio Bassani's *Gli occhiali d'oro.*" *Italian Studies* 41, no. 1 (1986): 101–15. http://dx.doi.org/10.1179/007516386790509211.

Cingari, Salvatore. *Benedetto Croce e la crisi della civiltà europea.* 2 vols. Cosenza: Rubbettino editore, 2003.

Cohen, Dorrit. "The Second Author of *Death in Venice.*" In Mann, *Death in Venice,* translated and edited by Clayton Koelb, 178–94.

Conway, Daniel W. *Nietzsche and the Political.* London, New York: Routledge, 1996.

Cotroneo, Roberto. "La ferita indicibile." In Bassani, introduction to *Opere,* xi–lxviii.

De Angelis, Luca. *Qualcosa di più intimo: Aspetti della scrittura ebraica del Novecento italiano: da Svevo a Bassani.* Florence: Giuntina, 2006.

De Stefanis, Giusi Oddo. *Bassani entro il cerchio delle sue mura.* Ravenna: Longo, 1981.

Della Coletta, Cristina. "La cultura del giardino: Miti e appropriazioni letterarie nel *Giardino dei Finzi-Contini.*" *Modern Language Notes* 1 (1998): 138–63.

Di Napoli, Thomas P., ed. *The Italian Jewish Experience.* Stony Brook, NY: Forum Italicum, 2000.

Dolfi, Anna. *Giorgio Bassani: Una scrittura della malinconia.* Rome: Bulzoni, 2003.

———. "Meritare il tempo." In *Giorgio Bassani: Una scrittura della malinconia,* 167–79.

Dolfi, Anna, and Gianni Venturi, eds. *Ritorno al Giardino: Una giornata di studi per Giorgio Bassani, Firenze, 26 marzo 2003.* Rome: Bulzoni, 2006.

Eco, Umberto. Postscript to *The Name of the Rose.* Translated by William Weaver. New York: Harcourt, Brace, Jovanovich, 1984.

Erlich, Gloria Chiasson. "Race and Incest in Mann's *Blood of the Walsungs.*" *Studies in Twentieth-Century Literature* 2 (1978): 113–26.

Eskin, Stanley. "Sex and Jewishness in Giorgio Bassani." *Midstream* (June–July 1973): 71.

Farnetti, Monica. "Il tema di Micòl." In Dolfi and Venturi, *Ritorno al Giardino,* 111–16.

Fernandez, Dominique. Introduction to *Les Lunettes d'or et autres histoires de Ferrare,* by Giorgio Bassani, 7–17. Paris: Gallimard, 1962.

Ferretti, Gian Carlo. *Letteratura e ideologia: Bassani, Cassola, Pasolini.* Rome: Riuniti, 1964.

Ferroni, Giulio. "'Ma che sa il cuore?' I sentimenti e la storia." In Gaeta, *Giorgio Bassani: Uno scrittore da ritrovare*, 17–28.

Fink, Guido. "Growing up Jewish in Ferrara: The Fiction of Giorgio Bassani." In *Acculturation and its Discontents: The Italian Jewish Experience Between Exclusion and Inclusion*, edited by David N. Myers, Massimo Ciavollela, Peter H. Reill, and Geoffrey Symcox, 203–10. Toronto: University of Toronto Press, 2008.

Frandini, Paola. *Giorgio Bassani e il fantasma di Ferrara*. San Cesario di Lecce: Piero Manni, 2004.

Franklin, Peter. *The Life of Mahler*. Cambridge, New York: Cambridge University Press, 1997.

Freud, Sigmund. *Civilization and its Discontents*. Edited and translated by James Strachey. New York, London: W.W. Norton and Co., 1996.

———. "Family Romances." Translated by James Strachey. In *The Standard Edition of the Complete Psychological Works of Sigmund Freud*, vol. 9 (1906–8). Reprinted in *Jensen's "Gradiva" and Other Works*, 235–41. London: Hogarth Press and the Institute of Psychoanalysis, 1959.

———. *The Interpretation of Dreams*. Edited and translated by James Strachey. Harmondsworth: Penguin, 1976.

Furst, Lillian R. "The Potential Deceptiveness of Reading in *Death in Venice*." In Mann, *Death in Venice*, edited by Naomi Ritter, translated by David Luke, 169.

Gaeta, Maria Ida, ed. *Giorgio Bassani: Uno scrittore da ritrovare*. Rome: Fahrenheit 451, 2004.

Gay, Peter. *Freud: A Life for Our Time*. New York, London: W.W. Norton and Co., 1988.

Gilman, Sander. *Difference and Pathology: Stereotypes of Sexuality, Race and Madness*. Ithaca, London: Cornell University Press, 1985.

———. *Freud, Race and Gender*. Princeton, NJ: Princeton University Press, 1993.

———. "Heine, Nietzsche and the Idea of the Jew." In Golomb, *Nietzsche and Jewish Culture*, 76–101.

———. *The Jew's Body*. New York: Routledge, 1991.

———. "Sibling Incest, Madness and the Jews." In *Love+Marriage = Death and Other Essays on Representing Difference*, 134–55. Stanford, CA: Stanford University Press, 1998.

Girelli-Carasi, Fabio. "Contemporary Jewish Memorialists in Italy: The Reasons of a Recent Literary Phenomenon." In Di Napoli, *The Italian Jewish Experience*, 218.

Goldschlager, Alain, and Jacques Lemaire. *L'imaginaire juif*. Liège: ULG, Éditions de l'Université de Liège, 2007.

Golomb, Jacob, ed. *Nietzsche and Jewish Culture*. London, New York: Routledge, 1997.

——. "Nietzsche and the Marginal Jews." In *Nietzsche and Jewish Culture*, 158–92.

Golomb, Jacob, Weaver Santaniello, and Ronald Lehrer, eds. *Nietzsche and Depth Psychology*. Albany: State University of New York Press, 1999.

Grillandi, Massimo. *Invito alla lettura di Bassani*. Milan: Mursia, 1972.

Guerriero, Stefano. "Crocianesimo e antifascismo nella poetica di Bassani." *Otto/Novecento* 3 (2004): 149–60.

Güntert, Georges. "L'arte narrativa di Giorgio Bassani: Persuasione, ironia e distanza." *Levia Gravia* 3 (2001): 365–80.

——. "La riflessione letteraria di Bassani: Punti di riferimento." In Gaeta, *Giorgio Bassani: Uno scrittore da ritrovare*, 53–60.

Harrowitz, Nancy A., and Barbara Hyams, eds. *Jews and Gender: Responses to Otto Weininger*. Philadelphia: Temple University Press, 1995.

Hawthorne, Nathaniel. *The House of the Seven Gables*. Edited by Robert S. Levine. New York, London: W.W. Norton and Co., 2006.

Hayden, Deborah. "Nietzsche's Secrets." In Golomb, Santaniello, and Lehrer, *Nietzsche and Depth Psychology*, 295–316.

Heidelberger-Leonard, Irène. *The Philosopher of Auschwitz: Jean Améry and Living with the Holocaust*. London, New York: I.B. Tauris, 2010.

Heilbut, Anthony. *Thomas Mann: Eros and Literature*. Berkeley, Los Angeles: University of California Press, 1995.

Imberty, Claude. "Il lettore e l'opera di Giorgio Bassani." *Chroniques italiennes* 3 (1985). Accessed May 19, 2011. www.chroniquesitaliennes.fr/numeros/3.html.

"Intervista inedita a Giorgio Bassani" (Istituto Italiano di Cultura di New York, in cooperation with Radio Italiana, 1966). In Antognini and Blumenfeld, *Poscritto a Giorgio Bassani* , 611–23.

Joyce, James. *Dubliners*. Edited by Margot Norris. New York and London: W.W. Norton and Co., 2006.

Kertesz-Vial, Elizabeth. "Giorgio Bassani, entrevues et premiers essais critiques." *Chroniques italiennes* 2/3 (1999). Accessed May 19, 2011. www.chroniquesitaliennes.fr/numeros/58.html

——. "Interview de Giorgio Bassani, 15 mai 1984." *Chroniques italiennes* 2 (1985). Accessed May 25, 2011. http://chroniquesitaliennes.univ-paris3.fr/PDF/2/Kertez2.pdf.

——. "*Le jardin des Finzi-Contini*: Du langage au roman familial." *Familles italiennes dans la littérature aux XIX et XX siècles, Transalpina* 4 (2000): 109–24.

Kiernan, Susan. "Giorgio Bassani, Historian of the Heart." In *The Attractions of Fascism: Social Psychology and Aesthetics of the Triumph of the Right*, edited by John Milfull, 32–42. New York: Berg, 1990.

Kroha, Lucienne. "Giorgio Bassani's *Gli occhiali d'oro*: The Structures of Silence." *Italianist* 10 (1990): 71–102.

———. "Il corpo e la Storia: Lettura di *Dietro la porta*." In *Giorgio Bassani: la poesia del romanzo, il romanzo del poeta*, edited by Antonello Perli, 155–70. Ravenna: Giorgio Pozzi Editore, 2011.

———. "In the Aftermath: Modalities of Memory in *Il Romanzo di Ferrara*." In Antognini and Blumenfeld, *Poscritto a Giorgio Bassani*, 207–34.

———. "Judaism and Manhood in the Novels of Giorgio Bassani." In Di Napoli, *The Italian Jewish Experience*, 185–97.

———. "The Same and/or Different: Narcissism and Exile in the Novels of Giorgio Bassani." *Annali d'Italianistica* 20 (2002): 307–24.

Kuspit, Donald. "A Mighty Metaphor: The Analogy of Archaeology and Psychoanalysis." In *Sigmund Freud and his Art: His Personal Collection of Antiquities*, edited by Lynn Gamwell and Richard Wells, 133–51. London: Freud Museum, 1998.

Lefkowitz, Lori Hope. "'Demand a Speaking Part!': The Character of the Jewish Father." In *Answering a Question with a Question: Contemporary Psychoanalysis and Jewish Thought*, edited by Lewis Aron and Libby Henik, 289–312. Boston: Academic Studies Press, 2010.

Levenson, Alan. "Thomas Mann's *Wälsungenblut* in the Context of the Intermarriage Debate and the 'Jewish Question.'" In *Insiders and Outsiders: Jewish and Gentile Culture in Germany and Austria*, edited by Dagmar C.G. Lorenz and Gabriel Weinberger, 135–43. Detroit: Wayne State University Press, 1994.

Levi, Carlo. *Christ Stopped at Eboli*. Translated by Frances Frenaye. New York: Farrar, Strauss and Giroux, 1999.

———. *Cristo si è fermato a Eboli*. Turin: Einaudi, 1983.

Levi, Fabio. "Gli ebrei e l'Italia contemporanea." In *Minoranze religiose e diritti: Percorsi in cento anni di storia degli ebrei e dei valdesi (1848–1948)*, edited by Alberto Cavaglion, 99–110. Milan: Franco Angeli, 2001.

Luke, David. "Thomas Mann's 'Iridescent Interweaving.'" In Mann, *Death in Venice*, translated and edited by Clayton Koelb, 195–206.

Mann, Thomas. "The Blood of the Volsungs." In Robertson, *The German-Jewish Dialogue: An Anthology of Literary Texts, 1749–1993*, 153–78.

———. "The Blood of the Walsungs." In *Death in Venice and Seven Other Stories*, translated by H.T. Lowe-Porter, 292–319. New York: Random House, 1936.

———. *Death in Venice*. Norton Critical Edition. Translated and edited by Clayton Koelb. New York, London: W.W. Norton and Co., 1994.

———. *Death in Venice*. Edited by Naomi Ritter. Translated by David Luke. Boston, New York: Bedford Books, 1998.

Marcus, Millicent. "De Sica's *Garden of the Finzi-Continis*: An Escapist Paradise Lost." In *Filmmaking by the Book: Italian Cinema and Literary Adaptation*, 91–110. Baltimore and London: The Johns Hopkins University Press, 1994.

McGrath, William. "Mahler and the Vienna Nietzsche Society." In Golomb, *Nietzsche and Jewish Culture*, 218–32.

Mendelsohn, Daniel. Review of *The Charterhouse of Parma*, by Stendhal, translated by Richard Howard. *New York Times*, August 29, 1999. Accessed May 23, 2011. http://www.nytimes.com/books/99/08/29/reviews/990829.29mendelt.html

Meyer, Hans. *Outsiders: A Study in Life and Letters*. Translated by D.M. Sweet. Cambridge, MA: MIT Press, 1982.

Michelis, Meir. "The Holocaust in Italy." In *The Holocaust and History*, edited by Michael Berenbaum and Abraham J. Peck, 439–62. Bloomington, Indianapolis: Indiana University Press, 1998.

Millen, Rochelle L. "The Garden of Innocence? Nietzsche's Psychology of Women." In Golomb, Santaniello, and Lehrer, *Nietzsche and Depth Psychology*, 73–90.

Molinari, Maurizio. *Ebrei in Italia: Un problema di identità (1870–1938)*. Florence: La Giuntina, 1991.

Moloney, Brian. "Giorgio Bassani, James Joyce and the *Storie ferraresi*." *Journal of Anglo-Italian Studies* 5 (1997): 231–43.

———. "Tematica e tecnica nei romanzi di Giorgio Bassani." *Convivium* 5 (1966): 485–95.

Mosse, George. *The Image of Man: The Creation of Modern Masculinity*. Oxford: Oxford University Press, 1996.

Neiger, Ada. *Bassani e il mondo ebraico*. Naples: Loffredo, 1983.

———. "Storie di 'vite nascoste' in Thomas Mann e Giorgio Bassani." *Critica letteraria* 4 (2002): 699–707.

Nietzsche, Friedrich. *Beyond Good and Evil*. Translated by Helen Zimmern. Rockville, MD: Serenity Publishers, 2008.

———. *Ecce Homo: How One Becomes what One is; and The Antichrist: a Curse on Christianity*. Translated by Thomas Wayne. New York: Algora Publishing, 2004.

———. *On the Genealogy of Morality*. Translated by Carol Diethe. Edited by Keith Ansell-Pearson. Cambridge: Cambridge University Press, 1994.

——. *Thus Spoke Zarathustra*. Translated by Graham Parkes. Oxford and New York: Oxford University Press, 2005.

Olick, Jeffrey K., and Charles Demetriou. "From Theodicy to *Ressentiment*: Trauma and the Ages of Compensation." In Bell, *Memory, Trauma and World Politics*, 74–95.

Pampaloni, Geno. "L'airone." *Corriere della Sera*, October 28, 1968. Reprinted in *Il critico giornaliero: Scritti militanti di letteratura*, edited by Giuseppe Leonelli, 283–6. Turin: Bollati, Boringhieri, 2001.

Parussa, Sergio. "The Construction of the Narrative Jewish Subject." In *Writing as Freedom, Writing as Testimony: Four Italian Writers and Judaism*, 94–131. Syracuse: Syracuse University Press, 2008.

Pavan, Ilaria. *Il podestà ebreo: La storia di Renzo Ravenna tra fascismo e leggi razziali*. Bari: Laterza, 2006.

Pazzi, Roberto. "Lo sguardo di Farinata: La sfida di scrivere di Ferrara dopo Bassani." In Gaeta, *Giorgio Bassani: Uno scrittore da ritrovare*, 125–39.

Pellegrini, Ann. "Whiteface Performances: 'Race,' Gender and Jewish Bodies." In Boyarin and Boyarin, *Jews and Other Differences*, 108–49.

Pendas, Devin O. *The Frankfurt Auschwitz Trial, 1963–65: Genocide, History and the Limits of the Law*. Cambridge: Cambridge University Press, 2006.

Pick, Daniel. *Faces of Degeneration: A European Disorder c.1848–c.1918*. Cambridge: Cambridge University Press, 1989.

Pieri, Piero. *Memoria e Giustizia: Le "Cinque storie ferraresi" di Giorgio Bassani*. Pisa: Edizioni ETS, 2008.

Reed, T.J. "The Art of Ambivalence." In Mann, *Death in Venice*, translated and edited by Clayton Koelb, 150–77.

——. *"Death in Venice": Making and Unmaking a Master*. New York: Twayne Publishers, 1994.

Renda, Marilena. *Bassani Giorgio: Un ebreo italiano*. Rome: Gaffi editore, 2010.

——. "Lo spazio vischioso: Tracce weiningeriane in *Dietro la porta*." In Dolfi and Venturi, *Ritorno al Giardino: Una giornata di studi per Giorgio Bassani*, 127–42.

Ricciotti, Romano. *La ferita sanata: I patti lateranensi e l'accordo di Villa Madama fra storia, politica e diritto*. Rimini: Il Cerchio, 2004.

Rinaldi, Micaela. *Le biblioteche di Giorgio Bassani*. Milan: Guerini e Associati, 2004.

Robert, Marthe. *Origins of the Novel*. Translated by Sacha Rabinovich. Brighton: The Harvester Press, 1980.

Robertson, Ritchie, ed. *The German-Jewish Dialogue: An Anthology of Literary Texts, 1749–1993*. Oxford: Oxford University Press, 1996.

———. "Historicizing Weininger: The Nineteenth-Century Image of the Feminized Jew." In Cheyette and Marcus, *Modernity, Culture and "the Jew,"* 23–39.

———. *The "Jewish Question" in German Literature 1749–1939: Emancipation and its Discontents*. Oxford: Oxford University Press, 1991.

Rosenberg, Warren. "Jewish Masculinities." In *International Encyclopedia of Men and Masculinities*, edited by Michael Flood, Judith Kegan Gardiner, Bob Pease, and Keith Pringle, 349–51. London and New York: Routledge, 2007.

———. *Legacy of Rage: Jewish Masculinity, Violence and Culture*. Amherst: University of Massachussetts Press, 2001.

Roveri, Alessandro. *Giorgio Bassani e l'antifascismo (1936–1943)*. Sabbioncello San Pietro, FE: 2G Editrice, 2002.

———. *Tra Micòl e il Partito d'Azione: Le passioni del giovane Bassani*. Scandicci, FI: MEF Firenze Atheneum, 2009.

Santaniello, Weaver. "Nietzsche and the Jews: Christendom and Nazism." In Golomb, *Nietzsche and Jewish Culture*, 21–54.

———. *Nietzsche, God and the Jews*. Albany: State University of New York Press, 1994.

Schneider, Marilyn. *Vengeance of the Victim: History and Symbol in Giorgio Bassani's Fiction*. Minneapolis: University of Minnesota Press, 1986.

Schwartz, Guri. "The Reconstruction of Jewish Life in Italy after World War II." *Journal of Modern Jewish Studies* 8, no. 3 (2009): 360–77. http://dx.doi.org/10.1080/14725880903263093.

Sedgwick, Peter R. *Nietzsche: The Key Concepts*. London, New York: Routledge, 2009.

Shamir, Milette. *Inexpressible Privacy: The Interior Life of Antebellum American Literature*. Philadelphia: University of Pennsylvania Press, 2005.

Siciliano, Enzo. *Autobiografia letteraria*. Milan: Garzanti, 1970.

Siporin, Steve. "A Map to the World's First Ghetto." In DiNapoli, *The Italian Jewish Experience*, 1–14.

Slavet, Eliza. *Racial Fever: Freud and the Jewish Question*. Bronx, NY: Fordham University Press, 2009.

Tomasi di Lampedusa, Giuseppe. *Il gattopardo*. Milan: Feltrinelli, 2009.

"Treasure Seized in Bassani Battle." *Times Higher Education*, September 22, 2000. Accessed May 23, 2011. http://www.timeshighereducation.co.uk/story.asp?storyCode=153586§ioncode=26.

Vanelli, Paolo. "Il cerchio spezzato: Le radici ebraiche nelle *Storie ferraresi* di Giorgio Bassani." In *Le icone del testo: Saggi sulla narrativa italiana contemporanea*, 39–83. Genoa, Milan: Marietti, 2006.

Villa, Cristina. "Il silenzio dei vivi: La letteratura della deportazione razziale nell'Italia del Boogie-Boogie, della rivolta studentesca e del terrorismo." In *Narrativa italiana degli anni Sessanta e Settanta*, edited by Gillian Ania and John Butcher, 139–50. Naples: Libreria Dante e Descartes, 2007.

Winter, Jay. "Notes on the Memory Boom: War, Remembrance and the Uses of the Past." In Bell, *Memory, Trauma and World Politics*, 54–73.

Wittmann, Rebecca. *Beyond Justice: the Auschwitz Trial*. Cambridge, MA: Harvard University Press, 2005.

Wood, Nancy. "The Victim's Resentments." In Cheyette and Marcus, *Modernity, Culture and "the Jew,"* 257–67.

Woolf, Judith. "Micòl and Beatrice: Echoes of the *Vita nuova* in Giorgio Bassani's *Garden of the Finzi-Continis*." In *Dante's Modern Afterlife: Reception and Response from Blake to Heaney*, edited by Nick Havely, 167–84. Basingstoke: Macmillan; New York: St. Martin's Press, 1998.

Wright, Elizabeth, ed. *Feminism and Psychoanalysis: A Critical Dictionary*. Oxford: Blackwell, 1992.

Yovel, Yirmiyahu. "Nietzsche and the Jews: the Structure of an Ambivalence." In Golomb, *Nietzsche and Jewish Culture*, 117–36.

Zimmerman, Joshua D., ed. *Jews in Italy under Fascist and Nazi Rule, 1922–1945*. Cambridge, New York: Cambridge University Press, 2005.

Zuccotti, Susan. *The Italians and the Holocaust: Persecution, Rescue and Survival*. Lincoln, NE: University of Nebraska Press, 1987.

Index

"Altre notizie su Bruno Lattes," 223–8; airplane imagery, 229–30; family romance, 224–5; Holocaust allusions, 227; Jewish self-hatred, 223–4, 228; longing as theme, 223, 225, 229–30; masochism, 226–7; memory and smell of hay, 217, 223; passivity, 226–7

Améry, Jean, 189–90, 192, 285n23

anti-Semitism: caricatures, 91, 162, 167, 218, 283n6, 284n7, 285n13; competitors, 283n6; and death of Jesus, 35, 192; disease carriers, 78–9, 167, 172–3, 178; historical background, 15, 23–4, 265n46, 282n2; Lavezzoli's attack in *Gli occhiali*, 35, 92–3, 95–6, 192; mongrels, 176–7, 179, 284n9; and Nietzsche's resentment, 33–5, 272n40; Race Laws, 15; sexuality, 38–9, 167, 171, 188, 284nn7–8; trains and trauma, 108–9; wandering Jew, 163, 164–5, 219–20, 221, 241, 283n6. *See also* eastern Jew; Weininger, Otto

Appelfeld, Aharon, 194, 203

At the Mind's Limits (Améry), 190

Auschwitz Trials, 190, 240, 259. *See also* Holocaust

Bachelard, Gaston, 280n8

Bartleby (film), 148

Bassani, Giorgio, life: ancestors, 43, 218, 264n37; biographical overview, 3–4, 10–13, 15–16, 264n37; impact of Race Laws on, 11, 15–16; marriage and family, 15, 229, 230, 234–6; vignettes in "Les neiges d'antan," 231–4; vignettes in "Ravenna," 228–31; vignettes in "Tre apologhi," 235–8

Bassani, Giorgio, political life: Action Party member, 15, 236, 288n13; autobiographical aspects of works, 12–13, 259–60; his father's politics, 10–11; overview, 9–13, 15–16; Resistance member, 3, 9–13, 15, 29–30, 222; silences in his works, 12–13, 263n33; Socialist member, 236, 288n13; vignettes in "Tre apologhi," 236. *See also* Croce, Benedetto

Bassani, Giorgio, views: on autobiographical parallels, 5, 9, 262nn19–20, 262n22, 263n23; on Catholicism in Ferrara, 155–6; on Croce's influence, 249; on Fadigati and narrator, 278n33; on first-person narrator, 72–3; on Freud's influence, 27; on his anti-Fascist activities, 13, 29–30; on his family's politics, 10–11; on his poetry, 262nn22–3, 263n23; on historical writing, 13, 17–18, 63, 217–18, 238–9, 258; on the Holocaust, 266n48; inconsistencies, 8–9; on Jewish critical reception, 17–18; on levels of meaning, 3; on Malnate, 258–9; on Mannian doubles, 38; on patriotism, 11; on privacy of his characters, 9; on psychoanalysis, 271n14; on Pulga as homosexual, 251; on Resistance, 11–12; on rewrites, 9; on spiritual reality, 9–10; on status of Italian novel, 193, 259; on titles of works, 26–7. *See also specific works*

Bassani, Giorgio, works: *Le parole preparate*, 77–8; poetry, 9, 262nn22–3, 287n1. *See also Dentro le mura; Dietro la porta; Gli occhiali d'oro; Il giardino dei Finzi-Contini; L'airone; L'odore del fieno; Romanzo di Ferrara*

Bassani, Giorgio, as a writer: ambiguity, 8, 83, 188, 240, 250; character doubles, 38, 241; critical reception overview, 17–18, 240–1, 252–60, 258, 270n67, 275n11; distinction between narrator, protagonist, and author, 9, 73, 84, 85, 238, 247, 252, 262n19, 277n32, 278n34, 287n1; as Jewish writer, 240–1, 253; memory and trauma as themes, 16–17, 240–1; publication and rewrites, ix–x, 7–8, 9, 16, 256; publication of *Gattopardo*, 195, 246, 257; reviews of Mann's works, 75–6, 257; romance tradition, 18–19, 27; self-delusion as theme, 20; as social novelist, 27; stratification, 22; unreliable narrators, 21, 257; on Venice in literature, 77–8; views in "Laggiù, in fondo al corridoio," 238–9; views in "Tre apologhi," 236–8; writing as symbolic revenge, 55. *See also* Freud, Sigmund; Mann, Thomas; narrators; Nietzsche, Friedrich

Behind the Door. See Dietro la porta

Beyond Good and Evil (Nietzsche), 196–7, 268n60

Birth of Tragedy (Nietzsche), 23–4

Blood of the Walsungs (Mann). *See Romanzo di Ferrara, Blood of the Walsungs* as intertext

Booth, Wayne, 21

Born, Wolfgang, 79, 83

Boyarin, Daniel, 281n18

Bruno Lattes. *See* Lattes, Bruno (character)

Buchenwald. *See* Holocaust

Calogero, Guido, 9–10, 270n66

Cavaglion, Alberto, 24, 265n41

Champagne, John, 5, 251–2, 288n7

Charterhouse of Parma (Stendhal), 62

Chatman, Seymour, 85

Christ Stopped at Eboli (Levi), 177–8, 285n10

Civilization and Its Discontents (Freud), 118–19

Cohen, Dorrit, 83–4

concentration camps. *See* Holocaust

Così è (se vi pare) (Pirandello), 54

Cotroneo, Roberto, x, 8–9, 188, 250

Croce, Benedetto: contemplated sentiment, 21, 268n57; influence on Bassani, 9–12, 31, 222–3, 249, 266n53, 270n66; and Nietzsche, 31

D'Annunzio, Gabriele, 121
Dante Alighieri: Celestino in *Giardino*, 135; *contrappasso* in "Una notte del '43," 68, 69–70; Micòl as Beatrice, 136, 148, 149, 151, 244, 280n11
De Angelis, Luca, 253–5, 259
de la Barca, Calderòn, 222
De Stefanis, Giusi Oddo, 19–20, 266n53, 279n38
Death in Venice (film), 79
Death in Venice (Mann): anti-Semitism, 78, 276n23; Bassani on Mann's Venice, 77–8; critical reception, 75–6, 83–4, 244, 275n7; Fadigati/Aschenbach parallels, 74–7, 88, 243–4; Fadigati/Mahler parallels, 83; homosexuality, 75–6, 78, 244, 257, 275n4, 275n7; intertexts, 277n26; and Mahler, 79–81, 243–4, 276n19, 276n21, 276n23; narrator's position, 83–4; publication, 78. *See also* Mann, Thomas
Dentro le mura, 40–71, 241–3; narrator, 21, 241–2; overview, 241–3. *See also* "Gli ultimi anni di Clelia Trotti"; "La passeggiata prima di cena"; "Lida Mantovani"; "Una lapide in via Mazzini"; "Una notte del '43"
Die Sünde wider das Blut (Dinter), 187–8
Dietro la porta, 152–93, 245–6; anti-Semitism, 103, 153, 164–5, 167, 171–3, 245–6; autobiographical aspects, 5, 249; Bassani on, 5, 27–8, 192–3, 259, 263n23; character doubles, 153, 241, 245–6; critical reception, 5, 188; door and threshold imagery, 28–9, 153, 187, 245; "door" scene, 153, 176–82, 245; Holocaust allusions, 154, 189, 190, 240, 259; identity conflicts, 152–3, 174, 189, 246, 283n3; intertexts, 177–8, 187–8, 282n1; Jewish self-hatred, 162, 189; memory and trauma, 189–93; passivity, 152; political climate, 153–5, 164–5, 245, 259; thematic overview, 245–6; time period, 152, 153–4, 156, 189, 245; title, 29, 153, 187, 245
Dietro la porta, Cattolica: anti-Semitism, 153, 172–3; character doubles, 153, 173; church scene, 159–60, 190–2; as narrator's ego-ideal, 153, 158–60, 163, 173, 176, 183, 252
Dietro la porta, narrator: adolescent insecurities, 152, 156–7, 161; anti-Semitic stereotypes, 103, 171, 188; Bassani on, 5, 27–8; "behind the door" scene, 176–82; as consenting victim, 200; crucifixion allusion, 177; dreams and fantasies, 169–70, 175; first-person narration, 152–3; Freud's family romance, 29, 153, 159, 167, 171, 174–5, 182–5; Jewish identity and sexual maturity, 153, 170–1, 174, 180–4, 187, 188, 284nn7–8; man of resentment, 35–6, 155, 156, 187, 189; maternal presences, 157, 169–70, 184–5; mother/son relationship, 164, 166–7, 180–3; and Nietzsche's "going inside," 36; and Otello, 157,

159, 164, 183–4; physical appearance, 158; sexual anxieties, 168–72, 174–5, 181–2; sexual sublimation, 167, 170, 187; social class, 157; trial scene, 190; "wounds," 154–5, 185, 189. *See also Romanzo di Ferrara*, narrator

Dietro la porta, Pulga: anti-Semitic stereotypes, 153, 162, 167, 176–7, 178–9, 184, 221; character doubles, 153, 162–3, 165–7, 188; as figure of Jewish self-hatred, 162, 188, 228, 246; homosexuality, 251; Judas allusion, 245; narrator's dream, 169–70; as part of narrator's psyche, 162, 167, 175–6, 180–1, 188; physical appearance, 161–2, 167; at seashore, 185–6, 228; sexuality, 166, 167–9, 177, 180–1, 185–7; trial scene, 190; as wandering Jew, 163, 164–5, 221, 284n6; Weininger's sexual stereotypes, 24, 103, 168, 181–2, 188, 245–6

Dinter, Artur, 187–8

Divine Comedy. See Dante Alighieri

Dolfi, Anna, 4, 17, 217, 267n55, 277n32

Dubliners (Joyce), 40, 70–1

"Due fiabe" (Two Fables), 218–23; autobiographical aspects, 222–3, 247, 250; eastern Jews, 218–21, 223; intertexts, 222; Jewish masculinity, 223; Yuri as eastern Jew, 250; Yuri as symbol, 221

eastern Jew: and dignity in "Due fiabe," 218–21, 247; feminized Jewish male, 26; overview of stereotype, 167, 218; Pulga as, 167, 171, 178–9. *See also* anti-Semitism

Ecce Homo (Nietzsche), 268n61

Eco, Umberto, 265n45

Eros and Literature (Heilbut), 244

Eskin, Stanley, 4–5

Etruscan tombs, 19, 22, 34, 116–18, 122, 128–9. *See also Il giardino dei Finzi-Contini*, prologue and epilogue

"Family Romances" (Freud), 26–30; maternal imagery, 28, 101–3, 113, 274n10; Oedipal crisis, 102–3; overview of theory, 7, 28–30, 274n10; pre-Oedipal narcissism, 113–14; replacement of parents, 111–12; threshold imagery, 28–9

Ferrara: Bassani as historian, 13, 17–18, 62–3, 275n11; Bassani on Catholicism in, 155–6; complicity with Fascists, 5–6, 20, 24, 69–70, 231; critical reception of *Romanzo,* 17–18; executions and assassinations, 63, 66, 67–9; Finzi-Contini estate, 112–14, 119–20, 126; ghetto, 106; Jewish culture of exclusivity, 253–5; masochism, 5–6; maternal images, 113, 144, 279n2; men's lives in *L'odore del fieno*, 232–5; passivity, 5–6, 28–9, 241; postwar period, 24, 50–1, 54–5; prewar period, 50; Socialists, 56–9; working class, 126

Ferretti, Gian Carlo, 258, 278n32

Ferroni, Giulio, 268n62

Five Stories of Ferrara. See Dentro le mura; Storie ferraresi

"The Forgotten Mask" (Pirandello), 53–4

Freud, Sigmund: archaeology and memory, 118–19, 280n6; Bassani

on his use of, 27–8; *Civilization and Its Discontents* (Freud), 118–19; house as psyche, 118–19; *Interpretation of Dreams*, 25; *Moses and Monotheism*, 19; Nietzsche's influence on followers, 248–9; on passivity, 25, 250; theory of Jewishness, 19–20; trains and trauma, 108–9; "uncanny," 140. *See also* "Family Romances" (Freud)
Freytag, Gustav, 283n6
Furst, Lilian R., 83

The Garden of the Finzi-Continis. See *Il giardino dei Finzi-Contini*
Genealogy of Morality (Nietzsche), 30–3
ghettos: and eastern Jews, 218–19; ghetto identity in "La passeggiata prima di cena," 43, 45–7, 270n10; historical background, 13–14, 78, 276n11; Jewish fears in *Dietro la porta*, 156–7; and Jewish masculinity, 25–6
Giardino. *See Il giardino dei Finzi-Contini*
Gilman, Sander, 108, 218, 273n45, 285n13
Girelli-Carasi, Fabio, 252–3
Gli occhiali d'oro, 72–109, 243–4; Apollonian and Dionysian conflict, 77; autobiographical aspects, 73; Bassani on, 72–3, 84, 263n23, 278n33; feminized Jewish male, 26; Freud's family romance, 101–5; Holocaust allusions, 91, 107–8, 269n63; homosexuality, 74–5, 84–5, 86, 103, 244; implied author, 85–6; intertexts, 74–5, 88, 243, 282n21; Jewish cemetery, 34; political climate, 73–4, 76, 89–93, 96–7, 101, 103, 243–4; as rewrite of *Death in Venice*, 244; summer holiday scenes, 91–6; title, 74, 83, 86–7; trains and trauma, 108–9. *See* also *Death in Venice* (Mann)
Gli occhiali d'oro, Deliliers: anti-Semitic attack by, 96; community views of, 92–3, 94; and Fadigati, 74–5, 95–6; humiliation of Fadigati, 77, 90, 99–100, 104; in "Les neiges d'antan," 233; and narrator's conflicts, 105
Gli occhiali d'oro, Fadigati: anti-Semitic attack by Lavezzoli, 35, 92–3, 95–6, 192; Bassani on, 278n33; community views of, 86, 92, 94–5, 104, 106–7; as consenting victim, 92, 98, 99–100, 200; Freud's family romance, 102; intertexts (Mann), 74–7, 83–4, 88, 275n4, 282n21; and Mahler, 83; masochism, 76, 99–101, 105–6; as outsider, 55, 75; and "passing" in Christian society, 82, 244; solidarity with narrator, 98–9, 103, 278n32; suicide, 74, 83, 84, 85, 99–101
Gli occhiali d'oro, narrator: Bassani on, 72–3, 278n33; and Deliliers, 105; distinction between narrator, protagonist, and author, 73, 84, 85, 247, 277n32, 278n34; father's politics, 91–2, 96, 100, 103, 257; Freud's family romance, 101–5; identification with Fadigati, 21, 74, 76, 84–6, 91, 94–5, 103–7, 244, 278nn32–3, 279n38; Jewish identity, 92–3; Jewish masculinity, 103, 105–6; memory process, 87–90, 92; moral responsibility, 85, 88, 90–1, 93, 99,

107–9, 112, 244, 277n32; narrator/protagonist and Fadigati's death, 83; as outsider, 84, 87, 96; parallels with Fadigati, 93, 96–8; sexual experience, 104–5, 181; time of narration and action, 85, 87, 89–90; wandering Jew, 164–5. *See also Romanzo di Ferrara*, narrator
Gli occhiali d'oro (film), 278n33
"Gli ultimi anni di Clelia Trotti," 56–62; Bassani on, 242, 288n13; Freud's family romance, 57–60, 223, 242; intertexts, 62; man of resentment, 34–5, 61–2; quest narrative, 57, 242; social class, 60–1, 242; Socialism, 56–9, 223, 242; threshold imagery, 57, 60
The Gold-Rimmed Spectacles. See Gli occhiali d'oro
Golomb, Jacob, 34, 247–9
Guerriero, Stefano, 263n33, 270n66
Güntert, George, 21, 268n57

Hawthorne, Nathaniel, 18–19, 27, 274n5, 282n21
Heilbut, Anthony, 75, 82, 244, 275n7
The Heron. See L'airone
Hilberg, Raul, 5–6
history of Italy: Catholic and Italian identities, 14; Catholicism as state religion (1929), 154–6, 245; German alliance, 15–16; Race Laws, 15; Risorgimento, 14. *See also* Roman Catholicism
history of Jews in Italy: Catholicism and Jewish marginalization, 42, 154–6, 245; collective psyche, 22; culture of passivity, 25–6, 28–9, 241, 250–1; early history, 13–14, 19, 78; exodus through Switzerland, 203–4; Jewish and Italian identity, 14–15, 55; post-Risorgimento period, 14, 270n67; postwar period, 16–17, 195–6, 244, 259–60; prewar anti-Jewish propaganda, 90, 91; Race Laws, 15. *See also* anti-Semitism; ghettos; Holocaust; Jewish culture
Holocaust: Améry on, 189–90, 192, 285n23; Appelfeld on, 194, 203; Auschwitz Trials, 190, 240, 259; Bassani on, 6, 266n48; in Bassani's works, 154, 240–1; camp allusions, 22, 52, 109, 126, 220, 227; Dr Menghele, 107–8, 269n63; Finzi-Contini deaths, 117; Jewish and Gentile passivity, 241, 250–1; and memory, 194; postwar response in Italy, 16–17; Primo Levi on, 51, 189–90, 253, 285n23; and resentment, 189–90, 192–3, 272n25, 285n23; survivors, as characters, 50–5, 242–3; trains and trauma, 109. *See also* "Una lapide in via Mazzini"; "Una notte del '43"
homosexuality: Alberto as latent homosexual, 35, 38, 140, 142; Bassani on Pulga, 251; as metaphor for diseased social body, 4; queer studies, 5, 251–2. *See also Death in Venice* (Mann); *Gli occhiali d'oro*
The House of Seven Gables (Hawthorne), 18–19

Il fu Mattia Pascal (Pirandello), 52–3
Il gattopardo (Lampedusa), 16, 195, 246, 257. *See also L'airone, Gattopardo* as intertext
Il giardino dei Finzi-Contini, 110–51, 244–5; archaeology motif, 22, 245;

autobiographical aspects, 12–13, 19–20; Bassani on, 6–7, 38; critical reception, 4–5, 19–20, 251–2, 253, 288n7; denial of reality, 132–3, 137–8, 244–5; fantasy and reality, 144–7; Freud's family romance, 30, 111–12, 128–9, 141–7, 244–5, 271n21; Freud's "uncanny," 140; Holocaust allusions, 126; intertexts, 37–9, 148, 151, 244; isolation, intimacy, and exclusivity, 35, 37, 253–5; political climate, 110–11, 113–14, 126, 129–31, 143–4; as symbolic novel, 110–11; thematic overview, 244–5; time periods, 110, 116, 125, 129, 131, 268n56

Il giardino dei Finzi-Contini, estate: carriage and past, 124, 134–7, 140–1; carriage and sexuality, 124, 135–7, 140–1; elevator and past, 140–1; Garden of Eden imagery, 111, 112–14, 132, 136, 244–5, 252; and Hawthorne's romance, 19; history, 113, 114, 119–21, 126; house as psyche, 118–20, 244–5, 280n8; liminal space, 117–18; loss of history, 119–21; mounds and sexuality, 127–9, 169; Perotti and past, 124, 134–5

Il giardino dei Finzi-Contini, Finzi-Continis: Alberto and homosexuality, 35, 38, 140, 142; ancestral tombs, 34, 114, 121–2, 123; and anti-Semitism, 122, 124; as aristocrats, 110, 114–15, 122–4; Bassani on, 7; community views of, 121–3, 124–5, 130; denial of reality, 113–14, 122–3, 132–3, 137–8; Ermanno and past, 34, 123, 133–4, 137, 141–2; Ermanno as father figure, 124–5, 133–4, 141–2; Ermanno's voice, 125, 280n10; Freud's family romance, 141–2; identity as Jewish Italians, 122–5, 132–3; intertexts, 37–9; and Limentani, 286n4; private language, 37, 114, 255

Il giardino dei Finzi-Contini, Malnate: Bassani on, 7, 38, 258–9; intertexts, 38; as masculine role model, 142–4, 251; and Micòl, 38, 144, 146; outsider's perspective, 131

Il giardino dei Finzi-Contini, Micòl: Aryan features, 115–16, 125; as Beatrice, 136, 148, 149, 151, 244, 280n11; carriage and past, 134–7; carriage/canoe speech, 137–8; dreams about, 115–16, 138–9, 280n12; as Eve, 112–13, 136, 139, 148, 244, 252; Freud's family romance, 141, 145–7; her Hebrew name, 149; her *shaddài,* 116, 150–1; intertexts, 37–8, 148; mounds and sexuality, 127–9, 169; Nietzsche's "going inside," 249; Nietzsche's innocent woman, 148–9; and preservation of past, 134, 147; private language, 37, 114, 255; as strong daughter, 149–50

Il giardino dei Finzi-Contini, narrator: acceptance of racial difference, 111, 114–15, 245; acceptance of sexual difference, 112, 126–8, 135–8, 145–7, 151, 245, 252; anti-Fascist movement, 143–4; archaeology and memory, 117–20, 245; author and narrator distinction, 252, 277n32; autobiographical aspects, 143–4; Bassani on, 7; carriage and past, 134–7; carriage and sexuality, 135–8, 139; character doubles, 21; dream and sexuality, 138–9, 280n12; father and ethnic difference, 137–8; father's political views, 111, 129–30, 257; father's views of Finzi-Continis, 121–3, 124–5, 130; father/son relationship, 129–30, 141, 143–4; Freud's family romance, 111–14, 128–9, 135–9, 141, 143–7; house as psyche, 118–20, 245, 280n8; identification with bourgeoisie, 121; intertexts, 38, 151; Malnate as role model for, 142–4, 251; man of resentment, 121; psychosexual immaturity, 244–5. *See also Romanzo di Ferrara*, narrator

Il giardino dei Finzi-Contini, prologue and epilogue: ancestral visits, 34, 117–18, 122; archaeology metaphor, 22, 117; death imagery, 116–17, 128–9; epilogue, 116, 147; Etruscan tombs, 19, 22, 34, 116–18, 122, 128–9; Jewish historical perspective, 19, 34, 116; narrator's perspective, 116–18

"Il treno ha fischiato" (Pirandello), 53–4

The Interpretation of Dreams (Freud), 250

Jellinek, Adolf, 24

Jewish culture: collective Jewish psyche, 22; eastern Jew as Other, 26, 218–19; exclusivity and secrecy, 14–15, 179–80, 253–5; and Hebrew scriptures, 25–6, 124–5, 218–19; lack of military tradition, 5–6; masculinity and ghetto culture, 25–6; Micòl's *shaddài*, 116, 150–1; Nietzsche's influence, 247–9; passivity, 25–6, 28–9, 241, 250–1; permissible emotions, 32; postwar narratives, 252–3, 265n44; self-hatred, 34; sexuality, 150–1, 281n18; shame, 26; strong women, 149–50. *See also* ghettos

Joyce, James, 20, 40, 70–1, 201, 274n1, 274n7, 287n11

"Judaism in Music" (Wagner), 80

Kiernan, Susan, 270n67

"La maschera dimenticata" (Pirandello), 53–4

"La passeggiata prima di cena," 43–50; character doubles, 43, 48–50, 242; community's views, 44, 45, 64, 242; father-son confrontation, 47; Freud's family romance, 44, 49–50; Holocaust allusions, 46; house as metaphor, 45, 274n5; Jewish identity dilemma, 44–8, 270n10; man of resentment, 35, 44, 45, 47, 50; marriage and social class, 35, 43–6, 50, 242; science and faith, 47, 242, 270n10; spectator motif, 48–9

La scuola dell'uomo (Calogero), 9–10, 270n66

"Laggiù, in fondo al corridoio," 238–9

L'airone, 194–216, 246–7; Bassani on, 37, 197, 286nn4–5; birds as victims, 204–7; consenting victim motif, 199–200, 203; intertexts, 37, 195–6, 201; maternal imagery, 28, 37, 198, 211, 215, 247; political climate, 195–6, 198, 200–2, 246; thematic overview, 246–7; third-person narrator, 21, 194, 197; time period, 195, 246

L'airone, Gattopardo as intertext: dreams, 213; embalmed animals, 210–11; "false consciousness" of

Jewish bourgeoisie, 195–6; hunting scene, 204–5; Limentani as Prince Fabrizio, 195–6, 198, 246; Malvica/Ulderico parallels, 198; overview, 195–6, 246; political climate, 195–6, 246; third-person narrator, 197

L'airone, Limentani: arrested development, 211–13; autobiographical aspects, 197; Bassani on, 287n9; and Bellagamba, 200–3, 207–8; consenting victim motif, 199–200, 203; dreams, 209, 212–13; embalmed birds, 36, 208, 209–11, 216; Freud's family romance, 28, 215, 246–7; heron as symbol, 197, 205–7, 209, 246; heron hunting scene, 204–7, 209, 216, 286n5; hunter as the hunted, 55, 196, 207, 246, 286n6; marriage, 197–8, 211–12, 216; memory and trauma, 196, 197–8, 199–200, 203–5, 207, 241, 246; mourning process, 196, 199–200, 246; Nietzsche's symbolic vengeance, 196–7, 249; Nietzsche's "unmasking" and "overcoming," 36, 197, 249–50; passivity, 207–8; physical appearance, 211; self-hatred, 203, 204, 246–7; self-image, 211–12, 215–16, 246; sexuality, 211, 213, 215, 225; social class, 196, 197, 198–9, 211–12, 286n4; suicide, 36, 196–7, 209–10, 216, 246, 249–50, 287n9; suicide and resentment, 21, 36, 55; symbolic confrontation with Fascists, 196, 200–2, 207–8, 246; and Ulderico, 198–9, 203, 211–15

The Late Mattia Pascal (Pirandello), 52–3

Lattes, Bruno (character): autobiographical aspects, 230, 242, 247; Bassani on, 242; in *Giardino*, 131–2, 254; and *Gli occhiali*, 228. *See also* "Altre notizie su Bruno Lattes"; "Gli ultimi anni di Clelia Trotti"

The Leopard. *See Il gattopardo* (Lampedusa); *L'airone*, *Gattopardo* as intertext

"Les neiges d'antan," 231–4, 239

Lessing, Theodor, 34

Levi, Carlo, 177–8, 252, 284n10

Levi, Primo, 51, 189–90, 253, 285n23

"Lida Mantovani," 40–3; autobiographical aspects, 42; character doubles, 50, 242; corridor motif, 42, 239; David as man of resentment, 35, 43, 50, 221; Freud's family romance, 28, 40–1, 43, 48–9, 242; Jewish male psyche, 50, 241–2; marriage and social class, 40–3, 50; political climate, 42

literature, Jewish. *See* Jewish culture

L'odore del fieno, 217–39, 247; autobiographical aspects, 217–18, 228–34, 247; Bassani on, 217–18, 247; narrator, 21–2, 247, 287n1; thematic overview, 247; title, 217, 223. *See also* "Altre notizie su Bruno Lattes"; "Due fiabe"; "Laggiù, in fondo al corridoio"; "Les neiges d'antan"; "Ravenna"; "Tre apologhi"

Luke, David, 83

Mahler, Gustav, and Thomas Mann, 79–84, 243–4, 276n19, 276n21, 276n23

man of resentment. *See* resentment (Nietzsche's *ressentiment*)

Mann, Thomas: Bassani's affinity for, 37–9, 244, 257–8; homosexuality, 75–6, 81–3, 244, 275n7;

identification with Jews, 81–3; and Mahler, 79–84, 243–4, 276n19, 276n21, 276n23
Mann, Thomas, works: *Doctor Faustus*, 71; *A Man and His Dog* (Mann), 76; *Mario and the Magician*, 75–6; "On the Jewish Question," 81–2. *See also Death in Venice; Romanzo di Ferrara, Blood of the Walsungs* as intertext
Manzoni, Alessandro, 22, 62–3, 142, 268n55
Mario and the Magician (Mann), 75–6
masculinity, Jewish: feminization, 23–6; gender categories, 23; and ghetto culture, 25–6; in *Gli occhiali*, 103, 105–6; and Hebrew scriptures, 25–6; historical background, 23–6, 250–1; Malnate as role model in *Giardino*, 142–4, 251; masochism, 5–6; and Nietzsche's resentment, 4, 6–7, 32–3; passivity, 5–6, 25–6; in *Romanzo*, 3–5, 220–1, 241; and voice, 125, 280n10. *See also* "Family Romances" (Freud)
Melville, Herman, 148
Meyer, Hans. *See* Améry, Jean
Moloney, Brian, 278n34
Moses and Monotheism (Freud), 19

Narrative of Arthur Gordon Pym (Poe), 67
narrators: distinction between narrator, protagonist, and author, 9, 73, 84, 85, 238, 247, 252, 262n19, 277n32, 278n34, 287n1; and history, 267n55, 268n62; implied authors, 85–6; overview of types, 20–2; questions presented by, 278n34; unreliability, 21, 257. *See also Dietro la porta*, narrator; *Gli occhiali d'oro*, narrator; *Il giardino dei Finzi-Contini*, narrator; *Romanzo di Ferrara*, narrator
Neiger, Ada, 271n11, 275n4
Neusser, Jacob, 32
Nietzsche, Friedrich: Améry on *ressentiment*, 190; forms of vengeance, 55, 196–7; and Freud, 248–9; "going inside," 22, 36, 249, 268n60; identity, art, and self-creation, 247–8, 258; influence on Jews, 247–9; influence on Mahler, 80; and Jewish men, 23–4, 241, 247–8; "loving one's fate," 239; on Old Testament, 47; "self-overcoming," 3, 13, 80, 249, 261n2; "slave revolt in morality," 30–2, 47, 285n23; "unmasking," 22, 36, 197, 249, 268n61; on women, 148–9, 281n15; psychology as hunt, 196–7. *See also* resentment (Nietzsche's *ressentiment*)
Nietzsche, Friedrich, works: *Beyond Good and Evil*, 196–7, 268n60; *Birth of Tragedy*, 23–4; *Ecce Homo*, 268n61; *The Gay Science*, 148–9; *Genealogy of Morality*, 30–3, 249; *Thus Spoke Zarathustra*, 80

"On the Jewish Question" (Mann), 81–2
Otto Weininger in Italia (Cavaglion), 24

Le parole preparate, 77–8
Parussa, Sergio, 274n5, 277n26, 278n32, 282n21
passivity: in "Altre notizie su Bruno Lattes," 226–7; in Ferrara, 5–6, 28–9, 241; Freud on, 25, 250;

and Jewish culture, 5–6, 25–6, 28–9, 241, 250–1; and Limentani in *L'airone*, 207–8; and Nietzsche's resentment, 32–3, 190; and paralysis in "Una notte del '43," 34, 63, 69–71, 210–11, 243; in *Romanzo*, 28–9, 35–6, 241
Pazzi, Roberto, 275n11
Pellegrini, Ann, 23
Pieri, Piero, 256–7
Pirandello, Luigi, 20, 52–4
Poe, Edgar Allan, 67, 282n1
primal imagery in *Romanzo:* doors and thresholds, 28–9, 104, 153, 212, 214, 245–7; seeing with the eye, 48, 64
Promessi sposi (Manzoni), 142

Race Laws, 11, 15–16
Rank, Otto, 23
Rappacini's Daughter (Hawthorne), 274n5, 282n21
"Ravenna," 228–31
Reed, T.J., 83
Renda, Marilena, 188
resentment (Nietzsche's *ressentiment*), 30–6; and anti-Semitism, 33–5, 272n40; and Holocaust, 189–90, 192–3, 272n25, 285n23; Jewish masculinity, 4, 6–7, 32–3; noncontradictory ambivalence, 272n40; overview of theory, 31–3; passivity and, 32–3, 190; and revenge, 50, 190, 196–7; "slave revolt in morality," 30–2
Ricciotti, Romano, 283n3
Robert, Marthe, 30
Robertson, Ritchie, 23–4, 81–2, 188
Roman Catholicism: Bassani on, 155–6; church scene in *Dietro*, 159–60, 190–2; church scene in "Ravenna," 230; and Jewish marginalization, 42, 154–6, 245; as national identity, 14, 154, 245, 283n3
Romanzo di Ferrara: archetypal imagery, 22; autobiographical aspects, 3–4, 9–13, 252, 257–8; Bassani as historian, 13, 17–18; Bassani on revisions, 9; character doubles, 21, 42, 241; corridor motif, 42, 238–9; critical reception, 4–5, 17–18, 270n67; epigraphs, 22; four stories in, 252; frame (prologue and epilogue) in *Giardino*, 116; Freud's family romance, 26–30, 38, 252; intertexts, 4, 7, 36–9; levels of meaning, 3–4, 8, 263n36; magnolia tree motif, 42, 99, 174, 184; Mann's influence, 36–9; as meditation on Jewish masculinity, 3–5, 220–1; Nietzsche's influence, 22, 30–6, 249; overview, 241, 263n36; passivity, 28–9, 35–6, 241; power and erotic dynamics, 38–9; publication and rewrites, ix–x, 7–9, 16, 22; romance tradition, 18–19, 27; time period, 3; title, 18–19, 26–7. *See also Dietro la porta*; *Gli occhiali d'oro*; *Il giardino dei Finzi-Contini*; *L'airone*; *Romanzo di Ferrara*, narrator
Romanzo di Ferrara, Blood of the Walsungs as intertext, 36–9; anti-Semitic discourses, 38–9; Bassani on, 6; in *Giardino*, 37–8; homosexuality, 38; incest, 36, 38, 273n45; and Jewish identity, 4, 36–7, 244; and *L'airone*, 37; power and erotic dynamics, 38–9; resentment of Gentiles, 37, 258–9

Romanzo di Ferrara, narrator: autobiographical aspects, 5, 13, 72–3, 249–50; Bassani on, 72–3; distinction between narrator, protagonist, and author, 9, 73, 84, 85, 238, 247, 252, 262n19, 277n32, 278n34, 287n1; man of resentment, 35–6; overview, 20–2, 252; physical appearance, 135; unreliable narrator, 21, 257. *See also Dietro la porta*, narrator; *Gli occhiali d'oro*, narrator; *Il giardino dei Finzi-Contini*, narrator
Rosenberg, Warren, 25–6, 250–1

Schneider, Marilyn, 4, 13, 280n12
Schwartz, Guri, 16–17
Segre, Dan Vittorio, 14–15, 265n39
Sex and Character (Weininger), 24, 168
sexuality: and anti-Semitism, 38–9, 167, 171, 188, 284nn7–8; estate in *Giardino*, 124, 127–9, 135–7, 140–1, 169; and Jewish culture, 150–1, 281n18; Limentani in *L'airone*, 211, 213, 215, 225; Micòl in *Giardino*, 127–9, 169, 280n12; narrator in *Giardino*, 135–9, 280n12; power and erotic dynamics, 38; Pulga in *Dietro la porta*, 166, 167–9, 177, 180–1, 185–7; and trauma in "Una notte del '43," 63, 69–70, 234. *See also* "Family Romances" (Freud); homosexuality; Weininger, Otto
Siciliano, Enzo, 255–7
The Sin against the Blood (Dinter), 187–8
Slavet, Eliza, 19
The Smell of Hay. *See L'odore del fieno*
social class: Finzi-Continis as aristocrats, 110, 114–15, 122–4; and Freud's family romance, 111–12; and marriage, 35, 43–6, 50, 242; resentment towards lower classes, 35; and self-delusion, 20; squatters in Finzi-Contini estate, 119, 121; working class, 41–2, 126, 230
Socialism: Bassani on, 288n13; in *Gli occhiali*, 96–7; in "Gli ultimi anni di Clelia Trotti," 56–9, 223, 242
Stendhal, 62
Storie ferraresi: Bassani on, 238–9, 247; rewrites, ix–x, 256; third-person narrator, 20. *See* also *Dentro le mura*

Thus Spoke Zarathustra (Nietzsche), 80, 261n2
Tomasi di Lampedusa, Giuseppe, 16, 246, 257. *See also Il gattopardo* (Lampedusa); *L'airone, Gattopardo* as intertext
"The Train Has Whistled" (Pirandello), 53–4
trauma: and memory in *Dietro la porta*, 189–93; and memory in *L'airone*, 196, 197–8, 199–200, 203–5, 207, 241, 246; in *Romanzo*, 241; and sexuality in "Una notte del '43," 63, 69–70, 234; as theme, 16–17, 240–1; and trains, 108–9
"Tre apologhi," 235–8
"Two Fables." *See* "Due fiabe" (Two Fables)

"Una lapide in via Mazzini," 50–5; community complicity, 24; Holocaust survivor identity, 50–3, 55, 242–3; intertexts, 52–4; revenge, 50–5, 242–3
"Una notte del '43," 62–71, 243; Bassani on, 63; Freud's family

romance, 68–9; historical realism, 62–3, 69; homosexuality, 4, 251; intertexts, 67, 68, 69, 70–1; narrator, 63–4; paralysis and passivity, 34, 63, 69–71, 210–11, 243; sexuality and trauma, 63, 69–70, 234; spectator motif, 63–5, 67–70, 234

Vanelli, Paolo, 263n36
Venice, Bassani on, 77–8

Wagner, Richard, 80, 284n9
Walter, Bruno, 80, 83
wandering Jew, 163, 164–5, 219–20, 221, 241, 284n6
Weininger, Otto: Jewish sexual stereotypes, 24, 103, 148, 168, 181–2, 188, 245–6, 284n8
"William Wilson" (Poe), 282n1

Yovel, Yirmiyahu, 272n40

www.ingramcontent.com/pod-product-compliance
Lightning Source LLC
LaVergne TN
LVHW040152080826
844660LV00014B/929/J

* 9 7 8 1 4 4 2 6 4 6 1 6 2 *